WHAT IS PARENTHOOD?

Families, Law, and Society Series
General Editor: Nancy E. Dowd

Justice for Kids: Keeping Kids Out of the Juvenile Justice System
Edited by Nancy E. Dowd

The New Kinship: Donor-Conceived Family Communities
Naomi Cahn

What Is Parenthood? Contemporary Debates about the Family
Edited by Linda C. McClain and Daniel Cere

What Is Parenthood?

Contemporary Debates about the Family

EDITED BY
Linda C. McClain and Daniel Cere

NEW YORK UNIVERSITY PRESS
New York and London

NEW YORK UNIVERSITY PRESS
New York and London
www.nyupress.org

© 2013 by New York University
All rights reserved

References to Internet Websites (URLs) were accurate at the time of writing. Neither the author nor New York University Press is responsible for URLs that may have expired or changed since the manuscript was prepared.

Library of Congress Cataloging-in-Publication Data
McClain, Linda C.
What is parenthood? : contemporary debates about the family / Linda C. McClain, Daniel Cere.
p. cm.   Includes bibliographical references and index.
ISBN 978-0-8147-2915-1 (hardback)   ISBN 978-0-8147-5942-4 (paper)
ISBN 978-0-8147-2448-4 (ebook)   ISBN 978-0-8147-8942-1 (ebook)
1. Parent and child (Law)—United States.   2. Parenthood—United States.
3. Adoption—Law and legislation—United States.
4. Gay parents—Legal status, laws, etc.—United States.
5. Custody of children—United States.   I. Cere, Daniel.   II. Title.
KF540.M33   2013
346.7301'5—dc23   2012028502

New York University Press books are printed on acid-free paper, and their binding materials are chosen for strength and durability. We strive to use environmentally responsible suppliers and materials to the greatest extent possible in publishing our books.

Manufactured in the United States of America

C 10 9 8 7 6 5 4 3 2 1
P 10 9 8 7 6 5 4 3 2 1

Contents

Acknowledgments	vii
Introduction	1
Linda C. McClain and Daniel Cere	

Part I: What Is Parenthood? Proposing Two Models

1. Toward an Integrative Account of Parenthood	19
Daniel Cere	
2. A Diversity Approach to Parenthood in Family Life and Family Law	41
Linda C. McClain	

Part II: Institutions: Is Parenthood Separable from Marriage (or Couplehood) When It Comes to Fostering Child Well-Being?

3. Uncoupling Marriage and Parenting	65
Judith Stacey	
4. The Anthropological Case for the Integrative Model	85
Peter Wood	

Part III: Rights: What Rights Are at Stake? How Should the Rights of Adults and Children Shape the Law of Parenthood?

5. Legal Parenthood, Natural and Legal Rights, and the Best Interests of the Child: An Integrative View	105
Don Browning	
6. Family Diversity and the Rights of Parenthood	124
David D. Meyer	

Part IV: Child Outcomes and Forms of Parenthood: Does One Model Produce, on Average, Better Outcomes for Children? For Society?

7. A Case for Integrated Parenthood	147
Margaret F. Brinig	
8. Developmental Outcomes for Children Raised by Lesbian and Gay Parents	171
Fiona Tasker	

Part V: Attachment: (How Much) Does Biology Matter?

    9. Biological and Psychological Dimensions of Integrative Attachments   193
    Terence E. Hébert, Ellen Moss, Daniel Cere, and Hyun Song

    10. Parenting Matters: An Attachment Perspective   214
    Howard Steele and Miriam Steele

Part VI: Gender Equality, Gender Difference, and Parenthood: Are There Gender Differences in Parenting? Should Difference Make a Difference?

    11. Gender and Parentage: Family Law's Equality Project in Our Empirical Age   237
    Susan Frelich Appleton

    12. Can Parenting Be Equal? Rethinking Equality and Gender Differences in Parenting   257
    Andrea Doucet

Part VII: Globalization and Parenthood: How Do Family Immigration and Transnational Parenting Shape Parenthood? How Should They Inform Debates over Parenthood?

    13. Transnationalism of the Heart: Familyhood across Borders   279
    Carola Suárez-Orozco and Marcelo M. Suárez-Orozco

    14. Transnational Mothering and Models of Parenthood: Ideological and Intergenerational Challenges in Filipina Migrant Families   299
    Rhacel Salazar Parreñas

Part VIII: Now What? Given Current Indicators, Can the "Toothpaste Go Back in the Tube"? Should It?

    15. Of Human Bonding: Integrating the Needs and Desires of Women, Men, and the Children Their Unions Produce   321
    Elizabeth Marquardt

    16. The Other Side of the Demographic Revolution: Social Policy and Responsible Parenthood   340
    June Carbone and Naomi Cahn

    Epilogue   361
    Daniel Cere and Linda C. McClain

    About the Contributors   373

    Index   377

ACKNOWLEDGMENTS

Linda C. McClain and Daniel Cere

This book had its genesis in a conversation between the editors, Linda McClain and Daniel Cere, about why and how we differed in our understandings of and convictions about family and marriage and how these differences seemed to turn on contrasting underlying models of parenthood. As we examined these issues further, and decided to pursue them in the present volume, we learned much from valuable conversations with our contributors, whose different disciplinary perspectives helped to shape the volume. We thank them for their dedication to this project. Reading and editing their chapters has deepened our own understandings of the many facets of parenthood.

We thank Deborah Gershenowitz, senior editor at NYU Press, and Nancy Dowd, editor of the Families, Law, and Society series, for giving this book such a wonderful home. We have appreciated Nancy's sustained enthusiasm as well as her constructive comments on all the chapters. We thank Deborah for her editorial comments. We also thank the anonymous reviewers for their instructive comments on the manuscript. Finally, we thank Alexia Traganas at NYU Press, for her careful work on the production of this book.

Producing this book required the sustained assistance of a number of people at Boston University School of Law. For vital help with research and cite checking, we thank Stefanie Weigmann, assistant director for Research, Faculty Services, and Educational Technology, and librarian Jennifer Ekblaw, at the Pappas Law Library, and law students Christine Dieter, Avalon Johnson, and Hallie Van Duren. A special thank-you to Sue Morrison, senior administrative assistant, for working tirelessly on the revisions and formatting of every chapter. Thanks also to Leanne Chaves and William Kaleva for help with chapter revisions. The Paul M. Siskind Research Scholar fund and a BU Law summer research grant supported this project.

We are grateful to the Institute for American Values, especially David Blankenhorn, for facilitating the public conversation out of which this book grew—a panel on Linda's book *The Place of Families: Fostering Capacity, Equality, and Responsibility* (Harvard University Press, 2006). The Institute supported the project by helping to fund a planning conference, held at Princeton University, and a working conference, held at the University of Virginia, at which some of the book's contributors shared early drafts of their chapters. Robby George, at Princeton, and Brad Wilcox, at Virginia, graciously hosted those events. At the Virginia working conference, Jim Dwyer, Vivian Hamilton, and Robin Wilson provided instructive commentary on some of those early drafts. Charlotte Patterson also offered valuable criticism. We thank Elizabeth Marquardt, at the Institute, for useful conversations about this project and for shepherding the late Don Browning's chapter through the final revision stage.

In addition, Linda wishes to thank Jim Fleming for moral and practical support as this book took shape, including thoughtful editing of her work. Dan wishes to thank those researchers and supporters who contributed to an early exploratory discussion of questions about parenthood in "The Future of Parenthood Workshop" held in Montreal in December 2005.

Introduction

Linda C. McClain and Daniel Cere

Extraordinary changes in patterns of family life—and family law—have dramatically altered the boundaries of parenthood and opened up numerous questions and debates. What is parenthood and why does it matter? How should society define, regulate, and support it? Despite this uncertainty, however, the intense focus on the definition and future of marriage diverts attention from parenthood. Further, demographic reports suggesting a shift away from marriage and toward alternative family forms keep marriage in constant public view, obscuring the fact that disagreements about marriage are often grounded in deeper, conflicting convictions about parenthood.

What Is Parenthood? asks bold and direct questions about how to think about, support, and regulate parenthood.[1] We begin with the institutional question: Is parenthood separable from marriage—or couplehood—when society seeks to foster children's well-being? We then turn to other issues: What is the better model of parenthood from the perspective of child outcomes? How should the rights of adults and of children shape the law of parenthood? How do children form secure attachment to parents, and how significant is biology to that process? How do gender equality and gender difference shape the law and social practice of parenthood? Are there gender differences in parenting, and, if so, should difference make a difference? What are the implications for the meaning of parenthood and family life of immigration and its giving rise to forms of transnational parenting? Finally, given the significant changes in patterns of family life, what directions should family law and public policy concerning parenthood take?

The book brings together an interdisciplinary group of distinguished scholars to investigate these questions and debates about parenthood in contemporary society. For each question, the book provides two responses from experts with different perspectives, who are, generally, from different disciplines. Law, admittedly, is the disciplinary center of gravity, but the volume brings into conversation scholars from law, anthropology, globalization and immigration studies, medicine, psychology, religious ethics, and sociology. This interdisciplinary approach allows competing perspectives on critical issues pertinent to parenthood. In addressing these issues, our contributors also offer different perspectives on related questions, such as the role of empirical research and evidence in debates over parenthood and the family.

As an organizing device, we use two contrasting models of parenthood: the *integrative model* and the *diversity model*. We offer them as a guiding framework subject to refinement, rather than as rigid constructs describing two polarized camps. Indeed, within this book, there are creative tensions over whether it is possible to delineate two contrasting models. There is a considerable amount of nuance and plasticity within what we call these integrative and diversity approaches, but we nonetheless believe that the models are helpful and avoid many of the available reductive dichotomies, such as for and against, liberal versus conservative, modern versus traditional. Therefore, we use the two models to elucidate the challenging tensions within academic discourse and public debate about parenthood.

Generally, for each question posed, one response approaches the question from the perspective of the integrative model and the other, from that of the diversity model.[2] Many collections on family issues gravitate toward the conservative, liberal, or feminist pole. By contrast, this book deliberately brings together scholars from different points along the spectrum. We offer the two models as an organizing device, and many contributors vigorously defend or criticize one or the other model. Some contributors also illuminate tensions in family life and family law between these two models. However, some contributors challenge the utility of this two-model approach and propose alternative frameworks.

The Integrative and Diversity Models and Their Usefulness

The *integrative model* of parenthood (as elaborated by Daniel Cere in chapter 1) reflects a traditional, and still common, understanding of parenthood as a natural relation following from biological reproduction by one man and one woman within marriage (or legal adoption within marriage). We call this view *integrative* because it regards marriage—between one man and one woman—as the central social institution for integrating sexuality, reproduction, and parenthood so that children grow up with their two biological parents. Proponents of the integrative model describe it as a *conjugal model* to emphasize that it is a male-female model of parenting and assumes a certain social ecology of adult pair-bonding, sex difference, and adult-child relationships. Although some appeal to religious convictions to justify the integrative model, many eschew explicit appeal to religion and find support for the model in academic fields like evolutionary psychology, kinship studies, and biological anthropology.

The integrative model emphasizes the importance of biological connection, the significance of sex difference, and the need—indeed, the right—of children to two biological parents: their mother and father. It urges caution about the growing use of assisted reproductive technology (ART) because of the separations this technology introduces between biology and parenthood and, often, between marriage and parenthood. Generally, its proponents oppose opening up civil marriage to same-sex couples because this change will weaken the basic idea that each child should have a mother and a father.³ However, some support second-parent adoption for same-sex couples because formal ties between parents and children better foster child well-being than informal ones. The role of law, in the integrative model, is to assist in channelling human bonding and reproduction toward the institution of marriage in a way that integrates the many biological and social goods of parenthood.⁴ Some proponents of the integrative model, nonetheless, now support same-sex marriage in light of other goods at stake (such as fairness and the dignity and equal citizenship of gay men and lesbians). They call for exploring possible coalitions between straight people and gay men and lesbians on strengthening marriage as an institution, embracing a norm of marital parenthood as best for children, and thinking carefully about the use of ART.⁵

The *diversity model* (as elaborated by Linda McClain in chapter 2) recognizes and responds to the growing diversity in patterns of family life. It acknowledges various pathways to parenthood. It often includes a normative judgment that this diversity has value. It defines parenthood more by reference to the quality of the relationship—or, to use a psychological concept, attachment—between adult and child than to whether a marital relationship exists between two opposite-sex adults or a biological tie between adult and child. It recognizes that adult-adult intimate relationships often produce and may be linked to parent-child bonds, as in marriage. However, it also recognizes that adult-adult intimate bonds are not always the anchor of parent-child bonds; some parent-child bonds form and flourish outside of marriage or other adult intimate relationships.

The diversity model tends to focus on family *function* rather than family *form*. The legal category of parent, on this model, properly includes persons who function as parents even if they lack a biological or formal connection to a child. It also stresses adult autonomy and responsibility and the basic right of children to healthy attachments and good parenting, rather than a basic right to biological parents or parents who satisfy certain formal requirements. This model embraces family law's gender revolution away from hierarchical, fixed gender roles for spouses and parents and toward equality as a basic norm.[6] It de-emphasizes the significance of sex difference and gender complementarity and is skeptical of claims that every child needs a mother and a father for optimal development. The role of law, on the diversity model, is to recognize and support the diverse array of contexts in which bonded parent-child relationships may arise. To be sure, the diversity model is a big tent. There is considerable disagreement among those who agree that the integrative model is too narrow in its approach to parenthood. Some proponents of the diversity model share with the integrative model the conviction that marriage is a valuable way to integrate intimate adult bonds and parent-child bonds; however, for them, this is a reason to support, rather than to oppose, marriage by same-sex couples. Other proponents criticize family law's focus upon marriage and urge that society should support a broader range of intimate adult relationships. Still other diversity proponents contend that, given the vicissitudes of adult intimate relationships, society should focus on and support parenthood—and the needs of children—rather than on integration of intimate and parenting bonds.

These models of parenthood often coexist in uneasy tension with one another. Public opinion surveys report both notable recognition of family diversity and considerable ambivalence about it. A Pew Research Center survey, *The Decline of Marriage and Rise of New Families*, found that majorities of Americans define "family" in a way that includes family forms that clearly do not fit into the integrative model of parenthood—married, heterosexual parents (by biology or adoption). To be sure, nearly 99 percent of those surveyed deem a married couple with children a family. Yet very large majorities also recognize family forms that depart from the integrative model and move toward the diversity model: 86 percent consider a single parent with children a family, 80 percent, an unmarried couple with children. Moreover, a sizable majority (63 percent) considers a same-sex couple with children a family.[7] These survey responses suggest, as the report notes, that although "the portrait of the American family circa 2010 starts where it always has—with mom, pop and the kids . . . the family album now includes other ensembles."⁸ However, recognition that greater family diversity exists does not translate in all cases to acceptance of such change. The survey found that 69 percent of respondents view with concern the trend of more single women having children. The public is more divided over other forms of family diversity, with a large minority (43 percent) believing that the trends of more unmarried couples and more gay and lesbian couples raising children are bad for society, while an equally large minority say that they are neither good nor bad. Further, different segments of the public (based on gender, age, religiosity, and race) hold different views about whether children need a home with both a mother and a father.⁹

This book is also pertinent to contemporary debates over the legal regulation of marriage. It attempts to provide a balanced and critical overview of the ways in which different conceptions of parenthood shape debates over marriage. An instructive example is provided by the ongoing legal and political struggles in the United States over whether states should open up civil marriage to same-sex couples. State courts that have rejected the constitutional challenges brought by same-sex couples have presupposed the integrative model of parenthood.¹⁰ State courts that have accepted such challenges have rejected this model to the extent it would limit marriage to opposite-sex couples, stressing the equal capacity of same-sex couples to be spouses and parents. Instead, the latter courts have recognized the diversity of pathways to becoming a parent and concluded that research indicates that gay and lesbian parents are as effective as heterosexual parents at rearing children and that parental effectiveness is not related to sexual orientation.¹¹ Further, as state legislatures wrestle with the marriage issue, the underlying role of competing models of parenthood is evident.¹² As elaborated in chapter 2, claims about the irrelevance of gender to parental capacity and child outcomes played a critical role in the successful federal constitutional challenge brought by same-sex couples to California's Proposition 8. Competing models of parenthood are also critical to ongoing legal challenges to the federal Defense of Marriage Act (DOMA) and to congressional debate over whether to repeal DOMA. By posing a range of questions about parenthood, this volume avoids focusing only on what gets the most airtime in debates over parenthood: family form. To be sure, it does ask whether family form matters, but it also asks many other questions concerning critical, but often overlooked, aspects of contemporary parenthood.

Overview of the Book

In part I, we offer the working hypothesis that the integrative and diversity models of parenthood provide a fruitful framework for making sense of contemporary debates about parenthood and addressing the significant questions about parenthood taken up by our contributors.

In chapter 1, Daniel Cere argues that developments in the fields of attachment theory, kinship studies, and evolutionary psychology resonate with an integrative approach to parenthood, which emphasizes the importance of human pair-bonding and kinship bonds and the evolutionary roots of attachment.[13] He looks closely at what these fields suggest about the critical importance of attachment and kinship bonds for human development. He contends that this research suggests significant convergence on a "substantive set of principles" across lines of debate over parenthood concerning the needs and rights of children, the duties of adults, and the obligation of society and the state to facilitate adults' capacity to meet children's needs. He then identifies some likely areas of disagreement between proponents of the integrative and diversity models about further implications of this research. Canvassing recent scholarship, he elaborates several features of human kinship systems and explains their import for the integrative model. He concludes by examining how this research might inform parenthood debates and translate into legal arguments about the "unique web of rights associated with childhood."

In chapter 2, Linda McClain sets forth the diversity model of parenthood.[14] She looks first at social practice, canvassing diverse pathways to parenthood, and then at family law, showing the law's evolution toward more diversity in defining and supporting parenthood. She acknowledges the continuing hold of an integrative model in public opinion (if not always in practice) and in family law. She explains the normative foundations of the diversity model as well as how changes in constitutional, criminal, and family law, and in women's economic status in society, have facilitated greater family diversity. Government, she argues, should recognize and support different forms of family, and she identifies different perspectives within the diversity model over questions of law and policy, such as the continuing place of marriage and whether and how closely to link adult-adult intimate bonds to parent-child bonds. She also sketches diversity (or disagreement) within the integrative model. She proposes that, given variations within both models, the image of a continuum might better help to map competing conceptions of parenthood in contemporary debates about family life and family law and what is best for adults, children, and society.

Part II takes up the question of institutions supporting parenthood: Is parenthood separable from marriage (or couplehood) when it comes to fostering child well-being? Sociologist Judith Stacey, in chapter 3, argues that the terms *singular* (or *universalist*) and *pluralist* better describe the contrasting perspectives on family change and family diversity.[15] She demonstrates the ethnographic character of the institutional question by drawing on field research on the matrilineal Mosuo culture of southwestern China and polygamy in South Africa—two radically different examples of family systems that do not presume that child welfare depends upon monogamous, heterosexual marriage. She criticizes the exaggerated emphasis that the integrative perspective places on the role of marriage in promoting child welfare and argues instead for greater social responsibility to enable successful parenting in all of its diverse forms.

In chapter 4, anthropologist Peter Wood also takes up the example of the Na (or what Stacey calls the Mosuo) in defending the opposite point: societies are generally and preferentially organized to provide each child with an acknowledged mother and father who bear responsibility for raising the child.[16] This proposition about the normative structure of human societies, he argues, does not deny that the actual arrangements societies employ to nurture, provide for, and educate children are diverse or that various external constraints sometimes compromise the underlying preferential pattern for assigning each child a mother and father. He argues, however, that while all human societies have "fictive kin" arrangements to address these exceptional circumstances, these are better understood as exceptions to the fundamental pattern than as evidence that the postulated pattern is an inaccurate generalization. He illustrates with two ethnographically documented cases of extreme deviations from the pattern of assigning a child a single mother and a single father: the Na and the Nayars of nineteenth-century India. He also addresses other ethnographic departures from the integrative model of parenthood.

Part III addresses the critical question of rights: What rights of adults and children are at stake in defining and regulating parenthood? Do adults have a right to a child? Do children have rights to their biological parents? How do human rights instruments, such as the Universal Declaration of Human Rights (UDHR) and the Convention on the Rights of the Child (CRC), illuminate these questions? Religious ethicist Don Browning and legal scholar David Meyer both consider the UDHR, the CRC, and the rights of parents and children in family law, but they reach different conclusions as to how they bear on models of parenthood.

In chapter 5, Browning develops an integrative view of children's rights based upon the natural law tradition in Christian thought.[17] He reconstructs this tradition to address two questions: How should we ground the rights of children, especially in light of the rights of parents? What can Christianity contribute to answering that question? He contends that the natural law tradition (which integrated and used many non-Christian sources, such as notions of kin altruism) emphasizes the biological relatedness and marriage of a child's parents as central to the rights of children, both legal and religious. Law and religion, he argues, should cooperate in maximizing the possibility that the reproductive rights of adults are realized in ways that protect the rights of children to be raised by the parents who conceived them and to ensure that this happens within legally institutionalized marriage. He shows the prominence of this view in major international human rights documents, such as the UDHR and the CRC. Browning also criticizes family law's move away from this natural law tradition and toward a diversity model.

In chapter 6, David Meyer asks whether the rights of children or adults require the state to enlarge the concept of parenthood to accommodate an expanding universe of family forms (as the diversity model would support) or, instead, aggressively to channel child rearing into the traditional, marital, two-parent, mother-father model of parenthood.[18] He concludes that the rights of children and those of adults do not require adherence to any single model of parenthood, whether oriented around biology, marriage, adult intentions, or any other polestar. Children's rights and those of adults do put modest constraints on the state's choices in defining the parent-child relationship, but the limits are broad, evolving, and multidimensional. Basic rights inevitably require some diversity in parenthood, but they do not compel public acquiescence in whatever child care arrangements upon which adults may agree. Resort to rights talk, Meyer argues, cannot spare society the need to grapple with the fundamental policy questions that must guide the exercise of democratic choice. He illustrates his thesis by examining the rights of children in the CRC, the rights of adults and children in the UDHR and the European Convention on Human Rights, and judicial constructions of parenthood in U.S. constitutional law.

In part IV, contributors address the question of child outcomes and parenthood: Does one model of parenthood produce, on average, better outcomes for children or for society? What light does social science shed on the parenthood—and family forms—debates? In chapter 7, legal scholar Margaret Brinig makes a case for the integrative model of parenthood and for supporting the formal, legally recognized statuses of husband/wife and parent/child.[19] Drawing on the existing literature and on her own research on different-sex couples, she argues that, in general, children do better in the short and long term if they live with married parents and if they are biological or adopted children of these parents. Using mixed-race marriages as an example, she explains the importance of different factors for child outcomes, such as the stability and permanence of relationships and parental warmth. She also explains the importance of community, which includes the formal community denoted by legal status, the family's religious community, and the peer community, which particularly influences older children. For example, black children seem to be affected by formal legal relationships far less than other racial groups in the United States, and she concludes that the reason may be the support provided by the mother's religiosity. She also considers that stable marriages may provide a buffer for fathers who, on their own, may prefer sons to daughters, as the reported cases involving relocation by custodial parents suggest.

In chapter 8, psychologist Fiona Tasker looks at developmental outcomes for children raised by lesbian and gay parents.[20] She observes that, for policy makers, whether or not children brought up in nontraditional family structures are disadvantaged, unaffected, or even advantaged in their development has been a key concern in whether to change the law to recognize and support lesbian and gay parenting. She first canvasses the pathways to parenthood by gay men and lesbians (such as adoption, the use of ART, and after heterosexual separation or divorce), and the extent to which current legal regimes support those pathways. She then provides an overview of key studies of children brought up by lesbian and gay parents, pointing out limitations in prior studies and how more recent studies provide probative evidence that children reared by lesbian and gay parents do not fare worse than children reared by heterosexual or opposite-sex parents. These studies generally are consistent with the diversity model's claim that family form in and of itself makes little difference to child well-being; instead, what matters are quality of parenting, access to resources, and the social systems surrounding the family. She concludes that further legal change is necessary to support different routes to family formation and to recognize and meet the needs of children in diverse families.

Part V turns to the question of how children form secure attachment to their parents or other caregivers—a vital component of child development. How much does a biological connection between parent and child matter to this process? What sort of factors foster and hinder secure attachment? Psychoanalyst John Bowlby's pioneering work on attachment provides a point of departure for both chapters in this part. However, the chapters contrast sharply in their basic or "take-home" messages about fashioning public policy about parenthood informed by the literature on attachment.

In chapter 9, an interdisciplinary group of authors from medicine, psychology, and religious ethics—Terence Hébert, Ellen Moss, Daniel Cere, and Hyun Song—explore the biological and psychological bases of attachment.[21] First explaining the biological bases of attachment relationships at a molecular, cellular, and genetic level, they contend that the intricate interconnections between pair-bonds and developmental processes are consistent with Bowlby's original theories of the biological bases of the attachment system and its evolutionary function. Then, they offer a more organismic, behavioral and social focus upon attachment. They identify and interpret qualitatively different child-parent attachment patterns within an evolutionary framework and the role of secure and insecure attachment relationships in promoting survival of offspring. What are the implications, they ask, of psychological research findings for child welfare policy and attachment-based intervention models? Finally, they call for rigorous research on attachment, but also conclude that the evidence concerning the evolution of complex biological and kinship patterns makes a strong case for caution with respect to changes in parenting structures and practices that would promote freedom, equality, and diversity in family forms without attention to the effects of such policies on children.

In chapter 10, psychologists Howard Steele and Miriam Steele strike a tone of confidence about what is known concerning human attachment, based on fifty years of systematic research since Bowlby's pioneering work, and how this attachment research may assist public policy. Attachment security, they argue, overrides any particular mode of conception and allows any child to thrive if she or he receives consistent sensitive care from at least one adult who assumes parental responsibility.[22] Bowlby's work frames their discussion of what the literature demonstrates about what contributes to a parent meeting a child's needs for secure attachment and the lifelong relevance of these concepts for healthy child, adolescent, and adult development. They highlight research showing how parents demonstrate an ability to rise above adverse experiences in their past. Considering attachment in the contexts of one- and two-parent families, adoptive and foster care families, and of children conceived by the new reproductive technologies, they also conclude that a burgeoning literature on nontraditional families firmly supports a diversity model of parenthood. Their take-home message is that the interior emotional and cognitive qualities of parents matter most to effective parenting and to children's adjustment and well-being.

Part VI tackles questions about gender equality, gender difference, and parenthood: Are there gender differences in parenting? Should such difference make a difference to understanding, regulating, and supporting parenthood? Both contributors addressing this question—legal scholar Susan Frelich Appleton and sociologist Andrea Doucet—share a commitment to gender equality and support such policy goals as facilitating women's equal participation in the workplace and men's and women's more equal participation in the home. Both locate themselves within the diversity approach to parenthood. However, there are fruitful and creative tensions between them as to how much a commitment to gender equality requires gender neutrality.

In chapter 11, Appleton makes the case for a legal regime based on the diversity approach to parenthood.[23] This model, she argues, supports recognition of a diverse range of parent-child relationships, without regard to sex or gender. Indeed, she challenges the constitutional validity of parentage laws that would impose an integrative model. She argues that this model and its underlying normative premises rest on gender stereotypes that equal protection jurisprudence and family law have repudiated. She also questions the reliance upon empirical claims about the effect of various familial arrangements on children to support or oppose one model of parenthood over another. Indeed, she argues that empirical data purporting to show that the normative one-mother/one-father configuration serves most children well would not justify enshrining it in parentage rules applicable to all children. Appleton engages with Doucet on the question of whether gender-neutral parental leave policies are up to the task, pointing out the comparatively less family-friendly environment in the United States than in the countries Doucet discusses. In concluding, she calls for a law of parentage rooted in a robust pluralism, a commitment to gender equality, and on common ground between the models on the paramount value of children's interests. She reminds readers that, whatever approach one takes, parentage rules are important because they invest authority over children in adults.

In chapter 12, Andrea Doucet begins with the points on which she and Appleton agree.[24] She agrees, in general, with Appleton's arguments about the limited role that gender differences should have in law. However, she brings a different set of lenses to the question of gender and parenthood, including sociological, ethnographic, and feminist theoretical work. In contrast to the integrative model, she does not emphasize biological connection. However, she does place critical importance on embodiment to men's and women's experience of parenthood. She contends that arguing for gender neutrality, as a legal principle, does not necessarily translate into an erasure or absence of gender differences in the everyday identities, practices, and responsibilities of parenting. She draws on her ethnographic work with Canadian families to illustrate differences in how fathers and mothers experience the emotional, moral, and community responsibilities of parenting and what factors contribute to those differences. She argues for a shift in focus from measuring gender equality in parenting to making sense of differences. She illustrates her approach by examining whether and how gender differences in parenting should inform parental leave policies.

Part VII considers the implications of global migration of families across national borders for parenthood and family life. As immigration and psychology scholar Carola Suárez-Orozco and immigration and anthropology scholar Marcelo Suárez-Orozco detail in chapter 13, hundreds of millions of families experience and conduct family life across national borders, giving rise to transnational parenting, with reverberations for children, parents, and extended family.[25] They examine what they call "familyhood" through multiple lenses—in its biological, functional, and symbolic complexities. They ask: What does it mean to be a parent, a child, or even a "family unit" in transnational circumstances of global migration? Explaining how immigration is often a *family* project, they point out the gap between the ideal of an integrative family—with parents and children in one household—and the reality of protracted separations between parents and children, with extended kin and fictive kin providing caretaking. They address the complex challenges families face at reunification and offer some guidelines for public policy.

In chapter 14, sociologist Rhacel Salazar Parreñas examines some dynamics of transnational families in the context of the Philippines, one of the largest source countries of migrant workers in contemporary globalization.[26] She focuses, in particular, on how young adult children of migrant mothers interpret their transnational life. She, too, identifies the challenges that geographic distance poses for transnational families, including marital strain, emotional distance, and the pain of family separation. However, she contends that the dismissal of transnational mothering as a viable means of parenting exacerbates these challenges and constraints. Public opinion in Philippine society, she finds, negatively views transnational mothers because their families depart from an integrative ideal of parenthood, and such views intensify the struggles faced by transnational family members. By contrast, her perspective on such families embraces a diversity model, which assumes that the geographic separation of mothers from their children need not prevent the formation of healthy intergenerational relations between them and rejects the idea that biological mothers are the only or ideal caregivers for their children.

Finally, part VIII poses the "Now what?" question. Given demographic changes in family life, and current patterns of family formation and parenting, what direction should family law and family policy take? Should the proverbial toothpaste go back in the tube, that is, by taking measures to link parenthood more tightly to marriage and discourage the growth in alternative families? Could it? Or should attention shift from family form as such to other matters, like whether persons who become parents are prepared for the responsibilities of parenthood and how law and policy could foster such responsibility? Family researcher and Family Scholars blog director Elizabeth Marquardt and legal scholars June Carbone and Naomi Cahn offer sharply diverging answers to the "Now what?" question.

In chapter 15, Marquardt argues that society can and should seek to renew marriage as a uniquely important integrator of male-female, mother-child, and father-child bonds.[27] She grants that there are many good aspects of recent family change, among them greater professional, educational, and leadership opportunities for women and girls; residential fathers' increased emotional involvement with their children; reduced tolerance for domestic violence; greater acceptance of diversity within families; and growing acceptance of gay and lesbian persons. However, some recent family changes have been negative and hurt children. She contends that there is much we still do not know, empirically, about same-sex marriage and parenting and child outcomes, and discusses findings from her own study of children conceived with donor sperm. She concludes that society should pursue greater integration, for the sake of children, and that doing so would not undermine the positive aspects of family change.

She challenges Carbone and Cahn's argument (in chapter 16) that a focus on "responsible parenthood" is a better strategy.

In chapter 16, Carbone and Cahn propose to resolve the evident tension between the integrative and diversity models by advancing the "responsible parenthood" model, which would support responsible parenthood irrespective of family form.[28] They elaborate the "critical principles" that support responsible parenthood: emphasize education for men and women; postpone childbearing until adults reach a measure of financial independence and emotional maturity; adopt more flexible attitudes toward gender roles in the home and workplace; and respect the life and reproductive choices of mature and independent persons. They note a central irony in the "family values" debate: in the more liberal, or "blue," states, which have moved toward this responsibility model, there is little preaching of traditional family values, but the two-parent, marital family flourishes. By contrast, families in "red" states, which emphasize steering sexuality and reproduction into marriage, have higher rates of teen births and divorce, and worsening prospects for the next generation. Disagreement over models of parenting, they contend, is less about the ideal—healthy, stable families—and more about the means for achieving that end and how to address the gap between ideal and reality. Wholesale demographic and economic changes, they argue, are shaping family formation and family life and making the "red" model more difficult to sustain.

In our epilogue, we offer some concluding reflections on this book's investigation of critical questions about parenthood and propose directions for further inquiry. Cere addresses several misleading critiques of both integrative and diversity accounts of parenthood to help readers identify lines of attack that obscure the complexity of the issues these accounts raise. McClain observes that the interplay of the contributors' various disciplinary perspectives reveals challenging methodological and normative questions that require consideration in shaping the law of parenthood and family policy. She identifies three issues that illuminate points of agreement and disagreement between the integrative and diversity models and warrant further attention: assessing the fact and value of family diversity and the role of law in addressing that diversity; determining the relevance of natural science and social science to models of parenting and to family law and policy; and addressing the role that public values and the normative commitments of family law and constitutional law should play in fashioning the law of parenthood.

Notes

1. We use the term *parenthood* rather than *parentage*, which refers typically to the legal determination of who is a parent. We use the broader term *parenthood* to encompass questions of legal definition, as well as other questions about the experience, institution, and regulation of parenthood.

2. In part VI, both authors locate themselves within the diversity model but take different approaches to questions about gender equality, gender difference, and parenthood.

3. See, e.g., The National Organization for Marriage, "Marriage Talking Points," http://www.nationformarriage.org (accessed Jan. 16, 2012).

4. For a helpful explanation of family law's channelling function, see Carl E. Schneider, "The Channelling Function in Family Law," *Hofstra Law Review* 20 (1992): 495.

5. We refer here to David Blankenhorn, president of the Institute for American Values and a prominent witness for the proponents of California ballot initiative Proposition 8 in the 2010 federal trial over the initiative's constitutionality. See David Blankenhorn, "How My View on Gay Marriage Changed," *New York Times*, http://www.nytimes.com/2012/06/23/opinion/how-my-view-on-gay-marriage-changed.html?_r=2&hp&pagewanted=print (accessed June 23, 2012); Mark Oppenheimer, "David Blankenhorn and the Battle Over Same-Sex Marriage," http://www.yourpublicmedia.org/content/wnpr/david-blankenhorn-and-battle-over-same-sex-marriage (accessed June 25, 2012).

6. See Linda C. McClain, *The Place of Families: Fostering Capacity, Equality, and Responsibility* (Cambridge: Harvard University Press, 2006), 60–61, 117–154; Susan Frelich Appleton, "Missing in Action? Searching for Gender Talk in the Same-Sex Marriage Debate," *Stanford Law and Policy Review* 16 (2005): 97, 110.

7. Pew Research Center, *The Decline of Marriage and Rise of New Families*, Nov. 18, 2010, http://www.pewsocialtrends.org/2010/11/18/the-decline-of-marriage-and-rise-of-new-families/ (accessed Nov. 15, 2011), 40–41.

8. Ibid., 40.

9. Ibid., 54–56, 62–67. For a subsequent analysis of these different segments, see Pew Research Center, *The Public Renders a Split Verdict on Changes in Family Structure*, Feb. 16, 2011, http://www.pewsocialtrends.org/2011/02/16/the-public-renders-a-split-verdict-on-changes-in-family-structure/ (accessed Nov. 15, 2011).

10. See, e.g., Hernandez v. Robles, 855 N.E.2d 1 (N.Y. 2006); Lewis v. Harris, 875 A.2d 259, 276 (N.J. Super. Ct. App. Div. 2005) (Parrillo, J., concurring) (discussing "conjugal" model of marriage), *affirmed in part and modified in part*, 908 A.2d 196 (N.J. 2006). An oft-discussed dissenting opinion articulating the role of marriage in linking heterosexual sexuality to responsible parenthood (cited favorably in *Hernandez*) is Goodridge v. Department of Public Health, 798 N.E.2d 941, 995 (Mass. 2003) (Cordy, J., dissenting).

11. See, e.g., Varnum v. Brien, 763 N.W.2d 862 (Iowa 2009); *Goodridge*, 961–964; In re Marriage Cases, 183 P.3d 384 (Cal. 2008). Proposition 8, which amended the California Constitution to define marriage as between one man and one woman, overturned the California Supreme Court's ruling. A federal district court subsequently held that Prop

8 violated the federal constitution and, after a lengthy trial, made extensive findings about the irrelevance of gender to marriage and parenthood and the equal capacity of heterosexuals and homosexuals to be spouses and parents. Perry v. Schwarzenegger, 704 F. Supp. 2d 921 (N.D. Cal. 2010), *affirmed sub nom.* Perry v. Brown, 671 F.3d 1052 (9th Cir. 2012).

12. The New York legislature's debate over the recently enacted Marriage Equality Act (2011), opening up civil marriage to same-sex couples, is one example.

13. Daniel Cere, "Toward an Integrative Account of Parenthood" (this volume).

14. Linda C. McClain, "A Diversity Approach to Parenthood in Family Life and Family Law" (this volume).

15. Judith Stacey, "Uncoupling Marriage and Parenting" (this volume).

16. Peter Wood, "The Anthropological Case for the Integrative Model" (this volume).

17. Don Browning, "Legal Parenthood, Natural and Legal Rights, and the Best Interests of the Child: An Integrative View" (this volume).

18. David D. Meyer, "Family Diversity and the Rights of Parenthood" (this volume).

19. Margaret F. Brinig, "A Case for Integrated Parenthood" (this volume).

20. Fiona Tasker, "Developmental Outcomes for Children Raised by Lesbian and Gay Parents" (this volume).

21. Terence E. Hébert, Ellen Moss, Daniel Cere, and Hyun Song, "Biological and Psychological Dimensions of Integrative Attachments" (this volume).

22. Howard Steele and Miriam Steele, "Parenting Matters: An Attachment Perspective" (this volume).

23. Susan Frelich Appleton, "Gender and Parentage: Family Law's Equality Project in Our Empirical Age" (this volume).

24. Andrea Doucet, "Can Parenting Be Equal? Rethinking Equality and Gender Differences in Parenting" (this volume).

25. Carola Suárez-Orozco and Marcelo M. Suárez-Orozco, "Transnationalism of the Heart: Familyhood across Borders" (this volume).

26. Rhacel Salazar Parreñas, "Transnational Mothering and Models of Parenthood: Ideological and Intergenerational Challenges in Filipina Migrant Families" (this volume).

27. Elizabeth Marquardt, "Of Human Bonding: Integrating the Needs and Desires of Women, Men, and the Children Their Unions Produce" (this volume).

28. June Carbone and Naomi Cahn, "The Other Side of the Demographic Revolution: Social Policy and Responsible Parenthood" (this volume).

What Is Parenthood?

Proposing Two Models

PART ONE

Toward an Integrative Account of Parenthood

Daniel Cere

Attachment theory and evolutionary kinship theory offer powerful and comprehensive theoretical accounts of the complex domain of human parenthood. Attachment theory emerged as a contribution to evolutionary psychology, but these trajectories of research had drifted apart. In recent years there have been efforts to reconnect these fertile explanatory approaches. This chapter discusses developments in these fields, what they suggest about the complex nexus of kin relationships and primal attachments, and how these findings may resonate with integrative lines of argument. The final section discusses tensions between the diversity and integrative approaches to parenthood and their implications for law and policy.

Integrative Attachments

Plato's *Republic* envisages a human society in which child care is fully disconnected from parenthood, allowing adult male and female progenitors to pursue their interests and careers freed from the burden of daily parental responsibilities. For Plato, the private (*idion*) realm of the familial is a dense domain filled with strong idiosyncratic passions and loyalties not easily ordered by the universal standards of justice.[1] *The Republic* argues for the deconstruction of this private sphere and its reorganization on transparent principles of rational justice. The nepotism of familial relationships must be replaced by an extensive system of public institutions dedicated to child care and rearing.

Modern culture has been the site for numerous experiments attempting to realize some version of this Platonic project. One significant example is the Israeli kibbutz experiment. Two key objectives of the kibbutz project were, first, an attempt to loosen the connection between the breeding and nurturing dimensions of parenthood and, second, the promotion of gender equality in the division of labor. Shepher and Tiger's classic study *Women in the Kibbutz* documents the diverse ways in which this experiment seemed to run up against entrenched features of human bonding. Despite the centrality of these child-rearing arrangements to the communal experiment, kibbutzim women demanded reversion to forms of mother-child attachment found in most, if not all, human societies.[2]

Jewish maternal resistance to this experiment in comprehensive child care could look to an influential body of research for support. Attachment theory has emerged as one of the most influential theories in contemporary psychology. Bowlby's early research on the disastrous effects of fragmented institutionalized child care led to a new awareness of the decisive importance of close attachment bonds for child development.[3] Ainsworth's fieldwork in Uganda underscored the cross-cultural significance of this emerging body of theory.[4] Decades later the legacy of Romania's institutionalized child care regime provided tragic data for extensive research into the traumatic impact of severe attachment deprivation and evidence for many of the basic claims of attachment theory.[5]

Attachment theory has its critics. One regular line of critique argues that attachment theory is an ideological paradigm that reflects the concerns of Western middle-class parenting culture.[6] However, an increasing body of interdisciplinary evidence points to the cross-cultural patterns of attachment. Primatological studies have underscored the applicability of attachment theory to non-human primates. The evidence points to the validity of a thick core of claims in attachment theory including the following:

1. the universal need of infants to become attached to a primary caregiver;[7]
2. the high degree of maternal sensitivity to an infant's attachment signals;[8]
3. elevated and enduring patterns of infant attachment behavior and maternal sensitivity in the higher primates;[9]
4. the high degree of infant sensitivity to changes in psychosocial attachments;[10]
5. the biological, hormonal, genetic, and epigenetic dimensions of social bonding;[11]
6. the significance of attachment security for competencies in cognitive, emotional, and social development;[12]
7. cross-cultural evidence for similar patterns of secure, insecure, and disorganized attachments;[13] and
8. the correlation of childhood attachment disorders to a number of adolescent and adult psychopathologies.[14]

A powerful set of research techniques have begun to uncover the biochemical interactions involved in maternal-infant attachments and the processes that regulate gene expression in the early development of infants.[15] This research has linked attachment theory to a system of gene regulation known as *epigenetics*.[16] Maternal-infant attachment bonds trigger epigenetic changes that initiate "long-term developmental effects lasting into childhood."[17]

There is a growing scientific consensus that early attachment bonds have long-term consequences across the life span.[18] Low attachment bonds result in heightened startle and defense responses, more intense responses to stress, and early, increased sexual activity—response patterns suitable to hostile unpredictable environments. Secure bonds result in a capacity for more explorative responses to novelty, lower levels of stress, and slower sexual development—traits suited to stable environments that offer diverse resources and opportunities.[19] Because attachment patterns typically reappear in future pair-bonding and parenting styles of these secure or insecure infants, they can, and regularly do, have a transgenerational impact. The impact of a mother's high or low attachment patterns is passed on to her daughters, shaping their future maternal responses. In short, patterns of parent-infant attachments are biologically encoded at the epigenetic level with long-term significance for adult attachments and, possibly, for their offspring.[20]

As evidence accumulated, Bowlby concluded that the formation of secure attachments occurs across the human life span.[21] According to Zeifman and Hazan, secure childhood bonds predispose individuals to develop stable attachments in adult relationships. Long-term pair-bonds anchor familial stability, enhance mutual support and parental collaboration, and tend to be associated with more secure attachments to the offspring of these pair-bonds. Individuals who have experienced stable attachments are more likely to adopt the committed long-term mating strategies important to reproductive success.[22]

Attachment theory's success in highlighting the crucial importance of attachment for human development, and the new discoveries into the biological mechanisms of attachment theory, raise some serious concerns. The social web of care for children emerges as the first and most fundamental developmental challenge for human relationships. This research has implications for law and public policy. There appears to be significant convergence on a substantive set of principles across lines of debate on parenthood:

- first, that children have a basic right to close, secure attachments with primary caregivers;
- second, that adults who are in relationships of parental responsibility for children have a duty to respond to their basic attachment needs;
- third, that society and the state should work to provide social, economic, and institutional contexts that facilitate and support, rather than erode or undermine, the capacity of adult caregivers to meet the basic attachment needs of children;
- fourth, there is a need to work toward the elimination of forms of child care that contribute to serious attachment deprivation.

Michael Rutter notes that attachment theory has already played a significant role in a number of major policy developments. Its findings contributed to the turn from institutionalized orphanages as the first-choice solution for children who have lost connection to parental caregivers. It has also contributed to changes in hospital practices dealing with children in situations of extended care.[23]

However, beyond these areas of convergence on some core principles and practices, there would be disagreement. To highlight the fluidity and elasticity of parenting arrangements, proponents of diversity emphasize the performative or functional character of attachment bonds. In this view, quality attachments are the result of good parenting practices. Performance is not tied to particular maternal or paternal kin-connected bonds. Adoptive parents, stepparents, foster parents, or same-sex caregivers should be able to perform the caregiving functions required to meet children's attachment needs.[24] Diversity proponents argue that the processes of attachment observed in secure mother-child bonds could also be provided by other consistent caregiving adults genetically unrelated to the child.[25] Highlighting the central significance of a particular form of parental attachment such as the "maternal-child" bond amounts to a form of essentialism that constrains the range of parenting possibilities and throws certain forms of parenting under a cloud of suspicion.

The integrative approach, in contrast, would have fewer reservations about highlighting the salience of particular parental bonds for the attachment needs of children. For example, it would be more willing to entertain evidence from primatology, evolutionary psychology, and attachment theory that points to the near-universal role of maternal-child ties as the primary attachment bond. Evolutionary psychology argues that across species females are far more likely than males to care for, invest in, and bond with their offspring.²⁶ As they move through gestation and birth, biological mothers are hormonally primed for parental sensitivity, investment, and attachment in ways that other adults are not.²⁷ These factors nudged Bowlby to suggest that the "elementary social unit" of our evolutionary development is the mother-child bond—and perhaps uterine bonds with her daughter's children (allomaternal)—rather than the co-parental bond.²⁸

In contrast, Sarah Hrdy's anthropological account of maternal caregiving seems supportive of a diversity line of argument.²⁹ She highlights the complexity of kinship systems and the significance of "fictive" or "manufactured" kinship and emphasizes "the advantages of casting the net of kinship as widely as possible."³⁰ She questions the significance of genetic relationship for parental attachment.³¹ Hrdy shares the Dutch primatologist Frans De Waal's fascination with the free-flowing mating and parenting styles of primates like the bonobos and the marmosets. Both scholars find these intensely promiscuous, sexually energized and good-natured primates far more attractive as fellow travelers in the trajectory of primate evolution than the "demonic," "xenophobic," and "compulsively possessive" parental behavior of chimps and gorillas typically cited as our closest and best primate templates for human patterns of parent-child attachment and caregiving.³²

Hrdy dismisses Bowlby's focus on the "sexually monandrous mother" as a narrow and "Victorian" account of the complexities of human mating and parenting.³³ Hrdy works the primatological data to highlight the elasticity of parental forms and the critical importance of cooperative breeding and alloparenting for human and nonhuman primate child care. The big idea permeating her work is one borrowed from Stephanie Coontz, namely, that "children do best in societies where childrearing is considered too important to be left entirely to parents."³⁴ The core elements of her argument lay out a primatological manifesto for good-quality child care:

> First, *there is no one, universal pattern of infant care among primates.* Second, far from being a hardwired primate-wide trait, *continuous-care-and-contact mothering is a last resort for primate mothers who lack safe and available alternatives.* Third, and perhaps most important so far as primates are concerned, *there is nothing evolutionarily out of the ordinary about mothers cutting corners or relying on shared care.*³⁵

According to Hrdy, human maternal-infant attachments, similar to those in a number of nonhuman species, form complex patterns of alloparenting, typically based on kin connection, that complement and assist maternal care.[36] This complexity provides human infants with a richer social matrix for development than the more possessive and "monotropic" maternal styles of chimps or gorillas.[37]

However, despite this shift of attention away from kin-connected bonds toward the more communal dimensions of parenting, in the final analysis her survey does not challenge "the central importance of mothers." "Of all the attachments mammalian babies form," Hrdy concedes, "none is more powerful than that between baby primates and their mothers."[38] Furthermore, her examination of the diverse forms of alloparenting (other parents) actually underscores the central role of kin-connected "allomaternal" supports (i.e., maternal grandmothering) as the most typical form of co-parenting in the human species.[39] In short, the continuity and quality of maternal-infant attachment still emerges as a critical factor in her anthropological and primatological research.[40] While it is important to recognize the supportive, or even replacement, role of secondary or subsidiary attachment figures in parenting, acknowledging the significance of these contributions cannot obscure the critical significance of biological mothering and kin-connected allomothering.[41]

Should legal significance be attributed to the mother-child bond? It would make sense for the integrative position to contend that, in principle, there should be some acknowledgment of the fundamental significance of these bonds. The specific legal and policy recommendations regarding the complex set of issues relating to maternity and maternal-child attachment are open to debate. However, it is significant that the motherhood/childhood nexus did receive formal recognition in the significant international human rights document of the modern era, the Universal Declaration of Human Rights (1948). Shortly before Bowlby's first formulation of attachment theory, the drafting committee for the United Nations declaration advanced the following provision: "Motherhood and childhood are entitled to special care and assistance" (Art. 25(2)). The International Covenant on Economic, Social, and Cultural Rights (1966) developed this principle by mandating that "special protection should be accorded to mothers during a reasonable period before and after childbirth. During such period working mothers should be accorded paid leave or leave with adequate social security benefits" (Art. 10(2)). These developments seem to be sound initiatives from the perspective of an integrative account sensitive to the concerns raised in attachment research.

Kinship Bonds and Pair-Bonds

Accenting the importance of mother-child attachments underscores the centrality of at least one kin-connected bond in the matrix of relationships important to an integrative approach. However, despite the early emphasis on the importance of kin connectedness in the work of Bowlby and Ainsworth, current attachment theory is shifting toward a stance of intellectual agnosticism on this question. Thus, in a prominent handbook on attachment, a survey of attachment theory contains only two references to kinship: a brief mention of possible differences between kin and non-kin foster care, and an equally brief discussion of research on evidence for kin-selective altruism among homosexuals.[42] This development marks a decisive shift away from Bowlby's attention to the significance of kinship and kin connection in evolutionary theory.[43] This shift has cut attachment theory off from the ongoing discussions of kin connection in evolutionary theory.[44]

Recognizing the significance of genetically related kinship bonds is clearly a vital element of the case for integrative conceptions of parenthood that tend to situate parenting within the wider web of kin relationships constituted by consanguineal bonds—both lineal (grandparents-parents-child-siblings) and collateral (cousins-uncles-aunts)—and the bilateral affinal bonds generated by stable pair-bonds (marriage). This interlocking nexus of kinship bonds constitutes a core feature of integrative conceptions that weave infant attachments (the parent-child bond) and adult attachments (adult pair-bonds) together into a dynamic kin-connected web of attachment bonds. Insofar as "the family" provides an integrative social nexus for both parent-child attachments and adult pair-bonds, Bowlby claims that it constitutes "the seat and centre" of our emotional life.[45]

However, as Eugene Burnstein points out, the current social science "orthodoxy" seems to be leaning in another direction, namely, pressing for an end to kinship discourse. Diverse sociological and anthropological theories argue that "there is nothing inherent to genetic relatedness that precludes unrelated individuals from developing equally close and demanding ties."[46] David Schneider's influential manifesto, *A Critique of the Study of Kinship*, is widely cited as heralding the end of kinship studies in modern anthropology.⁴⁷ Schneider's work did not sound the death knell for kinship studies, but it did ==signal a move from biologically based theories of kinship toward conceptions of kinship as pure cultural construct.==

Schneider argues that classical anthropological theories of kinship are based upon a number of flawed axioms: first, that kinship bonds are "natural ties" that are more "compelling and stronger than, and take priority over, other kinds of bonds";⁴⁸ second, that, at some level, these bonds are innate, "indissoluble," and biologically determined relations;⁴⁹ third, that kinship is the fundamental social bond, a foundational and "ordering principle" of society;⁵⁰ fourth, that kinship sets in motion an expanding genealogical matrix of human relationships based on sexual pair-bonding and reproduction;⁵¹ fifth, that the stable reproductive pair-bonds (marriage) are "the central feature of kinship" and the basis of all parenthood;⁵² and sixth, all the preceding axioms are based upon the assumption "that all human cultures have a theory of human reproduction or similar beliefs about biological relatedness, or that all human societies share certain conditions, which create bonds between genetrix and child and between a breeding couple."⁵³ Schneider rejects the argument that there are universals of kinship operative in all human societies and concludes that "there is no such thing as kinship" in this classic anthropological sense: "Robbed of its grounding in biology, kinship is nothing," that is, nothing more than an ideological construct of Western culture.⁵⁴

Post-Schneideran anthropologists have attempted to restore a discourse on kinship along more thoroughly constructionist lines. Janet Carsten speaks of kinship as "relatedness." In her view, "people become kin through living and eating together," not by mere reproduction.⁵⁵ Kinship is a cultural performance rather than a status derived from a singular event of biological reproduction. "Conceived in its broadest sense, relatedness (or kinship) is simply about the ways in which people create similarity or difference between themselves and others."⁵⁶

This deconstruction of kinship is not without critics. Anthropologist Ladislav Holy argues that strong social constructionist approaches fail to distinguish kinship as a category of human relationships distinct from other types of close interdependent relationships.⁵⁷ Robert McKinley criticizes Schneider for his refusal to acknowledge the universal appeal of the grammar of kinship in all human cultures. McKinley turns Schneider's argument on its head by arguing that this new anthropological fascination with "designer kinship" reflects the cultural bias of postmodern Western discourse.⁵⁸

However, the most telling critiques of strong deconstructivist approaches to kinship come from evolutionary theory and biological anthropology. Hamilton's influential theory of "inclusive fitness" represented a major development in modern evolution theory. Hamilton argues that all human and nonhuman social interactions display a critical evolutionary dynamic, namely, that levels of altruistic concern and investment increase with the degree of genetic relatedness.[59] Inclusive fitness is a dimension of behavior that works for the reproductive success of both individuals and their close relatives. Kin altruism represents personal investment for the sake of genetically related others: both direct descendants (lineal kin) or indirect descendants (collateral kin). The most significant site for displays of kin altruism is the domain of parental care and investment.[60] Almost all human societies structure family systems so that parental investment is directed toward close kin-related offspring.[61]

Marshall Sahlins attacks Hamilton's rule and ridicules the idea that behavior would be guided by the mental calculations of cost-benefit inclusive fitness central to Hamilton's theory.[62] However, Hamilton's approach takes issue with the assumption that human kinship behavior is a function of learned cultural belief systems. His theory of kin connection, discrimination, bias, and investment is grounded not on psychological or cultural dynamics but in the logic of evolutionary adaptation.[63] Richard Dawkins dismisses constructionist critiques of kin altruism and dubs them "Sahlins' Fallacy."[64] The fallacy resides in the presumption that all human behavior must be the result of implicit or explicit deliberations "informed by culture."[65]

Hamilton's theory, Burnstein argues, is now "well supported by ethnographic and experimental research, both of which consistently demonstrate that individuals are more likely to sacrifice for close kin than for distant kin and least likely to do so for unrelated individuals."[66] A growing body of research now concludes that kin relationships are "more precise, enduring, and inescapable . . . more intimate and taxing" than other types of human bonds.[67] The exact mechanisms of kin recognition are not fully understood, though there seems to be some consensus about the critical role of cues involving "familiarity" and "phenotype" recognition. However, there is growing consensus about the importance of the innate human orientation toward kin recognition and its critical role in shaping human behavior.

Neither classical nor contemporary theories of kinship seem up to the task of providing theoretical tools to adequately integrate the evidence and problematics emerging from new research in primatology, evolutionary theory, and biological anthropology. Doug Jones and Bernard Chapais have opened up new lines of theoretical exploration that are attracting scholarly attention. Jones suggests that many species, including humans, appear to operate with a precultural universal grammar of kinship. He argues that both human and nonhuman cognitive functions seem primed to recognize patterns of kin relatedness, to categorize relationships by their degree of genetic relatedness (close and distant kin, as well as non-kin), and to calculate and make higher and more sustained investments in close genetic relationships.[68] Humans are distinguished from other species in their capacity to construct more complex and variable systems of kin classification and kin-based social forms.[69] However, these levels of complexity and diversity, Jones argues, should not divert us, as Sahlins and Schneider insist that they should, from acknowledging the universal patterns of kin recognition, connectivity, and investment at play in these diverse constructions. Jones concludes that cultural anthropological polemics against evolutionary concepts of kinship cannot be sustained.[70]

Chapais's *Primeval Kinship* has been hailed as the first major revision of kinship theory since Claude Lévi-Strauss's seminal study, *The Elementary Structures of Kinship*.[71] Chapais positions his work in relationship to two major trajectories in kinship theory—structuralism and cultural relativism. In contrast to Schneider's stance of cultural relativism, Lévi-Strauss's structuralist account argued that there are a limited number of cross-cultural universals in kinship.[72] However, like Schneider, Lévi-Strauss maintains that kinship is grounded in structures of human cognition and culture rather than in biology. His basic thesis is that human culture breaks out from its animal matrix through the construction of the "incest taboo"—the foundation of all human kinship systems. Unlike animals, humans construct norms that prohibit sexual bonding between close consanguineal kin. This primordial cultural taboo, Lévi-Strauss argues, marks out the most elementary form of human social ordering—exogamous mating.

Chapais argues that evidence from the expanding body of new research in primatology disproves Lévi-Strauss's thesis that all animals, as well as all primitive hominids (prior to the emergence of incest taboos), engage in undiscriminating forms of sexual bonding.[73] All primates manifest incest avoidance. Evidence for the pervasiveness of incest avoidance was first put forward by Japanese primatologist Kinji Imanishi in the early 1960s, but his research was widely ignored.[74] However, numerous other studies have confirmed his findings. All nonhuman primates avoid incestuous relations between close kin (mothers-sons, brothers-sisters, grandmothers-grandsons). Both humans and nonhuman primates normally display sexual indifference toward close kin. There is an evolutionary logic to this pattern, since inbreeding is closely correlated with reduced reproductive success. The rare human and nonhuman exceptions to this rule typically are males or females who have experienced severe attachment deprivation or traumatic abuse in infancy.

Incest avoidance is closely associated with a second fundamental feature of both human and nonhuman primate kinship patterns: all primates display exogamous breeding patterns. Either males or females will disperse away from their natal group in order to mate.[75] Again, Lévi-Strauss erred in assuming that exogamy is distinctively human. Primatology has established that "in all sexually reproducing species the members of at least one sex disperse and breed outside their natal group."[76] Most species display a singular or monochromatic pattern of consistently male or female outbreeding. In this as in other areas of kinship, human cultures are characterized by more complex integrations of the varied patterns found in other primates.

A third feature of human cultures is stable pair-bonding. Chapais notes that "many sociocultural anthropologists take it for granted that marriage is a cultural construct with no biological underpinnings whatsoever."[77] However, there are numerous examples of patterns of durable opposite-sex pair-bonding, typically polygynous, among nonhuman primates. For most biological anthropologists and behavioral ecologists, stable pair-bonding is classified as "biological adaptation" similar to bipedalism or kin favoritism.[78] In this sense, Chapais argues, "stable breeding bonds in hominids have a biological basis, just as they have in other species, and they constituted the evolutionary precursors of marital unions."[79]

The constructionist perception of considerable conjugal variety across cultures is accurate when compared with the more uniform patterns in other primates.[80] However, the existence of cross-cultural variability and elaborate symbolic coding of marital bonds does not warrant the conclusion that these bonds are "intrinsically cultural." Chapais argues that the evidence points to definable "natural constraints" and, at a basic level, a definable "invariant core" or "stem pattern" to the family.[81] This stem pattern of durable male-female pair-bonding can include concurrent patterns of multiple pair-bonds evident in polygamy. However, no human society follows the free-flowing promiscuous patterns of mating characteristic of primate species like the bonobos or macaques.[82]

Fourth, enduring breeding bonds are linked to paternal recognition and interaction. In many nonhuman primate groups, kin recognition between mothers and offspring is well established, but paternity recognition is not.[83] This has tempted many anthropologists to conclude that fatherhood is a cultural construct. For example, Meyer Fortes asserts that "institutionalized fatherhood, unlike motherhood, comes into being not by virtue of a biological ... event, but by ultimately juridical, societal, provision, that is, by rule." "Fatherhood," he concludes, "is a creation of society."[84] Paternal kin recognition is a distinctive feature of human biparental families. Chapais suggests that father-child recognition is probably a function of "the father's long-term association with the mother" rather than a function of extensive paternal child caring.[85] However, this long-term association generates various forms of paternal parental investment.

According to Chapais, paternal connection and recognition are major features of human kinship systems independent of any cultural recognition of biological contributions by the genetic father. For example, although Trobriand Islanders do not have a "concept" of biological connection between fathers and children, paternal kin connections and recognition are still operative. "The important point," he argues, "is whether biological paternity in humans commonly translates into social situations that allow fathers and offspring to form preferential bonds." Fatherhood, as Fortes argues, may have diverse cultural, institutional, and symbolic meanings, but "institutionalized fatherhood is itself derived from biological fatherhood."[86]

Fifth, human societies are uniquely distinguished by their "bilateral" forms of kinship. According to Rodseth, "Humans are the only primates that maintain lifelong relationships with dispersing offspring," with both sexes remaining "embedded in networks of consanguineal kin."[87] Nonhuman outbreeding leads to a severance of kin relationships from their natal group.[88] This pattern holds for all outbreeding individuals, male or female, "in all known primate societies"—except for humans.[89] While kinship systems in primate species are always unilateral, in humans they are bilaterally structured through both maternal and paternal filiation. "Bifilial kin recognition," Chapais argues, "is the primary factor accounting for the unparalleled richness and complexity of human kinship networks.[90]

Sixth, human kinship systems operate in "stable bisexual groups" composed of multimale and multifemale members.[91] There are other examples of multimale/multifemale groups among primates, but these typically are associated with promiscuous breeding patterns. Human communities display a unique form of "multifamily community" featuring multimale/multifemale composition coexisting with stable breeding bonds.⁹²

Chapais's investigation of the thick array of kinship universals that constitute the "deep structure" of human societies includes other important features such as postmarital residential patterns, descent systems, agnatic and uterine kinship relations, sibling relations, and the distinctive place of the "brother-sister complex." He argues that this integrative complex of biologically grounded features actually facilitates more multifaceted forms of social organization, rather than constraining cultures within narrower frames:

> The genealogical unity of humankind includes, minimally, the following aspects: stable breeding bonds, motherhood, fatherhood, siblingship, intrafamilial incest avoidance, recognition of one's close matrilateral and patrilateral kin, recognition of one's in-laws and a propensity to treat them as allies, and certain kinship biases in mate selection. Taken together, these features define the *core kinship system of humankind*—itself an integral part of human society's deep structure—from which all known kinship systems have diversified. Depending on the circumstances, the system's basic elements may generate more complex phenomena.⁹³

All human societies integrate this array of primate practices into their kinship systems. This nexus of kinship universals does not simplify parental bonding but allows for more complex social possibilities. These complex integrations represent a break from the simpler parsed-out "atoms" of kinship characteristic of the more unidimensional kinship systems in nonhuman species.

Human kinship institutions create a complex set of centrifugal and centripetal social forces in human social organization that expand out lines of kin connection through bilateral affinal and consanguineal ties. However, the culture-shaping power of kinship does not mean that kinship should be viewed as "a cultural construct." According to Chapais, kinship is "composed of three basic bonds that have deep evolutionary roots: a kinship bond, a sexual bond, and a parental bond. This basic kinship structure is an integral part of human nature." The constituent features of kinship—kin-group outbreeding, incest avoidance, kin recognition, kin favoritism, opposite-sex pair-bonding, and bilateral kin connections—have "a biological foundation."⁹⁴ And it is within this complex nexus of kin relationships and primal attachments that the integrative approach begins to articulate its case.

Implications for the Parenthood Debate: Bonds and Rights?
In their exploration of recent developments in evolutionary theory, genetics, and anthropology, Linda Stone and Paul Lurquin draw the following observation:

> Every human culture in the world recognizes a set of special relationships—relationships that concern our most fundamental sense of identity, often involving our most basic rights and obligations—that we call kinship. Kinship is not only a human universal; it is also in all likelihood among the oldest of human cultural adaptations, probably preceding language.[95]

Stone and Lurquin's discussion of kinship studiously avoids any engagement with public debates on issues related to the family or parenthood. However, their suggestion that there is some linkage between the universal features of kinship in human culture and the language of rights does raise the difficult question of the relevance of these discussions to public policy.

The significance of the nexus of kin-connected attachments seems to be at the heart of tensions between diversity and integrative approaches to parenthood. Does research on attachment, pair-bonding, parental investment, and kinship raise concerns relevant to our most basic political commitments? One site for addressing these issues is the evolving debate over the unique web of rights associated with childhood. Martha Nussbaum and Bryan Turner have argued for a major theoretical expansion of political liberalism and the human rights tradition in order to address more effectively questions of human vulnerability.[96] Nussbaum points out that most liberal theory is anchored in a conception of human persons as rational, equal, self-determining agents.[97] However, this account overlooks the fact that vulnerability and neediness are fundamental and universal dimensions of human existence. Vulnerability is universally displayed in various stages of human life (childhood and old age) and in the various forms of disability—both temporary (illness/injury) and permanent (psychological, cognitive, or physical disabilities)—that afflict all stages of life.

According to Turner, children should be central to any discussion of rights and vulnerability. They are "the most vulnerable members of society

...dependent on adults, especially parents and other kin, through much of their early development."⁹⁸ Furthermore, women seem to be uniquely linked to this vulnerability through pregnancy, birth giving, and the significant levels of maternal investment involved in lactation and early infant attachment.⁹⁹ While Nussbaum and Turner cite the central significance of childhood for any discourse on vulnerability, neither attempts any substantive discussion of the complex issues surrounding vulnerability, rights and childhood. Nussbaum notes that there are two faces to rights and vulnerability, namely, the rights of "the cared-for" and the rights of those who care for them ("most often women").¹⁰⁰ But she focuses her attention on women's equality issues in the domain of vulnerability and caretaking.¹⁰¹ Her philosophical exploration of attachment theory does allude to the need to create "political facilitating environments" responsive to the neediness and vulnerability of children. The attachment needs of children could be viewed as one example of rights to "basic welfare" in any rightly ordered liberal society.¹⁰²

Turner argues that any concept of reproductive rights necessarily entails a discussion of the attachment rights of offspring: "If we grant full and effective reproductive rights to women (or, more generally, to parents), do children have comparable rights?"¹⁰³ If there are reproductive rights, are there rights of children to a secure future, intimacy and care?¹⁰⁴ He notes that current approaches to reproductive rights frequently conflict with children's rights. For example, technological developments are now creating new expansions of adult reproductive rights, including the reproductive rights of the elderly.¹⁰⁵ The extended menopausal phase of female development appears to be a unique and species-distinctive trait related to the lengthy period of child development and the ongoing availability of significant maternal and allomaternal (grandmothering) care in a child's life.¹⁰⁶ Trumping menopause with technology and legitimating the practice of geriatric motherhood may be increasing children's risks to "a future as orphans."¹⁰⁷

The United Nations Convention on the Rights of the Child (1989) raises some substantive concerns relating to rights, parenthood, and the vulnerability of children. It ensures "the right from birth to a name, . . . and, as far as possible, the right to know and be cared for by his or her parents," the right to remain in an intact family, and, if separation occurs, the right "to maintain personal relations and direct contact with both parents on a regular basis." The Convention also argues for the right of children to receive parental care attentive to their developmental needs and to be protected "from all forms of physical or mental violence, injury or abuse, neglect or negligent treatment, maltreatment or exploitation, including sexual abuse."[108] These provisions for the integrity and stability of the family and the rights of the child to parental caregiving do accent a number of rights consistent with an integrative vision of parenthood.

Childhood, in all its developmental complexities through gestation, infancy, and beyond, stands as the most vulnerable stage of human existence. Kinship systems and families have evolved as the primary social sites to meet the complex development challenges of childhood. Can the evolving body of research on attachment bonds, pair-bonding, and kinship systems be reformulated in the language of rights and vulnerability? Do children have a thick set of rights related to kinship patterns that have evolved in human societies? Do children have a right to a maternal bond? Do children have a right to know or be connected to their genetically related parents? Do children have a right to stable caregiving attachment bonds? Do children have a right to "stable" parental pair-bonds? Do children have a right to significant maternal and paternal investment? Do children have a right to connection with their close bilateral (maternal/paternal) kinship lines? Do children have a right, if required, to supportive kin-connected alloparenting? And, given Chapais's emphasis on the critical significance of close lineal kin in all human kinship systems, do children even have a soft right to siblings? Growing recognition of the significance of an integrative nexus of primary attachment and kinship bonds could be politically salient insofar as it feeds into an important and evolving discussion of the web of children's birth and attachment rights—a conversation that has already made some headway in the international rights tradition.

It would be misleading to suggest that current research in attachment, kinship, and evolutionary theory offers knockdown arguments for integrative accounts of parenting. However, important lines of theoretical inquiry and research are advancing lines of argument critical to integrative accounts of parenthood. Scholars, professional committees, or associations quick to pronounce that the verdict is in on questions concerning parenthood and child well-being would be wise to adopt a stance of intellectual caution in the face of the seriousness of the issues, the breadth and complexity of current research, and the range of core questions that still need to be explored by rigorous interdisciplinary research.

Given these constraints and the critical importance of parenthood to child development, a plug for the precautionary principle may be sound advice.¹⁰⁹ Human kinship systems have been evolving for millions of years. Today, vast new developments in science and technology have contributed to important advances in addressing issues relating to children's physical well-being, but we seem to be on shakier ground when it comes to issues relating to the social and psychological well-being of children. Sarah Hrdy's work does, in significant ways, support arguments for diversity in parenting and child care. However, she also sounds a cautionary, indeed ominous, note as she ends her exploration of maternal and alloparental caregiving. Hrdy is apprehensive that we may be shifting to patterns of child care increasingly devoid of "the art of nurture" critical to the formation of socially cooperative human beings. In the evolution of human society, children who lacked secure attachment bonds and kin connectedness rarely survived long enough for the "emotional sequelae of neglect to matter." "Today," Hrdy warns, "this is no longer true, and the intended consequences are unfolding in ways that we are only beginning to appreciate."¹¹⁰ She wonders whether new developments in technology and parenting may be setting in motion evolutionary trajectories that will progressively sideline those bonds of attachment, interdependence, and empathy that have been distinctive and defining features of the human species.¹¹¹

[handwritten: are we losing the art of nurture? who is nurturing the next generation?]

Notes

1. Jean Bethke Elshtain, *Public Man, Private Woman: Woman in Social and Political Thought*, 2nd ed. (Princeton: Princeton University Press, 1993), 22–23.

2. Lionel Tiger and Joseph Shepher, *Women in the Kibbutz* (New York: Harcourt Brace Jovanovich, 1976).

3. John Bowlby, *Attachment and Loss*, 3 vols. (London: Hogarth Press, 1969–1982). On the early development of attachment theory in Bowlby's work, see Suzan van Dijken, *John Bowlby: His Early Life, A Biographical Journey into the Roots of Attachment Theory* (London: Free Association Books, 1998).

4. Mary D. Salter Ainsworth, *Infancy in Uganda: Infant Care and the Growth of Love* (Baltimore: Johns Hopkins University Press, 1967).

5. Harvard neuroscientist Charles Nelson led the Bucharest Early Intervention Project, spearheading research into the effects of severe attachment deprivation on the psychological, cognitive, and physical development of Romania's orphans.

6. See Fred Rothbaum et al., "Attachment and Culture: Security in the United States and Japan," *American Psychologist* 55 (Oct. 2000): 1093.

7. John Bowlby, *Attachment and Loss*, vol. 1, *Attachment* (New York: Basic Books, 1969).

8. Ibid., 180–194 and passim.

9. Ibid., 177–209.

10. Mark V. Flinn, Carol V. Ward, and Robert J. Noone, "Hormones and the Human Family," in *The Handbook of Evolutionary Psychology*, ed. David M. Buss (Hoboken, NJ: Wiley, 2005): 552–580, 572.

11. Carol Sue Carter, "Biological Perspectives on Social Attachment and Bonding," in *Attachment and Bonding: A New Synthesis*, ed. Carol Sue Carter et al. (Cambridge: MIT Press, 2005), 85–100.

12. Jay Belsky, "Modern Evolutionary Theory and Patterns of Attachment," in *Handbook of Attachment: Theory, Research and Clinical Applications*, eds. Jude Cassidy and Phillip R. Shaver (New York: Guilford Press, 1999), 141–161.

13. Marinus H. van IJzendoorn and Abraham Sagi-Schwartz, "Cross-Cultural Patterns of Attachment: Universal and Contextual Dimensions," in *Handbook of Attachment: Theory, Research, and Clinical Applications*, 2nd ed., ed. Jude Cassidy and Phillip R. Shaver (New York: Guilford Press, 2008), 880–905, especially 881–882; see also H. Jonathan Polan and Myron A. Hofer, "Psychobiological Origins of Infant Attachment and Its Role in Development," in Cassidy and Shaver, *Handbook of Attachment*, 2nd ed., 158–172.

14. See Mary Dozier, K. Chase Stovall-McClough, and Kathleen E. Albus, "Attachment and Psychopathology in Adulthood," in Cassidy and Shaver, *Handbook of Attachment*, 2nd ed., 718–744.

15. Polan and Hofer, "Psychobiological Origins of Infant Attachment."

16. Ian C. G. Weaver et al., "Epigenetic Programming by Maternal Behavior," *Nature Neuroscience* 7 (Aug. 2004): 847.

17. Polan and Hofer, "Psychobiological Origins of Infant Attachment," 165.

18. Ibid., 159.

19. Ibid., 166–167.

20. Some attachment theorists argue that remedial work can be done in the second major attachment pattern, adult pair-bonding; see Susan M. Johnson, *Emotionally Focused Couple Therapy with Trauma Survivors: Strengthening Attachment Bonds* (New York: Guilford Press, 2002).

21. John Bowlby, *The Making and Breaking of Affectional Bonds* (London: Tavistock, 1979), 103.

22. Debra Zeifman and Cindy Hazan, "Pair-Bonds as Attachments: Reevaluating the Evidence," in Cassidy and Shaver, eds., *Handbook of Attachment*, 436–455.

23. Michael Rutter, "Implications of Attachment Theory and Research for Child Care Policies," in Cassidy and Shaver, *Handbook of Attachment*, 2nd ed., 958–974, 960.

24. Martha Nussbaum underscores the diversity of "transformational" attachment figures for children. See Martha C. Nussbaum, *Upheavals of Thought: The Intelligence of Emotions* (Cambridge: Cambridge University Press, 2001), 184.

25. Jay Belsky and R. M. Pasco Fearon make this argument in "Precursors of Attachment Security," in Cassidy and Shaver, *Handbook of Attachment*, 2nd ed., 295–316, 303–305.

26. David M. Buss, "The Problems of Parenting," in *Evolutionary Psychology: The New Science of the Mind*, 3rd ed. (Boston: Pearson, 2008): 200–202.

27. Flinn, Ward, and Noone, "Hormones and the Human Family."

28. Bowlby, *Attachment and Loss*, vol. 1, *Attachment*, 61.

29. Sarah B. Hrdy, *Mother Nature: A History of Mothers, Infants and Natural Selection* (New York: Pantheon, 1999); Sarah B. Hrdy, *Mothers and Others: The Evolutionary Origins of Mutual Understanding* (Cambridge: Harvard University Press, 2009).

30. Hrdy, *Mothers and Others*, 15–16.

31. "Of course, it takes more than one person to rear a child. However, studies have not been designed to determine whether that second person needs to be male and a genetic parent. . . . Are there multiple caretaker arrangements that are almost as good, just as good, or even better than two parents? We don't know, because we rarely asked." Ibid., 145.

32. Ibid., 21–23, 70.

33. Sarah B. Hrdy, "Evolutionary Context of Human Development: The Cooperative Breeding Model," in Carter et al., *Attachment and Bonding*, 9–32, quoted on 9–10.

34. Hrdy, *Mothers and Others*, 103.

35. Ibid., 85.

36. Human mothers do not engage in the kind of "compulsively possessive" mothering characteristic of orangutans or gorillas. Ibid., 70–79.

37. Ibid., 138–141.

38. Ibid., 68.

39. Ibid.

40. van IJzendoorn and Sagi-Schwartz, "Cross-Cultural Patterns of Attachment," 880–881; Hrdy, *Mothers and Others*.

41. Richard Bowlby, "Babies and Toddlers in Non-parental Daycare Can Avoid Stress and Anxiety If They Develop a Lasting Secondary Attachment Bond with One Carer Who Is Consistently Accessible to Them," *Attachment and Human Development* 9 (Dec. 2007): 307.

42. See Mary Dozier and Michael Rutter, "Challenges to the Development of Attachment Relationships Faced by Young Children in Foster and Adoptive Care," in Cassidy and Shaver, *Handbook of Attachment*, 2nd ed., 698–717; Jonathan J. Mohr, "Same-Sex Romantic Attraction," in Cassidy and Shaver, *Handbook of Attachment*, 2nd ed., 482–503, especially 485–486, 503.

43. Bowlby viewed his work as a major contribution to evolutionary theory. See his intellectual biography on Darwin, *Charles Darwin: A Biography* (London: Hutchinson, 1990).

44. This has prompted some scholars to argue for the need to retrieve Bowlby's project of integrating attachment theory into an evolutionary framework. See Jeffry A. Simpson and Jay Belsky, "Attachment Theory within a Modern Evolutionary Framework," in Cassidy and Shaver, *Handbook of Attachment*, 2nd ed., 131–157.

45. John Bowlby and Notre Dame Child Guidance Clinic, *Rediscovery of the Family and Other Lectures* (Aberdeen: Aberdeen University Press, 1981): 3.

46. Eugene Burnstein, "Altruism and Genetic Relatedness," in Buss, *Handbook of Evolutionary Psychology*, 528–551.

47. David M. Schneider, *A Critique of the Study of Kinship* (Ann Arbor: University of Michigan Press, 1984). For "after kinship" lines of anthropological research, see Janet Carsten, *After Kinship* (Cambridge: Cambridge University Press, 2004); Sarah Franklin and Susan McKinnon, eds., *Relative Values: Reconfiguring Kinship Studies* (Durham,

NC: Duke University Press, 2001); Marilyn Strathern, *Reproducing the Future: Essays on Anthropology, Kinship, and the New Reproductive Technologies* (Manchester: Manchester University Press, 1992).

48. Schneider, *Critique of the Study of Kinship*, 165, 188.

49. Ibid., 133, 166.

50. Ibid., 51.

51. Ibid., 113.

52. Ibid., 53–54.

53. Ibid., 119.

54. Ibid., vii, 112.

55. Carsten, *After Kinship*, 81, 139–141.

56. Ibid., 82.

57. Ladislav Holy, *Anthropological Perspectives on Kinship* (London: Pluto Press, 1996), 168.

58. Robert McKinley, "The Philosophy of Kinship: A Reply to Schneider's *Critique of the Study of Kinship*," in *The Cultural Analysis of Kinship: The Legacy of David M. Schneider*, ed. Richard Feinberg and Martin Ottenheimer (Urbana: University of Illinois Press, 2001), 131–167, quoted on 135.

59. William D. Hamilton, "The Genetical Evolution of Social Behavior," *Journal of Theoretical Biology* 7 (1964): 1–16.

60. Stuart A. West, Andy Gardner, and Ashleigh S. Griffin, "Kinship and Social Behavior," in *Foundations of Evolutionary Psychology*, ed. Charles Crawford and Dennis Krebs (New York: Erlbaum, 2008), 91–114, especially 94–95.

61. Daly and Wilson's research finds that stepchildren experience lower levels of parental investment and significantly higher rates of mistreatment and abuse. See Martin Daly and Margo Wilson, "Is the 'Cinderella Effect' Controversial? A Case Study of Evolution-Minded Research and Critiques Thereof," in Crawford and Krebs, *Foundations of Evolutionary Psychology*, 383–400.

62. Marshall Sahlins, *The Use and Abuse of Biology: An Anthropological Critique of Sociobiology* (Ann Arbor: University of Michigan Press, 1976).

63. David Buss, "Problems of Kinship," in *Evolutionary Psychology*, 3rd ed., 230–265.

64. Richard Dawkins, "Twelve Misunderstandings of Kin Selection," *Zeitschrift für Tierpsychologie* 51 (1979): 184; Richard Dawkins, *The Selfish Gene*, 2nd ed. (Oxford: Oxford University Press, 1989), 291–292.

65. Lee Cronk and Drew Gerkey, "Kinship and Descent," in *Oxford Handbook of Evolutionary Psychology*, ed. R. I. M. Dunbar and Louise Barrett (Oxford: Oxford University Press, 2007), 463–478.

66. Burstein, "Altruism and Genetic Relatedness," 547; see the overview of research by Cronk and Gerkey, "Kinship and Descent," 464–465; see also West et al., "Kinship and Social Behavior."

67. Burnstein, "Altruism and Genetic Relatedness," 528.

68. Doug Jones, "The Generative Psychology of Kinship: Part 1. Cognitive Universals and Evolutionary Psychology," *Evolution and Human Behavior* 24 (2003): 303.

69. Ibid., 315.

70. Ibid., 317–318.

71. Stone argues that the theoretical implications of the Chapais's study are "profound and far reaching," marking a decisive break with the social constructionist perspectives dominating kinship studies. Linda Stone, "Kinship Back on Track: Primatology Unravels the Origin and Evolution of Human Kinship," in *Evolutionary Psychology* 6 (2008): 557 (a review of Bernard Chapais, *Primeval Kinship: How Pair Bonding Gave Birth to Human Society* [Cambridge: Harvard University Press, 2008]).

72. Claude Lévi-Strauss, *The Elementary Structures of Kinship*, trans. James Harle Bell, John Richard von Sturmer, and Rodney Needham (London: Eyre and Spottiswoode, 1969).

73. Bernard Chapais, *Primeval Kinship: How Pair-Bonding Gave Birth to Human Society* (Cambridge: Harvard University Press, 2008), 77.

74. His research was originally published at Kinji Imanishi, "The Origin of the Human Family: A Primatological Approach," *Japanese Journal of Ethnology* 25 (1961): 119 (an English translation is available at Kinji Imanishi, "The Origin of the Human Family: A Primatological Approach," in *Japanese Monkeys: A Collection of Translations*, ed. Kinji Imanishi and Stuart A. Altmann [Edmonton, AB: Altmann, 1965], 113–140). See Chapais's discussion in *Primeval Kinship*, 60–61.

75. Chapais, *Primeval Kinship*, 62–63.

76. Ibid., 123; Lara Rodseth et al., "The Human Community as a Primate Society," *Current Anthropology* 32 (June 1991): 221, 234.

77. Chapais, *Primeval Kinship*, 158.

78. Ibid., 158–159.

79. Ibid., 158.

80. Ibid., 162.

81. Ibid., 159–160.

82. Ibid., 160.

83. Ibid., 167.

84. Meyer Fortes, *Rules and the Emergence of Society* (London: Royal Anthropological Institute of Great Britain and Ireland, 1983), 20; see also Meyer Fortes, *Oedipus and Job in West African Religion* (New York: Cambridge University Press, 1983).

85. Chapais, *Primeval Kinship*, 194–195. In societies with weak constraints on sexuality and high levels of paternity uncertainty, kinship systems do exhibit a tendency toward avuncular paternal investment. See Martin Daly and Margo Wilson, "Selfish Genes and Family Relations," in *Richard Dawkins: How a Scientist Changed the Way We Think*, ed. Alan Grafen and Mark Ridley (Oxford: Oxford University Press, 2006), 191–202, quoted on 198–199.

86. Chapais, *Primeval Kinship*, 197–198.

87. Lara Rodseth et al., "Human Community as a Primate Society."

88. Chapais, *Primeval Kinship*, 124.

89. Ibid., 124.

90. Ibid, 57.

91. Ibid., 127.

92. Ibid., 135.

93. Ibid., 56; see ibid., 126–130, for a more detailed summary of the twelve elementary components of human kinship systems.

94. Ibid., 307.

95. Linda Stone and Paul F. Lurquin, *Genes, Culture, and Human Evolution: A Synthesis* (Oxford: Blackwell, 2007), 216.

96. Martha C. Nussbaum, *Frontiers of Justice: Disability, Nationality, Species Membership* (Cambridge: Belknap Press of Harvard University Press, 2006); Bryan S. Turner, *Vulnerability and Human Rights* (University Park: Pennsylvania State University Press, 2006).

97. Nussbaum, *Frontiers of Justice*, 127–140.

98. Turner, *Vulnerability and Human Rights*, 69.

99. Ibid.

100. Nussbaum, *Frontiers of Justice*, 212.

101. Ibid., 212–216.

102. Nussbaum, *Upheavals of Thought*, 174–213, 227. Nussbaum shares Hrdy's emphasis on the value of multiple caregiving. Ibid., 184, 188.

103. Turner, *Vulnerability and Human Rights*, 83.

104. Ibid., 119.

105. Ibid., 83.

106. See Hrdy's discussion in *Mothers and Others*, chap. 8.

107. Turner, *Vulnerability and Human Rights*, 119.

108. Convention on the Rights of the Child, arts. 7:1, 9:1, 3, 19, 27.

109. See Terence E. Hébert, Ellen Moss, Daniel Cere, and Hyun Song, "Biological and Psychological Dimensions of Integrative Attachments," 207 (this volume).

110. Hrdy, *Mothers and Others*, 290.

111. Ibid., 294.

A Diversity Approach to Parenthood in Family Life and Family Law

Linda C. McClain

What is parenthood? How should we frame the competing models? Red versus blue (by analogy to red and blue states)?[1] "Traditional" versus "nontraditional"? Conservative versus liberal? Religious versus secular? Rural versus urban? Natural versus socially constructed? Simple answers are elusive. Indeed, "The definition of parentage—and with it the determination of which adults receive legal recognition in children's lives—has become the most contentious issue in family law."[2]

The most visible "family values" issues continue to be abortion and same-sex marriage. However, the definition and future of parenthood are important subtexts of those debates. Opposition to legal abortion often rests on a view that a fetus is a child and a pregnant woman is a mother who should accept the responsibilities of parenthood, or give someone else a chance to parent the child. Proponents of legal abortion counter that a pregnant woman should not be compelled to nurture a fetus and become a mother and that women have the constitutional right to decide whether to do so. Opponents of opening civil marriage to same-sex couples argue that supporting responsible procreation and child rearing is marriage's primary purpose and same-sex households are not optimal for children. Supporters of same-sex marriage challenge this primary purpose and counter that gay men and lesbians are capable parents and children in their households fare just as well as children reared by heterosexual parents.

This book proposes two models of parenthood—an *integrative model* and a *diversity model*—as an organizing device to make sense of complicated puzzles about family life and family law and to promote a constructive conversation about parenthood. In chapter 1, Daniel Cere suggests that recent developments in the natural and social sciences resonate with an integrative model and considers what implications kinship study has for the rights of parents and children.[3] In this chapter, I articulate a diversity model, situating it in social practice and family law. By social practice, I refer both to contemporary patterns of family life and to understandings of parenthood. I illustrate ways in which family law supports a diversity approach to defining legal parentage. This approach recognizes and supports pathways to parenthood in addition to heterosexual procreation within marriage and does not restrict parental rights and responsibilities to biological parents. In both social practice and law, there is considerable support for a diversity model. However, we also see the continuing hold of an integrative model and a mixture of public acceptance of *and* ambivalence about family diversity.

Ambivalence and acceptance seem equally apt in considering how family law grapples with defining parenthood and assigning parental rights and responsibilities as patterns of family life change and developments in technology make new methods of childbearing possible. Family law scholars speak of traditional legal definitions of parenthood as being "in a time of transition" and "uncertainty."[4] Due to "recent revolutions in family law," June Carbone explains, parental obligation to children may exist "independent" of marriage, raising the question of how best to secure adult responsibility for children.[5] David Meyer observes that, by contrast to an earlier model, in which "parenthood was understood to be largely a natural relation founded upon biological reproduction, and legal status as a parent followed easily from recognition of that natural fact," contemporary family law wrestles with "tensions between legal, biological, and social conceptions of parenthood."[6] He concludes that "there is no going back" from changing patterns of family life, yet there is no consensus about how to reconcile them with respect for traditional family ideals. Meyer predicts: "Until society itself comes to a clearer resolution of its own ambivalence about the respective roles of biology, care giving, contract, and tradition in defining parenthood, family law is unlikely to do much better."[7]

The mixture of integrative and diversity models in social practice and law suggests the image of a continuum, which may help to identify points of convergence in contemporary debates. Rather than poles, suggesting values polarization, a continuum suggests pulls toward different ideas along a spectrum. The integrative and diversity models harbor emphases, variations, or configurations. Working with a continuum may further this book's project of tackling the hard questions about what is best for adults, children, and society.

I illustrate how the integrative model features in debates over whether to extend civil marriage to same-sex couples and whether, when individual states *do* allow such marriages, the federal government should recognize them for purposes of federal marriage benefits and obligations, or refuse to do so (as the Defense of Marriage Act [DOMA] requires).[8] This model is congruent with some traditional concerns of family law but at variance with certain features of contemporary family law. I then elaborate the diversity model, beginning with social practice. I discuss demographic studies on the changing place of marriage, the rise of alternative family forms, and public attitudes about such developments. Turning to family law, I sketch the evolution toward a diversity model of parenthood, drawing on judicial opinions, state laws, and, again, the debate over DOMA. I identify diversity within the diversity model with respect to whether to link the parent-child bond to adult-adult intimate bonds and whether to expand marriage or disestablish it. I explore possible points of convergence by integrative and diversity proponents on troubling trends of family and marital inequality. I conclude by suggesting the value of envisioning a continuum of approaches to parenthood.

An Overview of the Two Paradigms
The Integrative Model
One answer to the question, Who is a parent?, emphasizes parenthood as an incident of marital procreation. Some argue that this has been, historically, the core normative understanding of parenthood. In contemporary debates over redefining marriage, appeals to traditional understandings stress the link between marriage and parenthood and the importance of the "channelling function" of family law: historically, family law supported the *social institutions* of marriage and parenthood and steered men and women to participate in them.[9] Under this view, the social institution of marriage combines, in one package, heterosexual sex between one man and one woman, reproduction resulting from such sex, and parenthood. Thus, Cere, in a report for the Council on Family Law, describes this as a "conjugal model" of marriage, stressing that what makes marriage "unique" is "the attempt to bridge sex difference and the struggle with the generative power of opposite-sex unions"—namely, that "heterosexual sex acts can and often do produce children." He contrasts an alternative model of marriage as a "close relationship," under which "marriage and children are not really connected" and marriage is not uniquely tied to the "sexual ecology" of human life.[10]

If there is a "pure" form of this conjugal model, perhaps it is certain orthodox religious views of the goods and purposes of marriage. According to the "Manhattan Declaration" (signed by more than a hundred "Orthodox, Catholic, and evangelical Christian leaders"), the "one-flesh union" of one man and one woman as husband and wife is "the crowning achievement of God's creation," and marriage is "the first institution of human society." The declaration affirms marriage's procreative purpose and its "sexual complementarity": marriage's "objective reality" is a "covenantal union," which is "sealed, completed, and actualized by loving sexual intercourse in which the spouses become one flesh . . . by fulfilling together the behavioral conditions of procreation."[11] Thus, demands by same-sex couples for marriage as a matter of "equality of civil rights" are mistaken: homosexual relationships cannot be marriages because they are not one-flesh unions fulfilling these conditions. This implicates parenthood: "rearing of children" who are the "fruit" of their parents' union is one of the "profound reasons" for marriage.[12]

Proponents of the integrative model sometimes appeal to the *congruence* of a conjugal view of marriage, the purposes of family law, and the role of religious institutions in reinforcing civil marriage.[13] This is one reason they oppose same-sex marriage. However, there is a notable lack of congruence between some forms of the integrative model and contemporary constitutional and family law. After all, *Griswold v. Connecticut*, which spoke loftily of marriage as a "noble" association, "intimate to the degree of being sacred," upheld the right of a married couple to *use* contraception.[14] In addition, the legal right to abortion allows women (married or unmarried) to terminate their pregnancies. State high courts that have accepted constitutional challenges by same-sex couples to civil marriage laws have rejected the argument that procreation is the primary purpose of marriage. Moreover, they have concluded that allowing same-sex couples to marry furthers the state's interest in providing an optimal setting for child rearing.[15] Similar conclusions about child well-being—and the salutary role of marriage in promoting family stability—feature in legislative arguments as states like New York pass laws allowing same-sex marriage.[16]

To be sure, the large majority of states have defense of marriage acts that define marriage as the union of one man and one woman—a definition congruent with the integrative model. Some state DOMAs declare a "compelling" state interest to "nurture and promote" traditional marriage for its "unique contribution to the rearing of healthy children."[17] Indeed, when Congress enacted the federal DOMA, it embraced the integrative model's articulation of the unique, "conjugal" role of marriage in managing heterosexual procreation: "Were it not for the possibility of begetting children inherent in heterosexual unions, society would have no particular interest in encouraging citizens to come together in a committed relationship."[18] However, a significant minority of states (including some with DOMAs)—invoking a governmental interest in family stability—allow same-sex partners to enter into an alternative legal status (civil union or domestic partnership), entitling them to all the parental rights and responsibilities linked to marital status.

These developments suggest a significant tension in a growing minority of states between the integrative model and the law of parenthood. This tension is evident in the views of some prominent proponents of the integrative model: for example, David Blankenhorn, president of the Institute for American Values, initially proposed civil unions for same-sex couples as a principled compromise to the marriage controversy—extending to same-sex partners whatever parental rights and responsibilities spouses enjoy due to marital status.[19] Three years later, in June 2012, in the face of a clear "emerging consensus" in America in favor of same-sex marriage, Blankenhorn had come to find that compromise unworkable and announced: "the time has come for me to accept gay marriage and emphasize the good that it can do." Although he stated that he still firmly embraced the integrative model's view that marriage is a unique institution "whose core purpose is to unite the biological, social and legal components of parenthood into one lasting bond," he identified a number of goods at stake in legally recognizing gay and lesbian couples and their children, including dignity, equal citizenship, "basic fairness," and comity.[20] Proponents of the integrative model, he concluded, had not persuaded the public of their view about marriage's relationship to parenthood, nor did he find any signs that fighting gay marriage was helping to bring about a "positive recommitment to marriage as an institution." Instead, he found it "profoundly disturbing" that "much of the opposition to gay marriage seems to stem, at least in part, from an underlying anti-gay animus." Thus, Blankenhorn's new position might be seen as a willingness to bring same-sex couples who support marriage within an integrative big tent: he seeks common ground between straight people and gay men and lesbians on strengthening marriage as an institution, shoring up as "vital" a cultural norm of "marrying before having children," and reflecting on whether children born through the use of ART have certain rights to know their biological parents.[21] By contrast, Maggie Gallagher, a prominent ally of Blankenhorn's in the marriage and integrative parenthood movements, swiftly countered that giving up "the truth" about the good of marriage (that is, its unique integrative role in uniting one male and one female) is "too high a price to pay" for comity and living with each other.[22]

Even in some states that do not afford same-sex partners a formal legal status for their adult-adult relationship, adoption laws allow them to establish formal legal relationships with a child (whether the biological child of one partner or a nonbiological child adopted by both).

Adoption would seem to challenge the integrative model, since it departs from the unity of biological and social parenthood. However, proponents of the model answer that adoption is simply a humane and necessary way to establish a parental relationship when biological parents cannot or will not care for children. In this volume, Elizabeth Marquardt calls adoption "an inspiration" and evidence that "biology is not everything" when it comes to fostering child well-being.[23] By contrast, the integrative model's proponents find troubling the use of assisted reproductive technology (ART) to produce children. Catholic teaching objects that ART commodifies the human person by implying a "right" to have a child and separates the unitive and procreative aspects of "the conjugal act."[24] Other critics object that creating a child by using donated egg or sperm deliberately severs biological from social parenthood. For example, the Commission on Parenthood's Future, in a report published by the Institute for American Values, insists that every child has a moral right to his or her two biological parents, and (echoing a recent French parliamentary report) that adults do not have a right "to" a child, if that means that they produce that child in a way that deviates from a marital/procreative model.[25]

Recognizing adoption as a pathway to parenthood raises the question, Who should be permitted to adopt? For the integrative model, the ideal adoptive family is a married, heterosexual couple, replicating the dyad found in a biological mother-father home. Nonetheless, in opposing the creation of parenthood rights by courts through doctrines of "functional" or "psychological" parenthood, some proponents support formal adoption (through second-parent adoption) for gay and lesbian couples as "preferable for children" to after-the-fact judicial bestowal of such status.[26] However, this support seems in tension with the integrative model's opposition to same-sex marriage.

Some proponents of the integrative model argue that it is better for society because it channels sexuality and procreation into marriage, helping men become responsible, productive members of society and securing for mothers the paternal investment needed to help children and families thrive.[27] Marriage rectifies a natural asymmetry between the sexes in parental investment. A vivid example of this argument appears in Justice Cordy's dissent in *Goodridge v. Department of Public Health*:

> Whereas the relationship between the mother and child is demonstrably and predictably created and recognizable through the biological process of pregnancy and childbirth, there is no corresponding process for creating a relationship between father and child.... The institution of marriage fills this void by formally binding the husband-father to his wife and child, imposing on him the responsibilities of fatherhood.

An alternative society, without the institution of marriage, "in which heterosexual intercourse, procreation, and child care are largely disconnected processes, would be chaotic."[28] New York's highest court, in *Hernandez v. Robles*, drew on Cordy's dissent in concluding that the legislature had a rational basis for limiting marriage to opposite-sex couples. Emphasizing that heterosexual sexual relationships can lead to accidental pregnancy, while homosexual ones cannot, it contends that marriage provides an "inducement" to opposite-sex couples, whose sexual relationships resulting in children are "all too often casual or temporary," to "make a solemn, long-term commitment to each other."[29] Notably, Congress's defense of DOMA against constitutional challenge invokes *Hernandez*'s rationale.[30]

Proponents of the integrative model also stress that it takes seriously sex difference and gender complementarity.[31] Biological difference provides a child with two differently sexed parents who provide models for being male and female and who parent in different ways. (*Hernandez* stated: "Intuition and experience suggest that a child benefits from having before his or her eyes, every day, living models of what a man and woman are like.")[32] Thus, proponents are concerned with families headed by a single parent and by gay or lesbian parents. To the extent family law permits and facilitates these forms of parenthood and does not consider gender differences salient for assigning parental rights and responsibilities (as Susan Frelich Appleton elaborates),[33] it is in tension with the integrative model.

The Diversity Model
A diversity approach to parenthood begins with recognition of the *fact* of diversity in patterns of family life in contemporary society.[34] There are

diverse pathways to becoming a parent and diverse family forms in which people parent. As one survey concludes, "The portrait of the American family circa 2010 starts where it always has—with mom, pop and the kids," but "the family album now includes other ensembles." Thus, along with the nuclear family—the marital, two biological parent family, but also a marital family with adopted children—are families formed by a single parent (whether due to divorce or the absence of marriage), families formed by two unmarried biological parents, by lesbian and gay parents, and by foster parents, blended families formed when divorced parents remarry or cohabit with new partners, and extended families (where a grandparent or other relative serves as caretaker, with or without the biological parents present in the household). A growing family form is the transnational family, with caretaking arrangements that, "while still kin-based, complicate the paradigm of mother/father/children integrative family life."[35]

Some diverse family forms are relatively new, such as a same-sex couple and their children living openly as a family. Others have historical antecedents: the extended family, the family formed by common-law marriage, and the single-parent family. The point is that majorities of Americans include, in their definition of "family," family forms that clearly do not fit the integrative model, although they have varying assessments of whether this diversity is good, is bad, or makes no difference.[36] In addition, while the integrative model views marriage's unique (indeed, universal) role as ensuring two biological parents for children, significantly fewer people view "having children" as a "very important reason to get married" compared with "love," "making a lifelong commitment," and "companionship."[37] Public opinion seems to hew less closely to the integrative view than to the *Goodridge* court's conclusion that "exclusive and permanent commitment," not procreation, is the most important element of marriage.[38]

The diversity model entails a belief about the *value* of diversity. Generally, its proponents regard some degree of diversity in family forms and parenthood not as evidence of deviance or decline but as the inevitable by-product of persons exercising their greater freedom to live out their vision of a good life, facilitated by changes in constitutional, criminal, and family law, and in women's economic status in society.[39] Elsewhere, I have drawn upon the political liberalism of John Rawls to develop a liberal feminist account of the family.[40] Translating liberal toleration to the realm of family law, the basic idea is that, given the fact of reasonable pluralism, achieving uniformity of family form could be done only with a degree of coercion that is unacceptable in a modern constitutional democracy.

Instead, as people exercise their moral capacity to decide the best way to live, they will adopt different family forms.

Political liberalism does not dictate that the family must take a particular *form* (e.g., the marital, heterosexual family), so long as the family can carry out its *functions* (e.g., the task of social reproduction) in a manner consonant with relevant public values.[41] A commitment to family diversity emphasizing function over form and the important personal and public goods furthered by families is consonant with feminist and liberal principles. From this commitment comes a conviction that government should recognize and support different forms of family.

To be sure, recognition of the *fact* of greater family diversity does not translate into accepting or *valuing* all such diversity. One way to interpret the evidently greater acceptance of gay and lesbian couples than single mothers is that the public is more accepting of diverse family forms that include *two* parents, even if not married or not opposite-sex, than of single-parent families. What are the concerns about single mothers? That (1) a child needs both a mother and a father; (2) a child needs two parents (such that two moms would not be as worrisome); or (3) a single mother is likely to be poor and to require public assistance? If single motherhood signifies poverty, would public opinion be more favorable toward "single mothers by choice" who are well educated, are financially self-supporting, and often form communities of support with other single mothers?[42] Or, instead, might some view "*all* practices of single motherhood" as "deviant" (to borrow Martha Albertson Fineman's term)[43] simply because of their singleness?

Could the integrative model's emphasis on gender complementarity in parenting explain public opinion? The Pew survey does not inquire as to ideal styles of parenting but does indicate growing acceptance of "the dual income/shared homemaker model" as the better template for marriage.[44] Moreover, far from supporting gender complementarity, responses to the question, What makes a good partner? "are . . . notable for how closely the public's evaluations of the two gender roles [husband and wife] are aligned."[45] If we can extrapolate from attitudes about partners to attitudes about parents, this suggests considerable support for what Appleton describes as family law's "equality project," that is, the move away from fixed gender roles to gender neutrality with respect to spousal and parental roles.[46]

We can glean from the Pew survey both recognition of family diversity and mixed views on how to evaluate it. A finer-grained analysis suggests an American public "sharply divided in its judgments" about changes in the structure of the American family: "About a third generally accepts the changes; a third is tolerant but skeptical; and a third considers them bad for society."[47]

Family Law's Evolving Embrace of the Diversity Model

Family law embraces a diversity model when it recognizes and supports diverse family forms. In 2000, the U.S. Supreme Court observed, in *Troxel v. Granville*, a case strongly affirming parental rights: "The demographic changes of the past century make it difficult to speak of an average American family. The composition of families varies greatly from household to household."[48] (Notably, the mother whose rights the Court protected was trying to stabilize her children's place in a complex, blended family.)[49] The Court spoke, decades earlier, of the "venerable" roots of the tradition of the multigenerational family—"of uncles, aunts, cousins, and especially grandparents sharing a household along with parents and children"—and opined: "Decisions concerning child rearing, which [earlier precedents] have recognized as entitled to constitutional protection, long have been shared with grandparents or other relatives who occupy the same household—indeed who may take on major responsibility for the rearing of children."[50]

The fact that marriage is not the exclusive source of parental rights and responsibilities provides one indication that contemporary family law embodies a diversity approach. For example, paternity laws support society's interest in ensuring sources of financial support for children, and most states are strict in holding persons responsible for the reproductive consequences of sex.[51] Thus, the integrative model stresses *marriage* as the social institution that deals with problems of accidental or unintended pregnancy, but it is not the only mechanism family law uses to compel financial responsibility for children.

Family law's recognition of parental rights and responsibilities outside of marriage also reflects the influence of federal constitutional guarantees of equal protection for nonmarital children, on the rationale that they should not be punished for the "irresponsible sexual liaisons" of their parents.[52] Additionally, the Supreme Court's "unwed father jurisprudence" accords biological fathers who show the requisite degree of responsibility a say in their children's lives.[53] These examples illustrate that contemporary family law finds ways to impose parental responsibilities and recognize rights apart from marriage. Integrationists might counter that the law's approach to the practical problems posed by nonmarital childbirth does not necessarily indicate a departure from a normative preference for formalizing parental status through marriage. However, there are also ways in which family law affirmatively supports parental status apart from marriage.

Adoption provides an example. If family law supported only an integrative model, it would confine adoption to married, heterosexual couples. However, this is not what most states do, and even "outlier" states have moved toward a diversity model. For example, a gay man (who had been an exemplary foster parent) recently challenged in court Florida's adoption law, which expressly prohibited homosexual persons from adopting a child.[54] To the state's argument that the ban had a rational basis because it furthered Florida's goal of providing children with "better role models" in "non-homosexual households, preferably with a husband and wife as parents," the state court countered that more than a third of Florida's adoptions are by single parents. Florida itself, in other words, supported a diversity of family forms. Moreover, the Department of Children and Families agreed that "gay people and homosexuals make equally good parents," and the appellate court reiterated the lower court's findings that the social science evidence was "robust" on the point that "there are no differences in the parenting of homosexuals or the adjustment of their children."[55]

A diversity approach is also evident in the evolution of a functional—rather than formal—approach to defining family and parenthood. Some state courts and legislatures employ such notions as functional parent, de facto parent, and psychological parent to assign parental rights and responsibilities to a person who is otherwise a "legal stranger" to a child (as Appleton and David Meyer elaborate).[56] Furthering the best interests of the child is a primary reason for doing so.

Family law's deviation from the integrative model is evident in use of notions of "intentional parenthood" in resolving disputes arising from use of ART, as well as in conferring rights and obligations on persons with no biological connection to a child. For example, the California Supreme Court interpreted its child support statutes to apply to a woman who agreed to the conception of her lesbian partner's children, lived with them, supported them, and held out to the world that they were her children. Family law's protective function explains this ruling: the children get the support of two parents, thus reducing the state's public welfare burden.[57]

Admittedly, courts sometimes stress that they are responding to—rather than valuing—diversity in family life. Sometimes, they invite legislatures to make laws indicating how to manage this diversity and sort out legal parenthood.[58] However, courts sometimes acknowledge the value of diversity: they articulate a belief that supporting diverse family forms is consistent with family values.[59]

A strong indication that contemporary family law in a significant minority of states embraces not only the fact but also the value of diversity is the emphasis on "fairness to families" and on the state's interest in supporting *all* families in the new generation of laws allowing same-sex couples access to civil marriage (Massachusetts, Connecticut, New Hampshire, Iowa, Vermont, the District of Columbia, and New York), civil unions (New Jersey, Illinois, Hawaii, Maryland, and Delaware), or expansive domestic partnership laws (as in California, Oregon, Washington, and Nevada).[60] The spur to such change in some states was a successful constitutional challenge by same-sex couples to state marriage laws.[61] However, a number of legislatures have acted without the spur of such a judicial ruling, including, most recently, New York (several years after an unsuccessful constitutional challenge). In 2012, both Maryland and Washington enacted marriage equality laws, which, however, will only take effect if they survive a voter referendum. When the respective state governors signed these laws, they stressed the positive benefits to children of gay and lesbian parents from the message sent that their families are worthy of dignity and equal protection, rather than being "separate but equal."[62]

Some states have acted even in the face of a state DOMA. Consider Oregon, whose Family Fairness Act accords same-sex domestic partners the same benefits, obligations, and protections as spouses and married parents.[63] The act declares: "This state has a strong interest in promoting stable and lasting families, including the families of same-sex couples and their children. All Oregon families should be provided with the opportunity to obtain necessary legal protections and status and the ability to achieve their fullest potential."[64]

The move by some legislatures, such as in Oregon, to give as much legal protection as possible under the existing state constitutional regime to families that do not fit an integrative model suggests not only the recognition of the fact of family diversity but also the appreciation of its value. These examples suggest the coexistence of the integrative and diversity models, with tenacious support for preserving "traditional" marriage side by side with a strong impulse to protect and be fair to all families. Some courts, notably California's and Connecticut's high courts, have resolved this evident tension by ruling that domestic partnerships or civil unions (respectively) did not afford same-sex couples the "equal dignity and respect" for their family life to which they are entitled under the state's constitution.⁶⁵ Further, some legislatures that chose civil unions as a compromise to preserve traditional understandings of marriage while protecting families formed by gay men and lesbians (e.g., Vermont and New Hampshire) have recognized that "separate is not equal" and opened civil marriage to same-sex couples to promote family stability and fairness.⁶⁶

The ongoing debate over the provision of the federal DOMA that defines marriage, for purposes of federal law, as the union of one man and one woman affords another example of tension between the two models and movement toward the diversity model. The Obama administration announced it would no longer defend DOMA in certain constitutional challenges brought by same-sex couples married under state law. It observed that the legislative record of DOMA was filled with expressions of "moral disapproval of gays and lesbians and their intimate and family relationships" and reflected "precisely the kind of stereotype-based thinking and animus the Equal Protection Clause is designed to guard against."⁶⁷ Expressly rejecting an integrative argument (offered in the congressional report) that DOMA, by limiting marriage to opposite-sex couples, "serves a governmental interest in 'responsible procreation and child-rearing," the attorney general stated: "Since the enactment of DOMA, many leading medical, psychological, and social welfare organizations have concluded, based on numerous studies, that children raised by gay and lesbian parents are as likely to be well-adjusted as children raised by heterosexual parents."⁶⁸ As Congress considers bills to repeal DOMA and to support federal recognition of valid state marriages, lawmakers and witnesses stress the capability of same-sex parents as well as marriage's role in fostering family stability.⁶⁹

When legislatures pass laws facilitating diverse pathways to parenthood, such laws arguably reflect a judgment that these new models are in children's best interests and are consistent with family law's protective functions. Some of these developments seem to fall along a continuum rather than fitting pure integrative or diversity models. For example, civil union laws might be consistent with an integrative model in reserving marriage for opposite-sex couples. Yet, civil unions afford to same-sex partners *all* the spousal benefits and obligations and parental rights and responsibilities that flow from marriage. In this sense, they *integrate* the intimate bond between adults with the parent-child bond for families that differ from the "conjugal" family.

Family law in the United States is not uniform. Among the states are salient differences, sometimes along the lines of red versus blue states, with red states more closely embracing integrative parenthood and rejecting forms of family diversity.[70] Nonetheless, one could reasonably conclude that much of contemporary family law more closely fits the diversity than the integrative model to the extent it allows the separation of legal parenthood from marriage, facilitates pathways to parenthood apart from biological procreation, recognizes parental rights and responsibilities for persons without a biological connection to a child, and, in a significant minority of states, allows same-sex partners access to institutions (whether civil marriage, civil union, or domestic partnership) affording them formal legal status as adult partners and parents.

Diversity within the Diversity Model

There are variations within each model. Proponents of a diversity approach differ about the implications of family diversity for law. Some (including me) believe that family law should continue to recognize and support the institution of marriage but in ways consistent with sex equality and opened up to include same-sex couples.[71] Such a model supports exploring whether a new civil registration scheme could foster stability in other households with children (such as cohabiting couples). Cynthia Grant Bowman points to the popularity of such a system, in other countries, among opposite-sex cohabitants, some of whom may seek to avoid the historical or religious symbolism of marriage.[72] Along these lines, a few U.S. states allow opposite-sex couples access to civil unions and expansive domestic partnerships.[73] A registration scheme, Judith Stacey proposes, might also help meet the needs of the more complex families formed by some lesbian and gay parents, when more than two persons have parental roles.[74] I have argued that a civil registration system could help to recognize and support other forms of committed adult relationships, such as adult siblings forming a household or friends aging with friends.[75]

By contrast, some proponents of a diversity model argue for dethroning marriage. An argument for "uncoupling marriage and parenting," advanced by Stacey, is that "our needs for both eros and domesticity are often at odds," so that tying parenting so tightly to marriage makes child well-being too vulnerable to "Cupid's antics."[76] Martha Albertson Fineman proposes to reorient family law around the caretaker-dependent relationship and attach the subsidies now linked to marital status to that dyad, shifting marriage to the realm of private contract.⁷⁷ Many scholars embrace this basic proposal.⁷⁸

But some scholars who share Fineman's view about ending state support for marriage resist her call to eliminate the state's role in regulating adult-adult relationships. Tamara Metz argues for disestablishing marriage and creating—and regulating—an "intimate caregiving union status," including "parents and children (biological and de facto); husband and wife; long-term cohabiting hetero- and homosexual lovers and partners; 'lesbigay' units; nonsexually intimate adult units or groups; adult siblings; adult children; and aging parents."⁷⁹ This model supports diverse forms of parenthood, while situating the caregiving of parents in the broader context of caregiving relationships. Such broader support for "intimate care in all its guises," Metz contends, is more just and more consistent with liberal commitments to liberty, equality, and stability.⁸⁰ This approach differs both from diversity approaches that would shift the focus to intergenerational caretaking relationships and from integrative approaches that contend that society's interest in encouraging committed adult relationships is confined to procreative unions.⁸¹ Thus, Maxine Eichner argues that state support is warranted because such adult relationships further "a broad range of important goods."⁸²

Another area of disagreement concerns the number of legally recognized parents. Multiple parenthood departs from the integrative model that, for each child, there should be one legally recognized father and one mother. How does the diversity model address the question whether children "can or should have more than two parents"?⁸³ As Nancy Dowd observes, some children already have more than two adults assuming parenting roles in their lives, due to patterns of marriage, divorce, cohabitation, and remarriage, as well as to open adoption and foster care. But, should more than two adults have legally recognized rights and responsibilities with respect to a particular child? In certain circumstances, family law has recognized three legal parents (e.g., a biological mother, her same-sex partner, and the sperm donor, or genetic father).⁸⁴ Some scholars view the recognition of multiple parenthood as consistent with family law's recognition of parental status due to social parenthood, apart from biology.⁸⁵ Dowd argues that recognizing multiple fatherhood would be consistent with the actual experience of many fathers and further the channelling function of family law.⁸⁶ Laura Kessler proposes that lifting the "numerosity requirement" with respect to parenthood would address situations in which children have "significant family ties" to *more than two adults* concurrently."[87] Proponents of a diversity model differ on these issues.[88]

Diversity or "Diverging Destinies"?
I turn now to trends toward inequality in family life and suggest possible common ground between the integrative and diversity models. My concern here is with what sociologist Sara McLanahan refers to as children's "diverging destinies" based on parental resources,[89] and what the Pew report describes as "a new 'marriage gap' in the United States . . . increasingly aligned with a growing income gap."[90] McLanahan warned of these "diverging destinies" nearly a decade ago. Commentators continue to identify the problem of "two classes, divided by 'I do'" as a troubling form of inequality between families—and the children within them.[91]

McLanahan argues that, while one trajectory for women, "associated with delays in childbearing and increases in maternal employment," results in "gains in resources" for children, the other, "associated with divorce and non-marital childbearing," "reflects losses" in resources for them.[92] She argues that society should care about "growing disparities in children's resources."[93]

Another inequality concern is a "class-based decline in marriage," with a dramatically larger gap in 2008 than in 1960 between marriage rates of college graduates (64 percent) and those with a high school diploma or less (48 percent).[94] Better-educated and economically successful people marry at higher rates (generally, to other well-educated and successful people), but lower down the economic spectrum, marriage rates are lower, nonmarital parenthood is more common, and divorce rates (often after early marriages) are higher.[95] The gap is not due simply to class-based views on the value of marriage. Rather, "Those with less income and education are opting out of marriage not because they don't value the institution or aspire to its benefits, but because they may doubt that they (or potential spouses) can meet the standards they impose on marriage."[96] Some men and women report that they are delaying getting married until they have the economic preconditions for a successful marriage.[97] Although low-income women value becoming a mother and say they value the institution of marriage, they may not view their male partner as a suitable marriage partner. They also believe they are capable of being a good parent without marriage.[98]

Wherever one falls on the continuum between integrative and diversity models, inequality in access to marriage, family life, and the successful transition to adulthood and the resulting forms of inequality for children are serious concerns. So, too, are the continuing high rates of teen pregnancy and early parenthood in the United States.

The problems of marriage inequality, unequal resources among children, and teen pregnancy and early parenthood suggest that not every current pattern of family life is one that proponents of a diversity model would celebrate. With proponents of an integrative model, they would find some of these trends and forms of inequality troubling. Although there would likely be differences concerning the best solutions, common ground is worth pursuing.

Conclusion: A Continuum Approach to Mapping Parenthood

I have suggested that the diversity model includes recognition of the fact of family diversity and appreciation of its value. It entails that diverse family forms should be supported by family law. I have illustrated that proponents differ on such matters as the continuing place of marriage and whether to link the adult-adult intimate relationship to the parent-child relationship. The diversity model captures the diverse pathways to parenthood in social practice. It also fits changes in family law giving legal protection to these pathways.

A premise of this volume is that using the integrative and diversity models is a fruitful way to wrestle with significant questions about parenthood. I have suggested that, given the differences within each model, it is helpful to locate positions about parenthood as points on a continuum rather than as a dichotomy. To give a few examples: people may accept the notion of family law's channelling function but draw different conclusions about what type of relationships the law should support and promote. Thus, people may share a belief in the importance of integrating adult-adult intimate and parent-child bonds but differ on whether parents must be opposite-sex or may also be same-sex. They may share a preference for establishing formal legal ties between parent and child but differ on what to do in concrete situations in which persons without formal legal ties are functioning as parents to children. They may harbor an intuition that family law's primary concern should be intergenerational relationships, of which the parent-child is the most fundamental, or they may envision the parent-child relationship as one in a family of relationships that the law should encourage and support. These are but a few of the matters we could productively map along a continuum of approaches to parenthood.

Notes

1. See Naomi R. Cahn and June Carbone, *Red Families v. Blue Families: Legal Polarization and the Creation of Culture* (New York: Oxford University Press, 2010).

2. June Carbone, "The Legal Definition of Parenthood: Uncertainty at the Core of Family Identity," *Louisiana Law Review* 65 (2005): 1295.

3. Daniel Cere, "Toward an Integrative Account of Parenthood" (this volume).

4. David D. Meyer, "Parenthood in a Time of Transition: Tensions between Legal, Biological, and Social Conceptions of Parenthood," *American Journal of Comparative Law* 54 (2006): 125; Carbone, "Legal Definition of Parenthood," 1295.

5. Carbone, "Legal Definition of Parenthood," 1297.

6. Meyer, "Parenthood in a Time of Transition," 125.

7. Ibid., 144.

8. Pub. L. No. 104-199, 1 U.S.C. sec. 7 (1996).

9. See Carl E. Schneider, "The Channelling Function in Family Law," *Hofstra Law Review* 20 (1992): 495; Linda C. McClain, "Love, Marriage, and the Baby Carriage: Revisiting the Channelling Function of Family Law," *Cardozo Law Review* 28 (2007): 2133.

10. Council on Family Law, *The Future of Family Law: Law and the Marriage Crisis in North America* (New York: Institute for American Values, 2005), 12–13, 14–15 (naming Daniel Cere as principal investigator).

11. Robert George, Timothy George, and Chuck Colson, "The Manhattan Declaration: A Call of Christian Conscience," Nov. 20, 2009, http://www.manhattan declaration.org (accessed Nov. 21, 2009).

12. Ibid., 5.

13. See, e.g., Brief Amici Curiae of the Church of Jesus Christ of Latter-Day Saints, California Catholic Conference, National Association of Evangelicals, and Union of Orthodox Jewish Congregations of America in Support of Respondent State of California in In re Marriage Cases, 183 P.3d 384 (Cal. 2008).

14. Griswold v. Connecticut, 381 U.S. 479 (1965).

15. Goodridge v. Department of Public Health, 798 N.E.2d 941 (Mass. 2003); In re Marriage Cases, 183 P.3d 384 (Cal. 2008). In response to the California Supreme Court's ruling that not allowing same-sex couples to marry (even though they could enter domestic partnerships) violated California's constitution, California voters, in November 2008, approved Proposition 8, amending the state's constitution to define marriage as between one man and one woman. Same-sex couples have prevailed in a federal constitutional challenge to Proposition 8 in federal district and appellate court, although the case may reach the U.S. Supreme Court. Perry v. Schwarzenegger, 704 F. Supp. 921 (N.D. Cal. 2010), *affirmed sub nom.* Perry v. Brown, 671 F. 3d 1052 (9th Cir. 2012).

16. See New York Marriage Equality Act, ch. 95 (2011).

17. Me. Rev. Stat. tit. 19-A, sec. 650 (1998 and Supp. 2011) (Maine's DOMA).

18. Committee on the Judiciary, Defense of Marriage Act, H.R. Rep. 104-664 (1996), 14 (also citing testimony by the Council on Families in America).

19. David Blankenhorn and Jonathan Rauch, "A Reconciliation on Gay Marriage," *New York Times*, Feb. 22, 2009, WK11.

20. See David Blankenhorn, "How My View on Gay Marriage Changed," *New York Times*, http://www.nytimes.com/2012/06/23/opinion/how-my-view-on-gay-marriage-changed.html?_r=2&hp&pagewanted=print (accessed June 23, 2012).

21. Ibid.; see also Mark Oppenheimer, "David Blankenhorn and the Battle Over Same-Sex Marriage," http://www.yourpublicmedia.org/content/wnpr/david-blankenhorn-and-battle-over-same-sex-marriage (accessed June 25, 2012).

22. Maggie Gallagher, "Bigotry, David Blankenhorn, and the Future of Marriage," http://www.thepublicdiscourse.com/2012/06/5759 (accessed June 25, 2012).

23. Elizabeth Marquardt, "Of Human Bonding: Integrating the Needs and Desires of Women, Men, and the Children Their Unions Produce," 325 (this volume).

24. Russell E. Smith, "*In Vitro* Fertilization—Fact Pattern, Roman Catholic Response," part IV.A of "Symposium: Roman Catholic, Islamic, and Jewish Treatment of Familial Issues, Including Education, Abortion, in Vitro Fertilization, Prenuptial Agreements, and Marital Fraud," *Loyola Los Angeles International and Comparative Law Review* 16 (1993): 9, 47–53.

25. Institute for American Values and Commission on Parenthood's Future, *The Revolution in Parenthood: The Emerging Global Clash between Adult Rights and Children's Needs* (New York: Institute for American Values, 2006). Elizabeth Marquardt is the principal investigator on this report.

26. Ibid., 24.

27. Council on Family Law, *The Future of Family Law; Marriage and the Public Good: Ten Principles* (Princeton, NJ: Witherspoon Institute, 2008).

28. *Goodridge*, 996.

29. Hernandez v. Robles, 855 N.E.2d 1 (N.Y. 2006).

30. See Memorandum of Law of Intervenor-Defendant the Bipartisan Legal Advisory Group of the United States House of Representatives in Support of Its Motion to Dismiss, Pedersen v. Office of Personnel Management, Case No. 3:10–cv.01750 (VLB), 49, http://www.glad.org/doma/documents (accessed Jan. 26, 2012).

31. Cere, "Epilogue" (this volume); Daniel Cere, "The Conjugal Tradition in Post Modernity: The Closure of Public Discourse?" (unpublished manuscript, 2003).

32. *Hernandez*, 7.

33. Susan Frelich Appleton, "Gender and Parentage: Family Law's Equality Project in Our Empirical Age" (this volume).

34. Judith Stacey, "Toward Equal Regard for Marriages and Other Imperfect Intimate Affiliations," *Hofstra Law Review* 32 (2003): 331.

35. Carola Suárez-Orozco and Marcelo M. Suárez-Orozco, "Transnationalism of the Heart: Familyhood across Borders," 280 (this volume); see also Rhacel Salazar Parreñas, "Transnational Mothering and Models of Parenthood: Ideological and Intergenerational Challenges in Filipina Migrant Families" (this volume).

36. Pew Research Center, *The Decline of Marriage and Rise of New Families*, Nov. 18, 2010, http://www.pewsocialtrends.org/2010/11/18/the-decline-of-marriage-and-rise-of-new-families/6/ (accessed May 1, 2011).

37. Ibid., 22 ("having children" is a "very important reason to get married": 59 percent of married persons, 44 percent of unmarried; "love" [married, 93 percent; unmar-

ried, 84 percent]; "making a lifelong commitment" [married, 87 percent; unmarried, 74 percent]; and "companionship" [married, 81 percent; unmarried, 63 percent]).

38. *Goodridge*, 961–962.

39. Here, I analogize to Rawls's idea of the "fact of reasonable pluralism" and the "fact of oppression." John Rawls, *Political Liberalism* (1993; repr., New York: Columbia University Press, 1996), 36–37.

40. Linda C. McClain, *The Place of Families: Fostering Capacity, Equality, and Responsibility* (Cambridge: Harvard University Press, 2006).

41. Ibid.

42. See, e.g., Emily Bazelon, "2 Kids + 0 Husband = Family," *New York Times Magazine*, Feb. 1, 2009, 30L; Rosanna Hertz, *Single by Chance, Mothers by Choice: How Women Are Choosing Parenthood without Marriage and Creating the New American Family* (New York: Oxford University Press, 2006).

43. Martha Albertson Fineman, *The Neutered Mother, the Sexual Family and Other Twentieth Century Tragedies* (New York: Routledge, 1995), 101–104.

44. Hertz, *Single by Chance*, 26.

45. Ibid., 30.

46. Appleton, "Gender and Parentage," 238–240.

47. Pew Research Center, *The Public Renders a Split Verdict on Changes in Family Structure*, Feb. 16, 2011, http://www.pewsocialtrends.org/2011/02/16/the-public-renders-a-split-verdict-on-changes-in-family-structure/ (accessed May 5, 2011).

48. Troxel v. Granville, 530 U.S. 57 (2000).

49. Ariela R. Dubler, "Constructing the Modern American Family: The Stories of *Troxel v. Granville*," in *Family Law Stories*, ed. Carol Sanger (New York: Foundation Press, 2008), 95–111.

50. Moore v. City of East Cleveland, 431 U.S. 494, 504, 505 (1977).

51. See Wallis v. Smith, 22 P.3d 682 (N.M. Ct. App. 2001).

52. Weber v. Aetna Casualty and Surety Company, 406 U.S. 164 (1972).

53. Lehr v. Robertson, 463 U.S. 248 (1983).

54. In re Adoption of X.X.G. and N.R.G., 45 So. 3d 79, 87 (Fla. Dist. Ct. App. 2010).

55. Ibid.

56. See, e.g., In re Parentage of L.B., 122 P.3d 161 (Wash. 2005) (en banc). See also Appleton, "Gender and Parentage"; David D. Meyer, "Family Diversity and the Rights of Parenthood" (this volume).

57. Elisa B. v. Superior Court, 117 P.3d 660 (Cal. 2005).

58. In re C.K.G., 173 S.W.3d 714 (Tenn. 2005) (defining motherhood in a surrogacy case, but concluding: "Given the far-reaching, profoundly complex, and competing public policy considerations . . . crafting a general rule to adjudicate all controversies [involving ART] is more appropriately accomplished by the Tennessee General Assembly"); K.M. v. E.G., 117 P.3d 673 (Cal. 2005) (Werdegar, J., dissenting) (urging that "only legislation defining parentage in the context of assisted reproduction is likely to restore predictability and prevent further lapses into the disorder of ad hoc adjudication").

59. V.C. v. M.J.B., 163 N.J. 200, 232 (N.J. 2000) (Long, J., concurring).

60. For an up-to-date overview, see "States," www.freedomtomarry.org/states (accessed Feb. 2, 2012).

61. *Goodridge*; Kerrigan v. Commissioner of Public Health, 957 A.2d 407 (Conn. 2008); Varnum v. Brien, 763 N.W. 2d 862 (Iowa 2009).

62. See Governor Chris Gregoire, "Marriage Equality Bill Signing," Feb. 13, 2012, http://governor.wa.gov/speeches/speech-view.asp?SpeechSeq=223 (accessed June 14, 2012); Office of Governor Martin O'Malley, "Marriage Equality Bill Signing," Mar. 1, 2012, http://www.governor.maryland.gov/blog/?p=4551 (accessed June 14, 2012).

63. Or. Rev. Stat. 106.990(2) (2003 and Supp. 2011).

64. Ibid.

65. *Marriage Cases*; see also *Kerrigan*, 418. Proposition 8 nullified the California Supreme Court's ruling that same-sex couples must be accorded access to civil marriage, not simply domestic partnerships, through amending the state constitution by ballot initiative. A federal district court ruled that Proposition 8 violates the federal constitution and was affirmed on appeal by the Ninth Circuit. Perry v. Schwarzenegger, 704 F. Supp.2d 921 (N.D. Cal. 2010), *affirmed sub nom* Perry v. Brown, 671 F. 3d 1052 (9th Cir. 2012). The Ninth Circuit indicated that it was deciding the case as narrowly as possible—based on the unique circumstances of California's law—and not ruling on the broader question of whether same-sex couples have a federal constitutional right to marry.

66. Vt. Stat. Ann. tit. 15, sec. 8 (2007 and Supp. 2011); N.H. Rev. Stat. Ann. sec. 457:1-a (Supp. 2011).

67. Eric Holder, Attorney General to Hon. John A. Boehner, Feb. 23, 2011, 4.

68. Ibid.

69. *The Respect for Marriage Act: Assessing the Impact of DOMA on American Families: Hearing on S. 598 before the S. Comm. on the Judiciary*, 112th Cong. (2011).

70. See Cahn and Carbone, *Red Families v. Blue Families*, 117–138.

71. McClain, *Place of Families*, 155–190.

72. See, e.g., Cynthia Grant Bowman, *Unmarried Couples, Law, and Public Policy* (New York: Oxford University Press, 2010), 221–230 (proposing registered partnerships).

73. For example, civil unions in Hawaii and Illinois and domestic partnerships in Nevada.

74. Stacey, "Toward Equal Regard," 346–348.

75. McClain, *Place of Families*, 191–209.

76. Judith Stacey, "Uncoupling Marriage and Parenting," 79 (this volume).

77. Martha Albertson Fineman, *The Autonomy Myth: A Theory of Dependency* (New York: New Press, 2004).

78. See, e.g., Nancy D. Polikoff, "Ending Marriage as We Know It," *Hofstra Law Review* 32 (2003): 201.

79. Tamara Metz, *Untying the Knot: Marriage, the State, and the Case for Their Divorce* (Princeton: Princeton University Press, 2010), 120.

80. Ibid.

81. See H.R. Rep. 104-664, 14.

82. Maxine Eichner, *The Supportive State: Families, Government, and America's Political Ideals* (New York: Oxford University Press, 2010), 101.

83. Susan Frelich Appleton, "Parents by the Numbers," *Hofstra Law Review* 37 (2008): 11.

84. Ibid., 12–13 (citing cases from Ontario and Pennsylvania).

85. Katherine K. Baker, "Bionormativity and the Construction of Parenthood," *Georgia Law Review* 42 (2008): 649.

86. Nancy E. Dowd, "Multiple Parents/Multiple Fathers," *Journal of Law and Family Studies* 9 (2007): 231; Melanie B. Jacobs, "My Two Dads: Disaggregating Biological and Social Paternity," *Arizona State Law Journal* 38 (2006): 809.

87. Laura T. Kessler, "Community Parenting," *Washington University Journal of Law and Policy* 24 (2007): 47, 50.

88. For concerns about legal attempts to protect "nontraditional caregiving relationships," see Emily Buss, "'Parental' Rights," *Virginia Law Review* 88 (2002): 635.

89. Sara McLanahan, "Diverging Destinies: How Children Are Faring under the Second Demographic Transition," *Demography* 41 (Nov. 2004): 607.

90. Pew Research Center, *Decline of Marriage*, i.

91. Jason DeParle, "Two Classes, Divided by 'I Do,'" *New York Times,* July 15, 2012, § 1:1. I cite this news article as a powerful example of such contemporary commentary, not to embrace entirely its analysis of the problem.

92. McLanahan, "Diverging Destinies," 608.

93. Ibid., 619.

94. Pew Research Center, *Decline of Marriage*, i.

95. McLanahan, "Diverging Destinies."

96. Pew Research Center, *Decline of Marriage*, 23.

97. McClain, *Place of Families*, 138–144; McClain, "Love, Marriage, and the Baby Carriage."

98. Kathryn Edin and Maria Kefalas, *Promises I Can Keep: Why Poor Women Put Motherhood before Marriage* (Berkeley: University of California Press, 2005).

Institutions

Is Parenthood Separable from Marriage (or Couplehood) When It Comes to Fostering Child Well-Being?

PART TWO

Uncoupling Marriage and Parenting

Judith Stacey

Women and men should not marry, for love is like the seasons—it comes and goes.

> Yang Erche Namu, Leaving Mother Lake

The genesis of this book lies in the American culture wars over family values. The root question posed to the authors in this part concerns institutions: Can parenthood be separated from marriage and couplehood? I was invited to make a case against the view that the modern nuclear family, composed of a married, heterosexual couple and their biological (or adopted) offspring, is the best family environment for promoting child well-being, and I promise not to disappoint. However, I want to begin with two core challenges to the basic conceptual apparatus and epistemological premise of the book.

Nomenclature

First, I take issue with the two terms, *integrative* and *diversity*, that the editors have chosen to frame the contrasting scholarly perspectives on parenthood and family. I think that these concepts mischaracterize the two poles in the culture wars over family and mistakenly imply that integration and diversity are antonyms, or at least distinctive perspectives. However, one can have an integrative perspective on family diversity, and there are diverse forms of integrative families. It is more accurate to depict the opposing perspectives in the family debate as *singular* (or, *universalist*) and *pluralist*. The former maintains that one family structure—a monogamous married, heterosexual couple and their biological children—is superior, both functionally and morally, to all others.[1] The latter rejects a hierarchy of family forms, values the quality and substance of familial relationships over their structure, and believes in the efficacy and moral value of diverse family structures. We are engaged, in essence, in ye olde structure versus process debate about family quality.[2]

Those who favor a singular or universalist perspective generally subscribe to an "essentialist" or foundationalist view of family structure. They consider the married, heterosexual couple and their biological children to be the superior family form, and to be (close to) universal historically and cross-culturally, a quasi-natural institution, virtually the core definition of family. Characteristically, in *The Future of Marriage*, David Blankenhorn insists that "the primary reason for the emergence of human pair-bonding was to ensure that mothers do not raise children alone. The evolutionary record suggests that men and women developed an unusual way of living together, primarily because the human infant needs a father and the human mother needs a mate."[3] A pluralist perspective, in contrast, is fundamentally antifoundationalist. Pluralists stress the variety and unavoidably changing character of family patterns across space, time, and culture. For example, family historian Stephanie Coontz points out: "Not until the mid-nineteenth century did the word 'family' commonly come to refer just to a married couple with their co-resident children"; "there is no universal definition of family that fits the reality of all cultural groups and historical periods."[4]

Confronting the vast anthropological and historical record of variation in parenting and intimate bonds, universalists perceive an underlying, fundamental structure beneath the creative clutter. Thus, Blankenhorn performs perceptual gymnastics to locate the contours of the married, procreative couple and their progeny amid alternative kinship tapestries in anthropological accounts of far-flung cultures, like the Trobriands, Nuers, and Azande, which seemingly challenge his thesis.[5] Matrilineal households, woman-woman marriages, and even polygyny retain the one-mother/one-father principle in his reading, whereas, for family pluralists, polygamy represents a radical, but not objectively inferior, departure from Blankenhorn's favored family form.

Social Science and Family Values

Ever since the late Daniel Patrick Moynihan's still controversial report, *The Negro Family: The Case for National Action*, appeared in 1965,[6] recurrent skirmishes between singular and pluralist perspectives have erupted over the significance of demographic trends indicating the decline of stable married, procreative-couple parenting. Rising rates of unwed motherhood (first among black women, later among whites) and divorce, and, more recently, struggles for lesbian and gay parenting (and unions) have incited some of the most polarizing conflicts.[7] Lesser flare-ups have concerned the ethics of who, if anyone, merits access to surrogacy, fertility services and assisted reproductive technologies, and the adoption of children, domestically and internationally.[8]

Each time a controversy surfaces, scholars and critics from singular and pluralist perspectives deploy social science evidence to support their divergent claims. However, I believe that research evidence neither is the source of either perspective, nor can it successfully adjudicate between them. Disputes express opposing values rooted in incommensurate religious, philosophical, and ideological convictions about gender, sexuality, and intimacy. Support for and opposition to same-sex marriage or lesbian and gay parenthood do not derive from disinterested assessments of the cumulative social science research. Mounting evidence (reviewed by Fiona Tasker in this volume)[9] that children raised by lesbian co-mothers fare at least as well as those from comparable heterosexual parent families does not diminish opposition from those convinced that homosexuality is sinful. No amount of social science evidence could persuade both intellectual camps that any one form of family or definition of parent is superior to all others, because what counts as a desirable developmental outcome rests on an inescapably subjective and cultural judgment. Data can compare average child outcomes on particular measures of adjustment, esteem, achievement, attitudes, interests, behavior, and the like but cannot establish the moral or social superiority of particular parenting configurations or child outcomes. Is a socially conforming child a positive or a negative outcome? What about a gender-conforming child, or a gay child? What about a religious, competitive, patriotic, chaste, ambitious, obedient, adventurous, deferential, independent, self-sacrificing, or fill-in-the-blank child? *what is a "good" child? what is healthy development?*

Social science research can demonstrate that different cultures seek to develop different behaviors, attitudes, beliefs, characters, and traits in their offspring; so, too, do different parents within a given culture. We can compare the relative effectiveness of groups in achieving particular outcomes. However, research cannot assess these outcomes or the family patterns that foster them according to a single, uniform, objective standard. The very notion that social science evidence could prove one family form or one definition of parent to be superior is a subjective, epistemological claim not amenable to objective proof. Unsurprisingly, I do not subscribe to that notion.

I suspect that parties to the family debates may be as incompatible in our temperaments, tastes, and sensibilities as we are in our political principles, even though the political causes and consequences of our views

competing values not evidence

are far from trivial. Some people spontaneously savor and favor change, variety, and innovation, while others prefer continuity, similarity, and tradition. If this hunch is correct, then despite our best efforts at collegiality and good faith dialogue, we are unlikely to shift our commitments to a singular versus a pluralist perspective in response to the quality of social science evidence marshaled or interpretations of data presented.

Perhaps the best we can do is understand more fully some sources and consequences of our incompatible frameworks, identify weaknesses in our respective uses of logic and evidence, and look for areas of common ground that do not violate our core convictions. What social science and historical research can contribute to this endeavor is empirical evidence about the range of parenting and family contexts that have existed historically and cross-culturally and that exist today. Research also can help identify the characteristic strengths and vulnerabilities of particular family patterns, although, here too, values questions inevitably come into play.

Parenting beyond Monogamous Heterosexual Marriage
With these more modest ends, I address the empirical question of whether or not it is possible to separate successful parenting from (monogamous heterosexual) marriage or couplehood by discussing two contemporary family systems that do just that. The first is rather exotic and seems almost a feminist fairy tale—the matrilineal Mosuo culture of southwestern China. The second, patriarchal polygyny, is far more prevalent and persistent historically, and closer to a feminist nightmare. I will depict its status in contemporary South Africa. Fortuitously for readers, Peter Wood, my designated intellectual sparring partner in this volume, also discusses Mosuo families.[10] (Woods refers to the Mosuo people as the Na, which is the name of the larger national minority group officially recognized by the Chinese government, but from which the Mosuo seek independent status. Our use of these different cultural terms hints at differences in our cultural frameworks.)

A Society without Fathers or Fatherlessness
In *The Future of Marriage*, Blankenhorn took on what he believed to be the greatest anthropological challenges to his universalist thesis about the married-couple (one-father/one-mother) family. Surprisingly, he overlooked the Mosuo people in the remote mountainous borderlands of China's Yunnan and Sichuan provinces. Approximately two millennia ago, Tibeto-Burman ancestors of the 30,000 to 50,000 surviving members

of this ancient Buddhist culture devised what is arguably the only documented family system in the anthropological or historical record not based on marriage. Mosuo kinship, in startling contrast with traditional Chinese patriarchy, is primarily matrilineal and matrilocal. "Happiness is defined as the ability to live in harmony with matrilineal kin," explains one of the anthropologists who know the Mosuo best.[11] ==Instead of marrying and sharing family life with spouses and genetic offspring, adult children remain in their natal, extended, multigenerational households with their mothers and maternal kin==. Together, family members rear all children born to the women of the household, care for aged and dependent members, and share property and labor. The culture does not assign social responsibility or status to male genitors.

Traditional Mosuo family values radically separate sexuality and romance from domesticity, parenting, and economic bonds. Sex life is strictly voluntary and nocturnal, while family life is obligatory and diurnal. The Mosuo practice *tisese*, a system of night visiting, which the Chinese misleadingly translate as "walking marriage." The Mosuo term literally means that a man "goes back and forth." Men live, eat, work, and parent with their maternal families by day but can seek entry into a woman's "flower chamber" for the night. Mutual desire alone governs romantic and sexual union for women and men. Because men generally do not live with or co-parent their biological progeny, their sexual behavior has no implications for their parenting careers or family size. Parents and kin do not concern themselves with the love lives of their daughters or sons because mate choice carries few implications for the family or society.

To assure its economic and social survival, a Mosuo matrilineal household needs each generation of women to bear at least one daughter and to produce collectively a gender mix of children. ~~The collective childbearing of their sisters, rather than their own procreative activity, determines men's parental roles. Mosuo men become social fathers to their nieces and nephews~~. Likewise, sisters jointly mother their collective issue, irrespective of individual fertility. ==Naru, the native language, employs the same word, *emi*, for both a mother and a maternal aunt==.[12] If biological paternity carries no inherent implications for kinship, today at least it is often a matter of common local knowledge. Male genitors of children who are born within exclusive *tisese* relationships often acknowledge their offspring, give them occasional gifts, and develop avuncular relationships with them. In a sense, Mosuo kinship reverses the social expectations assigned to fathers and maternal uncles in the West.

[margin note: same as Wood but less emphasis here]

[bottom note: Stacey - brilliant to excise family life from sex
Wood - cautionary, still goes back to M/F binary]

Although Mosuo kinship is not rooted in marriage, the culture has not entirely precluded the institution. Mosuo kinship has been a flexible system open to pragmatic adaptations that helped families to survive. One strategy to redress gender imbalances was to allow exceptions to the cultural rule against couples living together. Households short of males or of females might invite a lover of the desired gender to move in. Nonetheless, traditional Mosuo culture did not employ the idiom of marriage to depict such relationships or apply the categories of husband and father. Contemporary Mosuo informants regard *tisese* rather than marriage as their practice "since time immemorial," which, according to some scholars, extends back earlier than 200 BC.[13] There have been substantial changes in Mosuo family practices, particularly upheavals since the Communists came to power, but *tisese* remains the primary institution for sexual union and reproduction. It coexists with secondary forms of contemporary marriage and cohabitation.

With the surgical stroke of excising marriage, Mosuo kinship circumvented a plethora of familiar Western family traumas associated with what feminist family law scholar Martha Fineman refers to as "the sexual family."[14] A society without marriage is one with no divorce, no spinsters or bachelors, widows or widowers, or unmarried, solitary individuals of any sort. Nobody's social status or fate hinges on the success or failure of their love life or marriage, whether chosen or arranged. More pertinent to the question of parenting institutions, in a family system without marriage, no children are illegitimate, fatherless, or motherless, and few are orphaned. No marriage or divorce means no remarriage, and thus, no wicked (or benevolent) stepmothers, stepfathers, or Cinderellas. Rarely need anyone become a single parent, and even only children seldom grow up without playmates in their households. Perhaps that explains how the Mosuo achieved lower fertility and mortality rates than their neighbors long before they experienced the modern economic developments that generally propel that demographic transition.[15]

Polygyny, Modernity, and Plural Parenthood

The raid by state authorities on the polygamous Yearning for Zion compound in Eldorado, Texas, in April 2008[16] should remind us of the long history of another institutionalized exception to the putatively universal principle "For every child, a mother *and* a father. To meet this fundamental human need, marriage."[17] Patriarchal polygynous marriage, parenthood, family structure, and principles could scarcely be more antithetical to the matrilineal, sexually egalitarian, permissive, harmonious family ideals of the remarkable Mosuo. Disappointingly, however, from a Western feminist perspective, this was the world's predominant form of kinship before the twentieth century and remains widespread globally, both where it is legal and where it is not.[18]

Few Westerners are aware that postapartheid South Africa legally recognized polygamy. It is the only nation in the world that authorizes both plural and same-sex marriage and parenting rights.[19] The postapartheid society boldly configured its transition to democracy as a laboratory for utopian efforts to promote social justice. Among the least examined of these is its vanguard agenda for family democracy. The 1996 Constitution of the Republic of South Africa was the first to ban discrimination on grounds of culture and sexual orientation, and it embraced pluralist definitions of marriage and family. These historic innovations compel courts, citizens, and diverse communities to negotiate contradictions between protection for customary patriarchal prerogatives and commitments to full gender and sexual equality. Unique among the world's constitutions, the expansive equality clause of the Bill of Rights explicitly prohibits unfair discrimination on the grounds of marital status.[20]

After complex political negotiations over competing constitutional protections for gender equality and customary cultures, Parliament passed the Recognition of Customary Marriages Act (RCMA) in 1998.[21] An attempt to legitimate customary marriages among indigenous African cultures while protecting the interests of women and children within them, the RCMA offers legal recognition to "a marriage negotiated, celebrated or concluded according to any of the systems of indigenous African customary law which exist in South Africa."[22] Many customary cultures practice polygyny. It ruffled no legal feathers, therefore, when on January 5, 2008, Jacob Zuma, newly elected president of the African National Congress (ANC) and now president of South Africa, celebrated his polygamous marriage to a third wife in a customary Zulu ceremony. Since then, Zuma has married a fourth woman and paid *lobola* (bridewealth) for yet another wife.[23]

Despite the legal, quite visible practice of polygyny among some elite black men, few South Africans formally register their plural marriages, partly because the RCMA prohibits participants in a registered civil marriage from entering an additional customary marriage, and partly because men find little need or legal incentive to do so. Feminists and traditional leaders seem justified in anticipating that formal polygamy will continue to decline in South Africa, as it has done in most modernizing societies. Hybrid forms of de facto plural marriage, on the other hand, are proliferating. Some genres remain relatively traditional. Others encompass features of postmodern intimacy, including interracial and even some bisexual unions. While a few of these patterns are uniquely South African, others resonate in the United States and more globally and generate diverse forms of plural parenting.

Consider a Zulu family with one husband, two wives, and four children that I interviewed in 2007 in rural Kwa-Zulu Natal. Nobunto, the forty-six-year-old senior wife, and her husband, Marshall K, a migrant hotel service worker, had been married for twenty years in a monogamous, registered customary union before he initiated a second customary marriage with Lindiwe, a thirty-eight-year-old woman.[24] Traumatic personal events in the lives of both women made Mr. K's decision to do so seem at least partially altruistic. All four children born to Nobunto died in infancy, rendering her a tragic local figure who faced a dire social fate as she aged. Mr. K met his junior wife, Lindiwe, when she was working in a shebeen (informal tavern) near the hotel where he was employed during the week. At that time, she was a destitute, working single mother who had been literally seduced and abandoned years earlier by the father of her two children. She and her children were sharing cramped and tense quarters with a married brother and his wife and children.

Mr. K told his new love interest about his first wife soon after he began courting her. Lindiwe acknowledged to me how deeply disappointed she was to learn that her suitor was married. She claimed, however, that because she had begun falling in love with him and felt sympathy for his childless first wife, she did not end the relationship. After Lindiwe became pregnant with his child, Mr. K introduced her to Nobunto and proposed inviting Lindiwe and her children to join their family and home. Despite some feelings of jealousy and loss, Nobunto agreed to share her husband with a co-wife in exchange for becoming co-mother to the children. When I asked Nobunto how she felt about her co-wife when they first met, she said, "I liked her because she had children."

The co-wives spent one emotionally challenging year sharing their husband on alternate weekend nights in a crowded three-room residence, until Mr. K finished building a separate structure for Lindiwe. By then, she had given birth to two of his children and had moved with them into the adjacent cabin, while her two older children continued to reside with their new *umamkulu* (senior mother), Nobunto. Mr. K, who still lived at his hotel workplace during the week, spent one night in each household on the weekends. The two women shared parenting and occasional meals during his absence.

Thanks to the cultural legitimacy of polygynous marriage in South Africa, Nobunto became a mother again, and all four children received parenting from two full-time mothers and one weekend father. Both women claimed to love Mr. K. Each would have preferred to be married and parenting exclusively with him. However, both judged sharing this husband and these children to be a significant improvement over their former lives. I felt convinced that Nobunto, Lindiwe, and the children were much better off than when Mr. K had only one wife.

A universalist perspective on parenting might construe this polygynous family as conforming to the married-couple with children definition of parenthood.[25] From my pluralist perspective, however, it does not. These four children resided in two adjacent cabins with two full-time co-mothers and one weekend father. Reckoned from a singular Western perspective on kinship, the four children shared one biological ("real") mother and one stepmother or "fictive" mother, perhaps only to the two older children who resided with her. Their shared weekend dad is the biological father of only two of the four children and a stepfather to the others. Two children would count as full siblings, and two as half siblings. Within the South African context, the children suffer no social stigma, second-class status, or threat of intervention because their family form enjoys cultural legitimacy. In fact, their new senior mother grew up in a plural parenting family structure. Nobunto's father had married three wives who cooperatively reared their eleven children together without a father after their shared husband, Nobunto's father, died soon after she was born.

If polygamy were illegal in South Africa, Nobunto would have remained childless, while Lindiwe's children would have been raised by a single, working mother dependent on the indulgence and assistance of her brother and sister-in-law. For too many indigenous South Africans coping with the devastating AIDS crisis and the dire social and economic conditions of apartheid's legacy, such cooperative parenting structures offer children greater material and emotional support and security than do biological co-parent dyads.[26]

All Happy (and Successful) Families Are Not Alike
The two dramatically different contemporary family regimes depicted earlier provide strong empirical support for a pluralist perspective on family

structure and values. They demonstrate, persuasively, that it is possible to separate parenting that fosters child welfare from marriage or couplehood. The parenting and family practices of the exotic Mosuo likely pose the world's most potent challenge to the core convictions that underlie a universalist perspective. Their kinship system upends the claim that "the human infant needs a father and the human mother needs a mate"[27] and demonstrates that heterosexual marriage is neither the only nor the most reliable way "to ensure that mothers do not raise children alone."[28] Mosuo mothers are much less likely to raise children solo than are married mothers in the United States. They do so with the lifelong support of sisters, brothers, mothers, and uncles.

Because the Mosuo *do* radically separate parenthood from marriage and couplehood, their example undermines numerous popular beliefs rooted in a singular perspective—that the stability of a couple's marriage (or relationship) profoundly affects their children's welfare and security; that children generally, and boys particularly, need and yearn to live with their biological fathers; and, perhaps most radically, that parents who engage in multiple, extramarital sexual liaisons are irresponsible and threaten their children's emotional development.

Traditional Mosuo family life presents an exception that profoundly questions all these rules. *Tisese* separates sexuality and romantic love from kinship, reproduction, and parenting. It does so more completely than the "pure relationship" ideal of late modernity that sociologist Anthony Giddens endorses in *The Transformation of Intimacy*.[29] Mutual desire and reciprocal affection, unencumbered by responsibilities, govern traditional Mosuo sexual unions. Lovers do not share domiciles, finances, child rearing, labor, or kin. Because mate choice carries no implications for a family's resources, labor, security, or status, families need not intervene, approve, or even know when it occurs. Lovers may freely enter exclusive or multiple relationships, enduring or short-lived, and cross class, age, and ethnic boundaries, as they prefer.

Many features of *tisese* work to sustain romance, passion, and affection among lovers longer than is typical for married (or cohabiting) pairs. Couples who do not share residences, finances, child rearing, relatives, or other obligations bypass the primary triggers of marital conflict. Members of such couples need not adapt to each other's incompatible preferences, habits, and quirks. They never struggle over how many (if any) children to have, how to reward and discipline them, who does the dishes, what church (if any) to attend, how much money or time to spend on what, where, when, or with whom. The Mosuo I interviewed claimed that their "walking marriages" last longer than mainstream Chinese marriages because they generate so few sources of conflict.³⁰ Although no reliable data are available to support or undermine this claim, the crucial point is that the stability of parenting and the well-being of their children do not hinge on its veracity.

Giddens's idealized "pure relationship," entered into "for its own sake," and lasting only so long as it "deliver[s] enough satisfactions for each individual to stay within it,"³¹ has been legitimately criticized for ignoring its implications for parenting and caretaking.³² Fineman, in contrast, gives caretaking priority in her search for legal strategies for redefining family to avoid "tragedies" inherent in the "sexual family."³³ She employs that jarring concept to designate a family system generated by the adult sexual pair, the family structure promoted by the singular perspective informing the contemporary marriage promotion movement. Its tragic flaw, in Fineman's view, is making a family's economic and emotional security, and especially the welfare of women and children, vulnerable to the vagaries of Cupid's antics. Most of the seismic upheavals and divisive controversies in Western modern family life radiate from this fault line—tremblers over "the divorce revolution," unwed childbearing, "fatherlessness," same-sex marriage, lesbian and gay parenthood, and more.

Most premodern societies opted for patriarchal control of female sexuality and reproduction to manage conflicts between individual eros and collective (particularly male) family interests. This basic principle underlies polygyny. The remarkable Mosuo, in contrast, devised a brilliant, time-tested strategy, alternative both to patriarchy and to the modern sexual family. Mosuo *tisese* radically frees family fortunes and child well-being from the capriciousness of sexual and romantic love by eliminating marriage. Namu, likely the best-known contemporary Mosuo, expresses the worldview this way: "Women and men should not marry, for love is like the seasons—it comes and goes."³⁴

It would be easy to dismiss the Mosuo example as a fascinating piece of premodern kinship exotica of no relevance to debates about parenting in advanced industrial societies. Indeed, after surviving for two millennia, even despite Maoist efforts to eradicate it, Mosuo matrilineal kinship and *tisese* now face mortal threats from global market forces.³⁵ The system's success depended partly on geographic and economic continuity. However, while the most traditional form of Mosuo kinship is waning, we can detect echoes of Mosuo sexual and parenting practices emerging in subcultural pockets of many developed societies. Indeed, the marriage promotion movement, and the question posed for this chapter, would not exist if parenthood had not already become widely separated from marriage and couplehood. Thanks in part to the rising age of first marriages in modern societies, tacit principles akin to *tisese* now govern many contemporary sexual relationships. Unplanned premarital pregnancies are one inevitable consequence, as the political spectacle that surrounded unwed teenager Bristol Palin's pregnancy underscores.[36] This has generated a growing family form that echoes Mosuo matrilineal parenting. Grandparents raise or help raise their unmarried daughters' children so frequently (primarily, but not exclusively, in poor black families in the United States) that the federal government sponsors a clearinghouse website to coordinate available benefits and services for such families.[37]

Under the marriage-centric family ideology in the United States, however, these grandparent-headed families occupy a subordinate and deviant status—objects of pity or of patronizing respect. The singular perspective on families presumes that no sane, responsible unmarried adult ever would choose to parent in a three-generational matrilineal family. But many women, and some men, choose to do just that.

I am not suggesting that an advanced industrial society like the United States could or should replace our predominant, if challenged, marriage-based nuclear family system of parenthood with the Mosuo model. Nonetheless, we can learn much from the Mosuo practice of parenting. It could inspire creative thinking about models of successful parenting not dependent on the fragile bond of modern, romantic love–based marriage. At a minimum, it might encourage greater sympathy for a pluralist perspective that respects diverse parenting coalitions, including the three-generation, grandparent-headed families already in our midst. More creatively, we might envision ways of formally recognizing and supporting the broader range of child-rearing families that parents have been forging in the wake of marital instability and struggles against sexual discrimination. Necessarily, lesbian and gay parents have been at the forefront of these new chosen forms of family.[38] They challenge the law and social institutions to recognize plural forms of parenthood that cross conventional gender, race, sexual, and numerical borders. Hundreds of thousands of Heathers (and Harrys) with two or more lesbian mommies[39] and perhaps one or two sperm daddies, three or four sets of grandparents, and myriad additional blood and chosen kin have been growing up around us more rapidly than our laws, policies, and definitions of parent have adapted to recognize and serve them. A singular perspective on who should count as a parent makes their lives more difficult than is necessary or fair.

The South African example of plural parenthood within culturally legitimate polygynous marriages offers a less inspirational but more pertinent challenge to the singular perspective. Polygyny, once the world's predominant parenting context, remains widespread in parts of Africa, the Middle East, and Asia. It represents a fundamentally different structure of child rearing from the Western married couple–based family. Although plural marriage, unlike *tisese*, connects marriage to reproduction and parentage, it also generates complex plural parenting and kin relationships for children, quite unlike those idealized by the singular perspective.

In the United States, polygamy has long been despised and suppressed, in part because it was popularly associated with "barbaric," "Asian and Afriatic" societies.[40] Bigamy is illegal in all fifty states and a felony in many.[41] A 2005 Gallup poll reported that 92 percent of Americans surveyed viewed polygamy as "morally unacceptable."[42] Irrespective of its moral status, patriarchal polygyny does not mesh well with advanced industrial economies and liberal democracies, as its waning popularity in postapartheid South Africa indicates. Certainly, few feminists see much to mourn in its decline.[43] Nonetheless, in the United States, as in South Africa, informal forms of polygyny are widespread and may be proliferating. However, in contrast with South Africa, religiously rooted, legal, and social prohibitions foster deceitful, irresponsible sexual and parenting behavior subject to hypocritical, irrational consequences.

Under bigamy statutes in my state of New York, for example, Marshall K's marriage to his second wife and President Zuma's 2008 and 2010 marriages would be a felony, punishable by up to four years in prison.[44] In contrast, adultery is a misdemeanor, carrying a maximum sentence of three months in jail or probation, and a violation, as former New York City mayor Giuliani's tabloid behavior flaunted, that is rarely prosecuted. Although the sex and paternity scandal involving former Democratic presidential candidate John Edwards's secret second family derailed his political career, no penal consequences ensued. Because Edwards and his lover, Rielle Hunter, did not hold themselves out as a married couple, they did not commit bigamy under state law, but the much lesser offense of adultery.

Thus, engaging in clandestine plural unions and plural paternity is far less criminal or stigmatized in the United States than openly embracing these practices, as hundreds of Eldorado families can too readily attest.

After the Utah Supreme Court upheld the conviction of open polygynist Tom Green in 2001, one legal commentator aptly observed, "Green is not being punished for having children with several different women. He is being punished for sticking around,"⁴⁵ or perhaps, more accurately, for being open about doing so.

A few maverick feminists would rather encourage such fathers and lovers to stick around. Employing demographic logic similar to that offered by South African traditional leaders, critical race feminist theorist Adrien Wing interprets the prevalence of de facto polygyny among African Americans as a response to a dire shortage of marriageable men.⁴⁶ In June 2008, National Public Radio interviewed several articulate Black Muslim women in Philadelphia who similarly explained their decision to practice polygamy. "We're dealing with brothers who are incarcerated," one educated woman pointed out, and, "unfortunately, you have the AIDS and HIV crisis, where HIV has struck the African-American community disproportionately to others."⁴⁷ Wing proposes legal recognition of such families.⁴⁸

Such an approach might mitigate burdens faced by increasing numbers of families immigrating to North America from polygynous Islamic cultures. Current immigration laws exclude polygamous families, forcing men to choose between sequestering or abandoning some of their wives and children. In March 2007, a fatal fire in a crowded row house in the Bronx, New York City, brought this phenomenon into public view by exposing the secret plural marriage of its owner, Moussa Magassa, an American citizen born in Mali. Magassa's five children perished in the fire, while his two wives, who lived on different floors, survived.⁴⁹

In 2005, responding to the increasing incidence of polygamous, immigrant families, Status of Women Canada (SWC), a governmental organization that advises on policy in the interest of women and gender equality, commissioned research reports on polygamy. The prominent scholars who produced the reports provide competing proposals on how Canadian law should respond to the existence of illegal polygamous marriages within its borders.⁵⁰ All the reports recognize and oppose the patriarchal character of both Islamic and Fundamentalist Latter-Day Saints (FLDS) forms of polygamy, but they disagree over how best to erode it. While some defended Canadian antibigamy statutes, Martha Bailey and colleagues recommended decriminalizing polygamy and offering recognition to foreign plural marriages among immigrants.⁵¹ Their well-reasoned, but controversial, approach rests on the belief that "women [and I would add their children] are most likely to be in need of and most likely to benefit from further recognition."[52] Unrecognized wives, children, and families are unprotected.

The persistence of FLDS polygamous families in the United States, despite more than a century of persecution, like the indomitable resilience of the love that now dares to shout its name, demonstrates that the diversity of contemporary desires, unions, and families is here to stay. When a culture comes to presume that "love makes a family," love inevitably will make some families that transgress cultural conventions of gender, number, sexual identity, or race. Perhaps the South African experience can persuade supporters of family diversity, particularly feminists, to acknowledge that love (and tradition) also will make some families that reject gender equality. Equality advocates must come to terms with the enduring allure to women and men of religious ideologies committed to strong and sometimes unequal gender differences in parenting and family life.

To return to this chapter's central question, I have offered convincing historical and anthropological evidence that many cultures do successfully separate parenthood from marriage and couplehood. Nelson Mandela, for one illustrious example, grew up in a polygynous family. Barack Obama spent his childhood in three different family structures—with a divorced single mother; a remarried mother, stepfather, and half sister; and his maternal grandparents. Diverse cultures and families define child well-being differently. No universal standard of ideal family structure and parenthood can be derived from social science evidence.

The universalist or singular perspective, however well intentioned and self-consciously pro-child its advocates may be, is unwittingly ethnocentric, unrealistic, and harmful to many children and their parents. Insisting that one family form is superior for parenting unavoidably serves to diminish, stigmatize, and undermine all others. It fosters some of the deception, bad faith, and hypocrisy exposed each time a public official is caught responding to Cupid's antics by violating his (or, or less often, her) marital vows. It emboldens legislatures and courts to deny parenting rights to lesbians, gay men, and transgender people, leave foster children in anxious legal limbo, and remove hundreds of children from polygamous families in the absence of evidence of specific parental abuse or neglect.

We cannot will our desires or funnel them into a single, culturally prescribed domestic norm. But we can and should acknowledge that our needs for both eros and domesticity are often at odds. The singular perspective fails to address this dilemma. It also exaggerates the role that monogamous, heterosexual marriage plays in promoting child welfare. This diminishes efforts to provide greater social responsibility for all children. Even in the unlikely event that marriage promotion initiatives were to succeed in raising the percentage of children living with (heterosexual) married-couple parents, the cost to all other children, their parents, and society would be far too high.

Notes

1. The singular perspective typically makes allowances for married couples to adopt children as a compassionate, second-best situation for children.

2. For examples of the structural, or "singular," side of the debate, see David Popenoe, *Life without Father: Compelling New Evidence That Fatherhood and Marriage Are Indispensable for the Good of Children and Society* (New York: Martin Kessler Books, 1996); David Blankenhorn, *The Future of Marriage* (New York: Encounter Books, 2007); David Blankenhorn, Steven Bayme, and Jean Bethke Elshtain, eds., *Rebuilding the Nest: A New Commitment to the American Family* (Milwaukee, WI: Family Service America, 1990); Beau Weston, "Review: Allan Carlson, *Conjugal America: On the Public Purposes of Marriage*," *CHOICE: Current Reviews for Academic Libraries* 44 (Aug. 2007): 2184. For the processual, or "pluralist," perspective, see, e.g., Stephanie Coontz, *The Way We Really Are: Coming to Terms with America's Changing Families* (New York: Basic Books, 1997); Stephanie Coontz, *Marriage, a History: From Obedience to Intimacy, or How Love Conquered Marriage* (New York: Viking, 2005); Judith Stacey, *In the Name of the Family: Rethinking Family Values in the Postmodern Age* (Boston: Beacon Press, 1996); Judith Stacey, *Unhitched: Love, Marriage and Family Values from West Hollywood to Western China* (New York: NYU Press, 2011); Barbara J. Risman, ed., *Families as They Really Are* (New York: Norton, 2009); Nancy F. Cott, *Public Vows: A History of Marriage and the Nation* (Cambridge: Harvard University Press, 2000).

3. Blankenhorn, *Future of Marriage*, 86.

4. Stephanie Coontz, "The Evolution of American Families," in Risman, *Families as They Really Are*, 30–47, 31, quoted on 33.

5. Ibid.

6. U.S. Department of Labor Office of Policy Planning and Research (Daniel Patrick Moynihan), *The Negro Family: The Case for National Action* (Washington, DC: U.S. Government Printing Office, 1965).

7. During the 1992 electoral season, vice presidential candidate Dan Quayle criticized fictional TV character "Murphy Brown" for glamorizing unwed motherhood. Soon even liberal periodicals and politicians echoed the theme. See Barbara Dafoe Whitehead, "Dan Quayle Was Right," *Atlantic Monthly* 271, no. 4 (1993): 47; David Popenoe, "The Controversial Truth: Two-Parent Families Are Better," *New York Times*, Dec. 26, 1992, A21. For critique, see Judith Stacey, "Dada-ism in the 1990s: Getting Past Baby Talk about Fatherlessness," in *Lost Fathers: The Politics of Fatherlessness*, ed. Cynthia R. Daniels (New York: St. Martin's Press, 1998), 51–83. The literature debating the merits and forms of lesbian and gay family relationships is vast. For diverse affirmative views, see George Chauncey, *Why Marriage? The History Shaping Today's Debate over*

Gay Equality (New York: Basic Books, 2004); Andrew Sullivan, *Virtually Normal: An Argument about Homosexuality* (New York: Knopf, 1995); Evan Wolfson, *Why Marriage Matters: America, Equality, and Gay People's Right to Marry* (New York: Simon and Schuster, 2004); Judith Stacey and Timothy J. Biblarz, "(How) Does the Sexual Orientation of Parents Matter?," *American Sociological Review* 66 (Apr. 2001): 159. For critical perspectives, see, e.g., Blankenhorn, *Future of Marriage*; Lynn D. Wardle, ed., *What's the Harm? Does Legalizing Same-Sex Marriage Really Harm Individuals, Families, or Society?* (Lanham, MD: University Press of America, 2008); Stanley Kurtz, "Beyond Gay Marriage: The Road to Polyamory," *Weekly Standard* 8, no. 45 (2003): 26.

8. See, e.g., Lynn D. Wardle, "The Potential Impact of Homosexual Parenting on Children," *University of Illinois Law Review* 1997 (1997): 833; Barbara Katz Rothman, ed., *Encyclopedia of Childbearing: Critical Perspectives* (Phoenix, AZ: Oryx Press, 1993).

9. Fiona Tasker, "Developmental Outcomes for Children Raised by Lesbian and Gay Parents" (this volume).

10. Peter Wood, "The Anthropological Case for the Integrative Model," 90–95 (this volume).

11. Chuan-kang Shih, "*Tisese* and Its Anthropological Significance: Issues around the Visiting Sexual System among the Moso," *L'Homme* 154–155 (Apr.–Sept. 2000): 697, 704. I discuss the implications of the Mosuo family system for gender, eros, and domesticity in much greater detail in "Unhitching the Horse from the Carriage: Love and Marriage among the Mosuo," copublished by *Journal of Law and Family Studies* 11 (2009): 239 and *Utah Law Review* 2009 (2009): 287.

12. Cai Hua, *A Society without Fathers or Husbands: The Na of China*, trans. Asti Hustvedt (New York: Zone Books, 2001), 142.

13. Scholars disagree about the historical timing and genesis of marriage in Mosuo culture. See Chuan-kang Shih, "Genesis of Marriage among the Moso and Empire-Building in Late Imperial China," *Journal of Asian Studies* 60 (May 2001): 381, 403.

14. Martha Albertson Fineman, *The Neutered Mother, the Sexual Family, and Other Twentieth-Century Tragedies* (New York: Routledge, 1995).

15. Chuan-kang Shih and Mark R. Jenike, "A Cultural-Historical Perspective on the Depressed Fertility among the Matrilineal Moso in Southwest China," *Human Ecology* 30 (Mar. 2002): 21, 38.

16. The YFZ ranch is a Fundamentalist Latter-Day Saints community under the authority of Warren Jeffs, currently imprisoned for commanding the marriage of an underage girl to her cousin. In April 2008, Texas state authorities raided the ranch, taking hundreds of children away from their mothers and families into protective custody after receiving an anonymous phone call from a teenage girl who alleged sexual abuse. The Texas Supreme Court ruled that the state had exceeded its authority and ordered most of the children returned to their mothers. In re Texas Department of Family and Protective Services, 255 S.W.3d 613 (Tex. 2008). For contrasting feminist analyses, see Marci A. Hamilton, "Taking Stock of the 2008 Intervention at the Texas Fundamentalist Latter-Day Saints Compound on Its One-Year Anniversary: The Lessons We Must Learn to Effectively Protect Children in the Future," Apr. 16, 2009, http://writ.news.findlaw.com/ hamilton/20090416.html (accessed Feb. 11, 2010); and Catherine J. Ross, "Legal Constraints on Child-Saving: The Strange Case of the

Fundamentalist Latter-Day Saints at Yearning for Zion Ranch," *Capital University Law Review* 37 (2008): 361. For a description of FLDS polygamy and community, see Scott Anderson, "The Polygamists," *National Geographic*, Feb. 2010, http://ngm.nationalgeographic.com/2010/02/polygamists/anderson-text (accessed Feb. 11, 2010).

17. Blankenhorn, *Future of Marriage*, 88.

18. Coontz, *Marriage, a History*; Cott, *Public Vows*.

19. I conducted field research on the politics and practice of marital diversity in South Africa in June and July 2007. For more extensive analysis, see Judith Stacey and Tey Meadow, "New Slants on the Slippery Slope: The Politics of Polygamy and Gay Family Rights in South Africa and the United States," *Politics and Society* 37 (June 2009): 167; Stacey, *Unhitched*, chap. 3 and 4.

20. Const. of the Republic of South Africa, ch. 2, sec. 9(3), Feb. 4, 1997, http://www.info.gov.za/documents/constitution/1996/96cons2.htm#9 (accessed Jan. 3, 2012).

21. Republic of South Africa, Recognition of Customary Marriages Act, Dec. 2, 1998, http://www.info.gov.za/view/DownloadFileAction?id=70656 (accessed Feb. 11, 2010).

22. This law does not apply to Islamic plural marriages and does not legitimate polygyny for white men because these were not part of European customary culture. For a variety of complex political reasons, South Africa has not yet passed a law to regulate Islamic marriages.

23. Bongani Mthethwa and Subashni Naidoo, "Jacob Zuma in for a Bridal Shower," *The Times* (Johannesburg), Feb. 16, 2008; Monica Laganparsad and Yasantha Naidoo, "Four Better or for Worse," *The Sunday Times* (Johannesburg), Jan. 6, 2008; "Zuma's Fifth Marriage to Take Place 'One of These Days,'" *Mail and Guardian*, Jan. 5, 2009, http://mg.co.za/article/2009-01-05-zumas-fifth-marriage-to-take-place-one-of-these-days (accessed Jan. 3, 2012); Robyn Dixon, "South African President Jacob Zuma Marries Wife No. 5," *Los Angeles Times*, Jan 5, 2010, http://articles.latimes.com/2010/jan/05/world/la-fg-zuma-marriage5-2010jan05 (accessed Feb. 11, 2010).

24. I have assigned pseudonyms to all interview subjects.

25. Blankenhorn portrayed polygyny this way during his testimony as an expert witness in Perry v. Schwarzenegger, 704 F. Supp. 2d 921, 948 (N.D. Cal. 2010), *affirmed sub nom.* Perry v. Brown, 671 F.3d 1052 (9th Cir. 2012), the California same-sex marriage case prompted by Proposition 8. The district court observed: "Blankenhorn explained that despite the widespread practice of polygamy across many cultures, the rule of two is rarely violated, because even within a polygamous marriage, 'each marriage is separate.'" Ibid.

26. The 2008 South African National HIV Survey indicated an HIV prevalence rate of 13.6 percent for Africans, and only 0.3, 1.7, and 0.3 percent for whites, Colored, and Indians, respectively. Human Sciences Research Council, *South African National HIV Prevalence, Incidence, Behavior and Communication Survey, 2008: A Turning Tide among Teenagers?* (Cape Town: HSRC Press, 2008). The survey also indicated that women between the ages of fifteen and nineteen are three times more likely to be infected with HIV than men; between the ages of twenty and twenty-four, four times more likely; and between the ages of twenty-five and twenty-nine, twice as likely. Ibid. See also Stacey and Meadow, "New Slants on the Slippery Slope."

27. Blankenhorn, *Future of Marriage*, 88.

28. Ibid.

29. Anthony Giddens, *The Transformation of Intimacy: Sexuality, Love and Eroticism in Modern Societies* (Stanford, CA: Stanford University Press, 1992), 58.

30. Chuan-kang Shih, "The Yongning Moso: Sexual Union, Household Organization, Gender and Ethnicity in a Matrilineal Duolocal Society in Southwest China" (PhD diss., Stanford University, 1993), 157; and Shih, "*Tisese* and Its Anthropological Significance," 697, 704.

31. Giddens, *Transformation of Intimacy*, 58.

32. Lynn Jamieson, "Intimacy Transformed? A Critical Look at the 'Pure Relationship,'" *Sociology* 33 (Aug. 1999): 477.

33. Fineman, *Neutered Mother*, 143.

34. Yang Erche Namu and Christine Mathieu, *Leaving Mother Lake: A Girlhood at the Edge of the World* (Boston: Little, Brown, 2003), 7.

35. For discussions of the impact of tourism on the Mosuo, see Stacey, *Unhitched*, chap. 5; Eileen R. Walsh, "From Nü Guo to Nü'er Guo: Negotiating Desire in the Land of the Mosuo," *Modern China* 31 (Oct. 2005): 448; Louisa Schein, "Gender and Internal Orientalism in China," *Modern China* 23 (Jan. 1997): 69.

36. Visibly pregnant, Bristol Palin, daughter of right-wing Republican 2008 vice presidential candidate, Sarah Palin, adorned the dais of the party's nominating convention with her boyfriend and father of her child-to-be, Levi Johnston. Although they hastily announced an engagement, the couple broke up without marrying several months later amid considerable public conflict over custody of the child.

37. U.S. Government, "Grandparents Raising Grandchildren," Jan. 2, 2012, http://www.usa.gov/Topics/Grandparents.shtml (accessed Jan. 3, 2012).

38. See Judith Stacey, "Gay Parenthood and the Decline of Paternity as We Knew It," *Sexualities* 9 (Feb. 2006): 27; Judith Stacey, "Toward Equal Regard for Marriages and Other Imperfect Intimate Affiliations," *Hofstra Law Review* 32 (2003): 331; Abbie E. Goldberg, *Lesbian and Gay Parents and Their Children: Research on the Family Life Cycle* (Washington, DC: American Psychological Association, 2010).

39. See Lesléa Newman, *Heather Has Two Mommies* (Boston: Alyson Publications, 1989).

40. See Martha M. Ertman, "Race Treason: The Untold Story of America's Ban on Polygamy," *Columbia Journal of Gender and Law* 19 (2010): 287; Cott, *Public Vows*; and Stacey and Meadow, "New Slants on the Slippery Slope."

41. Bigamy is a misdemeanor in thirteen states. For examples of bigamy as a felony, see Mass. Gen. Laws ch. 272 sec. 15 (2000) ("Polygamy"); N.Y. Penal Law sec. 255.10 (2008) ("Unlawfully purporting a marriage," a misdemeanor), and N.Y. Penal Law sec. 255.15 (2008) ("Bigamy," a felony); Utah Code Ann. sec. 76-7-101 (2008) ("Bigamy," a third degree felony).

42. Eduardo Porter, "Tales of Republicans, Bonobos and Adultery," *New York Times*, July 2, 2009, A20, http://www.nytimes.com/2009/07/03/opinion/03fri4.html (accessed Feb. 11, 2010).

43. However, some feminists (e.g., black feminist law professor Adrien Wing in the United States and Afrikaans theology professor Cristina Landman in South Africa) argue for the advantages of polygamy for some modern women. See Stacey and Mead-

ow, "New Slants on the Slippery Slope." Moreover, the nineteenth-century history of U.S. feminism, monogamy, and polygamy was quite complex. Polygamy was arguably less oppressive to women than Victorian marriage. For example, Mormon polygamists granted women in the Utah territory the right to vote, but they lost the suffrage when the Mormons capitulated to demands that the church repudiate polygamy in order to enter the Union. See Joan S. Iversen, *The Antipolygamy Controversy in U.S. Women's Movements, 1880–1925: A Debate on the American Home* (New York: Garland, 1997); Cott, *Public Vows*.

44. See N.Y. Penal Law sec. 255.15.

45. Jacob Sullum, "Attacking Pluralism," *Reason*, May 29, 2001, http://www.reason.com/archives/2001/05/29/attacking-pluralism (accessed Jan. 3, 2012).

46. Adrien K. Wing, "Polygamy in Black America," in *Critical Race Feminism: A Reader*, 2nd ed., ed. Adrien K. Wing (New York: NYU Press, 2003), 186–194.

47. Barbara Bradley Hagerty, "Philly's Black Muslims Increasingly Turn to Polygamy," National Public Radio, June 2, 2008, www.npr.org/templates/story/story.php?storyId=90886407&sc=emaf (accessed Jan. 3, 2012).

48. Wing, "Polygamy in Black America."

49. Nina Bernstein, "Polygamy, Practiced in Secrecy, Follows Africans to New York," *New York Times*, Mar. 23, 2007, A1.

50. Angela Campbell et al., *Polygamy in Canada: Legal and Social Implications for Women and Children: A Collection of Policy Research Reports* (Ottawa: Status of Women Canada, 2005).

51. Martha Bailey et al., "Expanding Recognition of Foreign Polygamous Marriages: Policy Implications for Canada," *Queen's University Legal Studies Research Paper* No. 07–12, Oct. 23, 2007, http://papers.ssrn.com/sol3/papers.cfm?abstract_id=1023896#%23 (accessed Feb. 11, 2010).

52. Ibid., 41. But see Reference re: Section 293 of the Criminal Code of Canada, 2011 BCSC 1588 (concluding that Parliament's "reasoned apprehension of harm" to women, children, society, and the institution of monogamous marriage justifies Canada's criminal ban on polygamy).

The Anthropological Case for the Integrative Model

Peter Wood

Every viable society nurtures its children. In virtually all cases, the preferred form of bringing a child into the world and raising it is to provide a child with an acknowledged mother and father.

These fairly simple declarations have long been accepted fact among social scientists acquainted with the ethnographic record. Beginning in the 1980s, however, some anthropologists, influenced by postmodernism, began to express radical doubts about the very possibility of such generalization.

Seemingly simple declarations can indeed be complicated: definitions of "father" and "mother" are far from uniform across cultures. But I intend here to offer the case that these declarations are indeed valid.

The discipline of anthropology organized itself in the nineteenth century around the speculations of an American lawyer, Lewis Henry Morgan; a British Quaker, Edward Tylor; and, later in the century, a British classicist, Sir James George Frazer. Morgan made some fundamental contributions, which I will have occasion to refer to later, but he was dreadfully wrong on a key point. He imagined that human society—"Ancient Society," he called it[1]—arose in stages from a period of ancient promiscuity. Over time this promiscuity was transformed into "group marriage" in which a group of brothers married a group of sisters, and the children that resulted were common to the whole group.

Morgan's group marriage hypothesis was controversial. Among supporters were scholars who speculated a once-upon-a-time condition of primitive matriarchy.[2] The theory ran that no one could be certain about paternity, but maternity was seldom in doubt, and thus supplied the basis of a stable social order. Among the critics were scholars who argued that, on the contrary, primitive patriarchy must have been the primal human condition.[3]

Anthropology eventually discarded this debate as both fruitless and wrongheaded. We have no decisive evidence about the family structures of our Pleistocene ancestors, nor any reason to think that they all conformed to a single social pattern. Yet this long-discarded scholarly debate is not irrelevant to today's debates over the meaning of marriage and parenthood. Parts of it were absorbed into the larger culture via such works as Robert Graves's *The White Goddess*, and the theme of primitive matriarchy reemerged in the 1970s in a series of popular works that gave a patina of scholarship to what was essentially a feminist fantasy. Riane Eisler's *The Chalice and the Blade* (1987) is an example of this genre.[4]

It would be hard to say how many Americans currently entertain the idea that, once upon a time, villages really did raise children under the peaceful cooperative supervision of a group of wise women, and this golden age only came to an end because men introduced war, bloodshed, competition, and hierarchy. Nothing that we actually know from archaeology, human biology, and ethnography supports this picture, but it nonetheless seeps into our public discussion of marriage and child rearing. Imagine a society free from the oppression of the concept of "father." Imagine a world where raising children is the joyfully diffuse responsibility of a group. This imagining, it seems to me, lies behind much of the attempt to deny the plain fact that in virtually all societies the preferred form of bringing a child into the world and raising it is to provide a child with an acknowledged mother and father.

The ghost of a long-discredited anthropological hypothesis thus strangely haunts our contemporary debates over the legal and moral status of marriage and children.

Morgan, Tylor, Frazer, and other anthropologists who flourished during the epoch of anthropology's formative period eventually faced a stern tribunal of a new generation of anthropologists. In that court they were found guilty of guessing about the past; building their theories out of bits and pieces of data gathered the whole world over with little attention to local context; and paying little attention to how human societies actually work. The criticisms were overstated, but they did usher in an age of more exacting standards of ethnographic reporting, and we owe to figures like W. H. R. Rivers and Bronislaw Malinowski in Britain and Franz Boas in the United States the emergence of this new, systematic inquiry.[5] The results of the work they initiated are pretty much all we have to go on in answering the questions before us now, for, sad to say, their intellectual project was more or less terminated in the 1980s. The robust kind of ethnography that sought a systematic and holistic picture of individual societies is seldom pursued by today's anthropologists.

Anthropologists still engage in something they call "ethnography," but it bears little resemblance to that former quest to understand how human groups hold together and sustain themselves from generation to generation. Ethnography in the sense that now prevails gives pride of place to division, tension, discontinuity, disruption, diaspora, alienation, oppression, and psychosis. A good many anthropologists put themselves in the foreground of their work, writing a hybrid of autobiography and travel memoir; others ruminate in ornate prose on why the concept of "culture" is obsolete and how societies have melded into a boundless global everywhere.[6]

The historic change in the discipline of anthropology from holistic approaches often centered on the study of kinship to approaches that emphasize contention, struggle, and fragmentation bears directly on the debate between proponents of the *integrative model* and *diversity model* of marriage and parenthood. For one thing, it presents a possible confusion of terms that I want to forestall. The word *diversity* in this discussion could trip us up. Anthropology from its outset focused on the facts of human diversity. Should you want an account of the great variety of ways in which marriage and child rearing take place across the thousands of documented human societies, the place to look is the body of anthropological writing that includes abundant detail as well as strenuous analytical effort to make sense of the underlying patterns. But this documented *ethnographic* diversity must be distinguished from the *radical* diversity pictured by contemporary anthropologists who regard the concept of kinship itself as an ethnocentric Western imposition on the profound plurality of culture. This view was given its most famous enunciation by the anthropologist David Schneider, who after decades of scholarship on matrilineal kinship systems famously repudiated the whole field in these terms.[7] Ethnographic diversity poses a set of phenomena that we can strive to comprehend as the various manifestations of underlying principles. Radical diversity asks nothing from us but a kind of existential assent: yes, people over there really *are* different.[8]

That assent, however, has its purposes. It evokes a world in which humans are unconstrained inventors of their own realities, and it buttresses the political argument that we too should feel free to invent ourselves by dispensing with outworn institutions that have been falsely invested with a sense that they are rooted in human necessity.

Not all anthropologists support this picture of radical diversity, and the cohort of anthropologists who most strongly veer in another direction are those who are concerned with human evolution and the actual origins of ethnographic diversity. In this branch of anthropology, a lively debate has emerged drawing on clues from hominid fossils, linguistics, studies of living primates, analogies with contemporary hunter-gatherers, and other sources that has reawakened questions such as whether early humans were matrilineal or patrilineal. This debate, though inconclusive, bears on our topic.

For example, research on the genetics of hunter-gatherer groups in Africa has turned up a surprise. These groups are generally organized into patrilocal bands. But studies of matrilineally transmitted mitochondria and patrilineal Y chromosomes show that men are more likely to migrate than women and that hunter-gatherer women tend to stay near their mothers after they marry. These data are cited by those who argue that matrilineal organization is more fundamental than patrilineal organization,[9] but we need not take up that controversy to observe that in the case of hunter-gatherer societies, the underlying realities of kinship links exert a force that is a counter to the prevailing ideology of society. The bands conceive of themselves as bound together by links of sons to their fathers, but links of daughters to their mothers in practice may count even more.

The mitochondrial DNA studies reinforce the long-held view in anthropology that ties of filiation have social importance above and beyond their use in defining membership in key groups. In patrilineal societies, ties to the mother still count; in matrilineal societies, ties to the father still count. The anthropologist who gave the name to this seemingly paradoxical emphasis on the unemphasized parent was Meyer Fortes, who was prompted to consider it as he watched children among the matrilineal Ashanti carrying dinner to their fathers. He called it "complementary filiation."[10] It is a cumbersome phrase, but it has the merit of drawing attention to the center of the phenomenon. It is the filiation that completes the child. No matter that in these societies the links between a child and one of its parents are the crucial determinant of status; the link to the other parent is important too.

How far back does this go? How widespread is it? Linguistic reconstruction in Africa has shown that the proto-Khoesan people—the ancestors of most of today's hunter-gatherers in Africa—employed a kinship terminology that sharply distinguished fathers (and their siblings) from mothers (and their siblings) about 15,000 years ago.[11] This may sound like a trivial discovery, but it is not. Kinship terminologies tell us a great deal about social organization, and they have been studied systematically since the time of Morgan. What comparative philology has given us is a precious glimpse of social organization of the family deep in the past. Moreover, what that glimpse reveals is that the proto-Khoesans employed a system of classifying relatives that matches one familiar from the contemporary anthropological record. For our purposes, the details do not matter except for the focal emphasis on the difference between maternal and paternal kin. The timescale—15,000 years ago—puts this well before the domestication of crops and animal husbandry.

To reach back still further we must rely on various kinds of models and inferences. Some of the facts are simple. We know from the fossil record that species ancestral to our own had progressively larger brains, an evolutionary process known as *encephalization*. This put selective pressure on females to give birth after relatively short gestation, and this in turn meant caring for infants significantly less developed than the young of other species. Hence we can make a strong inference that the genus *Homo* evolved in a manner that ensured that infants at least some of them—would receive sustained care throughout a long period of maturation.

We know this happened over a period of about 2 million years—long before the development of a capacity for language. This gives some weight to the idea that behind the diversity of culturalized forms of kinship and family in contemporary *Homo sapiens* may lie a built-in biological pattern of instincts. Australopithecines appear to have matured quickly, but the larger-brained *Homo habilis* who was on the scene in East Africa making crude tools may well have required a longer period of dependence. In any case, our even larger-brained Pleistocene ancestor of the last 1.7 million years, *Homo erectus*, was undoubtedly devoted to caring for its children who could not otherwise survive. But the social arrangements to support this lie beyond what archaeologists can tell us.

Another line of inference comes from the study of the diets of contemporary hunter-gatherers. Work in this area shows that women in these societies over their lifetimes consume significantly more calories than they contribute through foraging. The deficit is estimated at 14.5 million kilocalories. After their childbearing years, at around age forty-six, women begin to produce a surplus, which, though it is not enough to make up the cumulated deficit, enables them to assist their children and grandchildren. On this basis, Kit Opie and Camilla Power argue that grandmothering may be a key to understanding hunter-gatherer social organization. Indeed, they go further, suggesting, "Grandmothering appears vital to our evolution,"[12] and offer a model of *Homo erectus* society based on a sexual division of labor with a key role for grandmothers. The idea has also been developed by the biological anthropologist Sarah Hrdy, who describes grandmothers as "allo-mothers."[13] Needless to say, the grandmothering hypothesis subsumes ideas about durable links of filiation.

When anthropology attempts to grapple with the large questions about who we are as a species and how we have become so, it still turns back to these fundamental matters of the relation between parent and child. Anthropologists who dissent are often those who, because they went into the discipline at a time when kinship studies were out of favor, do not know that much about the subject.[14] But putting aside such uninformed views, there are a handful of well-known ethnographic cases that seem to show that societies can get along perfectly well without *fathers*. Mothers may be indispensable nurturers; fathers perhaps not. The matrilineal Nayars in India in the nineteenth century and earlier, as reconstructed by Kathleen Gough fifty years ago, are the touchstone of this argument.[15] The more recently described Na of the Chinese provinces of Yunnan and Sichuan near the Burmese border provide another striking instance. We are fortunate to have an excellent ethnography of the Na by the French-trained Chinese anthropologist Cai Hua.[16]

These cases show the furthest possible extension of the principles of matrilineality and provide what might well be an insurmountable hurdle for theorists who see the whirring of a biological kin-selection engine beneath the surface of every social system. On the other hand, the existence of the Nayar and Na systems does not do much to weaken the general observations about the fundamental role of acknowledged mothers and fathers in nurturing children.

The Nayar were a warrior caste that lived in mixed-caste villages among the several kingdoms of the Malabar coast in southwest India.[17] They were organized into landed estates called *taravad*, which included a large, many-roomed house with a veranda and fields of cultivated land. Nayar men were trained in military exercises and went away for prolonged periods for exploits on behalf of the non-Nayar king. The agricultural work in Nayar fields was performed by workers of lower castes. The *taravad* were social units as well as houses and estates, and as such were strictly matrilineal. A boy and girl belonged to the *taravad* of their mother and remained so for life. They were also permanently resident in the *taravad* and were conceived by Nayars to share the physical substance of the Nayar estate. That is, the Nayars so identified with their *taravads* that they thought that the people and the soil shared substance.[18]

Shortly before puberty, Nayar girls participated in a ceremony in which each was ritually joined with a designated male from a linked section of another *taravad*. This relationship was not sexually consummated, and the man had no further obligation to the girl or she to him, except that she and her children were expected to perform a mourning ceremony for him at his death. After this symbolic marriage rite, the girl was free to commence sexual relations with any men who were Nayar but not members of her own *taravad*. She could also commence sexual relations with certain members of the Brahmin caste. There was no limit to the number of lovers she might take, and the lovers gained no rights over her or her property.[19]

A Nayar woman who became pregnant, however, stood in need of one of her lovers coming forward to acknowledge paternity by performing a public rite. If none did, it would be assumed that she had had sexual relations with a man of lower caste, and she would have been expelled from her *taravad*—stripped of social status and driven away. The acknowledged father of her child, however, bore no particular obligation to the child. Whether he had an informal relation with his children, we do not know, but Nayars put no cultural emphasis on paternity past the point of assuring themselves that caste purity had not been violated.[20]

The Nayar had a vestigial form of marriage and paternity. The Na appear to have neither. (Stacey's chapter in this volume refers to the Na as the Mosuo.)[21] They are a tribal group, numbering about 30,000, descended from Qiang immigrants who arrived in the area in the second century. In the eighth century, the Na's ancestors conquered some of their neighbors and formed a short-lived kingdom. The Na, along with three other tribes in Yunnan and Sichuan who speak related Tibetan languages, appear to be surviving fragments of the original ethnic group that created the Nan Zhao kingdom, but all four groups dispute this and claim distinct origins.[22]

The Na traditionally farmed oats, buckwheat, and flax and kept chickens and pigs. In the last century they expanded into other crops and acquired additional livestock. Currently 70 percent of their fields are devoted to rice. The Na were dry farmers who lived in villages and traded pork for salt, tea, cotton, and small luxuries.[23] Though not a prosperous group, they were stratified into three sections: an aristocracy consisting of members of the lineage of the Chinese government–appointed governor; commoner lineages; and servant lineages.[24] The Na have been under Han Chinese administration for 1,400 years. Like the Nayars, the Na cannot really be conceived as having an autonomous social system. Rather, they are an enclave subordinate to and dependent on a larger system. That status does not by itself explain the peculiar Na social structure but is probably a necessary precondition for it.

What makes the Na peculiar is their disdain for marriage. They are by no means ignorant of what marriage is or how marriage may be used to assign children to social groups. They see the practice carried on by their non-Na neighbors, and some Na in all three strata indeed marry. When men and women of the aristocratic Na stratum marry, the ordinary Na rule that assigns children to the lineage of their mother kicks into reverse. The children of a male aristocrat who marries belong to *his* matrilineage, and the children of a female aristocrat who marries belong to her husband's matrilineage.[25] This reversal holds even if the spouse is from a nonaristocratic lineage. It is as though a Na who chooses to marry has changed his or her sex.

The person who transmits to children his or her membership in a lineage is called an *ong*, which means "bone."[26] This too seems a little odd. In a great many cultures, fathers and mothers are conceived as contributing different substances to the formation of the child. Far more commonly, fathers are conceived as contributing bones, mothers the blood. The Na see no such mixture in the child; the parental contribution is all bone, and the mother normally provides it.

The normal Na pattern of procreation is for a man to visit a woman in her house for sexual intercourse but to remain resident in his own lineage's house.[27] Sometimes, however, a man and woman will cohabit for a period without getting married.[28] Children resulting from these cohabitations are assigned to lineages according to yet another peculiar set of rules. Male children from cohabitations are assigned to the lineage of the male, and female children to the lineage of the female. As a result, full siblings of opposite sex resulting from these unions belong to different lineages and are, in Na terms, unrelated. This rule, however, does offer a kind of social mobility. The son of a servant stratum woman by a commoner becomes a member of his progenitor's commoner lineage, and the son of a commoner stratum woman by a servant becomes a member of his progenitor's commoner lineage.

One can immediately see in these rules that Na are fully capable of building social realities on the basis of paternity, but for the purpose of the overall architecture of their social system, paternity is radically devalued and largely ignored. Most Na profess both ignorance about who their fathers are and indifference to the question. Male Na outside the context of marriage or cohabitation pay no particular attention to the children resulting from their liaisons. Consistent with this, Na women put no special restrictions on their sexual availability. Indeed, they show up in Marco

Polo's *Travels* as an object of merriment: "When a man of this region sees a foreigner come to his house to find lodging or anything else, he happily and joyously welcomes him.... All women—wives, daughters, sisters, the whole lot—give themselves freely."[29]

The Na definitely do not prefer to raise a child with an acknowledged mother and father. They prefer instead an acknowledged mother and mother's brother. The mother's brother, of course, plays an important role in the lives of his sister's children in all matrilineal societies. Occasionally the role of the father is much diminished in these societies, although the general rule is that Fortes's "complementary filiation" kicks in. Fatherhood is, in effect, split into two parts: the figure who bears the authority of the matrilineage to enforce rules, allocate resources, discipline the children, and make binding judgments, on one hand, and the solicitous, caregiving consort of the mother, on the other hand. The split runs down the middle of every man in a matrilineal society. One of the type cases is the Trobriand father who is legally bound to look after his sister's children but whose heart is always with his own children. Part of the lineage legacy he must guard and transmit to his sister's children is knowledge of clan magic, but he is perpetually giving away pieces of it to his own children.[30]

The Na has cured this internal division in men by erasing fatherhood. But the erasure is incomplete. Fatherhood keeps creeping back in as a kind of embarrassment that the Na have to acknowledge when lineage affairs do not work out right. A lineage needs a balance of male and female labor as well as female members to perpetuate itself. If it finds itself with only male heirs, contracting a marriage to bring a woman (and her potential children) into the lineage may be an unwelcome necessity. Likewise, a lineage with all daughters may sometimes seek a husband to acquire male labor. Men, knowing that they will bear a disproportionate share of the workload as well as the opprobrium of being married, shun this arrangement but can be brought to it by sheer need. A more common solution is for the lineage to go to an outside ethnic group to acquire a husband.

The Na system just barely accommodates the anomaly of marriage. The language lacks a word for father, and the children of a married woman refer to their mother's husband as *ewu*, the same word they use for maternal uncle. This makes sense, for their father is being assimilated to the role that their mother's brother would normally play: the male authority figure of the lineage to which they belong and the man they look to for male nurturance.

Can we accommodate the Na in any fashion with the proposition that "the preferred form of bringing a child into the world and raising it is to provide a child with an acknowledged mother and father"? Is the integrative model of parenthood doomed by the Na example? I suspect not.

Stacey draws a contrasting conclusion, but she also redefines the terms of the debate in a way that distorts what is really at issue. Stacey assigns to those who argue for the accuracy of the integrative model of parenthood both a moralistic motive and a pair of titles (*singular* or *universalist*) meant to characterize the position she disagrees with as ethnocentric and blind to the genuine variety of human social forms. She takes for her own position the term *pluralist*, to emphasize the openness of her view on the "changing character of family patterns across space, time, and culture."[31] But that changing character is in no sense in dispute. The issue is whether we can discern some underlying order in the great variety of social arrangements that humanity has contrived to govern parenthood. The matter hardly lies beyond the scope of fair-minded inquiry to resolve. Are forms of parenthood inventions that respect no natural limitations, or are they subject to systematic constraints? The answer does not come down to the "temperaments, tastes, and sensibilities" and "political principles" of the people asking the question. Rather, it comes down to how well we can explain the facts. For Stacey to characterize the Na (or Mosuo) as having a "brilliant time-tested strategy" begs a number of questions. A strategy for what? And who exactly has done the strategizing?

Terms like these may well apply to modern social movements such as the effort to establish gay marriage as a civil right, but they distort the historical and cultural situation of a group such as the Na. The Na, like most people most of the time, make choices within a system not of their own devising. If they choose to maintain that system against external pressure to change, they do so for reasons of their own and surely not because they share Stacey's view that their system "frees family fortunes and child well-being from the capriciousness of sexual and romantic love."[32] The Na may be many things, but they are not postmodern feminists.

My opening proposition about mothers and fathers is tethered to the qualification "in virtually all cases." The Na are the strongest exception in the ethnographic record and a perverse proof of principle. Instead of an acknowledged "father," the Na substitute an acknowledged male nurturer in a long-term and indissoluble relationship with the mother. Mother's brother is seen by the Na as the person best placed for this role, but mother's husband will do as a substitute. This does not so much invert the situation in most matrilineal societies as it does carry its logic to the furthest limits. Even there, the Na retain something very much like the integrative model of parenthood. The *ewu* is the child's steady and reliable provider, guardian, and male comforter—just not the sexual companion of the child's mother.

But even here, the Na exceptionalism comes at a price. Just as the ghosts of marriage and fatherhood haunt the system, so does the urge to integrate sexuality with the other aspects of a man's relationship with his sister. The Na testify to this by their strong taboos surrounding the brother-sister relationship. They live in the same house, for example, but are prohibited from being together in a dark room. From around age seven, brother and sister are prohibited from talking about emotional issues with each other or using coarse language in each other's presence. When incest does occur, the offending parties are executed, and the traditional Na form for this is to seal the brother and sister together in a cave. Brother and sister face a lifetime taboo on mentioning anything emotional or sexual in one another's presence.[33] The Na, who possess no particular sense of sexual jealousy, have turned the fear of brother-sister incest into a symbolic axis of their culture.

All in all, the Na seem to have banished the conscious idea of fatherhood only to have it return in various disguises. Why did this particular system develop when and where it did? Why has it endured despite numerous efforts by Chinese governments to suppress it? We do not know, but part of the answer is that the Na system of hypermatrilineality is one way of building a self-enclosed order inside the encompassing patrilineal order of Han Chinese society. Their system allows the Na to be totally open and accommodating to strangers at one level while remaining totally closed at another.

Having considered the Nayar and the Na, do we face a tide of other cases where parenthood is seriously in question? This is a matter of judgment. Those anthropologists who adopt the position of radical diversity are likely to point to numerous social arrangements that ostensibly do not fit with what I have called "the preferred form of bringing a child into the world," that is, with an acknowledged mother and father. Most of these cases, however, pose no real challenge. Let me briefly consider some of the conclusions about the family drawn from these cases.

The Nuclear Family Is Not Always the Primary Social Unit

That the nuclear family is not always the primary social unit is true and has been known to anthropologists since the beginning of systematic ethnographic inquiry, but it has no necessary bearing on whether the integrative model of parenthood is accurate. For example, in villages in India the common social unit is the joint family, in which brothers bring home their wives to a household in which the in-marrying wives share responsibilities under the often harsh supervision of their mother-in-law.[34] The shared responsibilities include child care, but mothers and fathers know who their own children are and pay special attention to them. Typically as the joint household ages, strains increase, and eventually the household breaks up as the brothers go their own ways with their wives and children.[35]

The Indian joint family is not an amalgamation of several nuclear families. It is a social unit in its own right expressed in the architecture of houses, customary law on marriage and inheritance, and child-rearing patterns. The shared components of female nurturance matter profoundly and are reflected, as Stanley Kurtz has pointed out, in the imagery of Hindu goddesses who, despite their different appearances and powers, are said ultimately to be a single entity.[36] "All the mothers are one," says the Indian villager, who at the same time knows that one particular mother stands out as his own.

Another South Asian family structure sometimes cited as evidence of the weakness of the integrative model of parenthood is the household based on fraternal polyandry that is found in parts of the Himalayas. For example, Luintel, writing on a Nepalese group that practices polyandry, concludes, "For the Nyinba, it does not matter so much who the biological father is, given that social fatherhood is a collective and symbolic expression of power configurations at large."[37] This is where several brothers will be married to and coresident with one woman. The joint wife in these cases takes care to know which of her husbands is the father of each child and generally gives priority to the oldest brother. Children of these families have only one father, and younger brothers typically spend great effort to acquire their own wives and eventually to move out of the shared household.

Polygamy in any form results in social units unlike the nuclear family, but it does not displace the child's need for both maternal and paternal care. In a polygynous household, women are mothers to their own children; in a polyandrous household, men are fathers to their own children.

Plural marriage creates situations of both cooperation and competition among co-spouses that may affect the emotional life and material circumstances of the child. Ethnographers have been highly attentive to this, and thus we know pretty clearly that, no matter the division of labor in plural marriage, parents form unique and powerful bonds with their own children.[38]

Some Matrifocal Societies Put Little Stock in Paternal Involvement
The observation that some matrifocal societies put little value upon paternal involvement is not exactly true. There are indeed societies in which men form weak and not very durable alliances with women, and children are raised, more often than not, in households where the mother is unmarried and the father unacknowledged or absent. This is familiar because of the exceptionally high out-of-wedlock birthrate in inner-city African American communities. Among the Nayar, male involvement in military expeditions meant prolonged absences. Communities dependent on long-distance trading or seafaring expeditions often created a situation in which children were fatherless for prolonged periods. It is an old story. Telemachus grew up waiting for Odysseus to return. Today, international migrant labor has created a new global system of matrifocal families supported by remittances and occasional visits by absentee husbands.

Women and children can get along without resident and reliable male support. That does not mean they generally want to or that they belong to a society that prefers that women bring children into the world without provision for paternal care. In most of these situations, the absence of fathers is felt acutely, and the male links that do exist become heavily invested with symbolic importance. Among African-Caribbean families 30 to 50 percent of households in the region are headed by women—Jamaica: 33.8 percent; Barbados: 42.9 percent; Grenada: 45.3 percent.[39] But these are also societies in which both women and men conceive that the roles of husband and father are enormously important.[40]

Fatherlessness can become widespread when a social order breaks down as when the Pakistani army in 1971 engaged in mass rape of Bangladeshi women and left many thousands pregnant. Many of these women were subsequently shunned by their husbands and families. The Bangladeshi government responded by offering abortions and adoptions, and the war babies were effectively "disappeared." The tactic, however, lives on—the Bangladeshi army itself has used mass rape since the 1970s against the restive Jumma tribal minority.

War, famine, severe impoverishment, and other external causes can force a society to suspend its moral expectations about how to bring children into the world, but it is much harder to find societies in which children are raised by preference without fathers. The Na are one case; perhaps our own society will provide another as in the case of women who voluntarily seek artificial insemination to bear children who come into the world without the prospect of fathers. Anthropology is not a source of moral rules or reflections on what a society ought to do, but only a systematic account of what societies actually do.[41]

But I would not rush to scrap our current understandings. Murphy Brown–style reproduction has not yet been institutionalized in the West. All human societies can be seen, in one sense, as experiments. Some fail; others thrive. The Na, by any standard, have shown their social order works within the political and material conditions of South China. On matters dealing with human reproduction, we should perhaps withhold a verdict on viability until a few generational cycles have run their course.

The West is a fecund source of social experimentation. Many of these experiments have indeed failed. Some we look back on as mere oddities—as in the Shaker attempt to build communities on the basis of total celibacy, or the Oneida Community's attempt to promote group marriage. In any case, we ought to see some evidence that a novel practice such as elective fatherlessness endures before writing it into theories of human nature.

Some Societies Have a Relaxed Approach to Giving Children Away for Adoption or Fostering

The observation that some societies freely rely upon adoption or fostering children to ensure their care is true and the ethnographic record extensive. Fostering children—sending them to live in another household without relinquishing the formal rights of the parents—is particularly common in West Africa, the Andes, and Micronesia.[42] The existence of mechanisms to assign children to the care of people other than their birth parents does not weigh against the proposition that the preferred form of bringing a child into the world and raising it is to provide a child with an acknowledged mother and father. Societies must have contingency plans for raising children whose parents die or become incapacitated. But fostering and adoption also occur for reasons that suggest that, in some societies, parents relinquish care of their children to others with relative ease—and this indeed points to a weakness in the integrative model.

When a single mother fosters a child because of financial hardship, and a married couple who already have many children relinquish a child who can be better cared for by another couple, the integrative model is not discomforted—and this appears to account for most of the West African cases. In that situation, fostering is a voluntary reallocation of children to improve their chances of thriving. Something similar appears to be the case in the Andes. One ethnographer recently calculated that about 10 percent of the children in the community she studied had been fostered, or "given," as the Bolivian peasants put it.[43] Though formal adoption is rare, the feeding of children is invested with symbolic importance. Feeding, along with other acts of nurturing, is said "to make a child into a son or daughter." The children "almost always" move from poorer to wealthier households, and frequently from young couples to older ones.

The Micronesian situation is more challenging. There we find the widespread practice of sending children to live and be raised in other households for no particular reason other than friendly relations among the adults.[44] The child in this kind of fostering appears not to suffer a decline in emotional or physical care, but we are left to ponder the seeming insouciance of the arrangement. It suggests that parents are, more or less, interchangeable in the eyes of Micronesians. Technically, the proposition that the children are brought into the world with an acknowledged mother and father is preserved; the acknowledged identity of a child who is fostered does not lapse, but with startling fluidity, the responsibility of nurturing the child can be transferred to another family.

Conclusion

The anthropological study of kinship is a searchlight that has been trained on a great variety of intellectual and humane problems over the last century and a half. In that time, it helped to transform our view of humanity.

Contemporary Westerners pride themselves on a cosmopolitan outlook that takes common humanity for granted and prizes cultural difference. The achievement owes much to the contributions of anthropologists who taught us to see human differences not as an unbridgeable gulf but as variations on a set of common themes. The most basic of these themes is kinship, and the most basic element of kinship is the relation of parent to child.

Having enthusiastically taken up the idea that everybody else in the world possesses his own practical way of doing things, his own view of the order of the world, and his own values, we are increasingly at a loss—once again—to see the common humanity.

Social and cultural differences are important, but we misread them if all we see in those differences is the human capacity endlessly to innovate new cultural forms. That innovation is bounded by numerous practical constraints, of which the most immovable is the need to bring each new generation to healthy maturity and to possession of the knowledge and motivation to carry on.

Nature, in stripping our species of many animal instincts and giving us instead a power of self-creation, leaves us vulnerable to cultural mistakes. We do not know how many societies have perished because they miscalculated their resource reserves; or burned their own houses and crops in a moment of millenarian delusion; or allowed their rate of reproduction to fall below the replacement level; or chose a path of child rearing that produced adults indifferent to the fate of their community. That a social order is extant at the moment is no guarantee that it can be sustained, and the world is full of middens marking where bygone groups once toiled.

The ethnographic record offers a cautionary tale. We see precious few instances in which societies depart from the integrative model of child rearing, which attempts to make out of each husband and wife, a committed father and mother. Societies can and do create socially approved exceptions, sometimes from necessity, and sometimes in a search for a wider field of social amity and security. But even the exceptions are bound by the search for ways to ensure that children receive paternal as well as maternal care.

Notes

1. Lewis Henry Morgan, *Ancient Society: Or Researches in the Lines of Human Progress from Slavery through Barbarism to Civilization* (Chicago: C. H. Kerr, 1877).

2. Johann Jakob Bachofen, *Das Mutterrecht: Eine Untersuchung über die Gyanikokratie der Alten Welt nach Ihrer Religiosen und Rechtlichen Natur*, ed. Hans-Jürgen Heinrichs (1861; repr., Frankfurt: Suhrkamp, 1975); Ernest Crawley, *The Mystic Rose: A Study of Primitive Marriage and of Primitive Thought in Its Bearing on Marriage*, rev. ed. by Theodore Besterman (1902; repr., New York: Meridian Books, 1960); Cynthia Eller, *Gentlemen and Amazons: The Myth of Matriarchal Prehistory, 1861–1900* (Berkeley: University of California Press, 2011).

3. John Ferguson McLennan, *The Patriarchal Theory*, ed. Donald McLennan (London: Macmillan, 1885).

4. Cynthia Eller, *The Myth of Matriarchal Prehistory: Why an Invented Past Won't Give Women a Future* (Boston: Beacon Press, 2000).

5. Alan Barnard, *History and Theory in Anthropology* (New York: Cambridge University Press, 2000).

6. Anna Lowenhaupt Tsing, *In the Realm of the Diamond Queen: Marginality in an Out-of-the-Way Place* (Princeton: Princeton University Press, 1993); Renato Rosaldo, *Culture and Truth: The Remaking of Social Analysis* (Boston: Beacon Press, 1989); Nicholas Thomas, *Colonialism's Culture: Anthropology, Travel and Government* (Princeton: Princeton University Press, 1994).

7. David M. Schneider, *A Critique of the Study of Kinship* (Ann Arbor: University of Michigan Press, 1984).

8. Cf. Marilyn Strathern, *Kinship, Law and the Unexpected: Relatives Are Always a Surprise* (New York: Cambridge University Press, 2005).

9. Chris Knight, "Early Human Kinship Was Matrilineal," in *Early Human Kinship: From Sex to Social Reproduction*, ed. Nicholas J. Allen et al. (Malden, MA: Blackwell, 2008), 61–82, especially 80; **Giovanni** Destro-Bisol et al., "Variation of Female and Male Lineages in Sub-Saharan Populations: The Importance of Sociocultural Factors," *Molecular Biology and Evolution* 21 (2004): 1673.

10. Meyer Fortes, *Time and Social Structure and Other Essays* (New York: Humanities Press, 1970).

11. Christopher Ehret, "Reconstructing Ancient Kinship in Africa," in Allen et al., *Early Human Kinship*, 200–231.

12. Kit Opie and Camilla Power, "Grandmothering and Female Coalitions: A Basis for Matrilineal Priority?," in Allen et al., *Early Human Kinship*, 168–186.

13. Sarah Hrdy, *Mother Nature: Natural Selection and the Female of the Species* (London: Chatto and Windus, 1999); Gillian Bentley and Ruth Mace, eds., *Substitute Parents: Biological and Social Perspectives on Alloparenting across Human Societies* (New York: Berghahn, 2009).

14. Warren Shapiro, "The Nuclear Family versus the Men's House? A Re-examination of Munduric Sociality," *Anthropological Forum* 21 (Mar. 2011): 57.

15. E. Kathleen Gough, "The Nayars and the Definition of Marriage," *Journal of the Royal Anthropological Institute of Great Britain and Ireland* 89 (Jan.–June 1959): 23.

16. Cai Hua, *A Society without Fathers or Husbands: The Na of China*, trans. Asti Hustvedt (New York: Zone Books, 2001).

17. C. J. Fuller, *The Nayars Today* (Cambridge: Cambridge University Press, 1976).

18. Melinda A. Moore, "A New Look at the Nayar Taravad," *Man*, n.s., 20 (Sept. 1985): 523.

19. Gough, "Nayars and the Definition of Marriage," 23.

20. Ibid.

21. Judith Stacey, "Uncoupling Marriage and Parenting," 68 (this volume).

22. Hua, *Society without Fathers or Husbands*, 35–37.

23. Ibid., 40–45.

24. Ibid., 49–54.

25. Ibid., 50.

26. Ibid., 51, 120.

27. Ibid., 185.

28. Ibid., 263–301.

29. Marco Polo, *Devisement du Monde—Le Livre des Merveilles* (repr., Paris: Editions La Decouverte, 1984), 296–297, quoted in Hua, *Society without Fathers or Husbands*, 23.

30. Bronislaw Malinowski, *Argonauts of the Western Pacific: An Account of Native Enterprise and Adventure in the Archipelagoes of Melanesian New Guinea* (1922; repr., New York: Dutton, 1961).

31. Stacey, "Uncoupling Marriage and Parenting," 66.

32. Ibid., 75.

33. Hua, *Society without Fathers or Husbands*, 125–128.

34. Oscar Lewis, *Village Life in Northern India: Studies in a Delhi Village* (New York: Vintage Books, 1958); David G. Mandelbaum, *Society in India* (Berkeley: University of California Press, 1970), 1:125–133.

35. Frederick G. Bailey, *Caste and the Economic Frontier: A Village in Highland Orissa* (Manchester: Manchester University Press, 1957), 88–89; M. N. Srinivas, *The Remembered Village* (Berkeley: University of California Press, 1976).

36. Stanley N. Kurtz, *All the Mothers Are One: Hindu India and the Cultural Reshaping of Psychoanalysis* (New York: Columbia University Press, 1992).

37. Youba Raj Luintel, "Agency, Autonomy and the Shared Sexuality: Gender Relations in Polyandry in Nepal Himalaya," *Contributions to Nepalese Studies* 31 (Jan. 2004): 43.

38. Nancy E. Levine and Joan B. Silk, "Why Polyandry Fails: Sources of Instability in Polyandrous Marriages," *Current Anthropology* 38 (June 1997): 375.

39. Joycelin Massiah, "Female-Headed Households and Employment in the Caribbean," *Women's Studies International* 2 (July 1982): 7.

40. Edith Clarke, *My Mother Who Fathered Me: A Study of the Family in Three Communities in Jamaica*, introduction by M. G. Smith (London: George Allen and Unwin, 1957); Jaipaul L. Roopnarine, "African American and African Caribbean Fathers: Level, Quality, and Meaning of Involvement," in *The Role of the Father in Child Development*, 4th ed., ed. Michael E. Lamb (Hoboken, NJ: Wiley, 2004), 58–97.

41. John Monaghan and Peter Just, *Social and Cultural Anthropology: A Very Short Introduction* (New York: Oxford University Press, 2000).

42. Arvilla C. Payne-Price, "Etic Variations on Fosterage and Adoption," *Anthropological Quarterly* 54 (July 1981): 134; Philip Kreager, *Traditional Adoption Practices in Africa, Asia, Europe, and Latin America* (London: International Planned Parenthood Foundation, 1980); Fiona Bowie, ed., *Cross-Cultural Approaches to Adoption* (New York: Routledge, 2004).

43. Krista E. Van Vleet, *Performing Kinship: Narrative, Gender, and the Intimacies of Power in the Andes* (Austin: University of Texas Press, 2008), 64.

44. Ward H. Goodenough, *Property, Kin, and Community on Truk* (Hamden, CT: Archon Books, 1966); Vern Carroll, ed., *Adoption in Eastern Oceania* (Honolulu: University of Hawaii Press, 1970); Ivan Brady, ed., *Transactions in Kinship: Adoption and Fosterage in Oceania* (Honolulu: University Press of Hawaii, 1976); Catherine A. Lutz, *Unnatural Emotions: Everyday Sentiments on a Micronesian Atoll and Their Challenge to Western Theory* (Chicago: University of Chicago Press, 1988); Dietrich Treide, "Adoptions in Micronesia: Past and Present," in Bowie, *Cross-Cultural Approaches*, 127–142.

Rights

What Rights Are at Stake? How Should the Rights of Adults and Children Shape the Law of Parenthood?

Legal Parenthood, Natural and Legal Rights, and the Best Interests of the Child

An Integrative View

Don Browning

The question to which I respond is this: How should contemporary family law define who is a parent in light of the rights of the parent, the rights of children, and the best interests of the child?

Overall, modern human rights thinking, as it pertains either to children or adults, stands largely devoid of critical grounding. The historically most influential tradition conveying human rights to the modern world—the natural rights and natural law traditions of Aristotelian and Stoic philosophy, Roman law, and the early Roman Catholic canonists—has been for the most part publicly rejected in the United States.

I will argue, however, that this influence lingers in the content of two major human rights documents whose intellectual history I analyze in this chapter: the Universal Declaration of Human Rights (UDHR) and the United Nations Convention on the Rights of the Child (CRC). These documents focus on the front door of family formation in striking contrast to so much of today's U.S. family law scholarship that focuses on the back door of family dissolution.

This chapter argues for the relevance of natural law and rational philosophical approaches, of which religious thinkers have been custodians, to today's questions about adults' and children's rights when it comes to legal definitions of parenthood. It suggests that religious language has functioned to stabilize insight gained from natural observation and philosophical argument. The chapter traces the natural law and rational philosophical roots of what we are calling the integrative tradition and its influence on significant human rights documents in international law.

In a paired chapter, legal scholar David Meyer ably examines how the rights of adults and the rights of children can come into conflict and identifies what he believes to be the limits of rights talk in deciding issues such as defining parenthood.[1] Meyer sees attention to the unique rights of both children and adults present in seminal international human rights instruments such as the UDHR and the CRC.

My approach, by contrast, is to reveal what I believe to be the deeper-seated intellectual history that led to these instruments, a background that helps us to understand the concern those drafting these documents had for the natural family and in particular the needs of children within it. This tradition, I believe, helps to shed light on contemporary discussions of how to define parenthood.

The chapter also offers contrasting examples of family law scholarship, with encouraging contemporary examples of scholarship attentive to the integrative tradition compared with other current, more pervasive approaches. Overall, the chapter affirms that marriage and biological relatedness should remain central in law's orientation to questions of defining parenthood, even as the law is and should be attentive to the varieties of families and parent-child relationships in special need of support.

The integrative tradition traced here begins with the later Plato and Aristotle, interacts with the doctrine of creation in Judaism and Christianity, appears in early medieval rights theory, gets synthesized with Roman law in the moral theology of Thomas Aquinas, and becomes transmitted to secular family law during the early years of the Protestant Reformation. Later, this tradition was mediated by Charles Malik and Jacques Maritain to the committee that wrote the UDHR, ratified in 1948. The tradition came to Malik and Maritain most directly from late nineteenth-century and early twentieth-century Roman Catholic social teachings.

Assumptions about Modernity

The question of modernity—its logic, power, and degree of inevitability—is important for understanding the decline of the integrative tradition. Western modernization is best characterized by the powerful dialectic between cultural individualism[2] and the spread of technical rationality, defined as the increasing use of means-end thinking and action to achieve a range of short-term life satisfactions.[3] Family law theories can be classified by whether they consider it the task of law to resist modernization (e.g., the work of Margaret Brinig, a contributor to this volume, which I shall discuss)[4] or conform to and possibly promote it (e.g., contributor to this volume June Carbone, as well as Martha Ertman, Martha Albertson Fineman, and the American Law Institute's *Principles of the Law of Family Dissolution*,[5] which I shall also discuss).

In the field of human sexuality, the forces of modernization have introduced a variety of separations—separations between marriage and sexual intercourse, marriage and childbirth, marriage and child rearing, childbirth and parenting, and—with the advent of assisted reproductive technologies—childbirth from sexual intercourse and biological filiation.[6] The integrative approach to parenthood views these separations with concern. Many sociologists and legal scholars, in contrast, hold that these modernizing forces are both inevitable and mostly benign. Rather than resisting them, law and public policy should accommodate and try to order the consequences.[7] The *diversity model* of parenthood reflects these latter convictions.

Thin and Thick Views of the Child's Best Interests

The concept of the best interests of the child floats in meaning. In law it sometimes refers to the child's right to basic nurturance and physical care or, at other times, the child's right to economic and social capital.[8] There is evidence, however, that law often narrows the child's best interests to thin and one-dimensional affective intersubjective relationships. This narrowing accounts for law's strong emphasis on the child's needs for continuity of relationships in the midst of the multiple separations in the sexual field that I listed earlier. I argue, however, that law's move in this direction overlooks other institutional, cultural, and biological factors deserving consideration in determining the best interests and rights of children.

Instead, the law should be guided, in both family formation and dissolution, by a thick, multidimensional model of the best interests of the child. The best-interests principle should entail simultaneously respecting the child's emerging personhood and working to actualize the basic goods (sometimes called *premoral goods*) needed for human flourishing. This view is both Kantian in its emphasis on respect for the emerging personhood of the child and Aristotelian in valuing the teleological goods required for healthy development. From a human development perspective, this view also acknowledges that the needs of the child emerge on a timetable in such a way that meeting early needs is foundational for the consolidation of later ones, as Erik Erikson, Robert Kegan, and others have shown.[9]

Reading the United Nations Convention on the Rights of the Child in Light of the Universal Declaration of Human Rights

Contemporary American family law has overlooked how the integrative tradition helped to define the rights and best interests of the child in modern human rights law. An excellent case study is found in the CRC, adopted in 1989 and ratified by all member states except the United States and Somalia and considered the definitive international document on children's rights (including within the United States, a nation deeply involved in drafting the document although it has not ratified it). There is a deep but poorly understood human rights tradition behind the CRC. This tradition is evident in the UDHR, which powerfully influenced the drafters of the CRC. In unearthing the historical sources of first the UDHR and then the CRC, we will gain insights into the multidimensional language of children's rights.

The UDHR devotes much attention to the rights of the family, in contrast to the rights of individual parents. It firmly establishes the priority of family rights and responsibilities when it states in Article 16(3), "The family is the natural and fundamental group unit of society and is entitled to protection by society and the State." This statement became a mantra in subsequent human rights statements. For example, it can be found in Article 10 of the International Covenant on Economic, Social, and Cultural Rights (1966) and in Article 23(1) of the International Covenant on Civil and Political Rights (1966).[10] But what do these words mean? Where did they come from?

Charles Malik, the highly influential Lebanese philosopher and statesman, was the source of the UDHR's emphasis on the family as the "natural and fundamental group unit of society." Originally, Malik had proposed a bigger idea. He wanted to insert the sentences "The family *deriving from marriage* is the natural and fundamental group unit of society. It is endowed by the Creator with inalienable rights antecedent to all positive law and as such shall be protected by the State and Society."[11] Malik believed that the inclusion of "natural" and "endowed by the Creator" assured that the marriage-based family would be seen as endowed by its own "inalienable rights," not viewed as a human invention subject to the caprice of either the state or current public opinion.[12] In Malik's original formulation, he tried to preserve the priority of the rights of natural parents, the importance of marriage-based parenthood, the prima facie rights of children to be raised by their natural parents, and a larger narrative that sanctioned and stabilized these values.

Malik was not successful in getting this stronger statement into the UDHR. Two of the four values he cherished were lost: the importance of marriage-based parenthood and a reference to the religious narrative historically used to support this institution. He was able to retain the emphasis on the "family as the natural and fundamental group unit of society," a phrase that then later influenced both parental and children's rights as framed in the CRC. This phrase, in effect, asserted that it was the role of society and the state to protect and enhance the family, but it also implied that neither society nor the state created the family or endowed it with its basic rights. The family has preexisting rights resident in its very nature and the functions it performs. In many ways, however, the UDHR's affirmation about the family as natural and fundamental hangs in midair as a bald statement of natural law devoid of the actual arguments, history, and narratives that motivated its original formulation.

Malik drew on the natural law and natural rights tradition mainly mediated by the Roman Catholic Church. His formulation asserts the idea that natural parents, on average, show more care and investment in their children than the state or other parental substitutes. This was not just a statement about the rights of parents to keep and invest in their children. The statement also asserted the rights of children to be born into a society that in principle protects their natural interest in being raised by those most likely to be invested in their well-being, that is, the individuals who conceive them.

The idea that the family is "the natural and fundamental group unit of society" drew on ancient insights into what evolutionary psychologists today call *kin altruism*. Aristotle provided much of the naturalistic and philosophical language for the centrality of kin altruism in family theory found in Western philosophy, law, and religion. Aristotle's arguments also influenced the powerful theory of subsidiarity that constitutes the philosophical core of Roman Catholic social teachings on the relation of family and state.

Kin altruism names our tendency as human beings to invest more of ourselves in those to whom we are biologically related. Aristotle, in his *Politics*, writes, "In common with other animals and with plants, mankind have a natural desire to leave behind them an image of themselves."[13] Aristotle rejected Plato's idea in *The Republic* that civic health would be improved if competing nepotistic families were undermined by removing children from their procreating parents and raising them in anonymity with nurses appointed by the state. Plato had hypothesized that if no one knew who their children or parents were, then all preferential treatment would end and pure justice would emerge.[14] Aristotle, by contrast, believed that if the state separated natural parents from their offspring, then love would become "watery" and diluted. The energy that fueled parental care would be lost. Violence would grow because the inhibiting factor of consanguinity would be removed.[15]

The great Roman Catholic theologian Thomas Aquinas renewed and expanded on this idea with a double language that was simultaneously bio-philosophical and religious. Aquinas's bio-philosophical view was informed by Aristotle, while his religious language principally came from the biblical book of Genesis and New Testament commentary on Genesis.[16] Aquinas's religious language functions to stabilize insight gained from natural observation and from philosophical argument found principally in Aristotle.

Aquinas's naturalistic view of parenthood recognized that human mothers become more easily attached to their infants because they carry them for months and expend enormous energy in giving birth to them. He also had insights into the natural conditions under which human males attach to their offspring. First, the long period of human infant dependency makes it very difficult for human mothers to raise infants by themselves. Aquinas believed that mothers, therefore, are inclined to turn to their male consorts for help.[17] The probable fathers are much more likely to attach to their infants if they have a degree of certainty that the infant is actually theirs and is therefore continuous with their own biological existence.[18] Males also attach to their offspring and consorts because of the mutual assistance and affection that they receive from the infant's mother.[19] He recognized that sexual exchange between mother and father helped to integrate the male into the mother-infant dyad. When fathers recognize, identify with, and comprehend their continuity with their offspring, they are more likely to take care of them as they would their own body, invest in them over a long period of time, and seek to preserve them into adulthood. These natural conditions listed by Aquinas strikingly parallel those now held by evolutionary psychologists to explain why humans, in contrast to most other mammals, form long-term attachments between fathers and mothers for the care of their infants and children.[20]

According to Aquinas and the ecclesial and civil law that he influenced, this tendency for fathers to bond with their recognized children, stabilized through sexual and help exchange with their children's mother, constitutes the natural grounds for the long-term commitment giving rise to the institution of marriage. Much later, Charles Malik affirmed the family as the natural group unit of society but also wanted to tie it to the reinforcements of marriage, something he failed to accomplish in the UDHR.

Malik's sources did not end with Aquinas. He drew on the theory of subsidiarity that began taking shape in the writings of Pope Leo XIII at the end of the nineteenth century, especially his Rerum Novarum (1891) on Catholic social teachings. The concept of subsidiarity was a philosophical idea nestled within a theological context but also analytically independent of it. Subsidiarity means that state and market should give support (subsidum) to both intact and disrupted families when they are in situations of special stress. But, at the same time, neither state nor market should do anything intentionally to disturb or take over the natural inclinations and capacities of parents and families to care for one another.

Leo XIII believed that humans should have certain prima facie rights and responsibilities to both the fruits of their bodily labor and the issue of their procreative labor. He understood these rights and responsibilities, which found expression in both Aristotle and Aquinas, to be laws of nature. With regard to natural parents, this law was true because parents by nature would see themselves in their children and thereby be more invested in them. Similarly, infants and children gradually would come to see themselves in their parents of conception and be more inclined to attach to, develop with, and follow their lead. Therefore, parents should have both the primary responsibility to discharge this care and the rights needed to do this without undue interference from society, state, and market.[21]

These ideas help to explain what Malik and the UDHR meant when they referred to the family as the natural and fundamental "group unit" that is "entitled to protection by both society and the State." The phrase "group unit" refers to the web of natural inclinations toward solidarity and deep attachment that spring from bonded relations between husband and wife and between parents and their offspring, as well as the offspring's inclination to identify with natural parents.

Subjective Rights, Objective Rights, and Aquinas

Given this history of the integrative tradition, what might be needed going forward? Human rights theory, particularly a theory about the rights of children, requires both some understanding of the subjective powers that humans have a right to exercise and some narrative about the purpose of life. Narratives about the purpose of life enable us to coordinate and pattern potentially conflicting subjective powers and rights.

The distinguished historian of medieval thought Brian Tierney tells us that when first elaborated in Western thought, subjective natural rights had to do with the exercise of our individual powers. On the other hand, objective natural rights were understood as the correct ordering of a "pattern of relations" between subjective rights,[22] or what we might understand as a pattern of mutually reinforcing subjective rights. From this perspective, the idea of the family as the "natural and fundamental group unit of society" is an objective right. It coordinates into a mutually reinforcing pattern the subjective rights of parents to their children and the subjective rights of children to care by their parents of conception.

A narrative view of the purpose of life is required for subjective powers to find their fully proper relation to one another in a theory of objective right. Nature gives hints of this objective order, but no theory of natural law, even when informed by contemporary scientific theories of nature, can by itself provide a theory of objective right sufficient to define the respective rights and obligations of parents, children, and the state.

Tierney believes that theories of objective natural rights were elaborated by Aristotle, Roman law, and Thomas Aquinas. But he also believes that eleventh- and twelfth-century Roman Catholic canonists introduced a theory of subjective natural rights that was later elaborated by William of Ockham. This theory of subjective natural rights eventually helped establish the individualistically oriented rights tradition of the last half century.

This intellectual history suggests that the doctrine of private ordering so prominent in American family law today—the right of adults to organize their lives as they see fit, rather than have the law impose terms upon them—is a contemporary manifestation of the tradition of subjective rights.[23] Modern human rights thinking is often guilty of obscuring the doctrine of objective rights, unfortunately leaving us with a disconnected and contradictory list of subjective rights. In contrast to most family law thinking today, both the UDHR and the CRC come closer to the earlier theory of objective rights, understood as a pattern of mutually reinforcing subjective rights.

We might also dwell more deeply on how the tradition of thought found in Aquinas can help us. A close reading of Aquinas reveals that the needs of children are assigned central weight in giving objective form to the relation of parents' and children's rights and the institutional pattern that they should take. This stance is dramatically different from the privileging of adult rights implicit in the doctrine of private ordering that is so central to much of family law today.

For Aquinas, the central need that controls matters of sexuality and affection between men and women is the long period of dependency that characterizes the human infant. Because of this prolonged period of vulnerability, the human child both requires and has a right to the long-term bonding of his or her parents and, indeed, its institutionalization in matrimony. But Aquinas tells us that the response of procreating parents to the needs of their offspring varies from species to species. It is worth pondering the following insightful words attributed to Aquinas:

> Yet nature does not incline thereto in the same way in all animals; since there are animals whose offspring are able to seek food immediately after birth, or are sufficiently fed by their mother; and in these there is no tie between male and female; whereas in those whose offspring needs the support of both parents, although for a short time, there is a certain tie, as may be seen in certain birds. In man, however, since the child needs the parents' care for a long time, there is a very great tie between male and female, to which tie even the generic nature inclines.[24]

In this tightly phrased paragraph we find a theory of both subjective and objective natural rights. It is the subjective need (and hence a subjective right) of the infant for care that puts pressure on the parents to form a "very great tie"—a tie that will, among other results, create the needed care for the infant. But, as we saw earlier, there is also a subjective need (and hence a subjective right) of both the mother and the father to care for that which they recognize as continuations of their own existence. When this parental recognition is consolidated, it forms the grounds for a bond—an attachment, to use the language of John Bowlby—that meets the infant's deep need for security, continuity, and affirmation at the point of family formation.[25]

Aquinas also added a narrative that gave these naturalistic insights a new meaning and order. He knew that the natural inclinations of human beings had their limits. He noticed that when males recognized a child was theirs and also enjoyed certain satisfactions of sex and mutual helpfulness with the child's mother, they might be inclined to remain attached to their infant. But Aquinas knew humans, especially males, had many other conflicting tendencies, such as desires "to indulge at will in the pleasure of copulation, even as in the pleasure of eating." He tells us that males tend to fight one another for access to females, and they "resist another's intercourse with their consort."[26] The affections and attachments of humans, especially males, are easily distracted. They are unstable. We might call this the *male problematic*. So, on the basis of natural inclinations alone, even parental attachments are likely to be unstable. What more is needed?

For Aquinas, a narrative was needed that justified the institution of marriage. In short, institutions stabilize human inclinations so that subjective rights can find form in objective rights—so that parents' rights, children's rights, and the corresponding rights and responsibilities of the state can be consolidated, signaled, and forcefully communicated from the beginning of family formation. Only marriage can institutionally pattern the subjective needs and rights of parents to attach to their offspring, the subjective needs of children to attach with their parents, and parents' subjective need for an intimate and bonding relation with another.

As is well known, Aquinas, as did Peter Lombard before him, absorbed marriage into the sacramental system of the Roman Catholic Church. This led the church at that time to make marriage a spiritually empowered and unbreakable sacrament. In later Protestant understandings marriage came to be seen not as a sacrament but rather as a covenant.[27] The long-term dependency needs of the child both contributed to and were consolidated by a narrative about the covenant status of marriage—a covenant that was increasingly seen as not only between the couple but also between the couple and society, the couple and their religion, and the couple and whatever transcendent power they believed in.[28]

Modern Trends toward a Diversity Model versus an Integrative Model

Today, I would argue there are three reasons for the drift of American family law away from the classic model described earlier. The first has to do with law's preoccupation with what I call the "back door" of family law, that is, the law of family dissolution, in contrast to the "front door" of family formation. The second is the pretension that law must be morally neutral, especially about the norms of family formation. Envisioning law as collaborating with other cultural spheres—education, the arts, religion, psychology, sociology, and economics, as examples—in contributing to a cultural work that might reintroduce a reconstructed classic integrative view is not popular in legal theory today but is worth pursuing. Third, much of family law theory believes modernization by necessity promotes private ordering and, for the most part, should be accommodated.

The American Law Institute's *Principles of the Law of Family Dissolution* reflects mainline legal thinking both in its approach to the rights of parents and children and in its alleged moral neutrality and commitment to family diversity.[29] The report is famous for two salient moves relevant to parental rights and children's rights and best interests. First, at the moment of family dissolution the report renders legal marriage and a range of cohabiting relationships equivalent before the law. Second, the report thinks about the rights and best interests of the child mainly from the angle of family disruption. Because of this, as noted previously, it views love and care largely as continuous of the child's relationships with caregivers in order to minimize the stress to the child of family breakdown and change. To advance the best interests of the child at the time of family dissolution, the *Principles* promotes "predictability in the concrete, individual patterns of specific families."[30] In situations of family dissolution, the continued participation in the life of the child of parents by estoppel and de facto parents may be "critically important for the child's welfare."[31]

This emphasis on the continuity of caretakers leads the *Principles* to formulate one of its strongest provisions: that dissolving families with children must file a "parenting plan" that outlines the role that parents (both biological and other caretakers) will take in the child's life on legal rights, decision-making rights, visitation rights, where the child will live, and how to resolve conflicts.[32] This plan is highly contextual and reflects what moral philosophers call a "situation ethics."[33] It is fine-tuned for the best interests of the child at the back door of family life—the point of family dissolution and reconfiguration. Even here the ambiguous borderline between what the report sometimes calls moral neutrality and at other times calls "fairness" requires that the plan be enacted without regard to "race, ethnicity, sex, religion, sexual orientation, sexual conduct, and economic circumstances of a parent."[34]

In dealing with the stress of family dissolution, chapter 6 of the *Principles* begins directly to shape the normative context of parenting—the front door of family formation—in part by addressing the rise of domestic partnerships. In an effort to induce fairness and responsibility between separating cohabiting partners and parents, the report's recommendations would virtually impose, without the consent of the couple, the same laws of dissolution applicable in legal marriage.[35] In effect, this stance makes cohabiting partners and married couples almost equivalent before the law.[36]

The *Principles* presents this parallel between cohabiting partnerships and marriage without acknowledging that the differences are significant, thereby obscuring the signaling power of institutions. Marsha Garrison points out that in marriage, in contrast to cohabitation, couples publicly *elect and consent* to the rules and in most cases treat marriage as a covenant of great seriousness to which they bind themselves before family, friends, community, and the state.³⁷ The work of Garrison is vastly different, for example, from the proposal by family law scholar Martha M. Ertman to replace the metaphors of status and covenant with the metaphors of what she calls the "implied contract" or implied "handshake."³⁸ Ertman's view is consistent with the *Principles* in injecting into family formation and child rearing a world of contingency without conscious intentions, commitments, promises, and covenants witnessed publicly by friends, community, and whatever metaphysical reality the couple might assume. Whatever this move might achieve for adult subjective rights in the questionable doctrine of private ordering, it stunningly disconnects the pattern of subjective rights between parents and children that made up the concept of objective family rights implicit in the UDHR and the CRC.

Martha Albertson Fineman and June Carbone

Trends embodied in the *Principles* are both fed by and reflected in the influential legal writings of family law scholars Martha Albertson Fineman and June Carbone. More than almost any other legal theorist, Fineman advances her position from the perspective of family dissolution. She sees contemporary society as an unpredictable place where "intimacies" between men and women—both inside of but more frequently outside of marriage—leave mothers with the care of their children, who are primarily envisioned as highly dependent infants and young children. The child's needs are defined primarily as a matter of holding, feeding, attaching, clothing, and cleaning human infants and children during a long period of dependency. While the classic integrative perspective on childhood dependency included the child's right to his or her father, Fineman uses her theory of dependency to de-emphasize a father's role in family formation and after separation or divorce.

Fineman argues that government and public policy should shift from supporting the "sexual family" in the institution of marriage to supporting actual caretakers of dependent persons.³⁹ She believes that the institution of marriage is disappearing and needs now to be de-legalized—no longer given explicit recognition and support before the law.⁴⁰ Couples can marry within the contexts of their religious traditions, if they wish, and they can regularize their unions with individually crafted and legally recognized contracts.⁴¹ Instead of supporting the institutional status of legalized marriage, law and public policy should give legal recognition, supports, and protections to caregivers and nurturers.⁴² The attachments of kin altruism would work only between mother and child. Fineman uses the mother-child dyad as a metaphor for the basic nurturing unit. The father is marginalized or excluded, except to the extent that he takes on a caretaking (understood as a mothering) role.

Carbone agrees with Fineman in holding that marriage should no longer be at the center of family law. She is not as aggressive as Fineman, however, in recommending that marriage be de-legalized. She contends that society and public policy must recognize family law's paradigm shift from emphasizing married partners to making the parent-child relationship central, whether parents are married or not.[43] Whereas Fineman marginalizes both marriage and the care provided by fathers, Carbone values the care of both mothers and fathers. She would, however, relinquish the institution of marriage and replace it with law's enforcement of parental responsibility and the subsidies of public welfare. For Carbone, moral obligations run primarily from the parent to the child and from the state to the parent-child relationship. There are few if any moral obligations between the parents as partners—married or not—that have implications for the rights and best interests of the child.[44]

Margaret Brinig: Covenant and Care

Family law professor Margaret Brinig offers a different and from the integrative perspective more encouraging point of view. Brinig draws upon Western legal, philosophical, and religious heritage and combines legal theory with empirical research. Her approach enables her family law scholarship to achieve a rich double language that both describes and retrieves the classical marital concepts of covenant and one-flesh union while also explaining the social functions of marriage with empirical data using the new institutional economics. Brinig opposes Fineman's desire to de-legalize marriage, Carbone's interest in replacing legal marriage with law's support of parenthood, and the *Principles*' concern to make domestic partnerships equivalent to legal marriage.[45]

Brinig preserves in fresh terms the accomplishments of older Jewish and Christian traditions of jurisprudence without becoming apologetic for them as such. Her position is theologically sensitive, consistent with the integrative model found in the classics on marriage and child care of Augustine and Thomas Aquinas, as well as with the latter's influence on the UDHR and the CRC.

Brinig achieves this synthesis by developing a phenomenology of covenant—a description of the model of marriage that historically has dominated Western thinking in law, culture, and religion. She then employs both the new institutional economics and evolutionary psychology in ways analogous to how Aquinas used the psychobiology and institutional theory of Aristotle to shape Roman Catholic marriage theory and much of the later Western legal tradition of marriage.[46] Brinig's approach illustrates how covenant thinking can be translated into secular law's rightful concern with the hard procreative, economic, and health realities of marriage and family.

Brinig argues that the post-Enlightenment contractual model of marriage that sees it as a freely chosen agreement is inadequate to both our experience of marriage and our past legal understandings of the institution. Western marriage has been viewed as a solemn agreement to a union of "unconditional love and permanence" through which the "parties are bound not only to each other but also to some third party, to God or the community or both."[47]

Brinig then turns to what is commonly called the "new institutional economics."[48] This perspective both builds on yet goes beyond the rational-choice view advocated by Nobel Prize–winning economist Gary Becker and law and economics theorist Judge Richard Posner. Marriage, Brinig argues, is more like a firm than an individualistically negotiated contract. A firm is an association organized to perform a specific function, achieve economies of scale, capitalize on special talents of individual participants, and relate to external parties as a collective unit. A firm is based on a prior agreement—something like a covenant—between the parties involved and the surrounding community about the purpose of the corporate unit. About the analogy between firms and covenantal marriage, Brinig observes: "This agreement does not purport to anticipate all future transactions among the firm members. In fact, one of the goals of the firm is the elimination of explicit interparty contracting and account keeping."[49]

The new institutional economics helps us see things in the firm and in marriages (especially marriages with children) that the older individualistic rational-choice economic model missed. The firm model enables us to grasp how marriages formed by settled public commitments (covenants) to each other, potential children, and society develop identifiable social patterns that convey trusted information, dependable access to known and valued goods, and valued reputations both within the marriage and between the marriage and the wider community.[50]

Marriages that result in children are more like a particular type of firm called a franchise. A set of imposed responsibilities come from the needs

(or subjective rights, to use the older terminology) of the child that cannot be totally dissolved even with legal divorce. Brinig believes that the inextricable one-flesh union and the shared family history do "not disappear" when the marriage ends or the child turns eighteen. She argues that "marriage persists to a certain degree in spite of divorce. To the extent that it persists, the family still lives on as what I call the franchise."[51]

Brinig's phenomenology of covenant and her institutional economics is supported by empirical research. Her empirical studies with sociologist Steven Nock lead her to assert (in this volume and elsewhere), in contrast to much of contemporary legal theory, that the status of parents in legal marriage is a leading positive asset for the well-being of children.[52] Brinig and Nock observe that abundant studies from both the United States and Europe show that cohabiting partnerships, even with children, are less stable than marriage.[53]

I make no claim that Brinig's view is the only example of the integrative perspective in contemporary family law. But in her perspective, we have a jurisprudence of marriage that meets the rationality test of legal theory, yet is both influenced by and broadly compatible with the outlines of the classic integrative view of marriage, parenting, and the best interests of both the child and his or her parent.[54] Her view respects the subjective rights of both children and parents but weaves them into an institutional pattern respecting and implementing the objective rights of the family, while also bridging the social space between secular law and the dominant models of love and marriage functioning historically in Western societies.

Conclusion

Overall, modern human rights thinking, as it pertains either to children or to adults, stands largely devoid of critical grounding. The historically most influential tradition conveying human rights to the modern world—the natural rights and natural law traditions of Aristotelian and Stoic philosophy, Roman law, and the early Roman Catholic canonists—has been for the most part publicly rejected in the United States.

This influence lingers, however, as seen in the content of the two major human rights documents that I have analyzed: the Universal Declaration of Human Rights and the United Nations Convention on the Rights of the Child. With regard to children and families, this international human rights tradition focuses on the front door, on family formation, in striking contrast to so much of today's U.S. family law scholarship that focuses on the back door of family dissolution.

The integrative tradition, with its deep natural law and rational philosophical roots, carried within religious thinking, helps us to see that institutions stabilize human inclinations. Institutions help subjective rights find form in objective rights, so that parents' rights, children's rights, and the corresponding rights and responsibilities of the state can be consolidated, signaled, and forcefully communicated.

Among institutions, only marriage can pattern the subjective needs and rights of parents to attach to their offspring, the subjective needs of children to attach with their parents, and parents' subjective need for an intimate and bonding relation with one another. Through marriage, the law recognizes that while biology is certainly not everything, biology does matter in the likelihood of fathers attaching to the mother-child dyad and bonding with their children, and in the propensity of children and parents to recognize and see something of themselves in one another. Even as the law supports the variety of families and parenting arrangements in special need, it should, I argue, resume its long-standing attention to the importance of marriage and biological relatedness in institutionalizing family formation and defining legal parenthood.

Notes

The editors with sadness wish to share that our friend and colleague Don Browning passed away on June 3, 2010, while this volume was under way (for a memorial tribute, see Disciples Divinity House of the University of Chicago, "In Memoriam: Don S. Browning," http://ddh.uchicago.edu/news/memoriam.shtml [accessed Dec. 11, 2011]). We are grateful to Elizabeth Marquardt for shepherding this chapter (with the permission of Don's literary executor, Chris Browning) through the editing process. This chapter incorporates, with permission, material from Don Browning, "Christianity and the Rights of Children: An Integrative View," in *Christianity and Human Rights*, ed. John Witte Jr. and Frank S. Alexander (New York: Cambridge University Press, 2010).

1. David D. Meyer, "Family Diversity and the Rights of Parenthood" (this volume).

2. For an important statement on the rise of cultural individualism in American society, see Robert N. Bellah et al., *Habits of the Heart: Individualism and Commitment in American Life* (Berkeley: University of California Press, 1985).

3. For the classic statement on the relation of technical reason and modernity, see Max Weber, *The Protestant Ethic and the Spirit of Capitalism*, trans. Talcott Parsons (New York: Scribner's, 1958), 182.

4. Other examples include the work of Milton Regan and Mission of Inquiry on the Family and the Rights of Children, *Parliamentary Report on the Family and the Rights of Children* (Paris: French National Assembly, 2006), http://www.assemblee-nationale.fr/11/rapports/r2832.asp (accessed Dec. 20, 2011).

5. American Law Institute, *Principles of the Law of Family Dissolution: Analysis and Recommendations* (Newark, NJ: Matthew Bender, 2002). Other examples include

Linda C. McClain, *The Place of Families: Fostering Capacity, Equality, and Responsibility* (Cambridge: Harvard University Press, 2006); Law Commission of Canada, *Beyond Conjugality: Recognizing and Supporting Close Personal Adult Relationships* (Ottawa: Law Commission of Canada, 2001); and the work of Daniel Friedman.

6. For an excellent discussion of these multiple separations, see Brent Waters, *Reproductive Technology: Towards a Theology of Procreative Stewardship* (Cleveland: Pilgrim Press, 2001).

7. In sociology, see Frank F. Furstenberg Jr. and Andrew J. Cherlin, *Divided Families: What Happens to Children When Parents Part* (Cambridge: Harvard University Press, 1991), 104–105; William J. Goode, *World Revolution and Family Patterns* (London: Free Press of Glencoe, 1964), 380. For family law, see Maria V. Antokolskaia, "Development of Family Law in Western and Eastern Europe: Common Origins, Common Driving Forces, Common Tendencies," *Journal of Family History* 28 (Jan. 2003): 52.

8. James S. Coleman, "Social Capital in the Creation of Human Capital," in "Organizations and Institutions: Sociological and Economic Approaches to the Analysis of Social Structure," supplement, *American Journal of Sociology* 94, no. S1 (1988): S95–S120.

9. Erik H. Erikson, *Identity, Youth, and Crisis* (New York: Norton, 1968), 93; Robert Kegan, *The Evolving Self: Problem and Process in Human Development* (Cambridge: Harvard University Press, 1982), 43, 56–57.

10. Ian Brownlie, ed., *Basic Documents on Human Rights*, 3rd ed. (Oxford: Clarendon Press, 1992).

11. Johannes Morsink, *The Universal Declaration of Human Rights: Origins, Drafting, and Intent* (Philadelphia: University of Pennsylvania Press, 1999), 254 (emphasis mine).

12. Ibid., 255.

13. Aristotle, *Politics*, in *The Basic Works of Aristotle*, ed. Richard McKeon (New York: Random House, 1941), 1127–1324, bk. I, ii.

14. Plato, *The Republic*, trans. Allan Bloom (New York: Basic Books, 1968), bk. V, par. 462.

15. Aristotle, *Politics*, bk. II, iv.

16. Thomas Aquinas, "Supplement," in *Summa Theologica* (London: R. and T. Washborne, 1917), 3: Q 42, A. 3.

17. Ibid., Q 41, A. 1.

18. Ibid.

19. Ibid.

20. For a summary of these four conditions as found in the literature of evolutionary psychology, see Don S. Browning et al., *From Culture Wars to Common Ground: Religion and the American Family Debate*, 2nd ed. (Louisville, KY: Westminster John Knox Press, 2000), 111–113. See also Don S. Browning, *Marriage and Modernization: How Globalization Threatens Marriage and What to Do about It* (Grand Rapids, MI: Eerdmans, 2003), 109–111. For a quick summary by leading evolutionary psychologists, see Martin Daly and Margo I. Wilson, "The Evolutionary Psychology of Marriage and Divorce," in *The Ties That Bind: Perspectives on Marriage and Cohabitation*, ed. Linda J. Waite et al. (New York: Aldine de Gruyter, 2000), 91–110.

21. Pope Leo XIII, *Rerum Novarum*, in *Proclaiming Justice and Peace: Papal Documents from Rerum Novarum through Centesimus Annus*, ed. Michael Walsh and Brian Davies (Mystic, CT: Twenty-Third Publications, 1991), para. 11 and 12.

22. Brian Tierney, *The Idea of Natural Rights: Studies on Natural Rights, Natural Law, and Church Law, 1150–1625* (Atlanta: Scholars Press, 1997).

23. Ibid., 39–42. Private ordering is defined as the right of adults to organize their intimate life as they see fit without the guidance of law; this includes the right of individual adults to conceive and raise children as they wish so long as no direct harm is done. In contrast, the intentionality of the law was central to the integrative tradition.

24. Aquinas, *Summa Theologica*, 3: Q 4.1.

25. John Bowlby, *Attachment and Loss*, vol. 1, *Attachment* (London: Hogarth Press, 1969).

26. Thomas Aquinas, *Summa Contra Gentiles*, trans. English Dominican Fathers (London: Burns, Oates and Washbourne, 1928), 3: ii, 117.

27. It is now well known by scholars that this absorption was based on a mistake in translation when the famous words of Ephesians (5:32) referring to Christian marriage as a great *mysterion* were rendered in the Latin Vulgate as *sacramentum* (sacrament) rather than mystery, which would have been more accurate to the original meaning. Although recognizing this undercuts the Catholic view that Christianity must, to be authentic, make marriage an unbreakable sacrament, it does not invalidate the deeper view, widely accepted in Judaism, Christianity, and other great religious and cultural traditions, that marriage should be like an enduring covenant.

28. These complex syntheses of naturalistic insights, philosophical argument, and narrative achieved in medieval Roman Catholicism constituted the blueprint of the Western cultural, legal, and religious heritage on marriage and family. See John Witte Jr., *From Sacrament to Contract: Marriage, Religion, and Law in the Western Tradition* (Louisville, KY: Westminster John Knox Press, 1997), 14–15.

29. American Law Institute, *Principles of the Law of Family Dissolution*, 6.

30. Ibid., 3.

31. Ibid., 6; see also ibid., 7.

32. Ibid., 7 (explaining the parenting plan).

33. William K. Frankena, *Ethics* (Englewood Cliffs, NJ: Prentice-Hall, 1973); Joseph Fletcher, *Situation Ethics: The New Morality* (Philadelphia: Westminster Press, 1966).

34. American Law Institute, *Principles of the Law of Family Dissolution*, 12. At this point, a moral philosopher would notice the tension between the report's situational ethic when considering the rights of children and its Kantian-Rawlsian ethic of fairness when weighing the rights and obligations of adults (e.g., as domestic partners).

35. Ibid., 913, 915.

36. Ibid., 920–922. This chapter does not make cohabiting couples equivalent before interstate agencies and the federal government.

37. Marsha Garrison, "Marriage Matters: What's Wrong with ALI's Domestic Partnership Proposal," in *Reconceiving the Family: Critical Reflections on the American Law Institute's Principles of the Law of Family Dissolution*, ed. Robin Fretwell Wilson (New York: Cambridge University Press, 2006), 305–330, especially 307–310.

38. Martha M. Ertman, "Private Ordering under the ALI Principles: As Natural as Status," in Wilson ed., *Reconceiving the Family*, 284–304, especially 293–300.

39. Martha Albertson Fineman, *The Autonomy Myth: A Theory of Dependency* (New York: New Press, 2004), 47–48.

40. Martha Albertson Fineman, *The Neutered Mother, the Sexual Family, and Other Twentieth Century Tragedies* (New York: Routledge, 1995), 228–230. On the statistical decline of marriage, see Fineman, *Autonomy Myth*, 110–112.

41. Fineman, *Neutered Mother*, 229.

42. See ibid., 9.

43. June Carbone, *From Partners to Parents: The Second Revolution in Family Law* (New York: Columbia University Press, 2000).

44. In this volume (chapter 16), June Carbone and Naomi Cahn propose that culture and family law focus primarily around preparing and encouraging young people toward "responsible parenthood" rather than focusing on marriage.

45. Margaret F. Brinig and Steven L. Nock, "Legal Status and Effects on Children," *University of St. Thomas Law Journal* 5 (2008): 548.

46. See John Witte Jr., *Law and Protestantism: The Legal Teachings of the Lutheran Reformation* (Cambridge: Cambridge University Press, 2002), 210–214, 230–240.

47. Margaret F. Brinig, *From Contract to Covenant: Beyond the Law and Economics of the Family* (Cambridge: Harvard University Press, 2000), 6–7.

48. Ibid., 6.

49. Ibid., 5.

50. Ibid., 6.

51. Ibid., 9.

52. See Margaret F. Brinig, "A Case for Integrated Parenthood" (this volume).

53. Ibid., 148; Brinig and Nock, "Legal Status and Effects on Children," 556–557. Brinig and Nock reached these conclusions through analyzing the database of the University of Michigan Panel Survey of Income Dynamics and its Child Development Supplement. Keeping children with natural mothers (both married and unmarried) constant, they measured child well-being from the perspective of the independent variables of income, family structure, legal relation of parents (unique to their study), parental warmth (close to Fineman's nurturance model), and mother's race and age. All these factors mattered for child well-being, but in contrast to the primary trend of contemporary family-law theory as exhibited by Fineman, Carbone, and the *Principles*, legal marriage and family structure count the most. See Brinig and Nock, "Legal Status and Effects on Children," 566–579.

54. Brinig's position has many concrete implications, more than I can discuss in detail. In view of the witness of both tradition and contemporary social science, Brinig contends that law should do what it can, in cooperation with other sectors of society, to encourage the marital franchise with children as the defining center of family formation.

Family Diversity and the Rights of Parenthood

David D. Meyer

The rapid expansion of nontraditional living arrangements has made the definition of family a flash point in public discourse. In recent years, that debate has moved beyond a focus on the meaning or availability of marriage, civil unions, and other adult relationships to include innovations in defining parenthood. As a small but growing number of states have recognized nontraditional caregivers as parents, even without the benefit of preexisting formal legal ties to the children in their care, judges, legislators, and commentators have debated whether legal notions of parenthood should be expanded to keep up with evolving patterns of child rearing.

A significant strand of this debate concerns the role of rights. Critiquing recent developments as nothing less than a "revolution in parenthood," the Commission on Parenthood's Future suggests that a focus on the rights of adults who aspire to parent drives the expansive redefinition of parenthood: "In law and culture, parenthood is increasingly understood to be an institution oriented primarily around adults' rights *to* children, rather than children's needs *for* their mother and father."[1] Broader parental diversity, in this view, is a by-product of society's acceptance of the rights claims of diverse adults—of infertile couples who wish to become parents through assisted reproductive technology, of gays and lesbians who wish to form families through marriage or adoption, and of single men and women who wish to become parents without the entanglements of a partner.

At the same time, some appeal to rights to argue for a return to the *integrative model* of parenthood. By this view, rights—especially children's rights—operate not as an accelerant to family diversification but as a brake. Some contend, for example, that children have a basic human right to be raised, "whenever possible . . . by the two people whose physical union made [them]."[2] In the previous chapter, Don Browning emphasizes the natural law foundations of early conceptions of parenting rights and shows their influence on modern human rights instruments such as the

Universal Declaration of Human Rights (UDHR) and the United Nations Convention on the Rights of the Child (CRC).³ This tradition centered rights in "the natural family" and understood them to emanate from roles and relations that were ordered by God or nature rather than socially constructed. Browning contends that renewed attention to these rights, and to the central role of marriage in ordering and effectuating them, should privilege understandings of parenthood centered on biological reproduction and marriage. Yet, even in pressing to recapture this traditional conception of parenting rights, Browning acknowledges that it has lost ground in an increasingly crowded field of rights claims from other perspectives favoring broader or alternative definitions of parenthood.

The question this chapter poses, then, is to what extent the rights of affected individuals limit society's choices concerning the construction of parenthood. Do the rights of children or adults require the state to enlarge the concept of parenthood to accommodate an expanding universe of family forms? Or do those rights require the state to channel child rearing more narrowly into the traditional "two-parent, mother-father model of parenthood"?⁴

I conclude that the rights of children and, in some cases, adults do constrain the state's choices in defining the parent-child relationship, but the limits are broad, evolving, and multidimensional. Consequently, they do not coalesce to compel adherence to any single model of parenthood, whether oriented around biology, marriage, adult intentions, or any other polestar. The rights of affected individuals will often require the state to justify its choices to deny parental status, especially when the state acts against established relationships. However, those rights do not reduce the state's choices in defining parenthood either to the integrative model or, at the other end of the spectrum, to an anything-goes model of parenting diversity. Basic rights inevitably require *some* diversity in parenthood but do not compel public acquiescence in whatever child care arrangements adults may agree upon. Instead, rights analysis leaves significant room for democratic choice in the construction of parenthood.

In the section that follows, I summarize recent developments leading to a broader definition of legal parenthood. I then turn to consider claims that the rights of children or adults might dictate the identity of parents, either compelling or disallowing further innovation in the law of parenthood. In doing so, I conclude that three essential features of rights analysis in this context—the potential for conflicting rightsholders, the potential for conflicting rights even of a single rightsholder, and the essential softness of parental rights—combine to ensure that rights cannot reduce the meaning of parenthood neatly to any single model, whether integrative or otherwise.

Diversity in Parenting

Patterns of parenting and child rearing have become markedly more diverse. The retreat of legal and social impediments to divorce and nonmarital child rearing has fueled a dramatic rise in both the number of single parents and the number of children being raised in part by adult caregivers who have no pretense of a biological connection. Many such caregivers lack any formal legal ties to the children in their care, either through adoption or through marriage to a parent of the children. Surveying the shifting landscape at the dawn of the twenty-first century, a plurality of the U.S. Supreme Court acknowledged that "the demographic changes of the past century make it difficult to speak of an average American family."[5]

In recent years, the growth rate in child rearing outside the nuclear family model appears to have leveled off. The locus of debate arguably has shifted from family life to family law, as courts and legislators have considered how to respond to the broader diversity of family living arrangements. The first responses were comparatively modest, granting unconventional caregivers legal standing to preserve a relationship with children as nonparents. Many jurisdictions have extended a qualified legal status to such caregivers through doctrines such as "equitable adoption," "in loco parentis," or "de facto parenthood." These doctrines generally confer limited relationship rights with children but stop short of classifying the caregivers as true parents.[6]

More recently, jurisdictions in the United States and abroad have begun innovating with the legal definition of parenthood, accommodating new family forms by conferring not just stand-in forms of quasi-parent authority but parenthood itself. In 2002, the American Law Institute called for recognition of new forms of parenthood based on caregiving and allowing for the possibility that a child might have three or more parents at once.[7] In 2005, the supreme courts of California and Washington each ruled that same-sex partners of biological mothers could be recognized as parents to children born during their relationship, even without adoption, based on the partners' joint undertaking to parent together.[8] The Delaware and Montana supreme courts extended this principle to recognize the parental interests of women who co-parented children adopted by their former partners.[9] The House of Lords arrived at a similar result in a British custody dispute between two former same-sex partners. In *In re G*, the Lords recognized "at least three ways in which a person may be or become a natural parent of a child": through a genetic connection, through gestation of a child, or through "social and psychological parenthood," that is, through the bonds of day-to-day caregiving over time.[10] By this definition, both the biological mother and her former partner qualified as "natural parents" in deciding custody, although the former's additional genetic and gestational ties were properly considered "an important and significant factor" in evaluating the child's best interests.[11]

Some states have opened new routes to parenthood based on the voluntary assumption of parental responsibility at birth. Pushed by federal welfare law, such states have recognized men as fathers based solely on a voluntary acknowledgment of paternity, even when all parties understand that the man is not the biological father.[12] Legal parenthood is established solely by agreement of adults, making adoption or marriage unnecessary. State laws providing for same-sex marriage, civil unions, or expansive domestic partnership laws allow both partners to be recognized as parents of a child born to one during the union, in the same way that husbands are presumed to be fathers of children born to their wives, though obviously without the same underlying assumption of a biological tie.[13]

While many of these changes de-emphasize biology, other changes simultaneously place new and unprecedented weight on biology in defining the identity of a parent. Aggressive efforts to collect child support for children receiving public assistance, requiring mothers to cooperate in identifying fathers and establishing their paternity, have supported an "emerging definition of fatherhood based solely on biology."[14] That understanding of fatherhood has been starkly reinforced by developments in a number of states permitting men to "disestablish" their paternity, even after many years of acting as a child's father, if DNA tests later rule out a biological connection.[15] Taken together, these developments confirm that "around the world, the two-person, mother-father model of parenthood is being fundamentally challenged."[16]

Diversity in Rights

The divisiveness of the "culture wars" over the family—with small prospects for finding basic agreement through political dialogue—has fueled resort to rights analysis to vindicate one's vision of family. Proponents of same-sex marriage, for example, have focused strategically on constitutional litigation, hoping to bridge the gulf dividing popular opinion by establishing a right to public recognition.¹⁷ Increasingly, appeals to rights analysis can be found in debates over parenthood as well, with alternating suggestions that the *integrative model* or *diversity model* of the family may be privileged by a proper understanding of constitutional or human rights.

In my view, however, rights claims cannot spare society the need to wrestle with the questions that divide us. Children and adults do have rights in the matter, but, for three basic reasons I shall elaborate, rights analysis only modestly constrains social constructions of parenthood. First, in at least some cases, questions of parental identity present a conflict among multiple rightsholders. Second, assigning parental status may implicate multiple and sometimes conflicting rights even of a single rightsholder, the child. The unavoidable need to resolve the tensions posed by the clash of multiple rights and rightsholders explains in part the third reason, the essential "softness" of parenthood rights. Any account of parenthood rights accepts that these rights are only prima facie, or presumptive, and ultimately are qualified by the need to accommodate competing relationship interests and by other compelling social objectives.

Multiple Rightsholders

Parenthood cannot be defined solely with reference to the rights of a single individual. The CRC focuses on the rights of children with respect to their parents. Article 8 guarantees "the right of the child to preserve his or her identity, ... including family relations." Article 7 recognizes the right of every child, "as far as possible, ... to know and be cared for by his parents." Backing these declarations are fundamental assumptions about the moral entitlement of children to the basic conditions necessary for their survival and development. "The first right of any child," writes Baroness Brenda Hale, "must be to be looked after, fed, clothed, housed, taken care of, and brought up to play his/her part in society."¹⁸ The CRC entrusts children to the care of their parents on the assumption that parents will be most capable of meeting their basic needs. Thus, Article 27(2) provides: "The parent(s) or others responsible for the child have the primary responsibility to secure, within their abilities and financial capacities, the conditions of living necessary for the child's development." The state has a supplementary duty to assist parents in ensuring that the child's basic needs are met, "particularly with regard to nutrition, clothing and housing."¹⁹

Similarly, the UDHR recognizes, in Article 16(3), that "the family is the natural and fundamental group unit of society and is entitled to protection by society and the State." Like the CRC, the UDHR contemplates that children will be raised within families and recognizes the state's obligation to respect and protect the integrity of the family. Additional regimes of fundamental human rights embody the same principle. The European Convention on Human Rights (European Convention), for example, declares in Article 8 that "everyone has the right to respect for his private and family life," a guarantee carried over in Article 7 of the 2000 Charter of Fundamental Rights of the European Union (Charter).[20] Indeed, the Charter goes further, including a separate article focusing on "the rights of the child." Like the CRC, it recognizes both children's "right to such protection and care as is necessary for their well-being" and the right of "every child ... to maintain on a regular basis a personal relationship and direct contact with both his or her parents, unless that is contrary to his or her interests."[21]

Yet, as some of these later provisions reflect, it is not *only* children who enjoy basic rights respecting family life; rather, "everyone" is entitled to the blessings of family life. Indeed, other provisions give more direct recognition that this includes the right to be a parent. The UDHR, for example, in addition to recognizing the family as "the natural and fundamental group unit of society," declares that "men and women of full age ... have the right to marry and to found a family" (Article 16(1)). The European Convention and the Charter similarly provide, albeit with greater qualification, that "the right to marry and to found a family shall be guaranteed in accordance with the national laws governing the exercise of these rights."[22]

The European Court of Human Rights (ECHR) has construed these guarantees to encompass a right of at least some adults to establish and maintain status as parents. It has acted, for example, to protect the right of unwed fathers to a relationship with their children. In 2008, it ruled that France's refusal to allow a lesbian to adopt a child internationally violated her rights under the European Convention. Although French law permits single persons to adopt, authorities refused to grant the woman authorization to adopt partly on the ground that she had no clear plan for providing the child access to a paternal figure, despite advice that "'all the studies on parenthood show that a child needs both her parents.'"[23] The ECHR stopped short of finding that Article 8's guarantee of "respect for [individuals'] private and family life" encompasses a fundamental right to adopt a child, but it held that the authorities' concerns with the woman's "lifestyle" and insistence on the availability of "a paternal role model" discriminated in relation to family life, in violation of the Convention. A dissenting judge, Antonella Mularoni, would have been even more direct in recognizing the rights of adults to become parents, whether by recourse to adoption or to artificial insemination.

The ECHR has not recognized a free-ranging right of adults to become parents under whatever terms they desire; it has, instead, sought to cabin adult rights in the parent-child relationship to more conventional circumstances. The European Convention's protection of family life "presupposes the existence of a family, or at the very least the potential relationship between, for example, a child born out of wedlock and his or her natural father[;] or the relationship that arises from a genuine marriage, even if family life has not yet been fully established[;] or the relationship that arises from a lawful and genuine adoption."[24] However, an essential point is that, at least in circumstances where society would commonly regard the claimant as a parent, tribunals recognize that the fundamental rights of adults, too, are implicated by state decisions to grant or deny parenthood.

The same understanding can be seen in judicial constructions of parental rights under the U.S. Constitution. Going back at least to the 1920s, the U.S. Supreme Court has recognized substantial constitutional rights in the relation of parents and children. "A parent's desire for and right to 'the companionship, care, custody, and management of his or her children,'" the Court has repeatedly held, "is an important interest that 'undeniably warrants deference and, absent a powerful countervailing interest, protection.'"[25] In modern constitutional parlance, the right of parents to raise their children is "fundamental," triggering heightened judicial protection when government seeks either to interfere in the parent-child relationship or to terminate it altogether.[26]

Significantly, the Constitution's protection of parenthood is not limited to incursions on established parent-child relationships; the Court has recognized at least qualified constitutional protection for some adults seeking to win initial recognition as parents. It has recognized that at least some unwed biological fathers—those who "accept[] some measure of responsibility for the child's future" by stepping forward to involve themselves in the child's life—are constitutionally entitled to be recognized as a legal parent.[27] Subsequent cases made clear that not all biological fathers are so entitled. Biological fathers who failed to show any real interest in their children, or who sought to impose on intact marriages, unsettling a husband's parental status, can be disregarded as parents.[28] Yet, in the right circumstances, the Court's cases appear to recognize the constitutional right of some who aspire to establish themselves as parents. These circumstances are only dimly defined. The unwed father cases make clear that biology is relevant, as is past caregiving, diligence, and the nature of the mother's relationships with the biological father and, if she is married, her husband.[29] However, no single criterion controls the constitutional definition of parenthood.

The absence of a single constitutional determinant of parental status stems partly from the absence of a single foundation for the Constitution's protection of parental rights. Instead, a multiplicity of rationales undergird parental rights: sometimes natural law (an approach that tends to confine rights to biological parents); more commonly (at least in recent decades), utility to children. It is assumed, for example, that "'natural bonds of affection lead parents to act in the best interests of their children.'"[30] This beneficial inclination might spring from nature, evolutionary biology, or simply the lived "intimacy of daily association."[31] Child-centered defenders of parental rights have justified such rights on the ground that freedom from state meddling is essential to encouraging unqualified parental investment in child rearing.[32]

In practice, despite incantations about the "paramount" interests of children, courts regularly rationalize parents' rights on the interests of parents themselves. This is clear enough from the long succession of court decisions holding that "parents' constitutional rights take precedence over the 'best interests of a child.'"[33] It is plain that adults, as well as children, have profound personal interests in the parent-child relationship. As James Dwyer has written, in examining welfare and autonomy rationales for adult rights of intimate association more generally, "a happy relational life is a prerequisite to effectuating our individual life plans and to developing our full humanity as autonomous persons."[34] Even if most would agree that a child's interests should predominate in the determination of parenthood, given the child's unique vulnerability and imperative developmental needs, it is implausible to suppose that the profound interests of would-be parents simply evaporate or count for nothing in the matter.

In modern constitutional doctrine, claims of fundamental, unenumerated rights are typically validated by reference to either historical or contemporary social consensus. Both theories favor recognition of the independent stake of parents in determinations of parenthood. The dominant, backward-looking test insists that fundamental rights be "deeply rooted in this Nation's history and tradition," as a means of giving democratic legitimacy to the judiciary's enforcement of unenumerated rights.[35] Given the powerful historical consensus favoring near-total power of parents over their children, an assumption of right sometimes analogized to a property right, this approach would support recognition of parenting rights for persons traditionally viewed as parents.

In some cases, the Court has set aside its focus on history and tradition and looked instead to contemporary assessments of the importance of the individual interests implicated by government action. In *Loving v. Virginia*, for example, the Court rested its recognition of a fundamental right to marry without regard to race not on historical consensus but on the essential importance of marriage to "the orderly pursuit of happiness by free men."[36] In *Lawrence v. Texas*, which struck down a ban on same-sex intimacy, the Court downplayed the importance of history and tradition before concluding that "in all events, we think that our laws and traditions in the past half century are of most relevance here."[37] The Court grounded constitutional protection in "an emerging awareness that liberty gives substantial protection to adult persons in deciding how to conduct their private lives in matters pertaining to sex."[38] This approach would likely support recognition of a constitutional right to parental status for at least some adults. Social understandings of who may qualify as a parent have plainly evolved in recent decades, reflecting appreciation of the increasing diversity and complexity of family living arrangements. There is, also, arguably an "emerging awareness" in the United States, Europe, and elsewhere that the interests of children must count for more in determinations of their family relationships.[39]

Finally, determinations of parenthood may implicate not only the rights of children and traditional parent figures in the integrative model but also those of more unconventional child-rearing relationships. Even if there is not a sound basis for recognizing a fundamental right of an aspiring parent to adopt an unknown child, as the courts have generally concluded both in the United States and abroad, far more substantial arguments support a right of both children and adults in established de facto parent-child relationships to formalize their family ties through adoption.[40]

The interests of all relevant rightsholders will often align in supporting recognition of a given parent-child relationship. In these happy cases, recognition that both children and adults have rights at stake reinforces, rather than complicates, the claim to parental status. In some cases, however, the claims of the different rightsholders may clash. For example, suppose that foster parents wish to adopt a seven-year-old girl they have cared for since she was a few months old, against the strong objections of the girl's mother, who has recently made substantial progress in overcoming a long-standing drug addiction. The mother, foster parents, and child might each have legitimate claims of right at stake in the proposed adoption.[41] Yet, because the contending rights point in different directions, they are of less help in producing an answer. A court cannot resolve the dispute on the basis of rights without balancing the conflicting interests, which likely will require the very policy judgments that rights analysis in other contexts might have avoided.

A recent Montana court decision, involving the dissolution of a cohabiting relationship between two women, illustrates the difficulty. During their decade together, one woman had adopted two children, whom both partners raised jointly as co-parents. When they separated, the adoptive mother asserted her constitutional rights as the children's only legal parent to cut off the children's relationship with her former partner. The court readily acknowledged the adoptive mother's constitutional rights, but reasoned that "while parental constitutional rights are important, the constitutional rights of the children are important as well."[42] In balancing the rights of parent and child, the court concluded that the former partner had "established a child-parent relationship, and [that] it is in the best interests of the children to continue that relationship."[43] Ordinarily, asserting a right will constrain the state's discretionary authority with respect to the protected interest. Where rights of two or more claimants conflict, however, the inescapable need to mediate the conflict effectively restores to the court a significant measure of discretion in balancing the contending interests.

The Multiple Rights of the Child
Even if the focus is narrowed to the rights of the child only, the child herself may have multiple, conflicting rights at issue in the determination of parenthood. The basic rights of children have won rapid formal international acceptance through the CRC, the Charter, and other accords, but the United States has generally lagged behind. Beyond its refusal to ratify the CRC, its courts also have been slow to recognize children's relationship rights as a matter of domestic constitutional doctrine. Nonetheless, the Supreme Court has signaled a growing receptiveness to extending constitutional protection to the independent relational interests of children. In *Troxel v. Granville*, even while reaffirming parents' constitutional right to rear their children free from state interference, a majority of justices qualified the strength of that right in recognition of the countervailing interests of some children in maintaining significant intimate relationships with other family members.[44] An increasing number of decisions in

state and lower federal courts, as in the recent Montana case, have even more directly raised the constitutional relationship rights of children as a counterweight to parents' rights.

Recognizing children's own rights relating to family life does little, however, to support any single definition of parenthood, integrative or otherwise. A basic feature of children's rights is that they are multidimensional and encompass distinctly different types of claims. James Dwyer distinguishes between "choice-protecting rights" of the sort usually accorded adults through family privacy doctrine and "interest-protecting rights."[45] Barbara Bennett Woodhouse differentiates between "capacity-based rights," rooted in children's emerging capacity to reason and speak for themselves, and "needs-based rights," reflecting children's entitlement to the resources and conditions necessary for their survival and development.[46] She contends that children possess both varieties of rights, though in varying degrees as they mature corresponding to their personal development. Five fundamental values, or principles, Woodhouse asserts, underlie children's basic rights: (1) privacy, (2) agency, (3) equality, (4) dignity, and (5) protection.[47]

Defining the "rights" of a given child is thus a complex business. Children's rights are not reducible to a universal prescription with respect to their upbringing. "Respect for intimate family relations" is "at the core of" the privacy principle, a "human rights value" readily apparent in provisions of the CRC (and other human rights instruments) barring state interference with the parent-child relationship.[48] Yet children's rights to family privacy would vary significantly with their age and capabilities. For younger children, Woodhouse notes, the privacy principle would inform a "needs-based" right that sought to protect the child's powerful developmental needs to stable attachments with caregivers. As children matured, however, the privacy principle might encompass a broader range of relationships of importance to older children (possibly including "relations with peers and adults outside the family circle"), shifting also to take account of the child's increasing "capacity to make choices about intimate relations."[49]

The various principles that give content to children's rights, Woodhouse further observes, are sometimes at cross-purposes even for a given child at a given time:

> Sometimes two principles or rights may come into conflict. For example, the agency principle often conflicts with the protection prin-

ciple. No matter how strongly felt and authentic the two-year-old's drive to cut his own meat, when he seizes a razor-sharp steak knife, the values of autonomy have to give way to the values of protection.⁵⁰

Similar internal tensions or conflicts are evident in the Charter's declaration of children's rights, as Clare McGlynn notes:

> Article 24(1) of the Charter is a curious mix of what might loosely be termed children's "protection" and "empowerment" rights, which are often found to be in conflict. The inclusion of the two elements in the one paragraph would appear to be an attempt at compromise and to balance the competing interests of paternalism and autonomy.⁵¹

The blending of what Woodhouse would call "needs-based" and "capacity-based" rights, moreover, leaves that balance to be worked out from case to case.

Similarly, McGlynn observes, Article 24(3), which declares the child's "right to maintain on a regular basis a personal relationship and direct contact with both his or her parents, unless that is contrary to his or her interests," "again balances interests between autonomy—the child's right to maintain contact—and welfare—the 'interests' of the child."⁵² That indeterminacy, moreover, is compounded by the likelihood that, "in practice," the child's rights under this article may be balanced against the parent's "right to contact" with children, derived from Article 7's "right to respect for private and family life" (in turn drawn from the European Convention).⁵³

The need to weigh a child's own autonomy interests and developmental needs in determining the balance of her rights—to say nothing of the need then to balance these rights against rights of other affected family members—suggests the improbability that children's rights hew to a single concept of parenthood. It seems likely that children's rights, defined exclusively as needs-based rights at the time of a newborn's birth, would generally favor assigning parenthood to the child's birth parents. Yet it is also easy to imagine scenarios under which the balance of a child's developmental needs might favor a different assignment—for example, cases in which the birth parents are demonstrably unfit to raise the child.⁵⁴ The possibilities expand as the child grows older, given the reality of family fracture and re-formation.

Some advocates of the integrative model of parenthood suppose that the modern diversification of parenthood is driven by a focus on adult rights claims and that recentering the issue on the needs-based rights of children would turn the tide.[55] However, given the diversity in children's family lives, it seems far from clear that the developmental needs of children would drive parenthood back toward a single model. Indeed, Dwyer observes, "A focus on children's welfare might lead to as much protection for nontraditional families as would increased deference to adults' choices."[56] Unless the state resorts to draconian means of regulating childbearing, "doing what is best for children [will often] mean[] recognizing and protecting a multiplicity of family forms."[57]

The "Softness" of Parenthood Rights

A final, related but distinct, consideration supports the conclusion that individual rights do not cabin parenthood to a single model. The rights in play are simply too malleable to produce a consistent answer reliably.

Virtually all conceptions of parenthood rights proceed on the assumption that they are only prima facie or presumptive. Human rights instruments often expressly reflect the qualified nature of these rights. The CRC, for example, states that the child's "right to know and be cared for by his or her parents" exists only "as far as possible."[58] After recognizing that every child has the right "to maintain on a regular basis a personal relationship and direct contact with both his or her parents," the Charter adds, "unless that is contrary to his or her interests."[59] Human rights instruments commonly recognize as a general principle that limitations on individual rights may be justified if necessitated by sufficiently powerful community interests. The UDHR, for example, contemplates that states may impose on individual rights as necessary to ensure "respect for the rights and freedoms of others and of meeting the just requirements of morality, the public order and the general welfare in a democratic society."[60]

Similarly, the Charter allows that, "subject to the principle of proportionality, limitations may be made only if they are necessary and genuinely meet objectives of general interest recognised by the Union or the need to protect the rights and freedoms of others."[61] The ECHR's principle of "proportionality" aligns with U.S. constitutional doctrine, where even a significant state incursion on a fundamental family liberty is not necessarily unconstitutional. Instead, the burden on the fundamental right simply triggers heightened judicial scrutiny, under which the individual's interest will be weighed against the state's asserted justification.

Just what showing of necessity must be made to warrant a limitation under the principle of proportionality remains ill defined. Yet, state limitations on individual rights are more easily justified in the context of parenthood and other family rights than in many contexts. Both the UDHR and the Charter make a special allowance for state limitations necessitated by "the need to protect the rights and freedoms of others."[62] Where individual rights conflict, the state must be allowed additional leeway to impose on the rights of each holder to reach an accommodation. U.S. constitutional doctrine effectively recognizes the same rule. The potential for conflicting individual rights may be found in many family privacy controversies, where validation of one party's rights in a family relationship necessarily has consequences for others in the family. Arguably, tacit awareness of that feature helps to explain the tendency of the Supreme Court and lower courts to apply a murkier and less strict form of scrutiny in family privacy cases.[63]

Rights in this context are malleable not only because they can be overcome by sufficiently strong countervailing interests but also because they are commonly held to be adaptable both over time and to specific cultures. Just as the U.S. Supreme Court has sometimes, as in *Lawrence* and *Troxel*, adapted the boundaries or substance of due process protection to keep pace with changing social conditions, the ECHR has taken the same approach to defining the scope of European Convention rights. In the *Case of E.B.*, finding protection for a lesbian seeking to adopt a child, the ECHR insisted that "the Convention is a living instrument, to be interpreted in light of present-day conditions."[64]

Courts and conventions also commonly make allowance for local adaptation of rights concerning the family. Even while broadly declaring the rights of children, for example, the CRC calls for "taking due account of the importance of the traditions and cultural values of each people for the protection and harmonious development of the child."[65] As Woodhouse observes, the nature of the CRC "places the design and implementation of human rights with local lawmakers and allows universal human rights principles to be adapted and molded to fit the contexts of nations with diverse legal, political, and social cultures."[66] Similarly, the Charter recognizes "the right to found a family," but only "in accordance with the national laws governing the exercise of these rights."[67] In keeping with this view, the French National Assembly's *Parliamentary Report on the Family and the Rights of Children* emphasized that, in defining family and parenthood, "every country is entitled to provide its own responses to the needs of its society, in accordance with its ethical principles, traditions and political choices."[68] Such a view, emphasizing the propriety of local variation in construing family rights, and their adaptability over time, seems at odds with an understanding of rights premised upon a truly "natural" or "universal" model of parenthood.

The ECHR has regularized this tolerance for local variation by commonly considering whether a state's seeming incursion on European Convention rights is nevertheless sustainable as within the state's "margin of appreciation." The ECHR, George Letsas observes, regularly uses the margin of appreciation doctrine in two different ways.[69] First, in the "substantive" concept of the doctrine, the ECHR uses it simply to describe the conclusion of its "proportionality" review—that the state's incursion on the individual was ultimately justified by overriding collective interests. The second, "structural" concept of the doctrine, however, captures the idea that the ECHR should leave states with "room to maneuver" in adapting Convention rights to local conditions and values.[70] The willingness to recognize a zone of reasonable discretion within which different states may interpret their Convention obligations differently further underscores the softness of parenthood rights.

A case decided under the European Convention in 2003 illustrates the considerable malleability of rights respecting parenthood. In *Odièvre v. France*,[71] a thirty-something woman challenged the French law (known as *accouchement sous X*) permitting women to give birth anonymously while surrendering the newborn for adoption. The woman challenged the law as a violation of her rights under the Convention to know her origins and parents. The Court agreed with her that Article 8, prohibiting state interference with "private and family life," encompassed a right of persons to know the circumstances of their birth and family origins. However, the Court found that the law did not violate France's obligations under the Convention. First, the child's right to know her origins must be balanced against the competing rights of other affected persons, including those of the birth mother and, potentially, the birth father, the adoptive parents, and "other members of the natural family."[72] Applying the proportionality principle, France was justified in seeking to strike a balance favoring the birth mother's desire to shed maternity over her child's right to know her origins. Second, France's contested policy judgment reconciling the competing interests fell within the allowable margin of appreciation. "In the absence of common European standards on matters of child abandonment in conditions of secrecy and anonymity," a concurring judge agreed,

"France enjoys a certain margin of appreciation in determining the modalities of divulging information on the identity of the parties."[73]

France's allowance for anonymous births "sous X" remains controversial and seems to fly in the face of the CRC's recognition that a child has, "as far as possible, the right to know and be cared for by his or her parents."[74] Indeed, as Ingeborg Schwenzer notes, "several other countries" have considered enacting similar laws but decided it "would run contrary to the child's right to know its own origins."[75] Nevertheless, the ECHR found, in effect, that even with a reasonably clear rights principle in the child's right to know her origins, France's interpretation of its European Convention obligations fell within the zone of reasonable disagreement.

The *Odièvre* decision illustrates how the nature of conflicting rights respecting parenthood can preserve discretionary authority for states to construct their own conceptions of parenthood. It also reveals a recurring feature of the ECHR's application of the margin of appreciation doctrine. The ECHR found that the European Convention did not preclude France's policy choice in part because France's policy did not defy an established social consensus in Europe concerning anonymous parenting. This resort to contemporary social consensus to identify the boundaries for permissible state regulation in defining parenthood recalls the practice of U.S. courts sometimes to consult contemporary social consensus in determining the boundaries of constitutionally protected family privacy.

In sum, the multiple and varying rights at stake in determinations of parentage are too indeterminate to compel adherence to any single "model" of parenthood. Determining the rights of each party and striking a balance ultimately requires sensitive attention to the circumstances of each family, emerging empirical knowledge concerning the developmental needs of children, and the shifting boundaries of social consensus concerning parenthood and family life. This means that if the state acts to deny parenthood in defiance of social consensus or powerful evidence of a child's most basic needs, the rights of the affected parties will impose on the state a heavy burden to justify its actions. The rights of the parties are too variable and fact-sensitive to produce brighter lines in defining the essential meaning of parenthood. In the end, notwithstanding the substantial individual rights at stake, there is no avoiding the hard and contestable social choices when it comes to determining who counts as a parent.

Notes

1. Elizabeth Marquardt, Commission on Parenthood's Future, and Institute for American Values, *The Revolution in Parenthood: The Emerging Global Clash between Adult Rights and Children's Needs* (New York: Institute for American Values, 2006), 15–16 (emphasis in the original). Elizabeth Marquardt, a contributor to this volume (chapter 15), authored this report.

2. Ibid., 16 (construing the United Nations Convention on the Rights of the Child).

3. Don Browning, "Legal Parenthood, Natural and Legal Rights, and the Best Interests of the Child" (this volume).

4. Marquardt, *Revolution in Parenthood*, 5.

5. Troxel v. Granville, 530 U.S. 57, 63 (2000).

6. See, e.g., Stadter v. Siperko, 661 S.E.2d 494, 499 (Va. Ct. App. 2008); Clifford K. v. Paul S., 619 S.E.2d 138, 148–158 (W. Va. 2005); Riepe v. Riepe, 91 P.3d 312, 316–317 (Ariz. 2004); Melanie B. Jacobs, "Micah Has One Mommy and One Legal Stranger: Adjudicating Maternity for Nonbiological Lesbian Coparents," *Buffalo Law Review* 50 (2002): 341, 355; Solangel Maldonado, "When Father (or Mother) Doesn't Know Best: Quasi-Parents and Parental Deference after Troxel v. Granville," *Iowa Law Review* 88 (2003): 865, 893–897, 910–912.

7. American Law Institute, *Principles of the Law of Family Dissolution: Analysis and Recommendations* (Newark, NJ: Matthew Bender, 2002).

8. See In re Parentage of L.B., 122 P.3d 161 (Wash. 2005); Elisa B. v. Superior Court, 117 P.3d 660 (Cal. 2005).

9. See Smith v. Guest, 16 A.3d 920 (Del. 2011); Kulstad v. Maniaci, 221 P.3d 127 (Mont. 2009).

10. In re G, 1 W.L.R. 2305, 2316 (House of Lords 2006).

11. Ibid., 2315; see also In re Parentage of J.A.B., 191 P.3d 71 (Wash. Ct. App. 2008).

12. See In re A.N.F., 2008 WL 4334712 (Tenn. Ct. App. 2008); Allison v. Medlock, 983 So.2d 789 (Fla. Dist. Ct. App. 2008); Burden v. Burden, 945 A.2d 656 (Md. Ct. Spec. App. 2008); Michael Higgins, "Meaning of Dad Widened by Judge: Man Ruled Father of Unrelated Boy," *Chicago Tribune*, Sept. 17, 2004, http://articles.chicago tribune.com/2004-09-17/news/0409170300_1_biological-father-paternity-legal (accessed Jan. 5, 2012); Nancy E. Dowd, "Parentage at Birth: Birthfathers and Social Fatherhood," *William and Mary Bill of Rights Journal* 14 (2006): 909.

13. See Susan Frelich Appleton, "Presuming Women: Revisiting the Presumption of Legitimacy in the Same-Sex Couples Era," *Boston University Law Review* 86 (2006): 227.

14. Jane C. Murphy, "Legal Images of Fatherhood: Welfare Reform, Child Support Enforcement, and Fatherless Children," *Notre Dame Law Review* 81 (2005): 325, 329.

15. See, e.g., State ex rel. Juvenile Department of Lane County v. G.W., 177 P.3d 24 (Or. Ct. App. 2008); Fla. Stat. sec. 742.18(3) (2008).

16. Marquardt et al., *Revolution in Parenthood*, 5.

17. See Michael J. Klarman, "*Brown* and *Lawrence* (and *Goodridge*)," *Michigan Law Review* 104 (2005): 431; David D. Meyer, "Fragmentation and Consolidation in the Law of Marriage and Same-Sex Relationships," *American Journal of Comparative Law Supplement* 58 (2010): S115, S118.

18. Brenda Hale, "Understanding Children's Rights: Theory and Practice," *Family Court Review* 44 (2006): 350, 353. Baroness Hale, originally a professor of family law at the University of Manchester, was also the author of the principal opinion in the House of Lords' disposition of *In re G*, discussed earlier.

19. Convention on the Rights of the Child, art. 27(3) (1990).

20. Article 7 of the Charter of Fundamental Rights alters the language of the European Convention slightly, declaring that "everyone has the right to respect for his or her private and family life, home and communications."

21. Charter of Fundamental Rights of the European Union (CFREU), art. 24 (2000).

22. Ibid., art. 9; Article 12 of the European Convention on Human Rights provides that "men and women of marriageable age have the right to marry and to found a family, according to the national laws governing the exercise of this right."

23. Case of E.B. v. France, App. No. 43546/02, para. 11–17 (Eur. Ct. H.R. 2008) (quoting recommendation of consulting psychologist).

24. Ibid., para. 41 (citations omitted).

25. Santosky v. Kramer, 455 U.S. 745, 787 (1982) (quoting Lassiter v. Department of Social Services, 452 U.S. 18, 27 (1981)).

26. See, e.g., *Santosky*; *Troxel*.

27. See Lehr v. Robertson, 463 U.S. 248, 262 (1983).

28. See, e.g., ibid.; Michael H. v. Gerald D., 491 U.S. 110 (1989).

29. See Katharine K. Baker, "Bargaining or Biology? The History and Future of Paternity Law and Parental Status," *Cornell Journal of Law and Public Policy* 14 (2004): 1, 34; David D. Meyer, "The Constitutionality of 'Best Interests' Parentage," *William and Mary Bill of Rights Journal* 14 (2006): 857, 872–873.

30. *Troxel*, 68 (quoting Parham v. J.R., 442 U.S. 584, 602 (1979)).

31. Smith v. Organization of Foster Families for Equality and Reform, 431 U.S. 816, 844 (1977).

32. See Emily Buss, "'Parental' Rights," *Virginia Law Review* 88 (2002): 635, 647; see also Martin Guggenheim, *What's Wrong with Children's Rights* (Cambridge: Harvard University Press, 2005); Elizabeth S. Scott, "Parental Autonomy and Children's Welfare," *William and Mary Bill of Rights Journal* 11 (2003): 1071.

33. E.g., *Stadter*, 498.

34. James G. Dwyer, *The Relationship Rights of Children* (Cambridge: Cambridge University Press, 2006), 120–121.

35. E.g., Washington v. Glucksberg, 521 U.S. 702, 720–721 (1997); Bowers v. Hardwick, 478 U.S. 186, 191–192 (1986).

36. Loving v. Virginia, 388 U.S. 1, 12 (1967).

37. Lawrence v. Texas, 539 U.S. 558, 571–572 (2003).

38. Ibid., 572.

39. See Clare McGlynn, *Families and the European Union: Law, Politics and Pluralism* (Cambridge: Cambridge University Press, 2006), 74–75; Dwyer, *Relationship Rights of Children*, 124–125; David D. Meyer, "The Modest Promise of Children's Relationship Rights," *William and Mary Bill of Rights Journal* 11 (2003): 1117, 1119–1120.

40. See David D. Meyer, "A Privacy Right to Public Recognition of Family Relationships? The Cases of Marriage and Adoption," *Villanova Law Review* 51 (2006): 891;

Barbara Bennett Woodhouse, "Waiting for Loving: The Child's Fundamental Right to Adoption," *Capital University Law Review* 34 (2005): 297.

41. Cf. Smith v. Organization of Foster Families for Equality and Reform, 431 U.S. 816 (1977).

42. Kulstad v. Maniaci, 23 (Mont. 4th Dist. Ct., Missoula County Sept. 29, 2008) accessible at 34 BNA Fam. L. Rep. 1543 (affirmed, 220 P.3d 595 (Mont. 2009)).

43. Ibid., 29.

44. I advance this reading of *Troxel* in David D. Meyer, "*Lochner* Redeemed: Family Privacy after *Troxel* and *Carhart*," *UCLA Law Review* 48 (2001): 1125, 1135–1155.

45. See Dwyer, *Relationship Rights of Children*, 127–133.

46. Barbara Bennett Woodhouse, *Hidden in Plain Sight: The Tragedy of Children's Rights from Ben Franklin to Lionel Tate* (Princeton: Princeton University Press, 2008), 34; see also Barbara Bennett Woodhouse, "'Out of Children's Needs, Children's Rights': The Child's Voice in Defining the Family," *BYU Journal of Public Law* 8 (1994): 321.

47. Woodhouse, *Hidden in Plain Sight*, 34.

48. Ibid., 36. See CRC, arts. 7, 8, 9, and 16 (providing that "[n]o child shall be subjected to arbitrary or unlawful interference with his or her privacy, family, or correspondence . . .").

49. Woodhouse, *Hidden in Plain Sight*, 36–37.

50. Ibid., 44.

51. McGlynn, *Families and the European Union*, 70.

52. Ibid., 71.

53. Ibid.

54. See James G. Dwyer, "A Constitutional Birthright: The State, Parentage, and the Rights of Newborn Persons," *UCLA Law Review* 56 (2009): 755.

55. See, e.g., French National Assembly, *Parliamentary Report on the Family and the Rights of Children* (2006), 6–7; Marquardt et al., *Revolution in Parenthood*, 15–16, 33.

56. Dwyer, *Relationship Rights of Children*, 134.

57. Ibid., 133–134.

58. CRC, art. 7(1).

59. CFREU, art. 24(3).

60. Universal Declaration of Human Rights, art. 29(2) (1948).

61. CFREU, art. 52(1).

62. Ibid.; see also UDHR, art. 29(2) ("respect for the rights and freedoms of others").

63. See David D. Meyer, "*Lochner* Redeemed: Family Privacy after *Troxel* and *Carhart*," *UCLA Law Review* 48 (2001): 1125, 1130–1135.

64. *Case of E.B.*, para. 92.

65. CRC, preamble.

66. Woodhouse, *Hidden in Plain Sight*, 33.

67. CFREU, art. 9.

68. French National Assembly, *Parliamentary Report on the Family*, 7.

69. George Letsas, "Two Concepts of the Margin of Appreciation," *Oxford Journal of Legal Studies* 26 (2006): 705.

70. Steven Greer, *The Margin of Appreciation: Interpretation and Discretion under the European Convention on Human Rights* (Strasbourg: Council of Europe, 2000).

71. Odièvre v. France, App. No. 42326/98 (Eur. Ct. H.R. 2003).

72. Ibid., para. 44.

73. Ibid., concurring opinion of Rozakis, J.

74. CRC, art. 7(1).

75. Ingeborg Schwenzer, "Tensions between Legal, Biological and Social Conceptions of Parentage," *Electronic Journal of Comparative Law* 11, no. 3 (2007): 1, 3, http://www.ejcl.org/113/article113-6.pdf (accessed Jan. 5, 2012).

Child Outcomes and Forms of Parenthood

Does One Model Produce, on Average, Better Outcomes for Children? For Society?

PART FOUR

A Case for Integrated Parenthood

Margaret F. Brinig

This chapter makes a case for the *integrative model* of the family and of parenthood. More specifically, it argues for supporting the formal, legally recognized statuses of husband/wife and parent/child. In general, children do better in both the short and long term if they live with married parents and if they are biological or adopted children of these parents. Children are particularly affected by the stability and permanence of their relationships, although they are famously resilient. Under any circumstances, parental warmth affects children significantly and positively. One of the more dramatic ways to see the influence of parental relationships involves mixed-race marriages because they tend to be of shorter duration. The mixed-race case, where children do fine only so long as their parents stay together, reveals the importance of community as well as intentions of parents for children's outcomes. Community includes the formal community denoted by legal status, the family's religious community (especially important for African American families), and the peer community, which particularly influences older children. Stable marriages may provide a kind of buffer for fathers, who on their own may prefer sons to daughters.

Marriage has been described in the literature as a gender factory.[1] It also serves as a factory for producing healthy children and contributing citizens, for children profit from stability, continuity, and love. In my earlier work, I note that families produce not only material goods or future workers for the labor force but also children who later will be able to love unconditionally.[2] The effects I will describe can thus be characterized as having both short- and long-run effects. Because children seem malleable and do not have effective political lobbies, it is easy for public policy makers to argue that what adults do does not matter as far as children are concerned. Parenthetically, this also makes it easier to sound politically correct and to seem to clearly separate poverty from intimate decision making (which, after all, is a constitutional right in the United States).[3]

So far, the empirical work I have done is limited to different-sex couples and parents. Other scholars can show, using some of the same data sets,

147

what happens if parents are of the same gender.⁴ In the next chapter, Fiona Tasker reviews this literature, concluding that this type of family form makes very little difference to child development, especially as compared with access to resources, social systems, and family dynamics (especially between co-parents).⁵ Further, most of my results necessarily cannot show causation, only relationships between variables. In these, causation may run in either direction, or the relationship may actually be caused by some variable that is not considered in my models. The results will at least be consistent with the hypothesis considered. Further, the small R^2 of the underlying equations (i.e., how much of the variance in the result is explained by the equation) shows that they do not explain all, or even a substantial part, of the variance in results. While I will begin with groups representative of society in general, I will have something to say about the African American subgroup, which displays quite different results. I also include some results for children whose race differs from that of one or more of their parents, who seem sensitive to family forms involving divorce or where their parents have never married, and who, unfortunately, are more likely than most children to see their parents divorce or their nonmarital relationship dissolve. Finally, because my results usually use large, longitudinal, nationally representative samples, while being scientifically more reliable, they may miss the individual stories that qualitative studies provide.

Literature on Formal and Informal Relationships
I begin with a very quick literature review. Many scholars, including some contributors to this book, have written about the negative effects of divorce on children.⁶ The consensus seems to be that when the vast majority of couples divorce—all those except couples in very high-conflict marriages—children do less well.⁷ While there is some debate about how long it takes children to recover from relationship disruption,⁸ it does seem to follow that children of divorce are less successful in their own marriages. They are more likely to cohabit and are more likely to divorce themselves. It is also clear that cohabiting relationships are less likely to be stable than married ones,⁹ even in countries where there is the same governmental support for both kinds of families, and even when there are children. Paul Amato has shown that, just as men seem to benefit from less than high-quality marriages, children do better even in unhappy marriages than when their parents divorce (except in cases where there is family violence to which children are exposed).¹⁰

There has also been significant writing on African American (black) families. One obvious observation is that fewer black children live with two

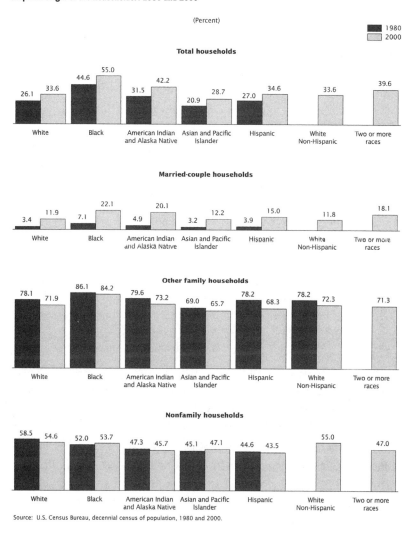

Figure 7.1 Percent Female Householders of Total Householders by Type of Household and Race and Hispanic Origin of the Householder: 1980 and 2000

Source: U.S. Census Bureau, decennial census of population, 1980 and 2000.

married parents. Their mothers are less likely to have married before they were born and are more likely to divorce even when they do marry (Figure 7.1). It is perhaps not surprising, given the fact that so many black children are born to unmarried parents or experience parental divorce, that marital status does not matter as much for these children as for other Americans. There has been less writing about interracial families of late, since the federal Multiethnic Placement Act[11] contradicted the movement by the National Association of Black Social Workers[12] to eliminate placements made solely or in stated part upon the race of child or parents. However, as national data sets such as the Panel Survey of Income Dynamics (PSID) show, many children in the United States have a different race than at least one of their parents. (See Table 7.1, in which the last line of results shows that figure at nearly 28 percent.) This may be because of intermarriage (while uncommon between blacks and whites, quite common between other racial groups)[13] or adoption of children, domestically or, particularly, internationally.[14] (See Table 7.2 for an idea of the numbers involved.) These children of interracial marriages, like most in America, do best living in married, intact families. Unfortunately, however, those of mixed-race marriages are particularly likely to experience their parents' separation or divorce (with marriages dissolving about 50 percent more often than those of racially homogeneous couples).[15] Children adopted transracially present particular challenges for the parents adopting them.[16]

Now we reach my own results. Most of these explore what I have called the short term: how the children are doing before they reach adulthood. What I have found using data sets like the National Longitudinal Survey of Adolescent Health (Add Health) and the PSID has been reported elsewhere but can be summarized here with reference to some key charts.[17]

Typically I have focused on a number of outcomes and have included not only family situation variables but also demographic information and, particularly, income and poverty. The outcomes of interest in this work are behavioral problems (external, which includes juvenile delinquency or like activities; and internal, including anxiety and depression); drug (marijuana), alcohol, and tobacco use; self-efficacy (or control over one's environment); and self-esteem. The adoption studies also use morbidity (fear of dying or of being killed young). Other researchers have looked at such things as grades in school and IQ. I have steered away from these measures because of my interest in basic character and relationship formation.

What I have found, unsurprisingly, is that children who live with their parents do far better than those living with foster parents. Of course, when children end up in foster care, which itself is disruptive and may provide less than optimum care,[18] whatever drove those parents to be unable to care for them has probably affected the children as well. Children who are adopted by their parents (and I do not know whether they were in foster care previously) typically cannot be distinguished on these measures from biological children. (See Table 7.3, "Adopted Child," and note the "ns," or not statistically significant, designations.)[19]

Table 7.1 Descriptive Statistics (PSID)

	N	Minimum	Maximum	Mean	Standard Deviation
Kid lives with 2 bio parents	2,681	.00	1.00	.6832	.46532
Kid lives with bio mom and no bio dad	2,681	.00	1.00	.1917	.39367
Kid lives with bio mom and adoptive dad	2,681	.00	1.00	.0063	.07922
Kid lives with bio mom and stepdad	2,681	.00	1.00	.0759	.26489
Kid lives with bio mom and other dad figure	2,681	.00	1.00	.0344	.18226
Kid lives with two adoptive parents	2,681	.00	1.00	.0086	.09219
Importance of religion to primary caretaker	2,672	1.00	3.00	2.6385	.59797
Age of mother or mother figure	2,582	20.00	81.00	41.9310	7.44560
Household income divided by census needs standard	2,583	.00	113.39	3.7756	4.78121
Mom married once, still intact	2,681	.00	1.00	.5833	.49311
Mom married and widowed at least once	2,681	.00	1.00	.0153	.12274
Mom married, divorced, remarried, still intact	2,681	.00	1.00	.1251	.33093
Mom married, divorced, remarried, now divorced	2,681	.00	1.00	.0316	.17483
Mom never married	2,681	.00	1.00	.1168	.32119
Mom married, divorced, never remarried	2,681	.00	1.00	.1176	.32221
Positive Behavior Scale 02	2,681	1.00	5.00	4.1270	.59692
Parental Warmth Scale 02	2,681	1.00	5.00	3.9271	.64020
Behavioral Problems Index - total score 02	2,650		30	8.58	6.442
BPI - externalizing score 02	2,667		17	5.53	4.116
BPI - internalizing score 02	2,659		14	3.23	3.193
Pearlin Self-Efficacy Scale 02	2,671	1.00	4.00	3.1054	.58953
Rosenberg Self-Esteem Scale 02	2,674	1.00	4.00	3.4036	.44345
Sex of CDS child	2,000	1.00	2.00	1.5107	.50001
Child age at time of mother's interview - years 02	2,681	5.52	19.25	12.3159	3.73311
Child's race different from one of parents	2,196	.00	1.00	.2788	.44852
Valid N (listwise)	1,551				

Table 7.2 Top Orphan-Issuing Countries

Country	IR3	IR4	TOTAL
China (mainland)	4,984	472	5,453
Guatemala	2,812	1,916	4,728
Russia	2,305	5	2,3310
Ethiopia	119	1,136	1,255
South Korea	3	936	939
Vietnam	783	45	828
Ukraine	606	0	606
Kazakhstan	540	0	540
India	44	382	265
Liberia	117	197	314
Colombia	310	0	310
Philippines	42	223	265
Haiti	112	78	190
Taiwan	127	57	184
Mexico	78	11	89
Poland	84	0	84
Thailand	12	55	67
Kyrgyzstan	32	29	61
Brazil	54	1	55
Uganda	7	47	54

Source: Statistics available at http://adoption.state.gov/about_us/statistics.php (last visited Dec. 16, 2011).

Most children living informally with relatives (grandmothers or aunts) are more similar to foster children than to children living with their biological families. However, for African Americans, this informal placement (so-called kinship care) seems indistinguishable from adoption, and therefore from living with biological parents. Why might this be so? For most children, adoption brings with it a sense of fully belonging in a family as well as an assurance of permanence and stability that foster children cannot claim. If there are biological children as well as the adopted child, being the same as far as legal status is concerned makes the children equals in a fundamental way. From their parents' point of view, adoption, with its finality, provides the opportunity for them to make a full investment in unconditionally loving these children.[20] They therefore are likely to do a better job. For African American children, as we will see, two things are at work. The first is that what this book calls the *integrative model* of family is really not the norm for them (see Table 7.1). The second does not emerge as readily from census data. African American children, like all children, do benefit significantly from external supports. For them,

Table 7.3 Effects of Adoption, Foster Placement, and Kin-Care by Race

Effect by Race	Depression	Drug Use (no./ month)	Juvenile Delinquency	Perceived Chance of Dying
Adopted child:				
White	0.466 ns	−0.013 ns	0.640 ns	0.012 ns
Black	1.434 ns	−0.163 ns	0.671 ns	0.003 ns
Asian	2.874*	−0.578 ns	0.660 ns	−0.005 ns
Native American	N/A	2.217*	0.252 ns	N/A
Other race	0.625 ns	2.095*	0.616 ns	0.021 ns
Fostered child:				
White	0.196 ns	2.884**	−0.682 ns	0.011 ns
Black	5.251**	−0.578 ns	0.086 ns	0.107*
Asian	5.585 ns	N/A	5.682**	0.363*
Native American	N/A	−2.034 ns	3.214 ns	N/A
Other race	6.461*	2.055 ns	6.500*	0.024 ns
Kin-care child:				
White	1.464*	0.467 ns	2.340**	0.017 ns
Black	0.164 ns	−0.097 ns	0.247 ns	−0.011 ns
Asian	3.092 ns	1.488*	4.003*	0.102*
Native American	N/A	1.315 ns	5.474*	N/A
Other race	3.236*	0.327 ns	2.128 ns	0.017 ns
R^2 / N				
White	.042**/9905	.057**/9745	.032**/9825	.023**/9882
Black	.048**/3135	.035**/3045	.028**/3090	.019**/3113
Asian	.068**/793	.050**/781	.086**/794	.049**/797
Native American	.075ns/253	.144**/248	.106*/248	N/A
Other race	.062**/1213	.056**/1188	.043**/1203	.036*/1213

Source: Margaret F. Brinig and Steven L. Nock, "How Much Does Legal Status Matter? Adoptions by Kin Caregivers," Family Law Quarterly 36 (2002): 449, 474, and Table 3.
Note: All equations control for household structure, child's gender, household income, mother's age, mother's current and previous marital status, mother's education, and mother's race.
** = Statistical significance is .01 or less.
* = Statistical significance is .05 or less.
ns = Not statistically significantly different from zero.
N/A = Insufficient number of cases or insignificant equation.

Figure 7.2

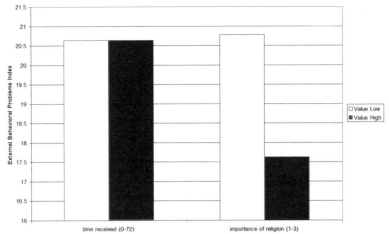

these supports may not always come in the guise of the formal family but frequently appear to be related to religiosity. (Figure 7.2 shows just one of many instances in which the parent's religiosity does matter significantly, and more than does the help provided by extended family.)

Are Diverse, or Intentional, Families as Successful as Formal Families?

Children living with their biological mothers form about 95 percent of all those included in these large data sets. Here, too, for most children, and controlling for other factors, their family status tells us much about how they do. As Figures 7.3, 7.4, and 7.5 show, American children taken as a whole always do better when their mothers were married at least once

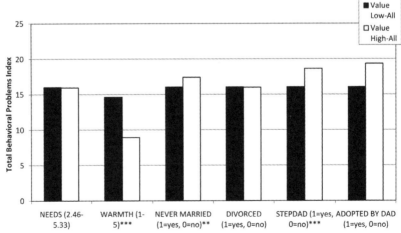

Figure 7.3 Total Behavioral Problems–All Kids

Figure 7.4

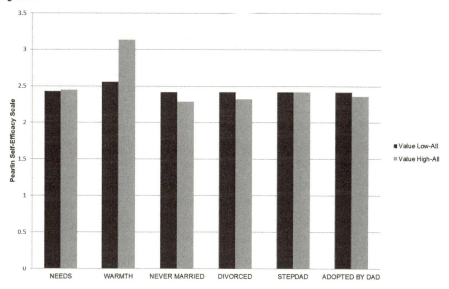

Figure 7.5

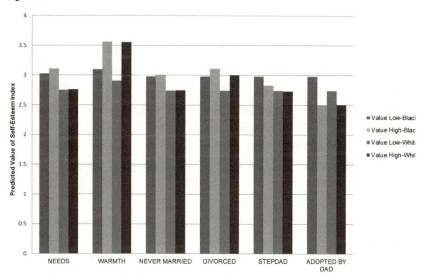

than if they never married, and divorce itself does not matter statistically once income is taken into account. However, living with a stepparent (which more often than not follows divorce) apparently increases behavioral problems and decreases feelings of self-efficacy and self-esteem. The other always significant and important ingredient is what the PSID calls "parental warmth": how often the parent praises the child, hugs the child, and talks positively about the child to others.

Over the long haul, family structure apparently matters as well. Adult children are slower to marry, more likely to cohabit, and quicker to divorce if their own parents divorced.[21] While some 70 percent do not exhibit major psychological problems as adults, nearly a third do have issues that are long-lasting.[22] Girls whose mothers never married are far more likely to have children without being married themselves.[23] Those whose mothers were on public assistance (typically because of nonmarital births or divorce) are more likely to end up on public assistance themselves.[24] They are less likely to finish high school or college and may find it more difficult to become employed.[25]

Figures 7.3 through 7.5 also show that living with stepparents (or stepparent figures, if there is no second marriage) tends to be associated with less good outcomes for children. While stepparents will reduce the financial problems typical for custodial mothers, they also typically signal a break in the child's relationships with the noncustodial parent, usually the father.[26] If it is the noncustodial parent who develops a new relationship, as most do, a similar break occurs. The remarried (or cohabiting) parent may be concentrating on the new relationship,[27] on blending a family of unrelated children who have not been raised together, or on starting a new family.[28] As we will see from the relocation cases we will look at presently, remarriage is frequently accompanied by a move out of the geographic area, and the physical distance may also affect the relationship.[29] Further, the second-order relationships (i.e., second, third, or subsequent marriages and cohabitation) are less stable—they are more likely to end in divorce or separation,[30] perhaps because, as demographer Andrew Cherlin put it thirty years ago, remarriage is an incomplete institution.[31] Further, there tend to be more problems with sexual and other abuse of children.[32]

Another way of looking at this phenomenon is through the lens of social capital and trust. If communities trust individual relationships (as they do marriage and legal parenthood), they imbue them with all sorts of help: legal protections, financial ones, and the sort of tangible help extended families often provide. On the other hand, for informal, less-recognized relationships, the couples or parents are to some extent on their own. While they may be successful, that success will come less frequently and will be more difficult to achieve.[33]

Children learn mimetically, that is, by imitating their parents (and, when older, their peers). They model adult relationships most closely on the one they experience firsthand—their parents'—and, secondarily, from those they see around them. Typically this learning by observation is a good thing, though it may be a precursor to "mimetic rivalry."[34] That is why children will marry later and divorce more often, independent of parental status, if they lived in a state with a higher divorce rate when they were sixteen.[35] But there seems to be a real difference between marriage and cohabitation, even when "everybody's doing it," and even when there are equal subsidies for both. As the first several lines of data in Table 7.4 show, even in Scandinavia, where living together without marriage has been practiced the longest, cohabiting relationships dissolve at a higher rate than married ones do, with or without children.[36] This may be because cohabitation, like remarriage, is incomplete, or because more religious couples tend to choose marriage (Table 7.5).[37] Religious institutions themselves provide community support for families and, in some communities, may substitute for formal families.[38]

Table 7.4 Relative Risk of Partnership Dissolution

Country	Married Directly	Cohabited, Then Married	Cohabited Only
Sweden	1.00	1.5+	3.96***
Norway	1.00	0.85	4.92***
Finland	1.00	1.12	3.44***
France	1.00	1.49**	6.04***
Austria	1.00	1.01	3.08***
Switzerland	1.00	1.11	4.84***
West Germany	1.00	1.38*	3.07***
East Germany	1.00	1.35*	1.55***

Source: Kathleen Kiernan, "Cohabitation in Western Europe: Trends, Issues, and Implications," in Just Living Together: Implications of Cohabitation on Families, Children, and Social Policy, ed. A. Booth and A. C. Courter (Mahwah, NJ: Erlbaum, 2002), 17, and Table 1.7. Reproduced with permission.

Table 7.5 Percentage of Women Aged 20 to 39 Reporting They Practically Never Attend Religious Services According to Type of First Partnership

Country	Married Directly	Cohabited and Married	Cohabited Only	Total
Sweden	38	61	73	66
Norway	51	71	78	62
Finland	22	33	43	34
Switzerland	24	41	55	41
West Germany	28	43	44	39
East Germany	68	80	78	77
Great Britain	41	47	56	46
Italy	8	9	28	9
Spain	50	65	74	57

Source: Kathleen Kiernan, "Cohabitation in Western Europe: Trends, Issues and Implications," Population Trends 96 (2001): 25.

Parenting and Divorce

I have already noted that their parents' divorce is typically not a good thing for children. There are a number of reasons given for this: that children of divorce are poorer,[39] that they may already have suffered because of whatever led to their parents' breakup, that divorcing parents are less able to parent well over the short term,[40] and that children may even in the best of circumstances have to negotiate between "two worlds."[41] Another, related to all the rest, is that parents frequently relocate after divorce.[42] In these cases, children typically endure not only some change in their relationships with their parents but also a geographic change. In the 819 reported relocation cases as of 2003, many of these other reasons emerge.[43] (Admittedly, these cases are not a completely unbiased sample, for they require a dispute that cannot be resolved out of court, some tenacity on the part of the parent who lost in the first instance, the expenditure of yet more funds to make an appeal, and a judge or judges who decide to publish their opinions.) More than half the time (53.3 percent), one or both of the parents have remarried. Frequently the custodial parent wants to relocate because of the new spouse's job or because the new spouse already lives outside the area. Sometimes the cases make it obvious that the move is simply to get away from the other parent, with whom the relationship ranges from acerbic to abusive. In other cases, the custodial parent wants to move because of (typically) her own employment or further education, or to move nearer to the support of her family: to begin life anew. But unless the noncustodial parent was physically abusive, these considerations, while completely understandable, are the parent's issue, not the child's. Unless the noncustodial parent was uninvolved before or had a bad relationship with the child, the question for the courts is whether the advantages offered *the child* by the move exceed the losses—in security and the relationship with the noncustodial parent. Although the arguments often revolve around parental rights, that is the problem. Parents at the time of divorce—and particularly at the time they begin new relationships—may not be putting the child first. The litigation demonstrates that fault may lie on either side or both sides. Sometimes the noncustodial parent is continuing a marital power struggle by objecting to what appears to be a perfectly reasonable move—for example, if the parents moved during the latter years of their marriage away from familiar territory and family supports, or if the poverty of the custodial spouse requires a move "home." This suggests that we should think carefully about parenting decisions when the parents are under such stress that they are putting their own interests before their children's.

One of the interesting observations about these reported relocation cases involves the gender of parent and child. When mothers are the custodial parents (508 cases), fathers object to their moves much more often when the children are sons than when they are daughters (69.29 percent compared with 55.7 percent). (In other words, more than 69 percent of the cases involved at least one boy, while more than 55 percent involve girls. This difference is highly statistically significant [$p < .001$].) In contrast, when fathers are the custodial parents (64 cases), mothers seek to block relocation equally as often for sons and daughters (59.38 percent compared with 60.94 percent). If what the objecting parents seek to do is provide gender role models for the children, one would suspect that the mothers would intervene more often with their daughters than with their sons. Perhaps the fathers' true preferences are emerging here, at a time when the parents' focus does not seem to be on their children. Perhaps mothers feel that they must continue to have contact with their children (of either gender) simply because they are mothers.

A similar issue of current legislative and judicial concern involves joint or shared parenting. Although for more than twenty years courts have been awarding fit parents joint decision-making authority, and the tendency to award equal physical custody has been on the rise for some time (see Figure 7.6 for the Oregon data), strong presumptions in favor of equal or nearly equal physical placement, trumpeted by the father's rights movement, are of quite recent vintage. The reason I say the issue is similar to relocation is that it, too, often reflects attention given to parents rather

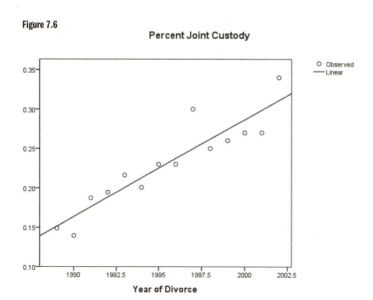

Figure 7.6

than to what is necessarily better for the children involved. That is not to say that agreed-upon shared parenting arrangements cannot work or that they cannot be beneficial to children. However, when they are the product of litigation, are sought to reduce child support payments or to exert power over the other parent, or reduce children to living out of suitcases on a continual basis, the emphasis at least seems wrong. An initial question for me is whether in fact more overnight visits with the noncustodial parent improve a child's welfare. Tables 7.6 through 7.9 indicate that on our by-now standard measures, it does not. While seeing fathers only several times a year has a negative effect, it does not seem to matter whether overnight visits occur once a month, many times a week, or somewhere in between. What does matter, and matters strongly, is the child's report of closeness to the parent. Closeness, while it probably is related to time spent together (or at least frequent communication), does not necessarily come from maintaining two households for the child.

Table 7.6 Depression

	Unstandardized Coefficients		Standardized Coefficients		
	B	Standard Error	Beta	t	Significance
(Constant)	14.237	1.811		7.863	0
KIDAGE Age at time of interview, 1995	0.194	0.085	0.052	2.272	0.023
KIDSEX	1.318	0.278	0.104	4.741	0
HHINC Household income in 1,000s	-0.004	0.005	-0.017	-0.742	0.458
MOMHISP Mom is Hispanic	2.148	2.621	0.018	0.82	0.413
MOMBLACK Mom is black	0.695	0.311	0.05	2.236	0.025
MOMASIAN Mom is Asian	0.156	0.938	0.004	0.166	0.868
MOMNATAM Mom is Native American	2.979	1.227	0.053	2.428	0.015
MOMOTHER Mom is other race	1.111	0.605	0.04	1.835	0.067
MOMEDUC Mother's years of schooling	-0.311	0.066	-0.108	-4.731	0
MOMAGE	-0.021	0.027	-0.018	-0.784	0.433
SELDOM Does kid stay with dad once or twice? 1=Y, 0=N	0.671	0.444	0.035	1.511	0.131
SEVERAL Does kid stay with dad several times? 1=Y, 0=N	1.33	0.422	0.078	3.153	0.002
MONTHLY Does kid stay with dad several times? 1=Y, 0=N	-0.024	0.573	-0.001	-0.043	0.966
WEEKLY Does kid see dad more than weekly? 1=Y, 0=N	-0.193	0.607	-0.008	-0.319	0.75
OFTEN	0.278	0.587	0.012	0.474	0.635
TALKBIOD Times last year kid talked with bio dad?	2.73E-03	0.004	0.018	0.671	0.502
HOWCLOSE How close kid feels to bio dad?	-0.595	0.124	-0.13	-4.814	0

CESD2 19-item Depression Scale; R2 (adj.) = .047.

Table 7.7 Drug, Alcohol, and Tobacco Use

	Unstandardized Coefficients		Standardized Coefficients		
	B	Standard Error	Beta	t	Significance
(Constant)	−0.685	1.107		−0.619	0.536
KIDAGE Age at time of interview, 1995	0.317	0.052	0.138	6.077	0
KIDSEX	−0.148	0.17	−0.019	−0.873	0.383
HHINC Household income in 1,000s	−0.004	0.003	−0.031	−1.349	0.178
MOMHISP Mom is Hispanic	−1.783	1.721	−0.023	−1.036	0.3
MOMBLACK Mom is black	−1.946	0.19	−0.228	−10.245	0
MOMASIAN Mom is Asian	−1.302	0.581	−0.048	−2.242	0.025
MOMNATAM Mom is Native American	−1.48	0.758	−0.042	−1.954	0.051
MOMOTHER Mom is other race	−1.172	0.368	−0.07	−3.181	0.001
MOMEDUC Mother's years of schooling	−9.07E-02	0.04	−0.051	−2.259	0.024
MOMAGE	−2.71E-04	0.016	0	−0.016	0.987
SELDOM Does kid stay with dad once or twice? 1=Y, 0=N	0.419	0.273	0.035	1.537	0.125
SEVERAL Does kid stay with dad several times? 1=Y, 0=N	0.429	0.257	0.041	1.672	0.095
MONTHLY Does kid stay with dad several times? 1=Y, 0=N	−0.629	0.349	−0.042	−1.8	0.072
WEEKLY Does kid see dad more than weekly? 1=Y, 0=N	0.346	0.37	0.023	0.936	0.349
OFTEN	−0.308	0.359	−0.022	−0.856	0.392
TALKBIOD Times last year kid talked with bio dad?	−1.05E-03	0.002	−0.011	−0.422	0.673
HOWCLOSE How close kid feels to bio dad?	−0.115	0.076	−0.041	−1.516	0.13

Times per month; R2 (adj.) = .80.

Table 7.8 Juvenile Delinquency

	Unstandardized Coefficients		Standardized Coefficients		
	B	Standard Error	Beta	t	Significance
(Constant)	16.556	2.098		7.892	0
KIDAGE Age at time of interview, 1995	−0.204	0.099	−0.048	−2.068	0.039
KIDSEX	−2.395	0.321	−0.166	−7.464	0
HHINC Household income in 1000s	−0.009	0.006	−0.036	−1.54	0.124
MOMHISP Mom is Hispanic	2.747	3.003	0.021	0.915	0.361
MOMBLACK Mom is black	−0.357	0.358	−0.023	−0.997	0.319
MOMASIAN Mom is Asian	−0.435	1.087	−0.009	−0.4	0.689
MOMNATAM Mom is Native American	1.211	1.406	0.019	0.861	0.389
MOMOTHER Mom is other race	1.861	0.697	0.06	2.669	0.008
MOMEDUC Mother's years of schooling	−0.142	0.076	−0.043	−1.872	0.061
MOMAGE	−0.017	0.031	−0.013	−0.552	0.581
SELDOM Does kid stay with dad once or twice? 1=Y, 0=N	0.372	0.514	0.017	0.724	0.469
SEVERAL Does kid stay with dad several times? 1=Y, 0=N	0.583	0.486	0.03	1.2	0.23
MONTHLY Does kid stay with dad several times? 1=Y, 0=N	5.37E-02	0.66	0.002	0.081	0.935
WEEKLY Does kid see dad more than weekly? 1=Y, 0=N	−0.162	0.7	−0.006	−0.232	0.816
OFTEN	−0.07	0.678	−0.003	−0.103	0.918
TALKBIOD Times last year kid talked with bio dad?	4.74E-03	0.005	0.028	1.014	0.311
HOWCLOSE How close kid feels to bio dad?	−0.584	0.143	−0.112	−4.089	0

Times last month (15-point scale); R2 (adj.) = .037.

Table 7.9 Morbidity

	Unstandardized Coefficients		Standardized Coefficients		
	B	Standard Error	Beta	t	Significance
(Constant)	0.177	0.046		3.833	0
KIDAGE Age at time of interview, 1995	2.44E-03	0.002	0.026	1.124	0.261
KIDSEX	1.15E-04	0.007	0	0.016	0.987
HHINC Household income in 1,000s	0	0	-0.035	-1.5	0.134
MOMHISP Mom is Hispanic	2.19E-02	0.073	0.007	0.299	0.765
MOMBLACK Mom is black	4.37E-02	0.008	0.125	5.533	0
MOMASIAN Mom is Asian	1.46E-02	0.024	0.013	0.611	0.541
MOMNATAM Mom is Native American	5.28E-02	0.032	0.037	1.663	0.096
MOMOTHER Mom is other race	5.53E-02	0.015	0.079	3.565	0
MOMEDUC Mother's years of schooling	-0.007	0.002	-0.094	-4.047	0
MOMAGE	2.47E-04	0.001	0.008	0.361	0.718
SELDOM Does kid stay with dad once or twice? 1=Y, 0=N	1.74E-02	0.011	0.036	1.539	0.124
SEVERAL Does kid stay with dad several times? 1=Y, 0=N	2.36E-02	0.011	0.055	2.201	0.028
MONTHLY Does kid stay with dad several times? 1=Y, 0=N	1.38E-02	0.015	0.023	0.948	0.343
WEEKLY Does kid see dad more than weekly? 1=Y, 0=N	-9.09E-03	0.016	-0.015	-0.584	0.56
OFTEN	6.46E-03	0.015	0.011	0.432	0.666
TALKBIOD Times last year kid talked with bio dad?	-8.44E-05	0	-0.023	-0.816	0.414
HOWCLOSE How close kid feels to bio dad?	-6.55E-03	0.003	-0.057	-2.079	0.038

Chances of dying or being killed young; R2 (adj.) =. 030.

Differences in Groups: Race and Age

As I mentioned previously, black children seem to be affected by formal legal relationships far less than other racial groups in the United States. Because the marital relationship typically receives so much more support from family members and the wider community than does cohabitation, I wondered what has taken the place of status for this subgroup of Americans. The answer seems to be religion: it is the importance of religion to the mothers of black children that, with warmth and income, makes the most difference as to how children turn out. Religion seems to matter more than, say, the hours of help provided by extended families, in particular, the maternal grandparents. These findings are reflected in Figures 7.7 and 7.8 (repeating the earlier Figure 7.2).

Finally, I would like to pay at least brief attention to the underlying question of how important parents are compared with peers. It turns out that intuition on this question is probably well founded. For young children, and for the essence of personality formed in early childhood, parents play the most critical role. For them, it is their parents' religiosity that keeps them out of trouble and provides essential optimism about life. For teenagers, the parents' role becomes less important and the peers' more critical. For them, their peers' religiosity determines whether or not they will engage in problem behavior such as delinquency. These findings are reflected in Figures 7.9 through 7.11.

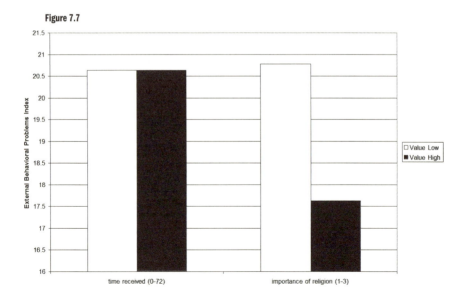

Figure 7.7

Figure 7.8

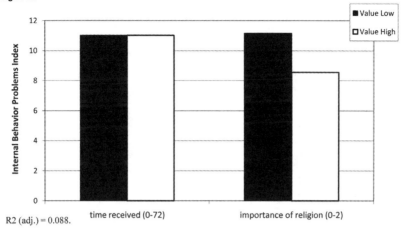

R2 (adj.) = 0.088.

Figure 7.9

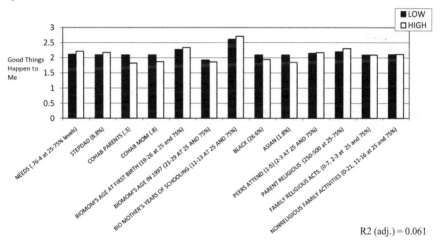

R2 (adj.) = 0.061

Figure 7.10

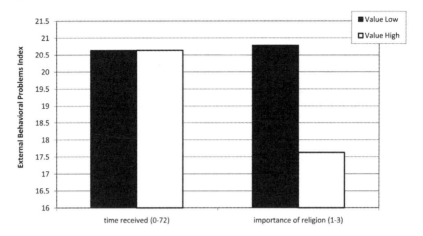

Figure 7.11

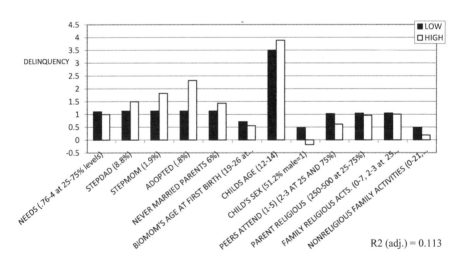

R2 (adj.) = 0.113

Conclusions and Recommendations for Policy

While even the premise of this book shows that the arguments I have made here are hotly contested, the case for privileging some families by giving them formal recognition is a strong one based not upon theory or adult ideals of equality of relationships but upon data. The fact that for most parts of society, formal families produce better results for children suggests caution in dismantling the legal protections given to marriage and biological or adoptive parenting. It suggests that relegating social institutions like marriage and adoption to religious spheres, while having surface appeal, might actually harm children, at least over the short run.[44] At least for now, the United States, at any rate, does not provide the massive social support through public welfare programs as do some Western European countries. However, empirical investigations do indicate that children in the United States may not all need formal families to the extent that the majority seem to. This cultural difference is one that should be respected when families in need turn to social services and parental rights are terminated. If the government cannot provide all the support these fragile families lack, it should allow kinship care rather than severing some children from their extended families.[45]

Notes

I acknowledge the many contributions of my coauthor and former colleague Steven L. Nock, with whom I wrote many of the published works from which tables for this piece are drawn.

1. Steven L. Nock, "Time and Gender in Marriage," *Virginia Law Review* 86 (Nov. 2000): 1971.

2. Margaret F. Brinig, *From Contract to Covenant: Beyond the Law and Economics of the Family* (Cambridge: Harvard University Press, 2000).

3. Lawrence v. Texas, 539 U.S. 558 (2003).

4. See, e.g., Charlotte J. Patterson and Jennifer J. Wainwright, "Adolescents with Same-Sex Parents: Findings from the National Longitudinal Study of Adolescent Health," in *Adoption by Lesbians and Gay Men: A New Dimension in Family Diversity*, ed. David M. Brodzinsky and Adam Pertman (New York: Oxford University Press, 2012), 85–111.

5. Fiona Tasker, "Developmental Outcomes for Children Raised by Lesbian and Gay Parents" (this volume).

6. See, e.g., Elizabeth Marquardt, *Between Two Worlds: The Inner Lives of Children of Divorce* (New York: Crown, 2005). See also David Popenoe, "The Evolution of Marriage and the Problem of Stepfamilies: A Biosocial Perspective," in *Stepfamilies: Who Benefits? Who Does Not?*, ed. Alan Booth and Judy Dunn (Hillsdale, NJ: Erlbaum, 1994), 3–27; Maggie Gallagher and Joshua K. Baker, "Do Moms and Dads Matter? Evidence

from the Social Sciences on Family Structure and the Best Interests of the Child," *University of Maryland Law Journal of Race, Religion, Gender and Class* 4 (2004): 161; Norval D. Glenn, "Biology, Evolutionary Theory, and Family Social Science," in Booth and Dunn, *Stepfamilies*, 45–51.

7. Paul R. Amato and Bryndl Hohmann-Marriott, "A Comparison of High- and Low-Distress Marriages That End in Divorce," *Journal of Marriage and Family* 69 (Aug. 2007): 621.

8. Cf. E. Mavis Hetherington and John B. Kelly, *For Better or for Worse: Divorce Reconsidered* (New York: Norton, 2003), with Judith S. Wallerstein, Julia M. Lewis, and Sandra Blakeslee, *The Unexpected Legacy of Divorce: A 25 Year Landmark Study* (New York: Hyperion, 2000).

9. Larry Bumpass and Lu Hsien-Henn, "Trends in Cohabitation and Implications for Children's Family Contexts in the United States," *Population Studies* 54 (Mar. 2000): 29; Kathleen Kiernan, "The Rise of Cohabitation and Childrearing Outside Marriage in Western Europe," *International Journal of Law, Policy and the Family* 15 (2001): 1.

10. Amato and Marriott, "Comparison of High- and Low-Distress Marriages," 621.

11. See Howard M. Metzenbaum Multiethnic Placement Act of 1994, Pub. L. 103–382, sec. 551, 553, 108 Stat. 405–4057 (1994); *repealed by* Small Business Job Protection Act of 1996, Pub. L. 104–188 sec. 1808(d), 110 Stat. 1904 (1996). Section 1808(a)(3) of the Small Business Job Protection Act added similar language forbidding the denial of placements on the basis of race.

12. Leslie Doty Hollingsworth, "Symbolic Interactionism, African American Families, and the Transracial Adoption Controversy," *Social Work* 44 (Sept. 1999): 443, 445–446, discussing *Preserving African American Families: Position Statement* (Detroit: National Association of Black Social Workers, 1994).

13. Rose Marie Kreider, "Interracial Marriage and Marital Instability" (PhD diss., University of Maryland, 1999).

14. Kathy S. Stolley, "Statistics on Adoption in the United States," *Future of Children* 3, no. 1 (1993): 26 (indicating that 8 percent of adoptions were interracial as of the time of her writing).

15. Kreider, "Interracial Marriage."

16. Literature includes Rita J. Simon and Rhonda M. Roorda, *In Their Own Voices: Transracial Adoptees Tell Their Stories* (New York: Columbia University Press, 2000). For an extensive discussion, see Margaret F. Brinig, "Moving toward a First-Best World: Minnesota's Position on Multiethnic Adoptions," *William Mitchell Law Review* 28 (2001): 553.

17. See Margaret F. Brinig, "Children's Beliefs and Family Law," *Emory Law Journal* 58 (2008): 55; Margaret F. Brinig and Steven L. Nock, "The One-Size-Fits-All Family," *Santa Clara Law Review* 49 (2009): 137; Margaret F. Brinig and Steven L. Nock, "Legal Status and Effects on Children," *University of St. Thomas Law Journal* 5 (2008): 548; Margaret F. Brinig and Steven L. Nock, "Can Law Shape the Development of Unconditional Love in Children?," in *Best Love of the Child: Being Loved and Being Taught to Love as the First Human Right*, ed. Timothy P. Jackson (Grand Rapids, MI: Eerdmans, 2011), 317–346.

18. See, e.g., Stephen M. Christian and Lisa Ekman, *A Place to Call Home: Adoption and Guardianship for Children in Foster Care* (Denver: National Conference of State

Legislatures, 2001), 1–7 (Executive Summary); Gannett News Service, "Fixing a Broken Foster Care System," *Iowa City Press-Citizen*, June 18, 2003, A7.

19. Margaret F. Brinig and Steven L. Nock, "How Much Does Legal Status Matter? Adoptions by Kin Caregivers," *Family Law Quarterly* 36 (2002): 449.

20. Ibid., 469.

21. Sara McLanahan and Irwin Garfinkel, "Single Mothers, the Underclass, and Social Policy," *ANNALS of the American Academy of Political and Social Science* 501 (Jan. 1989): 92.

22. Hetherington and Kelly, *For Better or for Worse*.

23. Margaret F. Brinig and F. H. Buckley, "The Price of Virtue," *Public Choice* 98 (Jan. 1999): 111; Larry Bumpass and Sara McLanahan, "Unmarried Motherhood: Recent Trends, Composition, and Black-White Differences," *Demography* 26 (May 1989): 279.

24. Sara S. McLanahan, "Family Structure and Dependency: Early Transitions to Female Household Headship," *Demography* 25 (Feb. 1988): 1.

25. McLanahan and Garfinkel, "Single Mothers."

26. Jennifer F. Hamer, "What African-American Noncustodial Fathers Say Inhibits and Enhances Their Involvement with Children," *Western Journal of Black Studies* 22 (Summer 1998): 117.

27. Kristen Harknett and Jean Knab, "More Kin, Less Support: Multipartnered Fertility and Perceived Support among Mothers," *Journal of Marriage and Family* 69 (Feb. 2007): 237.

28. Alan J. Hawkins and David J. Eggebeen, "Are Fathers Fungible? Patterns of Co-resident Adult Men in Maritally Disrupted Families and Young Children's Well-being," *Journal of Marriage and Family* 53 (Nov. 1991): 958.

29. Sanford L. Braver, Ira M. Ellman, and William V. Fabricius, "Relocation of Children after Divorce and Children's Best Interests: New Evidence and Legal Considerations," *Journal of Family Psychology* 17 (June 2003): 206.

30. Lynn K. White and Alan Booth, "The Quality and Stability of Remarriages: The Role of Stepchildren," *American Sociological Review* 50 (Oct. 1985): 689.

31. Andrew Cherlin, "Remarriage as an Incomplete Institution," *American Journal of Sociology* 84 (Nov. 1978): 634.

32. Robin Fretwell Wilson, "Children at Risk: The Sexual Exploitation of Female Children after Divorce," *Cornell Law Review* 86 (2001): 251; Owen D. Jones, "Evolutionary Analysis in Law: An Introduction and Application to Child Abuse," *North Carolina Law Review* 75 (1997): 1117.

33. The paragraph is in some ways a summary of Margaret F. Brinig, "The Relationship between Trust and Community Recognition," chap. 2 in *Family, Law and Community: Supporting the Covenant* (Chicago: University of Chicago Press, 2010).

34. Margaret F. Brinig, "The Limits of Community and the Role of Autonomy," chap. 5 in *Family, Law and Community*.

35. Margaret F. Brinig and Steven L. Nock, "'I Only Want Trust': Norms, Trust, and Autonomy," *Journal of Socio-Economics* 32 (Nov. 2003): 471.

36. Kiernan, "Rise of Cohabitation"; Wendy D. Manning, Pamela J. Smock, and Debarun Majumdar, "The Relative Stability of Cohabiting and Marital Unions for Children," *Population Research and Policy Review* 23 (Apr. 2004): 135.

37. Kathleen Kiernan, "Cohabitation in Western Europe," *Population Trends* 96 (Summer 1999): 25.

38. See Brinig, *Family, Law, and Community*, 117–118.

39. Paul R. Amato and Jacob Cheadle, "The Long Reach of Divorce: Divorce and Child Well-Being across Three Generations," *Journal of Marriage and Family* 67 (Feb. 2005): 191.

40. Wendy Sigle-Rushton, John Hobcraft, and Kathleen Kiernan, "Parental Divorce and Subsequent Disadvantage: A Cross-Cohort Comparison," *Demography* 42 (Aug. 2005): 427.

41. Marquardt, *Between Two Worlds*.

42. Braver et al., "Relocation of Children after Divorce," 206.

43. Data and results for the following section are available from the author in SPSS format. By "reported cases in 2003," I mean reported on Westlaw. The first such case dates back to 1884.

44. On some of these proposals, see Linda C. McClain, "A Diversity Approach to Parenthood in Family Life and Family Law" (this volume).

45. See Brinig and Nock, "How Much Does Legal Status Matter?"

Developmental Outcomes for Children Raised by Lesbian and Gay Parents

Fiona Tasker

In recent decades we have seen an increasing diversity of family structures in which children grow up. Whether or not differences in family structure make a difference to parenting and child development has been a hotly contested debate in family policy. In his analysis of sociodemographic trends in the United States, sociologist Andrew Cherlin argued first that remarriage was an "incomplete institution,"[1] and second that marriage itself has become deinstitutionalized.[2] Key elements in Cherlin's arguments are the rate of divorce in the United States and the advent of widespread cohabitation (by heterosexuals and also by same-sex couples), resulting in an increasing number of adults bringing up children within households not headed by a married couple. In this chapter, I will focus in particular on one area of the deinstitutionalization of marriage from parenthood and examine how legal and social policy has begun to change to recognize the differing profiles of parenting by lesbians and gay men. I will argue that further change is necessary to recognize the diversity of families led by nonheterosexual adults, in terms of both supporting different routes to family formation and acknowledging differences in how families function effectively to nurture children.

For policy makers with a pragmatic rather than a moral focus, whether or not children brought up in nontraditional family structures are disadvantaged, unaffected, or even advantaged in their development in various psychosocial outcomes has been a key concern in whether to change legislation to recognize lesbian and gay parenting. Later in this chapter, I provide an overview of the extensive body of research on children raised in families led by a lesbian mother, a gay father, or by same-sex couples parenting together and consider whether there are consistent ways in which children's development is associated with parental sexual orientation.[3] This research supports the conclusion that it is parenting quality rather than family type, in and of itself, that matters to child well-being.

Profiles of Same-Sex Parenting

Data from national census surveys in the United States and elsewhere have begun to provide some information on the numbers of households headed by same-sex couples who have children. Gates and colleagues have estimated from the U.S. census 2000 (Census 2000) that nearly a quarter of same-sex couples had at least one child under eighteen residing with them, with proportionately more children living with two women than two men, same-sex couples recording lower levels of household income than heterosexual married couples with children,[4] and more children residing with African American and Hispanic same-sex couples than with white Americans.[5] Of the children recorded in same-sex-couple households, more than 70 percent were classified as either the "natural born" child or the "stepchild" of the householder.[6] Gates reasoned that a large proportion of these children were conceived in prior heterosexual relationships as people in same-sex couples who recorded previous heterosexual marriages were nearly twice as likely as those previously unmarried to have children.[7]

Data from Census 2000, and other household surveys relying on similar question wording, likely underestimate the numbers of men and women bringing up their children as a nonheterosexual parent. Census 2000 did not ask a direct question on sexual orientation, sexual attraction, or sexual behavior. It recorded same-sex-couple households if the householder designated another adult of the same sex as his or her "unmarried partner" or "husband/wife."[8] Parenting commitments can cut across household boundaries as well as biological, partnership, or marital relationships.

Legislation and Routes to Same-Sex Parenting

The official parameters of parenthood for lesbian and gay parents are crucially influenced by two aspects: the laws of the jurisdiction where they and their children reside, and the route through which they became a parent. How parenthood is legally defined crucially affects lesbian and gay parents' interactions with educational and health care systems.[9] While public opinion influences policy and legislation, legal frameworks also exert an influence on attitudes in mainstream society. Scholars have begun to undertake cross-national comparisons to examine the experience of lesbian parenting under more liberal versus more conservative jurisdictions. One study found that Canadian lesbian mothers reported fewer anxieties about legal status and discrimination, and lower levels of depressive symptoms, than did lesbian mothers residing in the United States.[10] Children growing up in lesbian-led families in the Netherlands appeared to be more open about their family to others and reported fewer incidents of homophobia compared with children growing up in similar lesbian mother families across the United States.[11] In comparison to lesbian parents in the U.S. sample, lesbian parents in the Netherlands also reported that their children had fewer behavioral or emotional problems on the Child Behavior Checklist (CBCL).[12] Differences in experience of homophobia accounted in part for this variance in CBCL scores.

Lesbian and gay parents will have taken any one of four routes to parenthood. Some will have had more than one child via different routes. First, parents may have conceived children in prior, or ongoing, different-sex relationships. Second, parents may have children who are biologically related to them who were conceived with donor gametes through assisted reproductive technologies (ART), such as donor insemination or surrogacy. Third, they may be the nonbiological parents of their same-sex partner's, or ex-partner's, child. Finally, another route to parenthood is adoption, either as a single lesbian or gay parent, or within a same-sex partnership.[13]

Lesbian and Gay Parenting after Heterosexual Separation or Divorce

Many of the principles invoked in policies and legislation involving same-sex parenting were thrashed out in hotly contested custody cases in the 1970s and 1980s. These custody cases were usually between a woman, who had conceived (or adopted) children within a heterosexual marriage and then subsequently come out as lesbian, and her husband, who was contesting custody or access. Typical cases are those in North Dakota in which lesbian mothers lost, and in more recent years won, rights to continue to parent as a lesbian mother.[14]

In most Western jurisdictions, decisions concerning parental responsibility and children's residency and visiting with or access to a nonresidential parent are made with reference to the "best interests of the child." For example, in England and Wales, Section 1 of the Children's Act (1989) details a welfare checklist that is referred to in family law court judgments.[15] Further, residency and access decisions in the United Kingdom, and in other countries that have signed the European Convention on Human Rights, are influenced by decisions made in the European Court of Human Rights (ECHR). In a test case brought to the ECHR in 1999,

Salgueiro Da Silva Mouta v. Portugal, judges overturned an earlier Portuguese court's decision to prevent a gay father from having custody of, or access to, his daughter on the basis of his sexuality. The judgment made by the ECHR referred to two articles of the European Convention: Article 8 (the right to respect for his family life) and Article 14 (the right to be free from discrimination).[16]

In some states in the United States, lesbian and gay parenthood following heterosexual separation and divorce is defined with reference to the nexus test. Under that test, parental behaviors, including aspects connected with parental sexual orientation, cannot be introduced as admissible evidence unless a direct connection can be established between the specific parental behavior in question and a negative effect on child development.[17] Thus, while many states have moved away from per se rules that restrict custody for gay and lesbian parents solely on sexual orientation, under the nexus test the "moral fitness" of a gay or lesbian parent may be scrutinized or the judge might be concerned to protect a child from homophobia.[18] For instance, some states have limited parents from having an unmarried partner in the home overnight, thus making postdivorce living arrangements particularly difficult for lesbian or gay parents if state laws also prohibit same-sex marriage or domestic partnership agreements. However, since *Lawrence v. Texas*,[19] custody rulings restricting a parent's consensual same-sex conduct in private or cohabitation are presumably unconstitutional; therefore, state courts would find it difficult to point to same-sex conduct as illegal and thus immoral.

Various commentators have identified a gradual change in legal attitudes so that parental sexual orientation per se is less likely to be an issue in maintaining parenting after separation or divorce in the United States, although it may still be a legal journey fraught with uncertainty.[20] Also, a change in legal attitudes is more evident for lesbian mothers than for gay fathers. Gay fathers potentially face a double dose of prejudice against men as primary caregivers, and against their sexual identity.[21]

Planned Lesbian or Gay Parenting through Assisted Reproductive Technology

Different sets of legal issues arise for lesbians and gay men achieving planned parenthood through use of donor gametes and other forms of ART. The Ethics Committee of the American Society for Reproductive Medicine (ASRM) issued a report in 2009 that concluded: "Ethical arguments supporting denial of access to fertility services on the basis of marital status or sexual orientation cannot be justified."[22] Nevertheless, some state regulations in the United States impose limitations and conditions under which insurance coverage is made available or have restrictions on permissible expenses. In practice these regulations may exclude certain groups like cohabiting same-sex couples, or single women or men with lower incomes, from using ART because these technologies require expensive treatments such as donor gametes plus surrogacy. In their overview of legislation pertaining to ART across the United States, Kindregan and McBrien observed: "Whereas a few states have attempted to regulate certain practices, for the most part ART is largely unregulated. Medical insurance of ART services, clinic reporting requirements, religious exemptions, medical evaluation of gamete donors, and standards of practice differ greatly throughout the country."[23]

Many states have accepted the principle of the Uniform Parentage Act (UPA; 1973) clarifying that a donor who provides semen to a licensed physician has no legal or financial obligation to any children conceived with his sperm. Some states have adopted the updated UPA (2000), which does not require the intercession of a licensed physician.[24] When the donor is known to the recipient, however, some states may impose some parental responsibilities upon the donor, and some known donors have sought parental rights.[25] In other states, such as California, the known donor does not acquire legal rights or responsibilities if a medical doctor conducts the insemination.[26]

Empirical research indicates that, in contrast to many heterosexual couples, many lesbian mothers prefer a known donor to an unknown donor. For example, studies in the United States have indicated that many lesbian mothers wanted a known donor, due in part to wanting to have male involvement in their children's lives.[27] Data from the U.S. National Longitudinal Lesbian Family Study (NLLFS) indicate that children with known or unknown donors are indistinguishable in terms of their subsequent psychological adjustment.[28] "Dad" doesn't matter

In recent decades, surrogacy has become a route to parenthood for some gay men, although some U.S. states prohibit it.[29] Clinic clients may either use a traditional surrogate, where the surrogate's own egg is fertilized, or a gestational surrogate with an egg donor. In either case, the egg is fertilized with the directed donor's sperm (i.e., the sperm of the man or male couple commissioning the surrogacy). Another surrogacy possibility is embryo donation where a resulting baby is not related to the client(s) or the gestational surrogate. As Greenfeld and Seli emphasize, there are several reasons to provide counseling prior to ART.[30] First, the proposed surrogate or gamete donor may be a friend or relative. Second, when both men in a gay couple may want to provide sperm to fertilize the eggs available for surrogacy, and if a twin pregnancy resulted, then each man would be a genetic father. In this scenario, clients must consider how they would feel about bringing up two children with a different genetic relationship to each of them. Further, if the transfer of mixed-sperm embryos resulted in a single pregnancy, the gay couple needs to consider the possibility of having a child who may, or may not, be their genetic offspring.

Many countries do not allow access to ART treatments or adoption by same-sex couples or single unmarried women whatever their sexuality.[31] Therefore, states in the United States, such as California, that do allow such access may be visited by "reproductive tourists" who have the financial means to pay for treatment.

While clients and participants in ART programs are required to have a legal contract in place prior to proceeding, depending on what U.S. state they come from (and what state the baby is delivered in), same-sex couples using ART services may, or may not, be able to have the names of both parents on the child's birth certificate.[32] Only some states allow same-sex couples to marry and consent together to be recipients of ART, or allow for both same-sex partners to register as parents under two-parent adoption law. Second-parent adoptions enable a co-parent (non–birth parent or social parent) to establish legal parent status without ending the legal rights or responsibilities of the child's other legal parent. Patterson reported that second-parent adoptions have been granted in twenty-six states and the District of Columbia.[33] The American Academy of Pediatrics recently reaffirmed its earlier policy statement on the medical value of co-parent or second-parent adoption by same-sex couples.[34]

Planned Lesbian or Gay Parenting through Adoption

Another route to parenthood for lesbian and gay parents has been adopting a biologically unrelated child who cannot be cared for by birth family members (stranger adoption). Adoption is often a first-choice route to parenthood for lesbians and gay men, in contrast to many heterosexual women and men who consider adoption only after finding that they could not have biologically related children.[35] Openly out same-sex couples have completed "stranger adoptions" in some U.S. states, for example, California, Massachusetts, and New York. Nevertheless, adoption law and practice vary among the states with regard to lesbians and gay men as potential adoptive parents.[36] In some states, single lesbian or gay parents have accomplished adoption only because their sexual orientation has not come to light.[37]

More than 100,000 children in the United States remain in foster care after having been legally approved for adoption. In particular, a disproportionate number of African American, Hispanic, or mixed-race children wait to be placed, as they exceed the number of racial minority prospective adopters available.[38] The available evidence suggests that lesbians wanting to become adoptive parents may be a source of potential homes as Caucasian lesbian couples waiting to adopt appeared to be more open to transracial adoption than were heterosexual couples.[39] Lesbians in Goldberg's study also pointed to diversity in their communities and the perceived likelihood of extended family support as reasons supporting their willingness to consider transracial adoption.

Around 60 percent of U.S. adoption agencies have approved nonheterosexual women and men as potential adopters, and nearly 40 percent of agencies record having placed children with them.[40] Goldberg, Downing, and Sauck found that many of the thirty-five lesbian couples they interviewed wanted to approach adoption agencies by being open that they were a lesbian couple seeking to adopt.[41] However, unless the couple was working with a GLBT-affirming adoption agency, being fully "out" during the adoption process risked losing the chance to adopt.[42] This led to couples compromising on being out, often to the disadvantage of their relationship, because of the legal and social realities they faced.

Lesbian or Gay Parenting and Children's Development

Research into lesbian and gay parenting has boomed in recent years. While many studies have focused on the parents' experiences in families led by lesbian mothers or gay fathers, other research teams have investigated children's psychosocial and psychosexual development. A number of influential reviews have evaluated and detailed the research on developmental outcomes and concluded that parental sexual orientation makes little difference to key developmental outcomes.[43] My approach in this chapter is not to review the field comprehensively. Instead, I have directed attention to key studies in the area. Mostly these studies have been able effectively to evaluate developmental outcomes for children, because they have directly compared outcomes for children brought up by lesbian or gay parents with outcomes for children brought up by heterosexual parents under matched (similar) circumstances.

Previously, one major criticism of research into developmental outcomes for children raised by lesbian or gay parents (as noted in chapter 15) was that the findings were based on small, self-selected samples of mainly Caucasian, university-educated, and relatively affluent lesbian-led families.[44] Relatively little was known about other demographic groups. Research studies now have begun to examine whether results are representative of the wider population. Examples include a study by Wainright and colleagues using the U.S. National Longitudinal Study of Adolescent Health (Add Health) database and a study by Golombok and colleagues of five- to seven-year-old children in the United Kingdom drawing about half of its lesbian-led families group from the Avon Longitudinal Study of Parents and Children database.[45]

Drawing from the Add Health national database of U.S. high school students, Wainright and colleagues found that forty-four adolescents from households headed by female same-sex couples were performing well in terms of school adjustment and standard measures of psychosocial adjustment[46] and displayed low levels of delinquent behavior, substance use, and rates of victimization.[47] Adolescents from same-sex-parented families recorded similar scores to a matched group of adolescents from heterosexual two-parent households on these outcome measures and also on measures of romantic relationships, sexual behavior, and positive parent-adolescent relationships. Thus, family type did not seem to be associated with developmental outcomes, but the quality of parenting did. Across different family types, parents who described closer relationships with their adolescent sons and daughters were less likely to have adolescents who reported delinquent behavior or substance use.[48] Furthermore, when parents reported more satisfying relationships with their adolescent offspring, their sons and daughters reported better engagement with their high school.[49]

Findings from these two reports from a nationally representative U.S. Add Health database have gone a long way to quell doubts over extrapolating from the results of convenience samples.[50] Moreover, most previous studies concentrated on investigating the well-being of younger children and were unable to examine whether parental sexual orientation would only later become an issue for their adolescent offspring. The Add Health studies suggest that adolescents do not have more difficulties growing up in female two-parent households than in heterosexual two-parent families.

Nevertheless, conclusions drawn from the Add Health database were limited in other ways, as the authors acknowledged: findings were based on parent and adolescent self-report standard questionnaires, gathered at a single point in time, and the small sample size did not permit investigation of demographic subgroups.[51] Moreover, survey questions did not ask about parental sexual identity. Thus identification of same-sex-parented households relied on parental reports of being in a marriage or marriage-like relationship with someone of the same sex. To utilize research findings to address legal and policy questions, it is essential to examine findings from small-scale surveys that investigate household composition and route to parenthood.

Lesbian and Gay Parenting after Heterosexual Separation and Divorce

Beginning in the 1980s, studies were published on the psychological well-being of children who had lived with their lesbian mother after their mother's and father's relationship ended. These studies focused on the quality of postdivorce parenting and children's emotional, social, and psychosexual development, as these aspects were debated in court cases when postdivorce custody and access were denied to lesbian mothers. The investigation by Green and colleagues was one of the largest and most rigorous of such studies.[52] Comparing questionnaire data from fifty single lesbian mothers with a matched control group of forty single heterosexual mothers across the United States, Green and his colleagues found much similarity in the parenting, marital history, and living situations of the mothers and no significant differences between boys or girls (aged three to eleven years) in either family group on intelligence test scores, perceptions of peer group popularity, or indications of emotional difficulties on a projective test. None of the children in the sample met criteria for gender identity problems, and boys from either type of family did not differ in their gender role development. However, girls in lesbian-led families tended to indicate a wider range of games, toys, leisure time activities, and job preferences than did girls from heterosexual mother families.

Other studies have reported similar findings. For example, Golombok and colleagues found no differences between lesbian and single heterosexual mother families after divorce on the psychological adjustment of either mothers or children.[53] Many children who participated in that study were reinterviewed as young adults in the British Longitudinal Study of Lesbian Mother Families.[54] Findings from this later study indicated that children from lesbian mother families continued to be in good mental health in adulthood. The sons and daughters studied generally retained the close childhood relationships they had with their mothers, and young people in lesbian-led households recorded more positive relationships with their mother's female partner than were reported by young people in the comparison group when they talked about their mother's new male partner. The majority of the young adults from lesbian mother families identified as heterosexual; only two young women identified as lesbian.[55] No family type differences were found between the two groups of families in overall rates of being teased or bullied. Nevertheless, young people from lesbian mother families, particularly young men rather than young women and those from working-class rather than middle-class backgrounds, tended to be more likely to recollect having been teased about their own sexuality, or were perhaps more sensitive to this issue.[56] These detailed analyses suggest that parental sexual orientation in and of itself had limited association with young adult developmental outcomes. What seemed to have a bigger influence on the way young persons experienced their family life was the wider social context in which they grew up and how their family handled this. For example, young adults who had difficulties accepting their mother's lesbian identity were more likely to have been teased by peers about their own sexuality, and this problem was more acute if their mother had not been empathetic to the young person's peer dilemmas.

A limited amount of research evidence has been collected on the development of children with gay fathers, possibly because most of the gay fathers surveyed in the United Kingdom or the United States were nonresidential parents with children visiting rather than residing with them.[57] This may have helped the children to manage possible peer group stigma. Few of the fathers in Barrett and Tasker's survey reported that their children had experienced any peer relationship difficulties.[58] Around 20 percent of children in Wyers's survey had experienced peer group problems, but around 75 percent of gay fathers reported that children had been concerned that they might have difficulties.[59] Bailey and colleagues found that most of the fathers they surveyed reported that their adult sons identified as heterosexual, with only 9 percent of the sample of just over eighty sons considered as gay or bisexual.[60]

To date no published study has systematically examined the psychological adjustment of children with gay fathers. However, questionnaire data from fathers and qualitative data from interviews with fathers or their adolescent and young adult offspring give no indication of mental health problems.[61] Bigner and Jacobsen conducted a postal survey of gay and heterosexual fathers parenting children after divorce.[62] Compared with the heterosexual fathers surveyed, the gay fathers tended to have a more appropriate, authoritative parenting style (i.e., were more responsive to their children's needs but also set stricter limits on their children's behavior). Gay fathers also reported being more cautious than the heterosexual fathers in showing physical affection to their partner if their children were present. Other reports have indicated that gay fathers with male partners report fewer parenting difficulties compared with unpartnered gay fathers and that integration of their gay partner into family life was associated with higher ratings of satisfaction with family life by gay fathers and their children.[63]

Planned Lesbian and Gay Parenting

To date, only a handful of published reports have focused on planned gay fatherhood.[64] These reports have mostly examined the perspective of the men parenting rather than assessed children's developmental outcomes and so have not been reviewed here.

Several studies have investigated the development of children born to lesbian mothers via donor insemination. For example, findings from the Contemporary Families Study detail the family relationships and well-being of boys and girls aged around seven who were conceived via donor insemination at a single clinic in California.[65] The sample comprised thirty-four families headed by lesbian couples, twenty-one families headed by single lesbian mothers, and thirty-five families headed by heterosexual couples or heterosexual single mothers. The groups sampled enabled controlled comparisons between parental sexual orientation and number of parents in the home. Parental and teacher reported scores on a standard measure of children's psychological adjustment were similar across all types of families and fell within the normal range of scores on the CBCL. What did seem to be associated with children's psychological adjustment problems were parental reports of higher levels of parenting distress, more difficult parent-child relationships, and, for couples in the sample, lower levels of satisfaction with their relationship with their partner. Findings from a study comparing lesbian and heterosexual two-parent families in the Netherlands also confirm that child adjustment is not associated with family type but is instead linked to quality of parenting and level of satisfaction with a partner's co-parenting.[66]

The Contemporary Families Study research team investigated the division of household labor in couple-headed families.[67] These statistical analyses revealed that lesbian couples shared child care tasks more evenly than did heterosexual couples. Other studies also note this more equitable division of labor.[68] This underlines the generally high levels of involvement in parenting by nonbiological parents in planned lesbian-led families.

A longitudinal study in the United Kingdom has compared the development of children raised in fatherless families (children raised in single- or two-parent lesbian mother families or by single heterosexual mothers) with the development of children raised in father-present two-parent families through childhood,[69] adolescence,[70] and early adulthood.[71] No group differences in adolescent self-esteem scores were found between children brought up in different types of families.[72] Earlier tentative findings of difference in children's self-perceptions of physical and cognitive competence were not repeated.[73] Both sets of children raised in fatherless families continued to retain closer relationships with their mothers than did children in heterosexual two-parent families, but birth mothers in fatherless families also reported more severe disputes with their early adolescent sons and daughters. MacCallum and Golombok did find differences related to family type on adolescent gender role development: adolescent sons in either type of fatherless family reported more feminine-type, but no less masculine-type, gender role behavior compared with sons brought up by heterosexual mothers and fathers.[74]

Data from the NLLFS collected when the children were age ten found that children with lesbian mothers generally did not have psychological adjustment difficulties.[75] Nevertheless, NLLFS ten-year-olds who had experienced peer group prejudice were more likely to have emotional and behavioral problems reported.[76] For adolescents in the NLLFS, at age seventeen the association between experience of peer group prejudice and psychological adjustment was neutralized by positive parent-child relationships.[77]

Findings from the sample recruited by Golombok and colleagues when the sons and daughters were followed up at around age nineteen indicated similar young adult outcome profiles on peer relationships and psychological adjustment across all three family types.[78] Mothers in fatherless families reported being more emotionally involved in the lives of the young adult children than mothers in heterosexual two-parent families. Nevertheless, young adults' perceptions of how close they were to their mother did not differ by family type. At the start of young adulthood, only one of the offspring interviewed identified as nonheterosexual (a bisexual woman from a lesbian-led family). Data from the NLLFS sample at age seventeen indicated that growing up in a lesbian-led family was associated with a later-than-average age at first heterosexual contact, while daughters from lesbian mother families were more likely to have a same-sex experience in comparison with a U.S. national sample.[79]

Reviewing the evidence from different studies, Biblarz and Stacey have argued that lesbian couples with children may be more likely to separate than heterosexual parents.[80] Nevertheless, it remains to be seen how changing legislative provisions for same-sex marriage or civil unions will influence this finding. Recent data from the NLLFS indicate that, if lesbian couples do separate, then most mothers are able to organize shared residency, which is more likely to happen if the co-mother had legally adopted their child.[81] Adolescent psychological adjustment did not vary with shared residency or co-parent adoption, but a higher percentage of adolescents reported closeness to both parents if co-mothers had adopted.

Lesbian and Gay Adoptive Parents

Carefully designed studies have examined the well-being of children adopted by lesbian or gay parents by comparing their developmental outcomes with those of a matched group of children adopted by heterosexual parents. Erich, Leung, and Kindle compared lesbian, gay, and heterosexual adoptive parents' reports of their children's behavior, finding no differences in levels of behavioral problems across the three types of family.[82] Parental sexual orientation also was not associated with how helpful adoptive parents thought their extended family support networks were. Another study, by Leung and colleagues, compared scores on standard family functioning tests as reported by lesbian or gay adoptive parents and heterosexual adoptive parents.[83] Generally, adoptive families were functioning effectively, and scores did not differ by family type. The only exception was families with late-adopted children, where lesbian or gay adoptive parents reported more positive family functioning scores than did heterosexual adoptive parents. Another study found that the lesbian and gay adoptive parents who reported the highest levels of family functioning also tended to be those who had adopted sibling groups and/or older children, often with preadoption histories of abuse.[84] Late-adopted children (often with preadoption trauma) or sibling groups are usually the hardest children to place for adoption.

Data from lesbian and gay adoptive parents analyzed by Ryan similarly have indicated that they generally report few parenting difficulties, despite many of the children in these families having experienced trauma prior to adoption.[85] In another study, Ryan and Cash found that the majority of lesbian or gay adoptive parents they sampled reported that their children had not been teased or stigmatized because they had been adopted or because of having lesbian or gay parents.[86]

Conclusion

My review has surveyed lesbian and gay parenting across the diverse circumstances of parenting after heterosexual separation and divorce, planned lesbian and gay parenting through ART, and parenting after adoption. General data on the psychological well-being of children brought up in families led by lesbian or gay parents have undermined arguments limiting access to ART, denial of adoption, and restricting custody and access on grounds of parental sexual orientation. Recent research indicates that parenting is on the future agendas of many young adult lesbians and gay men.[87]

In many states in the United States and countries under the European Convention of Human Rights, legislation has evolved to maintain the connection between lesbian and gay parents and their children from previous heterosexual partnerships. Laws are also moving slowly to acknowledge connections between nonbiological parents and children in families formed by lesbian and gay parents through adoption and ART. Further legal change is necessary to recognize the diversity of needs of children in families led by nonheterosexual parents. For example, it would be advantageous to develop a consistent legal framework on the position of a known donor regarding a child conceived via gamete donation. Given the research evidence on the contributions made by co-parents in children's lives, it would also be valuable to have a way of legally acknowledging the role of a nonbiological co-parent in the child's life, irrespective of the co-parent's marriage, civil partnership, or coresidency with the child's biological parent. In the United Kingdom, progress toward this has been achieved through the use of parental responsibility orders issued under the Children Act,[88] which enable more than one adult of the same sex simultaneously to hold parental responsibility.

Polikoff has argued that parenting and caregiving are the elements of family life that need to be prioritized in family law, which should focus on the varied needs of different types of families rather than regarding marriage (either same-sex or different-sex) as the bedrock of family policy.[89] Research on lesbian and gay parenting and child development is congruent with this position in that family type per se makes little difference to children's well-being. What matters instead are family processes, acces socioeconomic resources, and how the social systems that surround family respond.

Notes

1. Andrew Cherlin, "Remarriage as an Incomplete Institution," *American Journal of Sociology* 84 (Nov. 1978): 634.

2. Andrew J. Cherlin, "The Deinstitutionalization of American Marriage," *Journal of Marriage and Family* 66 (Nov. 2004): 848.

3. I focus on reviewing lesbian and gay parenting because published empirical research examining children's development so far has investigated outcomes only for children raised in families defined by lesbian and gay parents. Research addressing other ways of nonheterosexual parenting by bisexual or queer parents is vitally needed. Arlene Istar Lev, "How Queer!—The Development of Gender Identity and Sexual Orientation in LBGTQ-Headed Families," *Family Process* 49 (Sept. 2010): 268.

4. Gary J. Gates and Jason Ost, *The Gay and Lesbian Atlas* (Washington, DC: Urban Institute Press, 2004).

5. Gary J. Gates, "Diversity among Same-Sex Couples and Their Children," in *American Families: A Multicultural Reader*, 2nd ed., ed. Stephanie Coontz, Maya Parson, and Gabrielle Raley (New York: Routledge, 2008), 394–399.

6. Gary J. Gates and Adam P. Romero, "Parenting by Gay Men and Lesbians: Beyond the Current Research," in *Marriage and Family: Complexities and Perspectives*, ed. H. Elizabeth Peters and Claire M. Kamp Dush (New York: Columbia University Press, 2009), 227–243.

7. Gates, "Diversity among Same-Sex Couples."

8. Gates and Romero, "Parenting by Gay Men and Lesbians."

9. Virginia Casper and Stephen B. Schultz, *Gay Parents / Straight Schools: Building Communication and Trust* (New York: Teachers College Press, 1999); Fiona Tasker, "Lesbian Mothers, Gay Fathers and Their Children: A Review," *Journal of Developmental and Behavioral Pediatrics* 26 (June 2005): 224.

10. Danielle N. Shapiro, Christopher Peterson, and Abigail J. Stewart, "Legal and Social Contexts and Mental Health among Lesbian and Heterosexual Mothers," *Journal of Family Psychology* 23 (Apr. 2009): 255.

11. Henry M. W. Bos et al., "Children in Planned Lesbian Families: A Cross-Cultural Comparison between the United States and the Netherlands," *American Journal of Orthopsychiatry* 78 (Apr. 2008): 211.

12. Thomas M. Achenbach and Craig Edelbrock, *Manual for the Child Behavior Checklist and Revised Child Behavior Profile* (Burlington: University of Vermont Department of Psychiatry, 1983).

13. I have not included taking parental responsibility via fostering children in my review. Few studies exist in this important area. Stephen Hicks, "Maternal Men—Perverts and Deviants? Making Sense of Gay Men as Foster Carers and Adopters," *Journal of GLBT Family Studies* 2, no. 1 (2006): 93; Damien W. Riggs, "Developmentalism and the Rhetoric of Best Interests of the Child: Challenging Heteronormative Construc-

tions of Families and Parenting in Foster Care," *Journal of GLBT Family Studies* 2, no. 2 (2006): 57.

14. Cf. Jacobson v. Jacobson, 314 N.W.2d 78 (N.D. 1981) with Damron v. Damron, 670 N.W.2d 871 (N.D. 2003).

15. Children's Act, ch. 41, sec. 1 (1989).

16. Salgueiro Da Silva Mouta v. Portugal, 1999–IX Eur. Ct. H.R. 309.

17. Robert E. Oliphant and Nancy Ver Steegh, *Family Law: Examples and Explanations*, 2nd ed. (New York: Wolters Kluwer Law and Business Aspen Publishers, 2007).

18. Patricia M. Logue, "The Rights of Lesbian and Gay Parents and Their Children," *Journal of the American Academy of Matrimonial Lawyers* 18 (2002): 95.

19. Lawrence v. Texas, 539 U.S. 558 (2003).

20. Charlotte J. Patterson, "Children of Lesbian and Gay Parents: Psychology, Law, and Policy," *American Psychologist* 64 (Nov. 2009): 727.

21. Mark Strasser, "Fit to Be Tied: On Custody, Discretion, and Sexual Orientation," *American University Law Review* 46 (Feb. 1997): 841; Susan Golombok and Fiona Tasker, "Gay Fathers," in *The Role of the Father in Child Development*, 5th ed., ed. Michael E. Lamb (Hoboken, NJ: Wiley, 2010), 319–340.

22. The Ethics Committee of the American Society for Reproductive Medicine, "Access to Fertility Treatment by Gays, Lesbians, and Unmarried Persons," *Fertility and Sterility* 92 (Oct. 2009): 1190, 1190.

23. Charles P. Kindregan Jr. and Maureen McBrien, *Assisted Reproductive Technology: A Lawyer's Guide to Emerging Law and Science*, 2nd ed. (Chicago: American Bar Association Section of Family Law, 2011), 245.

24. See Uniform Parentage Act, sec. 5 (1973); Uniform Parentage Act, sec. 702 (2000).

25. Deborah Forman, *Using a Sperm Donor: Understanding the Legal Risks and Challenges*, May 9, 2011, http://www.theafa.org/article/using-a-known-sperm-donor-understanding-the-legal-risks-and-challenges/ (accessed Nov. 19, 2011).

26. Ibid.

27. Nanette K. Gartrell et al., "The National Lesbian Family Study: 1. Interviews with Prospective Mothers," *American Journal of Orthopsychiatry* 66 (Apr. 1996): 272; Abbie E. Goldberg and Katherine R. Allen, "Imagining Men: Lesbian Mothers' Perceptions of Male Involvement during the Transition to Parenthood," *Journal of Marriage and Family* 69 (May 2007): 352.

28. Nanette K. Gartrell et al., "The National Lesbian Family Study: 4. Interviews with the 10-Year-Old Children," *American Journal of Orthopsychiatry* 75 (Oct. 2005): 518.

29. Dorothy A. Greenfeld and Emre Seli, "Gay Men Choosing Parenthood through Assisted Reproduction: Medical and Psychosocial Considerations," *Fertility and Sterility* 95 (Jan. 2011): 225.

30. Ibid.

31. Deborah Smith, "What Are the Reproductive Options When a Same-Sex Couple Wants a Family?," *Sexuality, Reproduction and Menopause* 9, no. 3 (2011): 30.

32. Greenfeld and Seli, "Gay Men Choosing Parenthood through Assisted Reproduction."

33. Patterson, "Children of Lesbian and Gay Parents."

34. American Academy of Pediatrics, "Policy Statement: Coparent or Second Parent Adoption by Same-Sex Couples," *Pediatrics* 109 (Feb. 2002): 339; American Academy of Pediatrics, "Policy Statement—AAP Publications Retired and Reaffirmed," *Pediatrics* 125 (Mar. 2010): 444.

35. Gerald P. Mallon, "The Home Study Assessment Process for Gay, Lesbian, Bisexual, and Transgender Prospective Foster and Adoptive Families," *Journal of GLBT Family Studies* 7 (2011): 9.

36. Kimberly D. Richman, *Courting Change: Queer Parents, Judges, and the Transformation of the American Family Law* (New York: NYU Press, 2009).

37. Patterson, "Children of Lesbian and Gay Parents."

38. David B. Brodzinsky and Evan B. Donaldson Adoption Institute, *Expanding the Resources for Children III: Research-Based Practices in Adoption by Gays and Lesbians*, Oct. 2011, http://www.adoptioninstitute.org/publications/2011_10_Expanding_Resources_BestPractices.pdf (accessed Nov. 19, 2011).

39. Abbie E. Goldberg, "Lesbian and Heterosexual Preadoptive Couples' Openness to Transracial Adoption," *American Journal of Orthopsychiatry* 79 (Jan. 2009): 103.

40. Brodzinsky and Evan B. Donaldson Adoption Institute, *Expanding the Resources for Children III*.

41. Abbie E. Goldberg, Jordan B. Downing, and Christine C. Sauck, "Choices, Challenges, and Tensions," *Adoption Quarterly* 10, no. 2 (2008): 33.

42. Brodzinsky and Evan B. Donaldson Adoption Institute, *Expanding the Resources for Children III*.

43. Alicia Crowl, Soyeon Ahn, and Jean Baker, "A Meta-analysis of Developmental Outcomes for Children of Same-Sex and Heterosexual Parents," *Journal of GLBT Family Studies* 4 (2008): 385; Ellen C. Perrin and the American Academy of Pediatrics Committee on the Psychosocial Aspects of Child and Family Health, "Technical Report: Coparent or Second-Parent Adoption by Same-Sex Parents," *Pediatrics* 109 (Feb. 2002): 341; Fiona Tasker and Charlotte J. Patterson, "Research on Gay and Lesbian Parenting: Retrospect and Prospect," *Journal of GLBT Family Studies* 3, nos. 2–3 (2007): 9; Cynthia J. Telingator and Charlotte J. Patterson, "Children and Adolescents of Lesbian and Gay Parents," *Journal of the American Academy for Child and Adolescent Psychiatry* 47 (Dec. 2008): 1364.

44. Norman Anderssen, Christine Amlie, and Erling A. Ytteroy, "Outcomes for Children with Lesbian or Gay Parents: A Review of Studies from 1978 to 2000," *Scandinavian Journal of Psychology* 43 (Sept. 2002): 335. See also Elizabeth Marquardt, "Of Human Bonding: Integrating the Needs and Desires of Women, Men, and the Children Their Unions Produce," 326 (this volume).

45. Jennifer L. Wainright, Stephen T. Russell, and Charlotte J. Patterson, "Psychosocial Adjustment, School Outcomes, and Romantic Relationships of Adolescents with Same-Sex Parents," *Child Development* 75 (Dec. 2004): 1886; Susan Golombok et al., "Children with Lesbian Parents: A Community Study," *Developmental Psychology* 39 (Jan. 2003): 20.

46. Wainright et al., "Psychosocial Adjustment," 1895.

47. Jennifer L. Wainright and Charlotte J. Patterson, "Delinquency, Victimization, and Substance Use among Adolescents with Female Same-Sex Parents," *Journal of Family Psychology* 20 (Sept. 2006): 526, 527–528.

48. Ibid., 528.

49. Wainright et al., "Psychosocial Adjustment," 1893–1894.

50. Wainright and Patterson, "Delinquency, Victimization, and Substance Use"; Wainright et al., "Psychosocial Adjustment."

51. Wainright et al., "Psychosocial Adjustment."

52. Richard Green et al., "Lesbian Mothers and Their Children: A Comparison with Solo Parent Heterosexual Mothers and Their Children," *Archives of Sexual Behavior* 15 (Apr. 1986): 167.

53. Susan Golombok, Ann Spencer, and Michael Rutter, "Children in Lesbian and Single-Parent Households: Psychosexual and Psychiatric Appraisal," *Journal of Child Psychology and Psychiatry* 24 (Oct. 1983): 551.

54. Fiona L. Tasker and Susan Golombok, "Adults Raised as Children in Lesbian Families," *American Journal of Orthopsychiatry* 65 (Apr. 1995): 203; Fiona L. Tasker and Susan Golombok, *Growing Up in a Lesbian Family: Effects on Child Development* (New York: Guilford Press, 1997).

55. Susan Golombok and Fiona L. Tasker, "Do Parents Influence the Sexual Orientation of Their Children? Findings from a Longitudinal Study of Lesbian Families," *Developmental Psychology* 32 (Jan. 1996): 3.

56. Tasker and Golombok, "Adults Raised as Children," 210; Tasker and Golombok, *Growing Up in a Lesbian Family*, 87–88.

57. Helen Barrett and Fiona L. Tasker, "Growing Up with a Gay Parent: Views of 101 Gay Fathers on Their Sons' and Daughters' Experiences," *Educational and Child Psychology* 18, no. 1 (2001): 62; Norman L. Wyers, "Homosexuality in the Family: Lesbian and Gay Spouses," *Social Work* 32 (Mar./Apr. 1987): 143.

58. Barrett and Tasker, "Growing Up With a Gay Parent."

59. Wyers, "Homosexuality in the Family," 146.

60. J. Michael Bailey et al., "Sexual Orientation of Adult Sons of Gay Fathers," *Developmental Psychology* 31 (Jan. 1995): 124, 126.

61. Barrett and Tasker, "Growing Up With a Gay Parent"; Frederick W. Bozett, "Gay Fathers," in *Gay and Lesbian Parents*, ed. Frederick W. Bozett (New York: Praeger, 1987), 3–22; Frederick W. Bozett, "Children of Gay Fathers," in Bozett, *Gay and Lesbian Parents*, 39–57; Brian Miller, "Gay Fathers and Their Children," *Family Coordinator* 28 (Oct. 1979): 544.

62. Jerry J. Bigner and R. Brooke Jacobsen, "Parenting Behaviors of Homosexual and Heterosexual Fathers," in *Homosexuality and the Family*, ed. Frederick W. Bozett (Binghamton, NY: Haworth Press, 1989), 173–186; Jerry J. Bigner and R. Brooke Jacobsen, "Adult Responses to Child Behavior and Attitudes toward Fathering: Gay and Nongay Fathers," *Journal of Homosexuality* 23, no. 3 (1992): 99.

63. Barrett and Tasker, "Growing Up with a Gay Parent"; Margaret Crosbie-Burnett and Lawrence Helmbrecht, "A Descriptive Empirical Study of Gay Male Stepfamilies," *Family Relations* 42 (July 1993): 256.

64. Golombok and Tasker, "Gay Fathers."

65. Raymond W. Chan, Barbara Raboy, and Charlotte J. Patterson, "Psychosocial Adjustment among Children Conceived via Donor Insemination by Lesbian and Heterosexual Mothers," *Child Development* 69 (Apr. 1998): 443.

66. Henry M. W. Bos, Frank van Balen, and Dymphna C. van den Boom, "Child Adjustment and Parenting in Planned Lesbian-Parent Families," *American Journal of Orthopsychiatry* 77 (Jan. 2007): 38.

67. Raymond W. Chan et al., "Division of Labor among Lesbian and Heterosexual Parents: Associations with Children's Adjustment," *Journal of Family Psychology* 12 (Sept. 1998): 402.

68. Timothy J. Biblarz and Judith Stacey, "How Does the Gender of Parents Matter?" *Journal of Marriage and Family* 72 (Feb. 2010): 3.

69. Susan Golombok, Fiona L. Tasker, and Clare Murray, "Children Raised in Fatherless Families from Infancy: Family Relationships and the Socioemotional Development of Children of Lesbian and Single Heterosexual Mothers," *Journal of Child Psychology and Psychiatry* 38 (Oct. 1997): 783.

70. Fiona MacCallum and Susan Golombok, "Children Raised in Fatherless Families from Infancy: A Follow-Up of Children of Lesbian and Single Heterosexual Mothers at Early Adolescence," *Journal of Child Psychology and Psychiatry* 45 (Nov. 2004): 1407.

71. Susan Golombok and Shirlene Badger, "Children Raised in Mother-Headed Families from Infancy: A Follow-Up of Children of Lesbian and Single Heterosexual Mothers, at Early Adulthood," *Human Reproduction* 25 (Jan. 2010): 150.

72. MacCallum and Golombok, "Children Raised in Fatherless Families from Infancy," 1415.

73. Golombok et al., "Children Raised in Fatherless Families from Infancy," 788.

74. MacCallum and Golombok, "Children Raised in Fatherless Families from Infancy," 1415.

75. Gartrell et al., "The National Lesbian Family Study: 4. Interviews with the 10-Year-Old Children," 518.

76. Bos et al., "Children in Planned Lesbian Families."

77. Henry M. W. Bos and Nanette K. Gartrell, "Adolescents of the USA National Longitudinal Lesbian Family Study: Can Family Characteristics Counteract the Negative Effects of Stigmatization?," *Family Process* 49 (Dec. 2010): 559, 566–567.

78. Golombok and Badger, "Children Raised in Mother-Headed Families from Infancy."

79. Nanette K. Gartrell, Henry M. W. Bos, and Naomi G. Goldberg, "Adolescents of the U.S. National Longitudinal Lesbian Family Study: Sexual Orientation, Sexual Behavior, and Sexual Risk Exposure," *Archives of Sexual Behavior* 40 (Dec. 2011): 1199, 1202.

80. Biblarz and Stacey, "How Does the Gender of Parents Matter?," 11–12.

81. Nanette K. Gartrell et al., "Family Characteristics, Custody Arrangements, and Adolescent Psychological Well-Being after Lesbian Mothers Break Up," *Family Relations* 60 (Dec. 2011): 572, 576–577.

82. Stephen Erich, Patrick Leung, and Peter Kindle, "A Comparative Analysis of Adoptive Family Functioning with Gay, Lesbian, and Heterosexual Parents and Their Children," *Journal of GLBT Family Studies* 1, no. 4 (2005): 43.

83. Ibid.

84. Stephen Erich et al., "Gay and Lesbian Adoptive Families: An Exploratory Study of Family Functioning, Adoptive Child's Behavior, and Familial Support Networks," *Journal of Family Social Work* 9, no. 1 (2005): 17.

85. Scott D. Ryan, "Parent-Child Interaction Styles between Gay and Lesbian Parents and Their Adopted Children," *Journal of GLBT Family Studies* 3, nos. 2–3 (2007): 105.

86. Scott D. Ryan and Scottye Cash, "Adoptive Families Headed by Gay or Lesbian Parents: A Threat . . . or Hidden Resource?" *University of Florida Journal of Law and Public Policy* 15 (2004): 443.

87. Rachel G. Riskind and Charlotte J. Patterson, "Parenting Intentions and Desires among Childless Lesbian, Gay, and Heterosexual Individuals," *Journal of Family Psychology* 24 (Feb. 2010): 78.

88. See Children and Family Court Advisory and Support Service, "Contact and Residence," http://www.cafcass.gov.uk/about_cafcass/the_law_about_children/contact_and_ residence.aspx (accessed May 23, 2012) (discussing the use of parental responsibility orders in the United Kingdom under Sections 3 and 4 of the Children Act 1989).

89. Nancy D. Polikoff, *Beyond (Straight and Gay) Marriage: Valuing All Families under the Law* (Boston: Beacon Press, 2008).

Attachment

(How Much) Does Biology Matter?

PART FIVE

Biological and Psychological Dimensions of Integrative Attachments

Terence E. Hébert, Ellen Moss, Daniel Cere, and Hyun Song

John Bowlby's experiences with institutionalized orphans, severely deprived of maternal care, convinced him that prevailing theories were inadequate to explain the developmental sequelae he observed.[1] The leading explanation of the origins of the infant's relationship with primary caregivers maintained that the bond was a by-product of association of mothers with feeding.[2] However, serious short- and long-term socioemotional problems of children raised in institutions convinced him that substitute, multiple caregivers who provided adequate nutrition to infants could not replace biological mothers. He suggested that intact parent-child bonds were as important to child development as adequate physical care,[3] and that foster care could not adequately support cognitive, social, and emotional development.

In *Attachment and Loss*,[4] Bowlby posited that the "ultimate outcome" for all behavioral systems was "survival of the genes an individual is carrying," anchoring his theory in evolutionary biology.[5] Although a primary function of attachment is to protect infants by maintaining physical proximity to caregivers, it is also likely associated with wider adaptive goals, such as facilitation of social integration and nurturing. The social and cognitive skills necessary to accomplish this include learning cooperation and competition during preschool and school-age periods and creating intimate relationships necessary for reproduction and adequate parenthood.[6] Biologically based attachment has far-reaching implications for long-term development of individuals and kinship.

The quality of early attachment relationships is an important predictor of social, emotional, and cognitive development.[7] Further, recent work on the biological foundations of attachment relationships suggests that parenting is intrinsically connected to biological processes in both parent and child. Interconnections among genetics, epigenetics, and rearing experiences are far more intricate and complex than our description reflects, with continual interplay between behavioral, environmental, and/or biological mechanisms in both parent and child.

Here, we examine the biology of attachment, with a focus on the development of bonds between parent and child, reviewing literature regarding maternal attachment. Recent studies indicate that offspring-father interactions are important and may lead to changes in the neuronal architecture of fathers. Much of this work on attachment was recently summarized in an excellent book.[8] We are interested in framing the discussion in terms of possible long-term biological consequences of changing parental structures. We examine the role of secure and insecure attachment relationships in promoting offspring survival and maintenance of kinship. We strike a note of caution with respect to changes in parenting structures and practices that might threaten biological connections within kinship systems.

The Biological Bases of Attachment

The modern synthesis of evolutionary theory has become the centerpiece underlying the entire scope of biology. However, the rapid rate of scientific advances has not kept pace with societal changes and the policy decisions taken to engineer them. Significant changes in parenting structures have been made for a number of reasons—the need for both parents to work, wider separation of extended families as children seek work far from home, changes in divorce laws, changes in the definition of marriage, as well as the desire of same-sex couples to raise children.

Changes in parenting structures and in policies center upon adults and what is best or most desirable for them. They either assume the new arrangements have little or no impact on children or ignore children's rights completely. Liberalization of divorce laws to end "bad" marriages is one example that had wide-reaching and unexpected consequences for children and families. Few changes in policy or practice consider the relevant biological dimensions, especially regarding how environment and early life influences shape outcomes for offspring.

The Pair-Bond and Children

Monogamous arrangements occur when males and females mate exclusively (or almost) and generally undertake biparental care of offspring. One well-studied model of the physiology underlying monogamy in mammals compares closely related voles; the monogamous prairie vole is generally biparental while montane and meadow voles are nonmonogamous.[9] Two neuropeptide hormones, oxytocin (OT) and arginine vasopressin (AVP), have been identified as critical for partner preference formation. OT is also critical for mother-infant bonding in sheep,[10] while AVP has been implicated in a number of male-specific social behaviors, including parental attachment. Both hormones play roles in the formation of attachment in either sex, although OT seems to be more important in females while the converse is true for AVP.[11] Precise molecular mechanisms underlying gender differences remain elusive as levels of receptors for both hormones are similar in the relevant brain regions of males and females. Molecular complexities in the underlying signaling machinery associated with these receptors, when known, will reveal the basis for these differences. Interestingly, the distribution of receptors for these hormones is distinct in brains of monogamous versus nonmonogamous voles. Anatomical studies demonstrated higher levels of the oxytocin receptor (OTR) in two brain regions, the striatum (caudate putamen and nucleus accumbens), and higher levels of a particular subtype of receptor for AVP, the V1a receptor (V1aR) in ventral pallidum, medial amygdala, and mediodorsal thalamus in pair-bonding prairie voles. Pair-bonding also seems to involve conditioned learning and dopamine (especially within the nucleus accumbens) and is critical for partner preference formation in prairie voles.[12]

Oxytocin "knockout" or gene-deleted mice fail to recognize individuals to whom they have been previously exposed[13] and show numerous social defects,[14] while V1aR knockout animals show a complete loss of social recognition.[15] Other specific olfactory and neural processing events remain grossly intact. The relevance of these studies to humans is unknown. However, there are elevations in OT levels during female orgasm and increases in AVP levels during male sexual arousal.[16] Imaging studies indicate that brain reward circuits involving dopamine and neuropeptides are involved in human pair-bonding.[17] Many of the same pathways involved in pair-bond formation are involved in forming attachments between parents and offspring. In evolutionary terms, these two bonds are intimately connected.

Attachment: Reciprocal Changes in the Mother and Infant

There are obvious shortcomings in animal models when relating their findings to humans. The evolution of the human neocortex adds many layers of complexity with respect to controls on simpler neural circuits involved in pair-bonding and parent-offspring attachment. However, similarities exist across different species in formation of these attachments.[18] There are common core neuroanatomic features in lower brain systems and in the signaling machinery underlying their function conserved throughout mammalian evolution.

Reciprocal interactions between mothers and offspring bring about changes in cellular signaling systems.[19] Maternal experience results in profound changes in many maternal hormonal response systems—including stress-signaling pathways such as the hypothalamic-pituitary-adrenal axis (HPA). The postpartum period shows elevated levels in circulating glucocorticoids in rats in response to nursing pups, linked to changes in production of new neurons, or neurogenesis, in the hippocampus—a key brain structure involved in memory consolidation.[20] Neurogenesis in adults reflects the remarkable hippocampal structural plasticity,[21] appreciated recently in many species, including humans. Genetic ablation of new hippocampal neurons in transgenic mice resulted in altered contextual and spatial memory formation, suggesting that continuous neurogenesis is critical for normal brain function.[22] These changes also provide feedback to the HPA, altering subsequent stress responses postpartum. Cellular responses to glucocorticoids have metabolic consequences as well, diverting energy and resources for physiological effects such as increased milk production.[23] Changes in the mother are important in forming attachments to infants and have long-term consequences for how mothers interact with later offspring. Evidence in animal models suggests that some but not all foster parents also undergo responses elicited in biological parents by exposure to young.[24] Anecdotal evidence indicates this is likely true in human foster parents as well.

Changes in infants are also induced by *early interactions* with the mother. Although these events are involved in formation of initial attachments, the nature of these interactions for developing infants has marked and likely permanent consequences: many developmental switches are set during a critical time window in early attachment. There are strong precedents for long-term effects of missing environmentally sensitive developmental windows. Many of these involve early interactions between offspring and caregivers. Developmental consequences may thus be considerations in the timing of adoptions (i.e., the age of the child) for both homosexual and heterosexual couples. Maternal deprivation in animals leads to changes in their behavior as adults. There are parallel changes in neuroendocrine function and brain architecture, which probably underlie behavioral changes. Interestingly, prolonged maternal separation in the early postnatal period does not affect basal HPA function (i.e., in its role in physical growth). However, distinct alterations in HPA regulation are manifested following stressful experiences as adult animals. In rats previously subjected to long periods of maternal deprivation, stress responses, including release of corticotrophin-releasing factor (CRF), adrenocorticotrophin (ACTH), and corticosterone, increase significantly.[25] Individual differences in two forms of maternal behavior in rats (licking/grooming of pups [LG] and arched-back nursing [ABN]) are a model for variations in parental care.[26] As adults, offspring of high-LG/ABN mothers show decreased startle responses, increased open-field exploration, and shorter latencies to eat food provided in novel environments. Offspring of low-LG/ABN mothers show greater active responses to perceived threats. The consequences of variations in maternal behavior include alterations in sexual behavior of the offspring as adults. Offspring of low-LG mothers showed increased sexual receptivity, increased plasma levels of luteinizing hormone (LH) and progesterone, changes in the feedback loop between estrogen on LH production by the pituitary, and increased expression of estrogen receptors in certain brain regions.[27]

Maternal care significantly impacts behavior in later life. Greater anxiety, impaired maternal care, and diminished spatial navigation learning result from reduced maternal attention.[28] Maternal deprivation reduces pools of nascent neurons in the rat dentate gyrus, a hippocampal structure involved in memory formation.[29] Reduced neurogenesis may be linked with human psychiatric disorders, including depression.[30] Indeed, prolonged treatment with antidepressants increases neurogenesis in animals.[31] Maternal deprivation decreases the number of immature, but not mature, neurons added to the dentate gyrus in adulthood.[32] The functional consequences of early adverse experience may involve a diminished pool of nascent neurons in adult animals. Evidence suggests that immature neurons have a unique and important role in the functioning of the adult hippocampus. Immature granule neurons, for example, may be involved in anxiety regulation[33] and learning.[34] Maternally deprived rats show heightened anxiety and a diminished capacity to learn some tasks.[35] Decreases in adult-generated immature neurons associated with maternal deprivation may impair hippocampal function in HPA feedback (i.e., how stress systems are attenuated and regulated), which may also explain why these changes are linked to stress in adult animals and why depression is stress-induced. Researchers have only begun to assess the extent of gene expression (or, as we discuss later, epigenetic modifications) and cellular signaling changes that are altered by maternal deprivation. *Only large-scale longitudinal studies in humans will reveal the magnitude and* ultimate impact of these early changes on later responses to stress or altered susceptibility to disease.]

Changes in Fathers as Well?

The mother-infant bond has obviously received greater scrutiny than the father-infant bond. However, positive paternal effects on offspring outcomes, including acceleration of sexual maturation in females, have been demonstrated in multimate primate social groups.[36] Human fathers are more responsive to infant cues than are nonfathers.[37] This involves both hormonal alterations, as observed in mothers, and changes in neuronal architecture in the father's brain. For example, in marmosets, which, like human fathers, help raise their young, changes were detected in dendritic spine density on pyramidal neurons in the prefrontal cortex.[38] This certainly affects learning and memory formation. Interestingly, there is an increase in V1aR density in these spines as well. The mechanisms underlying these changes are not known, nor are environmental or biochemical signals that might induce these changes in fathers, although feedback changes in vasopressin signaling might be involved. Cues from offspring are not well understood either. Previous maternal experience, which shapes mothers' responses to subsequent offspring, may also occur in fathers. For example, experienced human fathers show increased prolactin levels and changes in testosterone levels compared with first-time fathers, suggesting that interactions with children result in lasting hormonal alterations.[39]

Environmental Effects on Gene Expression

The notion of developmental windows affected by environmental influences is well established. Quality of parental care is a key environmental determinant for correct development. In addition to changes in individual brain structures and the architecture of stress-related signaling, dependent on the amount and quality of parental care, there is now a recently recognized possibility that these changes may be *heritable*. Specific chemical modifications to regulatory regions of different genes are recognized as critical for genetic imprinting and silencing of genes from one of the two parental chromosomes.[40] These modifications do not require changes in coding sequences of the genes involved. Multiple stable gene expression states or phenotypes can thus be generated from the same sequence of DNA. This is referred to as *epigenetic* rather than genetic change.

These modifications were initially thought to be *static*, that is, switches thrown once, permanently, during embryonic development. It is now clear that changes in epigenetic status of different genes are quite *dynamic*.[41] Thus, DNA methylation and histone modification, the two primary epigenetic marks, are modified by experience, and changes can have lasting effects on gene expression for individuals. Further, changes in the *epigenome* can be inherited, in effect passing the consequences of environmental influences onto subsequent generations.

Are there examples of parent-offspring interactions that modify the epigenome? In fact, this occurs in a number of relevant ways.[42] Variations in maternal behaviors, which reflect different levels of sensory stimulation (especially tactile), had consequences over a critical period of neural development.[43] In offspring of high-LG/ABN mothers, there was greater expression of genes related to metabolic activity, receptors for the neurotransmitter glutamate, and a number of growth factors involved in controlling cellular function, compared with offspring of normal- or low-LG/ABN mothers. Differences in gene expression patterns that govern behavioral responses to novelty (and the stresses it engenders) in offspring can be directly linked to maternal care over the first week of life. This is mediated through alterations in the function of the HPA and affected cognitive and emotional development through changes in underlying neuronal pathways. Changes in expression of the hippocampal glucocorticoid receptor (GR) gene is a key mechanistic element. Maternal care regulates its expression by altering two aspects of the epigenomic status: the acetylation of histone H3 and the methylation of the consensus sequence in the promoter of the GR gene (where the transcriptional machinery is recruited to initiate gene expression). For example, the GR promoter region, methylated in low-LG mothers, is sensitive to a transcription factor called nerve growth factor-inducible protein A (NGFI-A). A recent study demonstrated that childhood abuse *in humans* is linked to epigenetic changes in the NGFI-A regulation of transcription from the GR promoter in brain tissue.[44] This again highlights how these mechanisms are conserved throughout mammalian evolution.

Epigenome dynamics are recognized as increasingly important for normal development and correct function of physiological systems. They are also important modulators of disease progression and responses to therapeutic interventions. At present, our understanding of molecular signaling pathways that modulate the epigenome is rudimentary. Sensory, hormonal, and neurotransmitter signaling can impact epigenetic marking of different genes. In the example discussed earlier, the neurotransmitter serotonin modulates a common cellular signaling molecule, cyclic adenosine monophosphate (cAMP), underlying changes in the epigenetic status of the GR.[45] Beyond this example, we have little information as to how the hundreds of other cellular signaling pathways responding to both internal and external cues might regulate epigenome dynamics.[46]

Long-Term Consequences of Changing the Nature of Parenthood

We believe long-term sequelae associated with changing the nature of parenting are unknown and that it is unwise to assume that such changes will be necessarily benign, especially if biology is ignored when engineering changes in parenting structures and practices. We should think seriously about the potential impact of further changes. Recent studies echo concerns about the pace and nature of societal changes. The view that individual patterns of gene expression fixed in the epigenome during development were stable (i.e., inherited with high fidelity between generations) has been challenged. This was demonstrated by comparing identical twins sharing the same genome who accumulate epigenomic changes leading to distinct patterns of stable gene expression.[47]

For epigenetic variation to affect inheritance, propagation of epigenetic marks in mitosis (i.e., the division of cells in the body) is insufficient. Transmission through the germ line is essential. During development, epigenetic marks from either parent are largely erased during early embryo cleavages.[48] This model of epigenetic resetting in early development reinforces a widely held view that epigenetic information accumulated over a lifetime is confined to a single generation. However, epigenetic erasure is incomplete in many different species, including mammals, suggesting that parental epigenetic status can be transmitted to offspring for multiple generations.[49] Significant epigenetic variation occurs within individuals—between different parental gene alleles—as well as between different individuals, and both types of variation are transmissible from parent to offspring.[50] Knowing that epigenomic changes can be passed onto offspring and that these changes figure significantly in early development of correct attachment strongly indicates that early interactions and environmental quality are important not only for children per se but possibly for *their children* as well. Transgenerational effects of environmental quality may have tremendous impact on human disease and human evolution.

Nonbiological parents may be able to foster some or all of the same developmental and epigenetic changes in children as biological parents. If so, however, the timing of these changes must be recognized as important for two reasons. First, the developmental effects of parental interactions with offspring occur from birth and in many cases earlier. Thus, even in foster parenting situations, timing of adoptions may be critical to ensure that developmental milestones are met.

The other timing issue—the rate of evolutionary change—may perhaps be more important given the pace of societal change. There is recent evidence in both simpler organisms (bacteria) and more complex metazoans such as mice and rats (likely humans as well) that the rate of evolutionary change can be significantly accelerated through epigenetic modifications.[51] According to the widely held consensus, most "selective" events in terms of evolution occur by choosing among genetic variations generated by either mutation or recombination, taking hundreds of generations for changes to become fixed in the genome. However, stable epigenetic changes can occur on a much more rapid timescale. Generation of novel phenotypes can occur as a response to selective pressures in the environment. The pace of evolution may thus be linked to the pace of environmental changes. This makes sense given the widely different rates by which different environmental changes occur (e.g., long-term changes in climate versus more rapid changes in food quality/availability). Because evolution requires phenotypic variation to work, epigenetic changes to children altered by parental deprivation may be heritable. Changes are no longer selected for or against on the basis of their contribution to the fitness of our species per se. If so, we cannot predict either immediate or long-term consequences to *Homo sapiens as a species*.

Over the course of evolution, distinct roles for mothers and fathers have come into play. Changes in gender-specific brain systems and cellular signaling pathways between parent and offspring induced by early interactions between them are reciprocal. It is unknown if foster or same-sex parents can engender these reciprocal changes. This should be considered before redefining long-established practices and social institutions relevant to children. Taken together, our understanding of the biology of attachment, although incomplete, suggests that caution is required before engineering massive changes in human social architecture.

Sociopsychological Dimensions of Attachment

How do attachment relationships promote survival of the offspring and maintenance of the kinship system? What is the evolutionary function of different attachment patterns that we identify in children? What are the implications for child welfare policy and attachment-based intervention models? Does psychological research on developmental sequelae of different attachment relationships lead us to similar conclusions as those suggested by recent biological research? Bowlby might not have imagined the primary attachment figure as a homosexual male raising a baby, conceived through surrogacy. When definitions of motherhood and fatherhood are stretched beyond simple biological and gender connections, is Bowlby still relevant?

Caregiver Sensitivity and Individual Differences in Attachment Relationships

Earlier formulations of attachment theory[52] emphasized physical proximity to the caregiver as the set goal of attachment, with emphasis on the attachment figure's accessibility. In his earlier writings, Bowlby noted that the simple presence of the attachment figure was a major source of security for children. However, subsequent observations by Ainsworth of different patterns of infant proximity seeking and maternal responses revealed that the maternal presence alone was insufficient to provide comfort and reduce distress.[53] Thus maternal responsivity and sensitivity to infant signals was incorporated into attachment theory to account for caregivers present but not adequately responsive to infant distress.

Attachment should be seen within a control system, regulated by behavioral homeostasis in much the same way that bodily functions such as blood pressure and temperature are regulated within set limits.[54] The set goal is to maintain adequate distance from caregivers depending on the context. In stress or danger, greater proximity is desired, whereas in relative safety, infants can distance themselves from caregivers to explore the environment independently. Thus, many other developmental systems are linked to adequate functioning of the attachment system. For example, for the exploratory system, the basis for cognitive development, to function effectively, infants must use attachment figures as a secure base.

Ainsworth identified three patterns of infant attachment behavior, one secure and two insecure, which arose from the desire for proximity to parents and functioned to protect the infant. In identifying these patterns, Ainsworth was inspired by ethological studies of adaptive patterns in animals that maintained proximity within family and larger social groupings. Sensitive mothers interpret infant signals and provide correct responses with appropriate timing, facilitating development of secure attachment relationships. Secure infants achieve a balance between attachment and exploration; when the infant is in a comfortable, nonthreatening situation, exploration is enhanced, but when feeling distressed, play and exploration decline and proximity seeking increases.

Infant insecure patterns, avoidance and ambivalence, observed in cross-cultural studies of mother-infant behavior, were interpreted as compensatory strategies to maintain proximity to nonoptimal attachment figures. Avoidant attachment is associated with inhibition of negative affect in mother-child interactions and child detachment from caregivers in stressful situations.[55] Child detachment develops from repeated rejection by caregivers. Conversely, ambivalent-dependent attachment is characterized by hypervigilant and overly involved child behaviors stemming from attempts to maintain proximity to inconsistently available caregivers.[56]

Attachment Strategies and Preservation of the Kinship System

The demanding nature of ambivalent children might reflect a contingent strategy designed to obtain, retain, or improve parental attention and care.[57] It is hard to ignore a child who is screaming, clinging, or having a tantrum. Avoidance may permit infants to stay in proximity to caregivers who do not respond positively to displays of distress, but prefer a child who is independent and emotionally undemanding. For these parents, exaggerated distress of the ambivalent kind might push the parent farther away.

Research on the impact of insecure attachment has not consistently shown that avoidantly and ambivalently attached infants develop behavior problems or cognitive deficiencies.[58] These attachment patterns, although not optimal for development, do permit children eventually to use the caregiver in resolving distress. Individual differences in child attachment patterns provide mechanisms for keeping vulnerable infants in close proximity to their caregivers, taking account of both infant and caregiver idiosyncrasies, permitting them to survive vulnerable periods of development.

Underlying behavioral expression of attachment relationships are internal representations consisting of expectations about the self and others, based on past experiences with attachment figures, and unconscious rules for processing attachment-related information.[59] Data indicate that parents induct their infants into relating in ways consistent with their own models of self in relationships. For example, the secure child, able to use the parent as a safe haven in times of need, develops a capacity for self-regulation and an internal model of being a competent individual and of others as being dependable.[60] On the other hand, lack of recognition of distress that characterizes interactions between avoidant children and their caregivers is internalized within a self-schema that permits the child to remove the rejecting demeanor of the parent and of the self from consciousness and continue functioning. These expectations, attitudes, and processing rules show continuity from childhood to adulthood as well as to subsequent generations in more stable populations.

Disorganized Attachment and Its Developmental Consequences

More recent work by Main and Solomon, Lyons-Ruth and Jacobvitz, and Moss and colleagues has identified a fourth attachment pattern, called disorganization.[61] Disorganized/disoriented infants are distinguished from those with more "organized" secure or insecure attachment strategies by their apparent failure to show coherent behavioral strategies for dealing with separation and reunion with their mothers. They display bouts or sequences of behaviors that seemingly lack goals and, in contrast to infants of other attachment classifications, do not demonstrate an organized attachment strategy for seeking proximity to caregivers in times of distress.[62]

Infants identified as "disorganized" experience the most dysfunctional caregiving when compared with other attachment groups.[63] Mothers of disorganized infants are often highly insensitive, with repeated episodes of hostile intrusiveness and/or emotional detachment.[64] These behaviors, in addition to others, such as maternal dissociative states, may frighten infants and interfere with processing of affective, social, and cognitive information.[65] Maternal behavior revealing helplessness and loss of control leaves children in momentary or prolonged states of feeling abandoned or unprotected.[66]

In attachment theory, mother-child interactive patterns both contribute to development of distinct attachment patterns and predict child adaptation.[67] It is unsurprising that disorganized attachment is consistently a significant risk factor for psychopathology, and longitudinally predicts maladaptation between early childhood and young adulthood.[68] In addition, disorganization is associated with cognitive deficiencies, particularly those involved in executive functioning and school performance.[69] Attachment disorganization is also prevalent among maltreated children, with some 32 to 86 percent classified in this category.[70]

Apart from cases where children have not encountered a consistent attachment figure in early childhood (a situation dramatically improved by reduction of institutional care for infants), most children develop strong attachment bonds. However, these bonds differ in quality and developmental correlates. Developmental risks associated with disorganized attachment cannot be simply attributed to societal changes that loosen kinship bonds and encourage maternal deprivation. Research on the etiology of disorganized attachment reinforces the notion that the mere presence of a biological parent is insufficient to ensure child-secure attachment. Further, certain forms of child-parent attachment may actually be "toxic" and significantly impede development. Children with disorganized attachment patterns internalize many of the dysfunctional characteristics associated with caregivers, just as secure children internalize positive ones. Repeated failure of disorganized children to receive comfort from caregivers leads to deficiencies in emotional, behavioral, and cognitive regulation, and lack of trust in others.[71] Biologically based attachment is a particularly intense form of social bond that impacts child development significantly. However, the nature of the bonds and their developmental outcomes can vary. All close kinship bonds may not be inherently healthy but are critical for the social ecology of human life.

Attachment Theory, Child Welfare Policy, and Parenting Intervention

Biological processes interact with rearing conditions in contributing to development of attachment relationships. Attachment relationships promote survival through the most vulnerable period of development and maximize chances that attachment-related characteristics of kinship survive cross-generationally. In the disorganized group, attachment may contribute to survival of the kinship group, with important biological and social costs for individuals, their offspring, and society in general.[72] Disorganized attachment relationships, often the underlying pattern in abusing and neglecting families, pose a dilemma for child welfare and clinical professionals. In some cases, nonintervention in biological kinship entails important risks for developing children and, perhaps, even for subsequent generations. However, removal of children from biological families is also risky, as research on developmental outcomes for foster children has shown.[73] It is difficult to evaluate how attachment might differ in non-biologically-related parenting contexts.

Are there approaches to the child welfare dilemma adaptive for both individuals and family units from an evolutionary perspective? Abusing and neglecting mothers who were at risk for losing custody of their children participated in an eight- to ten-week therapeutic program.[74] Using video feedback to observe and evaluate the mothers' interactions with their children, an attempt to promote greater maternal sensitivity was undertaken. Following only eight to ten weeks of a weekly two-hour intervention, remarkable changes occurred. Comparison of pre- and posttest results for intervention and control groups revealed significant improvements in parental sensitivity and child attachment security, and a reduction in child disorganization. Older children in the intervention group also showed fewer behavior problems following intervention. The children, given their greater developmental plasticity, often changed more rapidly than parents, which, in turn, stimulated positive changes in the parent. This adaptive "self-righting" tendency has been documented in longitudinal studies of disorganized children and in the literature on resilience.[75]

As the majority of children with disorganized attachment approach school age, they seek ways of assisting parents to assume a more appropriate parental role.[76] In the absence of intervention, this often leads to attempts to control an acquiescent parent, with role reversal as the result. Increases in controlling behaviors with the caregiver during the preschool period may be linked to attempts by disorganized children to reduce stress levels, which cannot be regulated through child dependency on the caregiver.[77] In the absence of intervention, the controlling child's strategy of orienting away from seeking comfort, protection, and the meeting of his or her own needs and toward maintaining engagement with the parent on the parent's terms is likely to increase the likelihood of child psychopathology.[78] Clearly, more research is needed to identify the mechanisms, both behavioral and biological, that underlie these changes.

Conclusion

In summary, a greater focus on the biological-evolutionary origins of attachment theory and its potential applications to understanding parenthood may have important implications, not only for knowledge development but also for policy and intervention with parents and their children. We do not have specific policies to suggest at this point, as research discussed in this chapter is still at relatively early stages of development. However, in our view, an emerging body of biological and psychological research does make a strong case for caution. Legal reform and public policy initiatives promoting commitments to equality, freedom, and diversity in family forms should not simply trump evidence for complex biological kinship and attachment patterns that have evolved over millennia. These legal and political commitments should not be the sole determinants of what is best for us, our children, or our species. Decisions taken primarily to expand adult choice and to promote greater diversity of family forms should consider first the effects that they may have on children, and neither simply view children as instrumental to these adult concerns nor presume that children will automatically benefit from expanded adult choice.

What are the long-term consequences of changes in parenting structures? We just don't know. Should we apply the precautionary principle to changes in traditional family structures? Should we err on the side of caution when changing core parenting structures until the biology is better understood? Are these new functional arrangements effectively benign with respect to child development? Recent decades have witnessed a growing and justifiable concern about the fragility of our natural ecosystems to aggressive human intervention. Should we be equally concerned about the fragility of complex social ecologies? The tensions, debates, and unresolved issues in scholarly research on core features of our social ecology (attachment, kinship, and parenthood) signal the need for caution. If there is one major public policy recommendation that we would put forward, it would be a call for public investment in rigorous large-scale multidisciplinary and cross-cultural research on the biological and psychological dimensions of childhood attachment bonds. A more forward-thinking, rigorous, proactive, and interdisciplinary approach to these questions may benefit not only us but future generations as well.

Notes

1. R. Rogers Kobak and Stephanie Madsen, "Disruptions in Attachment Relationships: Implications for Theory, Research, and Clinical Intervention," in *Handbook of Attachment: Theory, Research, and Clinical Applications*, 2nd ed., ed. Jude Cassidy and Phillip R. Shaver (New York: Guilford Press, 2008), 23–47.

2. Sigmund Freud, *The Standard Edition of the Complete Psychological Works of Sigmund Freud*, trans. and ed. James Strachey, vol. 11, *Five Lectures on Psycho-analysis, Leonardo da Vinci and Other Works* (1910; repr., London: Hogarth Press, 1957); Robert R. Sears, Eleanor R. Maccoby, and Harry Levin, *Patterns of Child Rearing* (Stanford, CA: Stanford University Press, 1957).

3. John Bowlby, *Maternal Care and Mental Health: A Report Prepared on Behalf of the World Health Organization as a Contribution to the United Nations Programme for the Welfare on Homeless Children* (Geneva: World Health Organization, 1951).

4. John Bowlby, *Attachment and Loss*, vol. 1, *Attachment* (New York: Basic Books, 1969).

5. Ibid., 56.

6. Nancy Humber and Ellen Moss, "The Relationship of Preschool and Early School Age Attachment to Mother-Child Interaction," *American Journal of Orthopsychiatry* 75 (Jan. 2005): 128.

7. Cassidy and Shaver, *Handbook of Attachment*, 2nd ed.

8. Carol Sue Carter et al., eds. *Attachment and Bonding: A New Synthesis* (Cambridge: MIT Press, 2006).

9. Thomas R. Insel and Larry J. Young, "The Neurobiology of Attachment," *Nature Reviews Neuroscience* 2 (Feb. 2001): 129; Larry J. Young and Zuoxin Wang, "The Neurobiology of Pair Bonding," *Nature Neuroscience* 7 (Oct. 2004): 1048; Larry J. Young, Zuoxin Wang, and Thomas R. Insel, "Neuroendocrine Bases of Monogamy," *Trends in Neuroscience* 21 (Feb. 1998): 71.

10. Keith M. Kendrick et al., "Neural Control of Maternal Behaviour and Olfactory Recognition of Offspring," *Brain Research Bulletin* 44 (1997): 383.

11. Bruce S. Cushing and Carol Sue Carter, "Peripheral Pulses of Oxytocin Increase Partner Preferences in Female, but Not Male, Prairie Voles," *Hormones and Behavior* 37 (Feb. 2000): 49; Thomas R. Insel and Terrence J. Hulihan, "A Gender-Specific Mechanism for Pair-Bonding: Oxytocin and Partner Preference Formation in Monogamous Voles," *Behavioral Neuroscience* 109 (Aug. 1995): 782; James T. Winslow et al., "Oxytocin and Complex Social Behavior: Species Comparisons," *Psychopharmacology Bulletin* 29 (1993): 409.

12. Brandon J. Aragona et el., "A Critical Role for Nucleus Accumbens Dopamine in Partner-Preference Formation in Male Prarie Voles," *Journal of Neuroscience* 23, no. 8 (2003): 3483; Maria Rosaria Melis, Antonio Argiolas, and Gian Luigi Gessa, "Apomorphine Increases Plasma Oxytocin Concentration in Male Rats," *Neuroscience Letters* 98 (Apr. 1989): 351; H. Peter Pfister and Janice L. Muir, "Influence of Exogenously Administered Oxytocin on Central Noradrenaline, Dopamine and Serotonin Levels Following Psychological Stress in Nulliparous Female Rats (Rattus Norvegicus)," *International Journal of Neuroscience* 45 (Jan. 1989): 221.

13. Jennifer N. Ferguson et al., "Oxytocin in the Medial Amygdala Is Essential for Social Recognition in the Mouse," *Journal of Neuroscience* 21 (Oct. 2001): 8278.

14. Yuki Takayanagi et al., "Pervasive Social Deficits, but Normal Parturition, in Oxytocin Receptor-Deficient Mice," *Proceedings of the National Academy of Sciences of the United States of America* 102 (Nov. 2005): 16096.

15. Jay Belsky and R. M. Pasco Fearon, "Precursors of Attachment Security," in Cassidy and Shaver, *Handbook of Attachment*, 2nd ed., 295–316.

16. Marie S. Carmichael et al., "Plasma Oxytocin Increases in the Human Sexual Response," *Journal of Clinical Endocrinology and Metabolism* 64 (Jan. 1987): 27; Michael R. Murphy et al., "Changes in Oxytocin and Vasopressin Secretion during Sexual Activity in Men," *Journal of Clinical Endocrinology and Metabolism* 65 (Oct. 1987): 738.

17. Andreas Bartels and Semir Zeki, "The Neural Basis of Romantic Love," *Neuroreport* 11 (Nov. 2000): 3829; Andreas Bartels and Semir Zeki, "The Neural Correlates of Maternal and Romantic Love," *NeuroImage* 21 (Mar. 2004): 1155.

18. James F. Leckman et al., "Group Report: Behavioral Processes in Attachment and Bonding," in Carter et al., *Attachment and Bonding*, 301–348.

19. That is, in the way that different cells and tissues transmit, receive, and exchange information.

20. Benedetta Leuner et al., "Maternal Experience Inhibits the Production of Immature Neurons in the Hippocampus during the Postpartum Period through Elevations in Adrenal Steroids," *Hippocampus* 17 (June 2007): 434.

21. This leads to the growth of dendrites, axons, and synapses.

22. Itaru Imayoshi et al., "Roles of Continuous Neurogenesis in the Structural and Functional Integrity of the Adult Forebrain," *Nature Neuroscience* 11 (Oct. 2008): 1153.

23. H. Allen Tucker, "Lactation and Its Hormonal Control," in *The Physiology of Reproduction*, 2nd ed., ed. Ernest Knobil et al. (New York: Raven Press, 1994), 2:1065–1098.

24. See, e.g., Michael G. Ruscio et al., "Pup Exposure Elicits Hippocampal Cell Proliferation in the Prairie Vole," *Behavioural Brain Research* 187 (Feb. 2008): 9.

25. Dong Liu et al., "Influence of Neonatal Rearing Conditions on Stress-Induced Adrenocorticotropin Responses and Norepinephrine Release in the Hypothalamic Paraventricular Nucleus," *Journal of Neuroendocrinology* 12 (Jan. 2000): 5, reviewed in Paul M. Plotsky and Michael J. Meaney, "Early, Postnatal Experience Alters Hypothalamic Corticotropin-Releasing Factor (CRF) mRNA, Median Eminence CRF Content and Stress-Induced Release in Adult Rats," *Molecular Brain Research* 18 (May 1993): 195; Michael J. Meaney and Moshe Szyf, "Maternal Care as a Model for Experience-Dependent Chromatin Plasticity?," *Trends in Neurosciences* 28 (Sept. 2005): 456.

26. Frances A. Champagne et al., "Variations in Maternal Care in the Rat as a Mediating Influence for the Effects of Environment on Development," *Physiology and Behavior* 79 (Aug. 2003): 359.

27. Nicole M. Cameron, Eric W. Fish, and Michael J. Meaney, "Maternal Influences on the Sexual Behavior and Reproductive Success of the Female Rat," *Hormones and Behavior* 54 (June 2008): 178.

28. Leuner et al., "Maternal Experience Inhibits the Production of Immature Neurons."

29. Christian Mirescu, Jennifer D. Peters, and Elizabeth Gould, "Early Life Experience Alters Response of Adult Neurogenesis to Stress," *Nature Neuroscience* 7 (Aug. 2004): 841.

30. Elizabeth Gould, "How Widespread Is Adult Neurogenesis in Mammals?," *Nature Reviews Neuroscience* 8 (Jun. 2007): 481; Luca Santarelli et al., "Requirement of Hippocampal Neurogenesis for the Behavioral Effects of Antidepressants," *Science* 301 (Aug. 2003): 805.

31. Sylvia Navailles, Patrick R. Hof, and Claudia Schmauss, "Antidepressant Drug-Induced Stimulation of Mouse Hippocampal Neurogenesis Is Age-Dependent and Altered by Early Life Stress," *Journal of Comparative Neurology* 509 (Aug. 2008): 372; see Chunmei Zhao, Wei Deng, and Fred H. Gage, "Mechanisms and Functional Implications of Adult Neurogenesis," *Cell* 132 (Feb. 2008): 645.

32. Mirescu et al., "Early Life Experience Alters Response."

33. Santarelli et al., "Requirement of Hippocampal Neurogenesis."

34. Mate D. Dobrossy et al., "Differential Effects of Learning on Neurogenesis: Learning Increases or Decreases the Number of Newly Born Cells Depending on Their Birth Date," *Molecular Psychiatry* 8 (Dec. 2003): 974; Elizabeth Gould et al., "Learning Enhances Adult Neurogenesis in the Hippocampal Formation," *Nature Neuroscience* 2 (Mar. 1999): 260; Elizabeth Gould et al., "Neurogenesis in Adulthood: A Possible Role in Learning," *Trends in Cognitive Science* 3 (May 1999): 186; Tracey J. Shors et al., "Neurogenesis May Relate to Some but Not All Types of Hippocampal-Dependent Learning," *Hippocampus* 12 (2002): 578.

35. Rebecca L. Huot et al., "Neonatal Maternal Separation Reduces Hippocampal Mossy Fiber Density in Adult Long Evans Rats," *Brain Research* 950 (Sept. 2002): 52.

36. Marie J. E. Charpentier et al., "Paternal Effects on Offspring Fitness in a Multimale Primate Society," *Proceedings of the National Academy of Sciences of the United States of America* 105 (Feb. 2008): 1988.

37. Alison S. Fleming et al., "Testosterone and Prolactin Are Associated with Emotional Responses to Infant Cries in New Fathers," *Hormones and Behavior* 42 (Dec. 2002): 399.

38. Yevgenia Kozorovitskiy et al., "Fatherhood Affects Dendritic Spines and Vasopressin V1a Receptors in the Primate Prefrontal Cortex," *Nature Neuroscience* 9 (Sept. 2006): 1094.

39. Fleming et al., "Testosterone and Prolactin"; Lee T. Gettler et al., "Longitudinal Evidence That Fatherhood Decreases Testosterone in Human Males," *Proceedings of the National Academy of Sciences of the United States of America* 108 (Sept. 2011): 16194.

40. Diane J. Lees-Murdock and Colum P. Walsh, "DNA Methylation Reprogramming in the Germ Line," *Advances in Experimental Medicine and Biology* 626 (2008): 1.

41. See Moshe Szyf, "Epigenetics, DNA Methylation, and Chromatin Modifying Drugs," *Annual Review of Pharmacology and Toxicology* 49 (2009): 243; Moshe Szyf, Patrick O. McGowan, and Michael J. Meaney, "The Social Environment and the Epigenome," *Environmental and Molecular Mutagenesis* 49 (Jan. 2008): 46.

42. Reviewed in Meaney and Szyf, "Maternal Care as a Model"; Moshe Szyf, "Early Life, the Epigenome and Human Health," *Acta Paediatrica* 98 (July 2009): 1082; Moshe Szyf, "The Early Life Environment and the Epigenome," *Biochimica et Biophysica Acta* 1790 (Sept. 2009): 878; Szyf et al., "The Social Environment and the Epigenome."

43. Eric W. Fish et al., "Epigenetic Programming of Stress Responses through Variations in Maternal Care," *Annals of the New York Academy of Sciences* 1036 (Dec. 2004): 167.

44. Patrick O. McGowan et al., "Epigenetic Regulation of the Glucocorticoid Receptor in Human Brain Associates with Childhood Abuse," *Nature Neuroscience* 12 (Mar. 2009): 342.

45. Ian C. G. Weaver et al., "The Transcription Factor Nerve Growth Factor-Inducible Protein A Mediates Epigenetic Programming: Altering Epigenetic Marks by Immediate-Early Genes," *Journal of Neuroscience* 27 (Feb. 2007): 1756.

46. Christine M. Colvis et al., "Epigenetic Mechanisms and Gene Networks in the Nervous System," *Journal of Neuroscience* 25 (Nov. 2005): 10379; Nadia Tsankova et al., "Epigenetic Regulation in Psychiatric Disorders," *Nature Reviews Neuroscience* 8 (May 2007): 355.

47. Mario F. Fraga et al., "Epigenetic Differences Arise during the Lifetime of Monozygotic Twins," *Proceedings of the National Academy of Sciences of the United States of America* 102 (July 2005): 10604; Zachary A. Kaminsky et al., "DNA Methylation Profiles in Monozygotic and Dizygotic Twins," *Nature Genetics* 41 (Feb. 2009): 240.

48. Hugh D. Morgan et al., "Epigenetic Reprogramming in Mammals," *Human Molecular Genetics* 14, no. S1 (2005): R47.

49. Natasha Lane et al., "Resistance of IAPs to Methylation Reprogramming May Provide a Mechanism for Epigenetic Inheritance in the Mouse," *Genesis: The Journal of Genetics and Development* 35 (Feb. 2003): 88; Alcino J. Silva and Raymond White,

"Inheritance of Allelic Blueprints for Methylation Patterns," *Cell* 54 (July 1988): 145; see Eric J. Richards, "Inherited Epigenetic Variation—Revisiting Soft Inheritance," *Nature Reviews Genetics* 7 (May 2006): 395.

50. Ryan McDaniell et al., "Heritable Individual-Specific and Allele-Specific Chromatin Signatures in Humans," *Science* 328 (Apr. 2010): 235.

51. Reviewed in Oliver J. Rando and Kevin J. Verstrepen, "Timescales of Genetic and Epigenetic Inheritance," *Cell* 128 (Feb. 2007): 655.

52. John Bowlby, *Attachment and Loss*, vol. 2, *Separation: Anxiety and Anger* (New York: Basic Books, 1973).

53. Mary D. Salter Ainsworth, "The Development of Infant-Mother Interaction among the Ganda," in *Determinants of Infant Behavior*, ed. B. M. Foss (New York: Wiley, 1963), 2:67–104.

54. Jude Cassidy, "The Nature of the Child's Ties," in Cassidy and Shaver, *Handbook of Attachment*, 2nd ed., 3–22.

55. Mary D. Salter Ainsworth et al., *Patterns of Attachment: A Psychological Study of the Strange Situation* (Hillsdale, NJ: Erlbaum, 1978); Mary Main, "Avoidance in the Service of Attachment: A Working Paper," in *Behavioral Development: The Bielefeld Interdisciplinary Project*, ed. Klaus Immelman et al. (New York: Cambridge University Press, 1981), 651–693.

56. Bowlby, *Attachment and Loss*, vol. 1, *Attachment*; Bowlby, *Attachment and Loss*, vol. 2, *Separation*; see Jude Cassidy and Lisa J. Berlin, "The Insecure/Ambivalent Pattern of Attachment: Theory and Research," *Child Development* 65 (Aug. 1994): 971.

57. Cassidy and Berlin, "The Insecure/Ambivalent Pattern of Attachment"; Belsky and Fearon, "Precursors of Attachment Security."

58. Michelle DeKlyen and Mark T. Greenberg, "Attachment and Psychopathology in Childhood," in Cassidy and Shaver, *Handbook of Attachment*, 2nd ed., 637–665.

59. Inge Bretherton and Kristine A. Munholland, "Internal Working Models in Attachment Relationships: A Construct Revisited," in *Handbook of Attachment: Theory, Research, and Clinical Applications*, ed. Jude Cassidy and Phillip R. Shaver (New York: Guilford Press, 1999), 89–111.

60. Inge Bretherton, "Attachment Theory: Retrospect and Prospect," in *Growing Points of Attachment: Theory and Research*, ed. Inge Bretherton and Everett Waters (Chicago: University of Chicago Press, 1985), 3–35.

61. Mary Main and Judith Solomon, "Procedure for Identifying Infants as Disorganized/Disoriented during the Ainsworth Strange Situation," in *Attachment in the Preschool Years: Theory, Research, and Intervention*, ed. Mark T. Greenberg, Dante Cicchetti, and E. Mark Cummings (Chicago: University of Chicago Press, 1990), 121–160; Karlen Lyons-Ruth and Deborah Jacobovitz, "Attachment Disorganization: Genetic Factors, Parenting Contexts, and Developmental Transformation from Infancy to Adulthood," in Cassidy and Shaver, *Handbook of Attachment*, 2nd ed., 666–697; Ellen Moss, Diane St-Laurent, and Sophie Parent, "Disorganized Attachment and Developmental Risk at School Age," in *Attachment Disorganization*, ed. Judith Solomon and Carol George (New York: Guilford Press, 1999), 160–186.

62. Main and Solomon, "Procedure for Identifying Infants as Disorganized/Disoriented."

63. Elizabeth A. Carlson, "A Prospective Longitudinal Study of Attachment Disorganization/Disorientation," *Child Development* 69 (Aug. 1998): 1107; Karlen Lyons-Ruth, Elisa Bronfman, and Elizabeth Parsons, "Maternal Frightened, Frightening, or Atypical Behavior and Disorganized Infant Attachment Patterns," *Monographs of the Society for Research in Child Development* 64, no. 3 (1999): 67; Ellen Moss et al., "Correlates of Attachment at Age 3: Construct of Validity of the Preschool Attachment Classification System," *Developmental Psychology* 40 (May 2004): 323; Marinus H. van Ijzendoorn, Carlo Schuengel, and Marian J. Bakermans-Kranenburg, "Disorganized Attachment in Early Childhood: Meta-analysis of Precursors, Concomitants, and Sequelae," *Development and Psychopathology* 11 (June 1999): 225.

64. Karlen Lyons-Ruth et al., "Infants at Social Risk: Relations among Infant Maltreatment, Maternal Behavior, and Infant Attachment Behavior," *Developmental Psychology* 23 (Mar. 1987): 223; Lyons-Ruth et al., "Maternal Frightened, Frightening, or Atypical Behavior."

65. Mary Main and Erik Hesse, "Parents' Unresolved Traumatic Experiences Are Related to Infant Disorganized Attachment Status: Is Frightened and/or Frightening Parental Behavior the Linking Mechanism?," in Greenberg et al., *Attachment in the Preschool Years*, 161–184.

66. Judith Solomon and Carol George, "Defining the Caregiving Systems: Toward a Theory of Caregiving," *Infant Mental Health Journal* 17 (Fall 1996): 3.

67. Mary Ainsworth, Silvia M. Bell, and Donelda J. Stayton, "Individual Differences in Strange-Situation Behaviour of One-Year-Olds," in *The Origins of Human Social Relations*, ed. H. Rudolph Schaffer (London: Academic Press, 1971), 17–57; Bowlby, *Attachment and Loss*, vol. 1, *Attachment*.

68. Lyons-Ruth and Jacobvitz, "Attachment Disorganization"; Ellen Moss et al., "Stability of Attachment during the Preschool Period," *Developmental Psychology* 41 (Sept. 2005): 773.

69. Ellen Moss and Diane St-Laurent, "Attachment at School Age and Academic Performance," *Developmental Psychology* 37 (Nov. 2001): 863; Teresa Jacobsen, Wolfgang Edelstein, and Volker Hofmann, "A Longitudinal Study of the Relation between Representations of Attachment in Childhood and Cognitive Functioning in Childhood and Adolescence," *Developmental Psychology* 30 (Jan. 1994): 112.

70. van Ijzendoorn et al., "Disorganized Attachment in Early Childhood."

71. Ellen Moss et al., "Understanding Disorganized Attachment at Preschool and School Age: Examining Divergent Pathways of Disorganized and Controlling Children," in *Disorganized Attachment and Caregiving*, ed. Judith Solomon and Carol George (New York: Guilford Press, 2011), 52–79.

72. Lyons-Ruth and Jacobvitz, "Attachment Disorganization."

73. Mary Dozier and Michael Rutter, "Challenges to the Development of Attachment Relationships Faced by Young Children in Foster and Adoptive Care," in Cassidy and Shaver, *Handbook of Attachment*, 2nd ed., 698–717.

74. Ellen Moss et al., "Efficacy of a Home-Visiting Intervention Aimed at Improving Maternal Sensitivity, Child Attachment, and Behavioral Outcomes for Maltreated Children: A Randomized Control Trial," *Development and Psychopathology* 23 (Feb. 2011): 195.

75. Ibid.

76. Mary Main and Jude Cassidy, "Categories of Response to Reunion with the Parent at Age 6: Predictable from Infant Attachment Classifications and Stable over a 1–Month Period," *Developmental Psychology* 24 (May 1988): 415; Moss et al., "Understanding Disorganized Attachment."

77. Moss et al., "Stability of Attachment during the Preschool Period."

78. Main and Cassidy, "Categories of Response to Reunion."

Parenting Matters

An Attachment Perspective

Howard Steele and Miriam Steele

This chapter examines how parenting has been defined and studied by attachment theory and research. Further, it describes reliable and valid attachment research tools that may assist public policy makers and judges with decision-making processes regarding parent custody, child protection, and the prevention of child abuse. In the frame of reference provided by John Bowlby's landmark trilogy, *Attachment, Separation,* and *Loss*,[1] parents are attachment figures on whom children depend as (1) a secure base from which the child explores (away) when feeling curious; and (2) a safe haven to which the child returns when frightened or otherwise distressed. There is an implicit interplay between the motivation to attach (in search of familiarity/safety) and the motivation to explore (in search of novelty/danger). Getting the balance right in one's personal and family life is an ongoing challenge for every parent (and child). This chapter reviews the psychological characteristics of the parent who meets the demands to serve as both a secure base and a safe haven, and the lifelong relevance of these concepts for healthy child, adolescent, and adult development. Bowlby's writings on parenthood are reviewed together with an account of the (high) extent to which his views from the 1950s and 1960s have been validated by fifty years of systematic research that includes results from studies of what are typical (nuclear) and less typical family groups (e.g., foster, adoptive parents), with reference to mainly human but also nonhuman animals.

Genetic and Social Influences on Parenting

Bowlby reckoned that social parenting influences on children may be at least as important as genetic influences.[2] For a contemporary account of contributions to parenting that arise from inherited biological characteristics at the level of temperament or gene polymorphisms, readers should see the previous chapter by Hébert, Moss, Cere, and Song.[3] The lively area of ongoing research concerning gene expression and parenting in animals and humans is relevant, but at the end of the day, a parent or family court judge is left to decide what type and quality of caregiving is best suited to the needs of a given child. Confidence in how to respond to this question is within our grasp, based on available research incorporating attachment research methods that rely on the observation of behavior and close attention to language concerning attachment, loss, and trauma—research measures with documented validity in multigenerational longitudinal studies, pursued in many different countries.[4]

Overcoming Adverse Childhood Experiences to Become a Good Enough Parent

Importantly, the chapter will highlight research showing how parents demonstrate an ability to rise above adverse experiences in their past and realize their ambitions to be competent caring parents. The relevance to this process of reflective functioning will be highlighted. Reflective functioning is a basic human capacity, present in childhood in only a nascent form but evolving with language and cognitive development, to enable an understanding of thoughts and feelings in self and others. While this process begins with the acquisition of a basic theory of mind in the preschool years, it grows into a fuller appreciation of the desires, beliefs (sometimes false, based on limited information), and intentions that are the causes and consequences of behavior. Over time, reflective functioning comes to include a developmental perspective, that is, the ability to distinguish between children's desires and beliefs and the multiple perspective-taking and higher-order reflections available to the adult mind. None of this happens in a vacuum. Vital to the process of overcoming adversity are ongoing supportive relationships, involving communication, clarification, and much listening by each party to the interaction. Only against this background may it be the case that trauma experienced in one generation is not revisited upon the next.

Attachment research over the last fifty years has produced a toolbox of reliable measures that permit identification of individual differences in parents' states of mind that influence child outcomes, including how parenting is experienced by children, and how such experiences by children are carried forward into new relationships in the school-age years, adolescence, and far beyond into the next generation. There is a massive volume of research based on attachment theory, which carries messages of import for public policy and legal decision-making processes that involve children and parents. Drawing on research on attachment in the contexts of one- and two-parent families, of adoption and foster care, and of children conceived with assisted reproductive technologies, we argue that attachment security, identifiable in diverse forms of the parent-child relationship, should be acknowledged as the optimal form of parent-child relationship quality that may be achieved by any parent with any child, given relevant support and empowerment. Attachment security makes it possible for any child to thrive, however conceived, provided he or she receives consistent sensitive care from at least one adult who assumes parental responsibility. Ideally, the adult is settled vis-à-vis the past, aware in respect of the present, and organized with regard to future plans. This research lends support to a *diversity model* of parenthood, where no external form of family, and no biological profile of child or parent, is privileged over others. Instead, internal qualities of the effective parent are emphasized, including inner balance, organization, and a devotion to repairing interactive errors, separations, and losses when they inevitably occur. When these qualities are present in parents, it is argued that the parenting provided by such adults will help their children thrive to the full limits of their potential.

quality NOT type matters

Bowlby's Trilogy on Attachment, Separation, and Loss

Bowlby's monumental trilogy[5] has been cited more than 10,000 times, more than any other book with parenting as a core focus, even more than Sigmund Freud's classic work *The Interpretation of Dreams*.[6] The attachment trilogy is well known to have grown out of John Bowlby's thinking honed prior to, during, and after World War II. Before the war he trained in psychology, psychiatry, and psychoanalysis. During the war he served as a psychiatrist refining interview techniques for the selection of officers. After the war he prepared a widely acclaimed book for the World Health Organization on the fate of separated, orphaned children.[7] At the same time (and through 1967), he chaired the Child and Family Department at the Tavistock Clinic, where his principle was "no therapy without research, and no research without therapy."[8] At the Tavistock Clinic, throughout the 1950s, Bowlby's practical concerns about parenting and child development led him to convene a series of seminars to which he invited specialists in the study of parenting. These included his research assistant, a recent PhD graduate from Canada, Mary Ainsworth, and established psychoanalysts, lawyers, and advocates of the new science of ethology, that is, observing animals in their natural habitat in order to identify fixed action patterns or species-specific behavior subserving survival. Representing this latter perspective was Robert Hinde, who introduced Bowlby to the work of Konrad Lorenz. Lorenz is famous for having suggested that the first animate object a gosling sees and hears is imprinted as mother. Bowlby embraced and elaborated on this idea by stating that the newborn's behavior in this regard is governed by the component instincts of the attachment behavioral system, hardwired in the central nervous system. When the attachment system is activated, Bowlby argued, newborns display "hardwired" responses reflecting adaptations to the environment in which we evolved (e.g., crying, rooting, reaching), aimed at ensuring contact with an attachment figure whose help is needed to secure the child's safety and survival.

The Relevance of Foster Care and Adoption Studies

Just how deeply "hardwired" these behaviors are has become evident via studies looking at children placed in foster or adoptive care after serious neglect or abuse. One study by Mary Dozier and colleagues looked at fifty foster children aged twelve to twenty-four months, observed with their foster mothers three months after the placement in the classic Ainsworth Strange Situation twenty-minute procedure.[9] The infants were significantly more likely to show secure patterns of attachment in normative proportions if the foster mother provided an organized, coherent state of mind in response to the Adult Attachment Interview (AAI).[10]

Similar findings concerning the power of the AAI to forecast children's adaptation in contexts where the child has no biological or genetic link to the parent were observed in our study of postadoption emotional development in fifty-eight children aged four to seven years at time of adoption.[11] Just as in the study by Dozier and colleagues,[12] the children we followed were more likely to give narrative responses that were classified as secure in response to a standardized doll play prompt if at least one of their new adoptive parents provided an organized secure response to the AAI.[13] Taken together these independent studies by Dozier and her team, and Steele and her team, demonstrate three important points: (1) babies as well as school-age children with a history of maltreatment appear capable of reorganizing their behavior and emotion-regulation strategies in connection with new caregivers; (2) this evolution toward security and adaptive development, against the background of adversity, progresses most easily if caregivers (the foster or adoptive parents) are settled, organized, and coherent with respect to their attachment history; and (3) these findings argue for a nongenetic mechanism for the intergenerational transmission of attachment in line with Bowlby's expectation.[14]

Children Born of the New Reproductive Technologies and Other Nontraditional Family Forms

Multiple independent studies by developmental psychologists, conducted on both sides of the Atlantic Ocean, have demonstrated that children raised by lesbian mothers have positive mother-child relationships and are overall well adjusted.[15] Of course, studies of children born by lesbian mothers often include children conceived by anonymous donor insemination, and questions have followed concerning the extent to which parent-child communication comes openly to include parents' sexual orientation and conception issues. Here there is evidence that openness about these issues is at once both more common than thirty years ago and linked to positive reactions from children, who typically come to a gradual understanding of their parent's or parents' sexual orientation and of their own conception.[16] This burgeoning literature on nontraditional family forms converges on the conclusion that it is interior psychological qualities of the parent (especially the capacity for warmth and open, clear communication matched to the child's ability to understand), rather than sexual orientation, or mode of conception of child, that is predictive of children's adjustment and well-being.[17]

For detailed information on what constitutes the roots of a secure child-parent attachment, and adaptive child outcomes, the chapter now turns to the findings from scores of reliable and valid independent studies, and data collected over decades, reflecting closely observed parents and the normative emergence of infant-parent attachment patterns.

The Normative Development of Infant-Parent Attachment Patterns

Over many thousands of interactions over the first months of life, the infant forms a set of expectations concerning how the parent will respond when the infant calls for him or her. This web of expectations and assumptions was called, by Bowlby, the internal working model of attachment (and self), thought to become organized and established in the child's mind during the second half of the first year of life. While the infant has rudimentary internal working models of attachment, reflecting his experience and guiding his feelings and expectations, each parent has long-established internal working models of attachment that govern how well the parent will respond to his or her child's attachment needs. In the case of the one-year-old child, inference about the child's internal working model of attachment is obtained by observing how a child behaves upon reunion with the parent after two brief separations.[18] For the parent, inference about the adult's internal working model of attachment is obtained via the AAI,[19] and verbal responses to the AAI are powerfully associated with infant responses to the Strange Situation across many thousands of observations.[20]

Internal Working Models of Attachment and Their Manifestations in Parent and Child Behavior

According to attachment theory, it is the parent's internal working model of attachment and caregiving, stemming from his or her childhood experiences, that appears to govern what the parent sees, hears, feels, and does in response to the child's distress. In the best of circumstances, the parent resonates with the child's distress *without* becoming distressed. This enables the parent to respond reflectively about what might be bothering the child, and so act in a way likely to assuage the child's concerns. In less optimal circumstances, the parent becomes distressed at seeing his or her child in distress. At least two possible courses of action may follow: (1) the parent will turn away from the child's distress, finding it too alarming (reminiscent perhaps of unmet attachment needs in his or her own past); or (2) the parent will rush in to help and miss out on the opportunity to connect in a calm way with his or her child. In both cases, the child's distress is likely to be amplified. In the former case, however, where parents turn away, children may learn from this to turn away from distress themselves (to deny it or otherwise pretend that the upset feeling belongs to someone else—perhaps a split-off dissociated aspect of the self). In the situation where parents rush in intrusively, children learn the necessity of remaining distressed insofar as (1) the parent has alarmed them further; and (2) the feeling of extreme distress becomes very familiar, associated as it is with the parent's close presence. Parent and child tussle and struggle to achieve a hard-won equilibrium. Here we see how patterns of flight (avoidance) and fight (resistance) may become habitual modes of relating between infants and parents. These infant-parent patterns of attachment were first noted by Mary Ainsworth,[21] and have since been observed in a huge array of contexts and cultures. These patterns are noteworthy because they have been observed to be more-or-less stable over time, unrelated largely to infant temperament, and so characterize patterns of parent-child interaction that persist over time and influence the child's relationships with significant others (e.g., in preschool, with teachers, with peers, and eventually with romantic partners) for better or worse.[22] The wealth of detailed longitudinal attachment data spanning more than twenty years, and well over a thousand individual lives, is considerable and includes three independent studies from the United States, one from the United Kingdom, two from Germany, and one from Israel.[23] This painstakingly detailed collection of interview and observational (videotaped) material is testament to the importance of parenting for a child from earliest development forward.

The Strange Situation and Its Correlates: The Gold Standard Measure of Mental Health in Infants and Toddlers

The rare two-or-more-decades-long longitudinal studies mentioned earlier, as well as a vast number of shorter longitudinal and cross-sectional studies, constitute a remarkably firm empirical base, validating attachment theory as a key resource for anyone seeking to understand parenting and the influence parents have, consciously and unconsciously, upon their children. The Strange Situation paradigm has quantified the nature of the child's attachment to a specific parent, classifying their reunion behavior, following two brief separations, into normative proportions of 60 to 65 percent secure, 20 to 25 percent insecure-avoidant (or flight as described earlier), 10 to 15 percent insecure-resistant (or fight as described earlier) or 10 to 15 percent disorganized/disoriented.[24] This is the distribution found in low-risk community samples. In high-risk samples, 50 to 80 percent of the children show the disorganized/disoriented response together with their best attempt at achieving an organized pattern of attachment, whether avoidant, resistant, or secure.[25] Disorganized/disoriented responses indicate an apparent lack of a consistent and coherent strategy for organizing a response to the need for comfort and security when under stress.[26]

Main and Hesse contend that when the potentially protective parent is also a source of fear, a disorganized attachment relationship may ensue.[27] Under these circumstances (i.e., fright without solution), the child is faced with an insoluble dilemma that prevents the development of an organized strategy for the use of the attachment figure when distressed or prompts a breakdown of an existing strategy. In the absence of an organized strategy for dealing with distress, odd, conflicted, contradictory, or inexplicable behaviors associated with disorganized attachment are displayed (e.g., stilling [becoming motionless], freezing, repeated incomplete approaches to the parent, or failing to approach the parent when distressed).[28] Mounting evidence suggests that a history of a disorganized attachment serves as a marker for later unfavorable mental health outcomes in childhood and adolescence.[29] A meta-analysis of twelve studies (n = 734) by van IJzendoorn, Schuengel, and Bakersmans-Kranenburg found a substantial association between disorganized attachment and later behavior problems.[30] In particular, disorganized attachment to the mother at one year is linked to concurrent elevated levels of the stress hormone cortisol[31] and child behavior problems at five years of age.[32] Longer-term sequelae of infant disorganization include symptoms of post-traumatic stress disorder at eight years of age,[33] dissociative symptoms in middle and late adolescence,[34] and adolescent psychopathology.[35]

While there is some suggestion that genetic vulnerabilities may predispose some children to heightened sensitivity to the caregiving environment, and so to disorganization if parenting is harsh or unpredictable, there are also recent reports that security of attachment can actually "override" or buffer the genetic predisposition to regulatory difficulties.[36] The case is thus robustly clear that there are multiple social, emotional, and overall health benefits to helping children develop secure infant-parent attachments. But how can parents be helped to achieve this outcome?

The Adult Attachment Interview: A Unique Measure of Parenting Competence

The adult parallel to the Strange Situation procedure is the gold standard measure of adult patterns of attachment known as the Adult Attachment Interview.[37] The AAI has been used extensively to demonstrate links between parents' narrative response patterns to questions about one's childhood and observed individual differences in their children's response to the Strange Situation.[38] In the years since 1995, the AAI has come to be applied in an increasing number of clinical studies such that, as of 2009, there were reports of more than 10,000 AAIs having appeared in print.[39] At the most global level, the AAI assesses the degree to which adults have "come to terms" with their childhood experiences and are able to provide a balanced, coherent, and reflective narrative about their attachment history.[40] When these capacities are evident, the interview is termed *secure-autonomous* (58 percent of community respondents). When these capacities are lacking because of an emotionally restricted style of narration, the interview is judged *insecure-dismissing* (24 percent of community respondents), whereas an overly involved (angry or passive) style of narration leads to a judgment that the interview is *insecure-preoccupied* (18 percent of community respondents). These are all organized patterns of response to the AAI distinct from the disorganized or unresolved response (19 percent of community respondents) where chronic grief is evident, stemming from past loss or trauma.[41] Table 10.1 provides a brief summary of these adult patterns and the infant-parent correlates observed in the Strange Situation procedure.

Table 10.1 describes the main overall patterns of parent responses to the AAI and child responses to the Strange Situation. Note that the typical frequencies of insecure and unresolved/disorganized responses are 50 to 70 percent of clinical referred samples. The description of the AAI in Table 10.1 includes mention of differing levels of reflective functioning, scored on an eleven-point scale, ranging from primitive immature and limited expressions of reflective functioning (e.g., hostile, disavowing, or

Table 10.1 Intergenerational Patterns of Attachment

Adult Attachment Interview	Strange Situation Procedure
Measures adults' current *thoughts and feelings* re past attachments, loss, trauma.	Measures child's current *behavior* in response to two brief separations from the parent with a focus on reunion behavior.
Secure-autonomous pattern: Speaker is balanced, coherent, and valuing of attachment, whether experiences recalled are favorable or not; moderate to high reflective functioning.	*Secure infant-parent attachment*: Child shows a clear preference of having parent in room and plays best when parent is there; happy to see parent upon reunion, and settles if child was distressed.
Dismissing pattern: Speaker is minimizing import of past, claims it was OK or fine with absent or weak supporting evidence; disavowing, hostile, or overly general quality to reflective functioning.	*Insecure avoidant infant-parent attachment:* Child looks away or moves away on reunion; actively attending to toys rather than parent; response to parent is unemotional.
Preoccupied pattern: Speaker is maximizing of past hurts, showing high current anger or passive ongoing involvement with past; hyperactive or bizarre quality to reflective functioning.	*Insecure resistant infant-parent attachment*: Child fails to settle on reunion, after crying on separation; protest may be angry or passive, whimpering; fails to return to play.
Unresolved re past loss or trauma: Speaker is absorbed in past loss or trauma such that the past hurt takes on a live quality; a marked failure in reflective functioning as the speaker adheres to an equivalence or pretend mode of thought (e.g., dead person is spoken about as alive, or abusive figure is spoken about as terrifying still, or is regarded as worthy for having taught a valuable lesson in respect).	*Disorganized/disoriented response:* Child may freeze with a trancelike expression; cry uncontrollably; hand to mouth on reunion is common; prostrating body; hiding under chair; child makes swimming movements; walks backward; combines avoidance with resistance; central core of all these behaviors is fear in the presence of the parent.

bizarre remarks) through low restricted levels (e.g., trite generalizations or hyperactive expressions) to moderate (thoughtful and generous remarks) to high expressions (sophisticated metaphors, spontaneous fresh formulations that show an understanding of the complex links between mental states and behavior, including the differences and similarities between a child's thoughts and feelings and those of an adult). These differing types of reflective functioning are reliably coded and described over an eighty-page manual.[42] In longitudinal research with the London Parent-Child Project, no feature of either maternal or paternal AAI responses was so powerfully predictive of child outcomes as reflective functioning.[43] Table 10.1 notes how unresolved anomalous responses to topics of loss or abuse are typified by "equivalence" and "pretend" modes of thought, conceived as the most primitive early prereflective mental efforts (akin to dreams). When operating according to the "equivalence" rule, inner psychic reality is equated with external reality (no difference is appreciated). What one wishes or believes is absolutely true, and the need or desire that is felt *must* be met. This is the core of unmitigated impulse. Think of the crying newborn who is only satisfied by being given the breast or bottle. Something must be done so that the desperate urgency of the demand is assuaged—that is, until next time. With development, the infant becomes a toddler and acquires rudimentary symbolic capacities. Entry into the world of pretense follows, and children work hard in this domain. Notably, it is an imaginative domain that involves retreat from reality as much as reworking past experiences, and preparing for future ones. One can be carried away by pretense. And this is precisely what happens as some adults tell the story of their experience of loss or abuse. They become absorbed and speak with excessive detail when recalling the past hurt, referring perhaps to a dead person as if he or she were alive. Mary Main calls this a lapse in the monitoring of reason (as it is unreasonable to refer to a dead person as living).[44] Yet it is also an understandable retreat to an early way of thinking, when what was wished for was true in the most immediate sense, and pretend was a welcome escape from the pressures of the external world. All of this gives some idea of how this unresolved state of mind interferes seriously with caregiving of an infant, who needs the adult to monitor his or her mental state and respond with sensitivity. Fear may overcome an infant who encounters a mother or father lost in reverie thinking about a lost parent (a grandparent the child will never know).

It was a landmark report by Main and Hesse that first suggested it was parents whose Adult Attachment Interviews were classified as unresolved with regard to their own experiences of loss and/or trauma who were more likely to have children classified as disorganized in the Strange Situation.[45] This finding has been replicated multiple times, with its robustness confirmed by meta-analytic summaries.[46] For clinicians working in parent-infant psychotherapy, against the backdrop of Fraiberg's words[47] and work on the infamous "ghosts in the nursery," the AAI has been shown to be a reliable measure of such ghosts, that is, unresolved traumatic experiences in the mind of the parent.[48]

For these reasons, the AAI may be administered pre- and posttreatment with a view to examining possible changes from disorganized to organized maternal states of mind over one year. This expectation is bolstered by the recent report of such positive changes in AAI status observed in adults being treated for personality disorder undergoing psychotherapy over one year.[49] At the same time, we are aware of how resistant adult attachment patterns are to change, such that it may be more prudent to anticipate changes in dimensional scores assigned to interviews (e.g., reflective functioning akin to coherence) rather than classification status per se.[50] Certainly, the AAI has a useful clinical role to play in revealing traumatic experiences and important losses likely to be unsettling to parents and a source of interference with their caregiving. At the same time, the AAI is capable of revealing the extent to which a parent has acquired reflective functioning, the capacity for showing an understanding of thoughts, feelings, intentions, and their links to behavior of the self or others. This functioning is a reliable indicator of an adult having resolved past loss or trauma—a vital step toward the prevention of child maltreatment, and a sign that family preservation may be a worthwhile decision/goal. Figure 10.1 shows how reflective functioning (RF) represents a restorative path out of adverse childhood experiences (ACE), including loss or trauma, away from what would otherwise be the intergenerational transmission of insecurity and disorganization arising from adverse parenting (AP). Optimal parenting (OP) is shown as the desirable outcome in Figure 10.1.

Figure 10.1 does not detail the wide range of sources that permit the emergence and capacity for reflective functioning leading to optimal parenting, despite adverse childhood experiences. These sources are various, including cognitive development, new compensatory relationships and the social support they provide (e.g., with a friend, teacher, or grandparent), making it possible for the child, adolescent, or adult to distance him- or herself from, and understand the origins of, adverse experiences that may otherwise preoccupy the mind. From such a position of moderate to

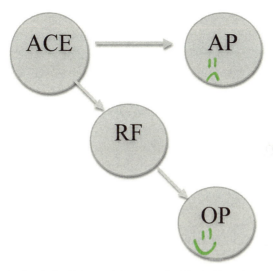

Figure 10.1 Reflective Functioning Moderates the Intergenerational Cycle of Adversity

Key:
- **RF** = Reflective Functioning
- **ACE** = Adverse Childhood Experiences
- **AP** = Adverse Parenting
- **OP** = Optimal Parenting

high reflective functioning, as Figure 10.1 suggests, an adult who did not receive sensitive caregiving becomes capable of providing what he or she did not know as a young child, but came to know later and acquire, the capacity for sensitive and responsive caregiving or optimal parenting. Notably, optimal parenting will vary depending on the age, temperament, and history of the child. What makes the parenting optimal is the way it is not unduly influenced by the parent's adverse history and instead represents a flexible, sometimes humorous, and supportive response to the child's needs. Will optimal parenting attempts sometimes fail? Certainly, but what makes these attempts optimal is the way parents, and so children as well, will rebound quickly in a nonjudgmental way so that child and parent are left with an enduring feeling of joy and resilience rather than despair or shame.

Maternal Sensitivity and Children's Mental Health

Sensitive maternal behavior is arguably the inverse of maternal neglect, rejection, or maltreatment. Maternal sensitivity is best briefly described as the capacity to respond promptly, with appropriate care and concern, to childhood distress. Bowlby posited that continuous sensitive maternal care promotes infant mental health, in both the near and the longer term.[51] Correspondingly, maternal sensitivity has been long thought (and shown) to be the primary determinant of infant-mother patterns of attachment.[52] This situation changed, however, with the advent of the Adult Attachment Interview.[53] The AAI altered the map, with recurrent findings demonstrating a 25 percent overlap of variance between maternal state of mind about attachment and infant-parent patterns of attachment, whereas maternal sensitivity ratings account for no more than 10 percent of the variance in these infant-parent patterns. This led to much discussion of the "transmission gap."[54] A resolution to this mystery has been posited by Slade and colleagues, who point to observed maternal sensitivity (caregiving behavior) being on the path between maternal reflective functioning and infant-mother attachment security.[55] In terms of social work practice, advice to parents, and policy or legal decision making, investing in programs that teach sensitivity *and* reflective functioning is likely to yield rewards for parents and children alike.

Can you teach sensitivity?

John Bowlby on Parenting

Bowlby was emphatic that roots of adult mental health lie in the quality of early experience for which parents are responsible and deserve much support. Evolution has predisposed us to sympathize with and adore a small child, while a parent struggling to cope is inevitably less attractive. But if we gain an appreciation for parents' wishes to safeguard the survival of their child(ren), and to become the kind of parent they wish to be (in their calm moments of hope and planning), then appropriate support of parents, even vulnerable ones with complicated adverse histories, may be realized. The importance of delivering services to vulnerable parents is underscored by the well-documented ACE studies.[56] In more than fifty reports from the ACE study of 17,000 largely middle-class adults in California who were participating in the same managed health care system, it was possible to isolate the multiple psychological and physical health risks that are associated with adverse (traumatic) childhood experiences. A brief perusal of these findings is enough to persuade one of the worth of delivering preventive services to vulnerable parents with adverse histories so the well-known cycle of disadvantage may be disrupted.

What? ?

The Inevitability of Adversity and the Problem with "Attachment Parenting"

If by adversity we mean disappointment and ill fortune, then such things are inevitable in life. In fact, the ACE studies in referring to adversity looked at neglect, physical abuse, sexual abuse, incarceration of a parent, mental illness or substance abuse of a parent, and so on. These types of adversity can be prevented, though hurt feelings, separations, and loss (of loved ones) are inevitable. Here it is important to distinguish Bowlby's approach to parenting from the popular websites that celebrate "attachment parenting." This attachment parenting movement, like the "bonding movement" of the 1970s, was founded by a pediatrician (William Sears), not a researcher, and it is based on a recitation of all the finer beautiful moments of parenting when things go well—sensitivity, warm discipline, caring—put together with an endorsement of natural childbirth, breastfeeding, bonding after birth, and all good things that promote healthy children.[57] Parents are told by followers of Sears to administer their parenting duties with pleasure. But what are parents to do when they find themselves not living up to these ideals, as inevitably will be the case? Would it not be far better to acknowledge up front that mental and interpersonal conflict is inevitable? From there we can talk about the importance of acknowledgment of distress and repair of ruptures.

Empirical work that calculated the proportion of insensitive exchanges between mothers and babies in relation to attuned sensitive interactions observed that in the best of circumstances, as good as it ever gets, it is only about 50 percent of the time that mothers and babies are "attuned."[58] In other words, half of all our attempts to connect with one another fail. And this is the source of hope, of belief in the value of interacting, clarifying, qualifying, and making things right, where they were recently felt to be wrong. For infants on an insecure (avoidant or resistant) path, it is probably the case that insensitive interactions outnumber sensitive ones by a margin of 3 to 1 or 4 to 1. Yet, for other infants on a trajectory involving serious neglect or maltreatment, governed by disorganization and disorientation, we would expect the insensitive interactions to outnumber the sensitive ones by as much as 10 to 1. This is hugely deflating, and understandably terrifying, for the baby. Recent painstaking longitudinal work by Beatrice Beebe and colleagues has demonstrated how filmed interactions of four-month-old babies and their mothers (in five-to ten-minute face-to-face interactions) reveal the distinctive anomalous multimodal patterns of interaction that foreshadow insecure (resistant) or disorganized infant-mother attachments at one year.[59] Bowlby's writing about parents and children seemed to have a prescient appreciation for what empirical science now takes as given: cycles of rupture and repair are inevitable in interpersonal interaction. Relationships are built up on moments of repair that hold one's mind together, and link one person to another, helping one to go forward with a solid sense of hope. *fluid*

Roots of Children's Mental Health Difficulties in Parents' Own Unresolved Childhood Experiences

When Bowlby spoke of parents' emotional problems, in place of constitutional factors (excessive libidinal or aggressive energies) unsettling a child's adaptation, he places parents' unresolved ambivalence from their own childhood experiences.[60] This is the culminating penultimate six-page section of his lecture entitled "Emotional Problems of Parents." Here Bowlby sketches what could be considered a blueprint for "ghosts in the nursery,"[61] and the development of the AAI as reported in "a move to the level of representation."[62] Bowlby remarks: "It seems plain that the feelings evoked in us when we become parents have a very great deal in common with the feelings that were evoked in us as children by our parents and siblings." He qualifies this observation: "I believe that the trouble does not lie in the simple recurrence of old feelings—perhaps a measure of such feelings is present in every parent—but in the parent's inability to tolerate and regulate these feelings."[63]

Bowlby reaches the peak of his concern for, and empathy with, new parents when he advocates for the kinds of efforts that would later become organized as the field of infant mental health: "The advantage of treating young children is now well-known; we are now advocating that parents, too, should be helped soon after they are 'born'!"[64] Pointing out how salient are new parents' feelings and wishes to get things right, Bowlby comments: "Relatively little help, if skilled and given at the right time, may thus go a long way."[65] In this comment, Bowlby anticipates the "less is more" finding that would be documented forty-eight years later in a meta-analytic review of eighty-eight interventions involving more than 7,500 mothers, where the aim was to enhance maternal sensitivity or infant-mother attachment security.[66] This "less is more" finding concerned the observation that brief interventions (six sessions) were observed to be more effective than longer-term interventions for garden-variety difficulties with parenting. Multiproblem families where trauma in the past and present is common are certainly in need of more intensive long-term treatments.

Conclusion

John Bowlby's attachment theory is arguably the most comprehensive and clear available account of the importance of parenting for a child's mental health and for the well-being of society at large. Bowlby's message for parents, penned in the middle of the twentieth century, continues to have penetrating relevance for all those concerned with how best to educate parents, and how best to inform those in positions of authority (e.g., family court judges) affecting the lives of parents and children. A tight summary of attachment research intended specifically for family court judges has recently been published in the *Family Court Review*.[67] This effort by Main and colleagues provides detailed suggestions for how the AAI, the Strange Situation, and a home observation technique may be combined in court-appointed work to facilitate family court judgments. It covers very well issues concerning confidentiality, procedures, and ethics. That article should be consulted if legal or public policy actions, as is hoped, will be inspired by this chapter.

A vital take-home message of this chapter is that the task of parenting well has much more to do with interior emotional and cognitive qualities of the parent than any characteristic of the child (e.g., mode of conception, prematurity, temperament, or disability), or external (superficial) characteristic of the parent (e.g., sexual orientation, foster status, adoptive status). In this respect, attachment theory and research lend firm support to a diversity model of parenting, privileging inner qualities of the mind (secure/balanced/reflective) of the parent that may be found in any cultural context.

Biology predisposes all children to form attachments, and the process is initially automatic, reflexive, and subcortical. By the time a child becomes a parent, however, a great deal of learning has happened. Attachment is by then largely cortical, a reflection of adaptations chosen or arrived at permitting control, redirection, and implying a strong measure of responsibility. The fate of children's attachments, therefore, lies initially and for some time to come with their parent(s) who in most circumstances will be responsible, caring, and effective. Yet all parents deserve support. In this connection, it is prudent to remember how John Bowlby ended many of his writings on parenthood, that is, with the admonition: "A society that values its children must cherish their parents."

Notes

1. John Bowlby, *Attachment and Loss*, vol. 1, *Attachment* (New York: Basic Books, 1969); John Bowlby, *Attachment and Loss*, vol. 2, *Separation: Anxiety and Anger* (New York: Basic Books, 1973); John Bowlby, *Attachment and Loss*, vol. 3, *Loss: Sadness and Depression* (New York: Basic Books, 1980).

2. Bowlby, *Attachment and Loss*, vol. 2, *Separation*.

3. Terence Hébert, Ellen Moss, Daniel Cere, and Hyun Song, "Biological and Psychological Dimensions of Integrative Attachments" (this volume).

4. See, generally, Klaus E. Grossmann, Karin Grossmann, and Everett Waters, eds., *Attachment from Infancy to Adulthood: The Major Longitudinal Studies* (New York: Guilford Press, 2005); Howard Steele and Miriam Steele, "On the Origins of Reflective Functioning," in *Mentalization: Theoretical Considerations, Research Findings, and Clinical Implications*, ed. Frederic N. Busch (New York: Analytic Press, 2008), 133–156.

5. Bowlby, *Attachment and Loss*, vol. 1, *Attachment*; Bowlby, *Attachment and Loss*, vol. 2, *Separation*; Bowlby, *Attachment and Loss*, vol. 3, *Loss*.

6. Sigmund Freud, *The Interpretation of Dreams: The Illustrated Edition*, ed. Jeffrey Moussaieff Masson (1900; repr., New York: Sterling, 2010).

7. John Bowlby, *Maternal Care and Mental Health: A Report Prepared on Behalf of the World Health Organization as a Contribution to the United Nations Programme for the Welfare of Homeless Children* (Geneva: World Health Organization, 1951).

8. Suzan Van Dijken, "The First Half of John Bowlby's Life: A Search for the Roots of Attachment Theory" (PhD diss., University of Leiden, 1996).

9. Mary Dozier et al., "Attachment for Infants in Foster Care: The Role of Caregiver State of Mind," *Child Development* 72 (Sept.–Oct. 2001): 1467. See Mary Ainsworth et al., *Patterns of Attachment: A Psychological Study of the Strange Situation* (Hillsdale, NJ: Erlbaum, 1978).

10. Carol George, Nancy Kaplan, and Mary Main, "The Adult Attachment Interview" (unpublished manuscript, 1985).

11. Steele and Steele, "On the Origins of Reflective Functioning."

12. Dozier et al., "Attachment for Infants in Foster Care."

13. Steele and Steele, "On the Origins of Reflective Functioning."

14. Bowlby, *Attachment and Loss*, vol. 2, *Separation*.

15. E.g., Raymond W. Chan, Barbara Raboy, and Charlotte J. Patterson, "Psychosocial Adjustment among Children Conceived via Donor Insemination by Lesbian and Heterosexual Mothers," *Child Development* 69 (Apr. 1998): 443; Susan Golombok et al., "Children with Lesbian Parents: A Community Study," *Developmental Psychology* 39 (Jan. 2003): 20.

16. See Madeleine Stevens, "Openness in Lesbian Mother Families Regarding Mother's Sexual Orientation and Child's Conception by Donor Insemination," *Journal of Reproductive and Infant Psychology* 21 (Nov. 2003): 347.

17. Charlotte J. Patterson, "Children of Lesbian and Gay Parents," *Current Directions in Psychological Science* 15 (Oct. 2006): 241.

18. Ainsworth et al., *Patterns of Attachment*.

19. George et al., "Adult Attachment Interview"; Mary Main, Erik Hesse, and Ruth Goldwyn, "Studying Differences in Language Usage in Recounting Attachment History: An Introduction to the AAI," in *Clinical Applications of the Adult Attachment Interview*, ed. Howard Steele and Miriam Steele (New York: Guilford Press, 2008), 31–68.

20. Marinus H. van IJzendoorn, "Adult Attachment Representations, Parental Responsiveness, and Infant Attachment: A Meta-analysis on the Predictive Validity of the Adult Attachment Interview," *Psychological Bulletin* 117 (May 1995): 387.

21. Ainsworth et al., *Patterns of Attachment*.

22. L. Alan Sroufe et al., *The Development of the Person: The Minnesota Study of Risk and Adaptation from Birth to Adulthood* (New York: Guilford Press, 2005).

23. For a summary of these studies, see Grossman et al., eds., *Attachment from Infancy to Adulthood*.

24. Ainsworth et al., *Patterns of Attachment*.

25. Karlen Lyons-Ruth and Deborah Jacobvitz, "Attachment Disorganization: Genetic Factors, Parenting Contexts, and Developmental Transformation from Infancy to Adulthood," in *Handbook of Attachment: Theory, Research, and Clinical Applications*, 2nd ed., ed. Jude Cassidy and Phillip R. Shaver (New York: Guilford Press, 2008).

26. Mary Main and Judith Solomon, "Discovery of an Insecure-Disorganized/Disoriented Attachment Pattern," in *Affective Development in Infancy*, ed. T. Berry Brazelton and Michael W. Yogman (Norwood, NJ: Ablex, 1986).

27. Mary Main and Erik Hesse, "Parents' Unresolved Traumatic Experiences Are Related to Infant Disorganized Attachment Status: Is Frightened and/or Frightening Parental Behavior the Linking Mechanism?," in *Attachment in the Preschool Years: Theory, Research, and Intervention*, ed. Mark T. Greenberg, Dante Cicchetti, and E. Mark Cummings (Chicago: University of Chicago Press, 1990), 161–182.

28. Mary Main and Judith Solomon, "Procedures for Identifying Infants as Disorganized/Disoriented during the Ainsworth Strange Situation," in Greenberg et al., *Attachment in the Preschool Years*, 121–160.

29. Elizabeth A. Carlson, "A Prospective Longitudinal Study of Attachment Disorganization/Disorientation," *Child Development* 69 (Aug. 1998): 1107; Karlen Lyons-Ruth, Lisbeth Alpern, and Betty Repacholi, "Disorganized Infant Attachment Classification and Maternal Psychosocial Problems as Predictors of Hostile-Aggressive Behavior in the Preschool Classroom," *Child Development* 64 (Apr. 1993): 572; Ellen Moss, Chantal Cyr, and Karine Dubois-Comtois, "Attachment at Early School Age and Developmental Risk: Examining Family Contexts and Behavior Problems of Controlling-Caregiving, Controlling-Punitive, and Behaviorally Disorganized Children," *Developmental Psychology* 40 (July 2004): 519; Helen Z. Macdonald et al., "Longitudinal Association between Infant Disorganized Attachment and Childhood Posttraumatic Stress Symptoms," *Development and Psychopathology* 20 (June 2008): 493; Judith Solomon, Carol George, and Annemieke De Jong, "Children Classified as Controlling at Age Six: Evidence of Disorganized Representational Strategies and Aggression at Home and at School," *Development and Psychopathology* 7 (July 1995): 447.

30. Marinus H. van IJzendoorn, Carlo Schuengel, and Marian J. Bakermans-Kranenburg, "Disorganized Attachment in Early Childhood: Meta-analysis of Precursors, Concomitants, and Sequelae," *Development and Psychopathology* 11 (June 1999): 225.

31. Gottfried Spangler and Klaus E. Grossmann, "Biobehavioral Organization in Securely and Insecurely Attached Infants," *Child Development* 64 (Oct. 1993): 1439.

32. Lyons-Ruth et al., "Disorganized Infant Attachment Classification and Maternal Psychosocial Problems."

33. Macdonald et al., "Longitudinal Association between Infant Disorganized Attachment and Childhood Posttraumatic Stress Symptoms."

34. Carlson, "Prospective Longitudinal Study."

35. L. Alan Sroufe et al., "Implications of Attachment Theory for Developmental Psychopathology," *Development and Psychopathology* 11 (Mar. 1999): 1.

36. See, e.g., Grazyna Kochanska et al., "Early Attachment Organization Moderates the Parent-Child Mutually Coercive Pathway to Children's Antisocial Conduct," *Child Development* 80 (July/Aug. 2009): 1288, 1297.

37. Mary Main, Nancy Kaplan, and Jude Cassidy, "Security in Infancy, Childhood and Adulthood: A Move to the Level of Representation," *Monographs of the Society for Research in Child Development* 50, nos. 1/2 (1985): 66; Mary Main, Ruth Goldwyn, and Erik Hesse, "Adult Attachment Classification System Version 7.2" (unpublished manuscript, 2003); Main et al., "Studying Differences in Language Usage in Recounting Attachment History."

38. See van IJzendoorn, "Adult Attachment Representations, Parental Responsiveness, and Infant Attachment," for a meta-analytic report of approximately 1,000 observed intergenerational associations.

39. Marian J. Bakermans-Kranenburg and Marinus H. van IJzendoorn, "No Reliable Gender Differences in Attachment across the Lifespan," *Behavioral and Brain Sciences* 32 (Feb. 2009): 22.

40. Main et al., "Studying Differences in Language Usage in Recounting Attachment History"; Steele and Steele, "On the Origins of Reflective Functioning."

41. Main et al., "Studying Differences in Language Usage in Recounting Attachment History."

42. Peter Fonagy et al., "Reflective Functioning Manual (Version 5) for Application to Adult Attachment Interviews" (unpublished manuscript, Nov. 1998).

43. Steele and Steele, "On the Origins of Reflective Functioning."

44. Main et al., "Studying Differences in Language Usage in Recounting Attachment History."

45. Main and Hesse, "Parents' Unresolved Traumatic Experiences."

46. van IJzendoorn, "Adult Attachment Representations, Parental Responsiveness, and Infant Attachment."

47. Selma Fraiberg, *Clinical Studies in Infant Mental Health: The First Year of Life* (New York: Basic Books, 1980).

48. Peter Fonagy et al., "Measuring the Ghost in the Nursery: An Empirical Study of the Relation between Parents' Mental Representations of Childhood Experiences and Their Infants' Security of Attachment," *Journal of the American Psychoanalytic Association* 41 (Nov. 1993): 957.

49. Kenneth N. Levy et al., "Change in Attachment Patterns and Reflective Function in a Randomized Control Trial of Transference-Focused Psychotherapy for Borderline Personality Disorder," *Journal of Consulting and Clinical Psychology* 74 (Dec. 2006): 1027.

50. Peter Fonagy et al., "The Relation of Attachment Status, Psychiatric Classification, and Response to Psychotherapy," *Journal of Consulting and Clinical Psychology* 64 (Feb. 1996): 22.

51. Bowlby, *Maternal Care and Mental Health*.

52. Ainsworth et al., *Patterns of Attachment*.

53. Main et al., "Security in Infancy, Childhood and Adulthood."

54. van IJzendoorn, "Adult Attachment Representations, Parental Responsiveness, and Infant Attachment."

55. John Grienberger, Kristen Kelly, and Arietta Slade, "Maternal Reflective Functioning, Mother-Infant Affective Communication, and Infant Attachment: Exploring the Link between Mental States and Observed Caregiving Behavior in the Intergenerational Transmission of Attachment," *Attachment and Human Development* 7 (Sept. 2005): 299.

56. E.g., Vincent J. Felitti et al., "Relationship of Childhood Abuse and Household Dysfunction to Many of the Leading Causes of Death in Adults: The Adverse Childhood Experiences (ACE) Study," *American Journal of Preventive Medicine* 14 (May 1998): 245.

57. William Sears and Martha Sears, *The Attachment Parenting Book: A Commonsense Guide to Understanding and Nurturing Your Baby* (Boston: Little, Brown, 2001).

58. Edward Z. Tronick, "Emotions and Emotional Communication in Infants," *American Psychologist* 44 (Feb. 1989): 112.

59. Beatrice Beebe et al., "Maternal Anxiety Symptoms and Mother–Infant Self- and Interactive Contingency," *Infant Mental Health Journal* 32 (Mar./Apr. 2011): 174.

60. John Bowlby, "Psychoanalysis and Child Care," in *The Making and Breaking of Affectional Bonds* (London: Tavistock, 1979), 1–24. See Howard Steele, "Test of Time: On Re-reading 'Psychoanalysis and Child Care', John Bowlby's Lecture Delivered in 1956 on the Centenary of Sigmund Freud's Birth," *Clinical Child Psychology and Psychiatry* 15 (July 2010): 453.

61. Selma Fraiberg, Edna Edelson, and Vivian Shapiro, "Ghosts in the Nursery: A Psychoanalytic Approach to the Problems of Impaired Infant-Mother Relationships," *Journal of the American Academy of Child Psychiatry* 14 (1975): 387.

62. Main et al., "Security in Infancy, Childhood and Adulthood."

63. Bowlby, *Making and Breaking of Affectional Bonds*, 17–18.

64. Ibid., 20.

65. Ibid.

66. Marian J. Bakermans-Kranenburg, Marinus H. van IJzendoorn, and Femmie Juffer, "Less Is More: Meta-analyses of Sensitivity and Attachment Interventions in Early Childhood," *Psychological Bulletin* 129 (Mar. 2003): 195.

67. Mary Main, Erik Hesse, and Siegfried Hesse, "Attachment Theory and Research: Overview with Suggested Applications to Child Custody," *Family Court Review* 49 (2011): 426.

Gender Equality, Gender Difference, and Parenthood

Are There Gender Differences in Parenting? Should Difference Make a Difference?

PART SIX

Gender and Parentage

Family Law's Equality Project in Our Empirical Age

Susan Frelich Appleton

This chapter joins the conversation about the place of gender in the law of parentage, an issue that looms large in today's "culture war,"[1] including the continuing battle in the United States over same-sex marriage. Here, in addressing not only the question, What is parenthood?, but also Who is a parent?,[2] I make the case for a legal regime based on the *diversity model*. This approach, which embraces gender equality, supports recognition of a diverse range of parent-child relationships, without regard to sex or gender. This approach contrasts with what this book calls the *integrative model*, in which parentage integrates biological and other parental functions and locates them within heterodyadic marriage. Because the integrative model relies partly on genetics, assumes gendered family performances, and privileges traditional marriage, its understanding of parenthood requires just one man and just one woman.

In advocating for a law of parentage that respects diversity, this chapter makes two contributions. First, it challenges the constitutional validity of laws that would impose an integrative model by showing how this model and its underlying normative premises rest on gender stereotypes that equality jurisprudence and contemporary family law have repudiated. Second, it questions recent arguments, both for and against laws based on the integrative model, that rely on empirical investigations of the effects of various familial arrangements on children. Even if empirical findings purport to show that the normative one-mother/one-father configuration serves most children well, such data do not justify enshrining this arrangement in a law applicable to all children.

Family Law's Equality Project
Gender's Place in Family Law

Family law long stood out as a site marked by inequalities, including differences based on economic class,[3] race,[4] and marital status.[5] Gender, however, accounted for the most pervasive and salient disparity of treatment, entrenched by the "vehicle" of marriage.⁶ ==The entire construction of family law as a field delineated a diminished "private" or domestic sphere belonging to women in opposition to the exalted "public" sphere of men.⁷==

In the 1970s, family law embarked on what I call an "equality project," designed to correct the manifold disparities of the past. Participants included scholars, activists, law reformers, and, ultimately, judges and legislators. Although this project proceeded on various fronts, for example, undoing most of the discrimination suffered by children born to unmarried parents⁸ and federalizing many disparate standards among the states,⁹ gender emerges as an especially conspicuous focus, challenging the field's fundamental assumptions. This aspect of the equality project achieved enormous success after the U.S. Supreme Court declared its allegiance, condemning traditional gender-based roles and stereotypes in its antidiscrimination jurisprudence.¹⁰

radical change

Because much traditional family law rested on such roles and stereotypes, the Court's decisions prompted reforms in the states, where family law is ordinarily made. In the remarkable transformation that followed, family law went from a regime that systematically and explicitly classified by gender and subordinated women, especially married women, to a body of rules that, with few exceptions, insists that gender must be formally ignored.¹¹

Caban v. Mohammed illustrates the doctrinal analysis producing such changes.¹² In seeking to have her husband adopt the children she bore during an earlier relationship, Maria Mohammed relied on a New York statute that did not require the consent of unmarried birth fathers, despite requiring such consent from married birth fathers and birth mothers, regardless of marital status. Abdiel Caban, the birth father of Mohammed's children, successfully challenged the statute on equal protection grounds. The Court determined that he and Mohammed were "similarly situated"¹³ in their parental relationships because both had lived with and cared for the children. The Court concluded that the statute embodied an "overbroad generalization," reflecting impermissible gender stereotypes.¹⁴

State responses moved beyond such cases. For example, the Supreme Court never directly confronted the place of gender in child custody adjudication or the traditional "tender-years" doctrine, which prefers maternal, over paternal, custody of young children.¹⁵ Yet signals from its cases about parentage, adoption consent, and marital roles were sufficiently clear that state legislatures, state courts, and law reform initiatives excluded gender as a factor for deciding child custody.¹⁶ Under contemporary statutes, neither a parent's nor a child's gender constitutes a legitimate consideration.¹⁷ The favored place of joint custody in many jurisdictions implements this principle.¹⁸

Today, family law facially treats men and women as similarly situated for purposes of family life, including parenting—with two noteworthy qualifications. First, Supreme Court opinions indicate that identical treatment is not required when "real differences" distinguishing men and women are relevant.¹⁹ True, the justices sometimes struggle to identify what counts as a "real difference" and what instead constitutes an "overbroad generalization" based on habitual stereotypes,²⁰ illustrated by their sharp division about whether birth abroad to a citizen father must be treated the same, for purposes of U.S. immigration law, as birth abroad to a citizen mother.²¹ Nonetheless, Mary Anne Case distills from the cases the doctrine that sex- or gender-based legal rules survive constitutional scrutiny only when the classification embodies a "perfect proxy," with the assumption reflected in the gender-based rule "true of either all women or no women or all men or no men."²² By contrast, gendered generalizations that, even if often true, are not always so will fail as unconstitutional discrimination.²³ Whatever the permissibility of rules distinguishing, say, pregnant women and expectant fathers,²⁴ justifications for different treatment abate after birth and, at least after lactation ends, become constitutionally unsustainable, as *Caban* shows.

Second, as my use of the term *project* suggests, family law's moves toward equality convey an aspirational tone. Consistent with the notion that family law performs a "channelling function,"²⁵ family law can be understood as an endeavor to shape family life. For example, in examining the federal Family and Medical Leave Act (FMLA)²⁶ in *Nevada Department of Human Resources v. Hibbs*,²⁷ the Supreme Court indicated that it shares with Congress the goal of combating gender stereotypes in both the workplace and the home. Accordingly, the FMLA and *Hibbs* reach beyond the elimination of employment discrimination to include an aspiration of "degendering" care work within the family itself.

At first, this channelling effort and aspirational approach to gender seem to cut against the grain of family law's oft-stated emphasis on "freedom of personal choice in . . . family life."²⁸ How can a legal regime actively seeking to influence behavior also claim to respect pluralism and autonomy? Yet, a closer look at gay rights litigation, for example, reveals how liberty and equality often work as mutually reinforcing values.²⁹ Accordingly, family law's efforts to displace gender stereotypes should promote individual dignity,[30] freeing men and women to create the family lives they choose. Such equal liberty, of course, allows those who prefer adhering to more traditional gender performances to do so, with ample support from culture, religion, and familiar social practices.

Reinforcement from Family Law's Functional Turn

If efforts to counter express discrimination first loosened the grip of traditional gender norms in family law, a second development strengthened the shift. Calls for family law to reflect "the reality of family life"[31] sparked a functional turn in the field—the rise of legal recognition for those who perform a family relationship, even in the absence of formal or biological connections.[32] These calls arose from the inequities resulting from discrimination against nonmarital families. The case for evenhanded treatment proved particularly compelling for children, who had no control over the behavior of the adults in their lives. From acknowledgment that punishing children for their biological parents' failure to marry is "illogical and unjust"[33] emerged more capacious concepts extending family law's benefits (and responsibilities) to once unrecognized affiliations. These concepts often emphasize the child's perspective, protecting a relationship with one whom the child regards as a parent despite the absence of traditional ties.[34]

Thus, familiar criteria for parentage, such as giving birth, marriage to a child's mother, or adoption, have been joined by newer understandings based on behavior and resulting dependencies and affective ties. Concepts such as de facto parents, parents by estoppel, psychological parents, intent-based parenthood, and in loco parentis status establish legal *parentage* based on *parenting conduct* under certain circumstances.[35] Significantly, the performances triggering such recognition do not depend on whether the performer is male or female, strengthening the equality project's rejection of gender-based classifications.

Attending to function and performance opens up the analysis in intriguing ways. For example, scientific research suggests that parental conduct can change biology, including sex-associated differences, so that what we do affects who we are[36]—a conclusion not far removed from theories of those who, like Judith Butler, understand gender itself as performance.[37]

Gender Neutrality and Beyond

The Court's precedents embrace a principle of formal equality, disestablishing gendered rules and expectations so that men have an equal opportunity to perform the family roles customarily performed by women and vice versa. In the parentage context, this approach means that conduct should produce the same legal consequences regardless of the actor's gender or a couple's combined gender. Thus, the traditional rule presumptively making a husband the legal parent of his wife's children should extend to same-sex couples who marry or enter functionally equivalent relationships.[38]

Other authorities use gender-neutral approaches designed to encourage performances against stereotype. As noted, the FMLA seeks to regulate the workplace in a way that influences decisions made "privately" in the home.[39] A stronger version can be found in countries that designate some leave for one parent while making additional leave available to the second parent on a "use it or lose it" basis.[40]

Gender neutrality, however, might provide just the beginning. More ambitious visions of egalitarian family law push beyond formal equality. Martha Albertson Fineman emphasizes that gender neutrality leaves mothers, children, and caretaking all underserved and undervalued.[41] Ultimately invoking a functional approach, Fineman and others, such as Barbara Katz Rothman, understand "mothering" as an activity or performance, which men too can execute.[42] By contrast, Laura Kessler advocates dismantling the very performances associated with mothers and fathers. Even the advent of female breadwinners, although defying traditional stereotypes, stops short, she argues, of achieving feminist ideals of equality.[43] Still others emphasize unique biological contributions that males and females make in reproduction, for example, the caretaking performed in gestation, either to challenge gender neutrality[44] or to call for forms of "affirmative action" to overcome disadvantages that might stem from such differences.[45] "Affirmative action" could include gender-specific legislation such as the designated paternity leave that Andrea Doucet (in the next chapter) situates within the diversity model.[46]

These variations demonstrate that family law's equality project remains a work in progress and a contested one at that. While discarding traditional assumptions, the project leaves considerable room for newer constructions to evolve. It does not leave room, however, for a return to the inequalities of the past.[47]

Such evolution forward will unfold in a dynamic process as legal developments shape public views while changing public views set the arc for law reform. A glimpse of such interaction emerges from the Pew Research Center's recent data, including findings that reflect a decreasing significance of gender and gender roles in public perceptions of marriage and understandings of "family."[48] Even if same-sex marriage sits at the edge of the equality project's present bounds[49] and remains the center of a "culture war," support for this family form has grown with its scattered legalization, with a narrow majority in the United States now favoring recognition.[50]

Testing the Normative Claims of the Integrative Model

Although articulations of the integrative model vary, all share a vision of parenthood in which biological or genetic connection stands out as a necessary, even if not sufficient, element. For example, Daniel Cere understands this model to "argue for the integration of the diverse aspects of parenthood: biological, intentional, gestational, paternal, maternal, social, sexual, and psychological."[51] Emphasizing maternal attachment,[52] Cere explains that "integrative accounts resist the fragmentation of parenthood into its diverse components."[53] Elizabeth Marquardt grounds reservations about same-sex marriage in the link between marriage and parenthood and the fact that "the two persons in a same-sex couple cannot both be the biological parents of the child."[54]

Certainly, in supporting "integration," Cere and Marquardt eschew doctrinaire arguments in favor of nuanced ones. Cere is open to expansive understandings of family that would include same-sex couples and sperm donors or "surrogate mothers," thus joining children with multiple adults who perform parental functions.[55] Marquardt expresses positive views about adoption, although it defies her integrative ideal.[56] Nonetheless, each privileges the family consisting of one mother, one father, and their biological children.

A search for the normative commitments animating the integrative account yields several readings. Yet, the equality project's established principles would doom a parentage law resting on any of them.

Under one reading suggested by Cere's reference to maternal and paternal "aspects," women and men play different family roles, children benefit from rearing by two adults who embody these roles, and family law should perpetuate such norms for future generations. Gender-based role modeling becomes part of family law's larger channelling function. Clearly, an "integrated" law of parentage with no additional justification could not survive constitutional challenge.[57]

A second reading of the underlying normative claim might welcome gender-atypical family behavior but contend that a female breadwinner and male caregiver remain models for gender performances—performances to be enshrined in the law of parentage. Yet, such thinking evokes the very stereotypes that family law's equality project now repudiates, shown by cases from the employment arena. In *Price Waterhouse v. Hopkins*,[58] the Supreme Court agreed that critical considerations of the employee's performance as a female—her language, mannerisms, vocabulary, clothing, and grooming style—constituted prohibited "sex stereotyping."[59] The legal links between the workplace and home, highlighted by the FMLA and *Hibbs*, demonstrate the relevance for family law of cases like *Hopkins*. These authorities bridge once "separate spheres," reminding us that any given individual, male or female, usually has a place in both. Hence, this second reading of the claim that parentage requires one mother and one father also stands at odds with the equality project.

A third reading might build on the opening reserved by the Supreme Court for consideration of "real differences." This space remains narrow, however, with the opinions articulating a sharp contrast between "mythical or stereotyped assumptions about the proper roles and relative capabilities of men and women," on one hand, and "'inherent differences' between men and women,"[60] on the other. Because "overbroad sex-based generalizations are impermissible even when they enjoy empirical support,"[61] one need not argue that women and men behave identically to require gender neutrality in parentage law. Besides, given the aspirational character of the equality project, family law seeks to reshape the way things are, not reinforce prevailing gender scripts.

What "real [sex-based] differences" would justify the integrative account's gendered parentage law? Contested theories that posit stark physical contrasts between "female brains"[62] and their male counterparts simply return us to the possibility that men and women perform parental functions differently. Moreover, even these physical differences can change with behavior.[63] Further, apart from an objective of role modeling, this argument fails to justify why any such differences *should matter* legally.

Probably, the role modeling envisioned is considered important preparation for heterosexual adulthood. Thus, an alternative argument for one mother and one father based on "real differences" could focus on the anatomical distinctions relevant in sexual activities themselves.[64] Anatomical differences and the procreative potential of a male-female couple's sexual relationship occupy a significant place in cases rejecting challenges to an exclusively heterosexual marriage regime.[65] However, *Lawrence v. Texas* casts a shadow on much discriminatory treatment of same-sex sexual activity.[66] Further, children are not expected to observe directly the sexual activities of those who rear them,[67] and the argument for dual-gender role models because of anatomical likeness would lose its force in families with only sons or only daughters[68]—even if we could assume that all parents practice physical immodesty with their children.

True, some sex-based anatomical differences may have implications for parentage law. Even under functional approaches, women perform gestational functions that men cannot. Yet, such differences must have limited and time-restricted consequences, as the Court's opinions make plain.[69] Attaching enduring legal effects to a woman's gestational contribution would make biology destiny—precisely the generalization that family law's equality project seeks to dismantle. Accordingly, privileging over the long term the "maternal-infant attachment bonds" that Cere celebrates[70] would contravene established precedents, including *Caban*.[71]

Another reading of "real differences" emphasizes genetic ties, as Marquardt does, when she criticizes donor insemination and argues that rearing by gamete providers (one male and one female) is uniquely beneficial for children.[72] This argument raises as many questions as it answers, however. First, it fails to explain why proponents of the integrative model have not joined forces with critics of the child welfare system, who point out how the state too often removes children from their homes even when more modest intervention or simple financial assistance could preserve such (genetic) families.[73] Second, it fails to confront the presumption of legitimacy, the traditional doctrine making the mother's husband a child's only legal father, to the exclusion of an interested and involved genetic father.[74] Indeed, Marquardt's discourse equates parenthood with genetics, without acknowledging law's well-established participation.[75] Third, several law reforms might promote the maintenance of genetic ties—from open adoption to required state notification of all adopted children about their status, even if their adoptive parents decided not to share such information.[76] Yet, proponents of integration do not advocate such measures (which would circumscribe parental autonomy). Indeed, some of them are among the strongest opponents of the emerging view that children might have more than two legal parents (often a biological mother, her same-sex partner, and the child's genetic father)—although these arrangements afford children a recognized relationship with a gamete provider who would otherwise be a legal stranger.[77]

Finally, emphasis on genetic ties might express a normative claim that the benefit of rearing by genetic parents lies in the messages conveyed about "personal responsibility,"[78] the link between sexual activity and parental obligations, and the association of sexual desire and pleasure with ongoing intimate relationships.[79] Parenting entails a sense of continuity, the transmission of values,[80] and decisions made with love, all of which genetic ties are said to promote.[81] This vision explains the integrative account's preference for dual-gender marriage, reflected in Marquardt's analysis, which signals a long-term arrangement in which gender-specific elements remain salient well past fertilization, pregnancy, birth, lactation, and other time-limited "real differences." Yet, to the extent that a gendered conceptualization of marriage occupies a central place in the integrative model, parentage becomes gendered, too, conflicting with precedents and the equality project.

The Contested Role of Empirical Evidence

The legal debate about gender and parentage has become increasingly empirical, with social scientists, legal scholars, and courts proceeding as if a definitive resolution lies in data about how children fare in various familial arrangements. For example, Cere cites for support of the integrative model multidisciplinary findings about attachment theory and kinship bonds. By contrast, recent meta-analyses of empirical data uncover no evidence for the superiority of an integrative model, concluding that neither parental gender nor sexual orientation affects child well-being.[82] Like Fiona Tasker's contribution to this volume,[83] recent judicial analyses of the data come down firmly on the no-harm side, determining that "there are no differences in the parenting of homosexuals or the adjustment of their children."[84]

Whatever view momentarily holds the upper hand, however, findings from the social sciences cannot answer the question whether gender should matter in the *law* of parentage. Whether my position presents a persuasive argument or simply a provocative thought experiment, I note the problems in using such data to craft parentage laws.

First, controlling judicial opinions unmistakably elevate equality values over findings about child welfare that implicate constitutionally impermissible considerations. The Supreme Court's famous case about race and custody, *Palmore v. Sidoti*,[85] held that the Fourteenth Amendment's anti-discrimination goals trump "the reality of private biases and the possible injury they might inflict" on a Caucasian child living with her mother, who began cohabiting with and later married an African American man—a situation subjecting the child to peer stigmatization. Conceding that the "effects of racial prejudice" might well be "real,"[86] the Court ruled off-limits such otherwise plausible considerations under the best-interests-of-the-child standard for custody, overturning the decision below changing custody to the father. The Court explained its decision not as a repudiation of the best-interests standard but rather as a refusal to give legal effect to discrimination. Thus, *Palmore* put aspirations of equality above assertions of possible harm, providing a legal frame for findings that Tasker reports about the effects of peer-group prejudice experienced by some children of lesbians.[87]

Second, even if we assume that scientific studies and empirical data about what is good for children and what is not ought to shape the law of parentage, several difficulties would follow. One difficulty is that such empirical data would provide information about children generally, presumably based on large samples and control groups. By contrast, authentic applications of the best-interests standard have always contemplated an individualized, fact-sensitive assessment concerning a particular child.[88] Even if data revealed that most children thrive in one setting rather than another, such data would fail to address what familial arrangement works best for a given child, based on her unique history, attachments, and needs. Thus, data like those cited by Marquardt about the risks some children face from stepfathers or mothers' cohabitants[89] cannot alone support the demise of de facto parentage as a legal option or an across-the-board rule making all stepfathers and mothers' cohabitants ineligible for such status.

Certainly, I do not mean to conflate the best-interests standard, typically used to decide custody disputes between "parents," with the logically prior inquiry about whom family law should recognize as parents in the first place. Still, arguments for enacting integrative parentage laws and excluding other possibilities have much to learn from the best-interests standard's assumption that children's needs differ from one case to the next. Despite the well-rehearsed difficulties of the indeterminacy of the best-interests standard,[90] its persistence signals not only family law's long-standing embrace of pluralism,[91] but also the allure of treating each child individually. Indeed, recently several broad parentage rules and policies—from the presumption of legitimacy to the disfavor of transracial adoption—have given way to more particularized approaches emphasizing the interests of the individual child in question.[92] One size does not fit all, so invoking data about the welfare of most children to make the case for a restrictive rule applicable to all necessarily leaves some children out.

Further, competing value judgments prevent empirical evidence and scientific studies from resolving the legal parentage debate. Interpretations of studies focused on the sexualities and gender performances of individuals reared in families headed by gay male and lesbian couples, compared with those reared in more traditional settings, necessarily depend on one's view of desirable and undesirable gender performances.[93] Although legislatures often make value judgments, as they are elected to do, something more than a preference for traditional gender stereotypes is required.[94] Moreover, counterevidence often emerges. For example, findings about the "male sex-typed traits" of girls reared by lesbian parents diverge in important ways from more recent data about the feminine career aspirations of this group.[95]

Similar problems plague a second type of study that focuses on overall child well-being, testing the superiority of one parental arrangement over another. As with other contentious issues, one can find evidence on both sides—with advocates pushing results they regard as favorable and pointing out flaws in studies producing different outcomes.[96] Although bias infiltrates all scientific and social-scientific investigations, the "culture war" in the United States about gender, marriage, and parenthood makes studies on these matters especially fraught.

Indeed, the prevailing wisdom might well change over time, as we see, for example, in radically changed expert opinions about secrecy versus openness in adoption[97] and in the on-again, off-again preference, after dissolution, for sole custody plus visitation versus joint legal and physical custody.[98] These illustrations demonstrate the fragility of a legal regime constructed on the basis of whatever happens to be today's scientifically supported conventional wisdom.

Finally, in studies of children's well-being, identifying the appropriate counterfactual proves problematic. If we take seriously family law's channelling function, signaling official approval and disapproval of certain conduct and domestic arrangements, then data about children reared within various settings do not permit the necessary comparisons. Comprehensive social-scientific investigations must also take into account the effect of the legal regime, that is, the impact on a child's lived experience of laws that marginalize his particular family arrangement, compared with laws that would accord it equal value and respect. Courts deciding same-sex marriage cases often cite the negative impact on child well-being resulting from the illegitimacy of certain family forms.[99] Such negative impact transcends the denial of tangible benefits and includes the psychic consequences of second-class citizenship, which courts have emphasized in explaining why civil union and domestic partnership laws, although providing marriage's material benefits to same-sex couples and their children, failed to go far enough.[100]

If children reared by same-sex couples are shown to be worse off than their counterparts reared in more traditional families, can we reliably disentangle the impact of gender from the impact of an inhospitable legal environment, including, for instance, recently passed "preservation of marriage" amendments to state constitutions and explicit discrimination at the federal level?[101] Indeed, until quite recently, discerning how children fare when reared by same-sex *married* couples would have been impossible, and even in Massachusetts and California, backlash or what Marquardt calls efforts "to put the toothpaste back in the tube,"[102] with all attendant publicity,[103] send a disapproving message. The concerns voiced in *Brown v. Board of Education* about children's "feeling of inferiority as to their status in the community"[104] because of legal segregation provide an analogy that resonates in this contemporary context.

The aspirational character of family law's equality project only accentuates the difficulties of basing restrictive parentage rules on general data that ignore the legal environment's effects. Such data-based rules are likely to reinforce customary and traditional ways (even "private biases") rather than to push forward, opening the path for the hoped-for opportunities and transformations.

Concluding Reflections

The legal problems posed by the overriding importance that proponents of the integrative model accord to gender and genetics, together with reasons to discount empirical evidence in crafting a law of parentage, clear the way to explore alternative conceptualizations. The diversity approach that I favor, though not developed here, contemplates a commitment to robust pluralism and equal liberty.[105] A legal regime based on these values would not stand in the way of those who choose traditional family forms and gender roles, but it would welcome with equal dignity those who organize their lives differently.[106] I envision parentage laws reflecting what

David Chambers called "supportive neutrality"[107] or what others have theorized as the "disestablishment" of sex and gender[108] (or protection for the "free exercise"[109] thereof). By contrast, the integrative model's heteronormativity naturalizes a gendered model, so that everything else becomes deviant, even if begrudgingly tolerated or accorded second-class status.[110]

Of all the noteworthy crosscurrents explored in this volume, I conclude by calling attention to two. First, Doucet, who shares my goal of unsettling entrenched gender inequalities, contends that gender-neutral laws are not up to the task. Using evidence from Sweden and parts of Canada, she argues that only gender-specific parental leave policies aimed at fathers can dismantle traditional gender norms.[111] I accept the need for such "affirmative action." Yet, the cultural environment Doucet cites contrasts sharply with that in the United States. For example, Canada has legalized same-sex marriage and supports families headed by gays and lesbians,[112] while Sweden has a gender-neutral marriage law.[113] In these jurisdictions, which rely on the diversity model to answer the question, Who is a parent?, refinements in parental leave policies develop against background commitments not evident in the United States. In the United States, the "culture war" about gender and marriage persists (notwithstanding family law's equality project), the integrative model retains traction in public and political discourse, and leave laws remain rudimentary, as illustrated by the FMLA, which promises only limited and unpaid leave.[114] The disparity between the gender neutrality that I urge and the gender specificity that Doucet advocates serves as a helpful reminder of how context shapes our understanding of gender—a point she properly emphasizes.[115]

Second, integrative accounts, such as those advanced by Cere and Marquardt, like my diversity approach, claim to promote children's interests—which I suspect that we all agree is a paramount value. In sharing concern for children's interests, however, our contrasting views play out against an age-old tension in family law. While children routinely occupy a revered place in family law's rhetoric, the field remains trapped between two unsatisfying ways to implement this rhetoric. Under one understanding, parents have plenary authority to speak for children, and intrusion by the state necessarily undermines their best interests.[116] Under another, parental autonomy and control advance adult interests at the expense of children's, and a skeptical state should have more leeway to challenge parents on behalf of children.[117] Although contemporary family law combines strands from both, each assumes that children cannot reliably speak for themselves or independently advance their own interests.

Whether based on an integrative or a diversity approach, parentage rules are important precisely because of the authority and responsibility that family law vests in those deemed parents and the relative lack of legal status and protection accorded to nonparents.[118] Further, the more flexible and individually tailored a parentage determination becomes, as illustrated by contemporary functional tests, the more room the law of parentage leaves for judicial determinations and hence state intervention. Awareness of law's limited capacity requires proceeding with caution.[119]

Nonetheless, all parentage rules, even those that are most familiar and traditional, reflect social and legal constructions. Because the state *necessarily* participates in the creation of such constructions[120] and *purposely* seeks to shape family behavior, I regard the equality project and its repudiation of gender stereotypes as indispensable tools and vital limits in developing legal answers to the questions, What is parenthood? and Who is a parent?

Notes

With thanks for comments and suggestions to Mary Anne Case, Adrienne Davis, Linda McClain, and Laura Rosenbury and participants in the Randall-Park Colloquium at the University of Kentucky College of Law and at the "What Is Parenthood?" working conference at the University of Virginia. Caitlin McGarr and Lindsay Smith assisted with research.

1. See Lawrence v. Texas, 539 U.S. 558, 602 (2003) (Scalia, J., dissenting).

2. I add the question, Who is a parent?, because my exploration of parenthood as a legal issue necessarily emphasizes whom law does or does not recognize as a parent. Although historically such matters went by a variety of names, such as *illegitimacy*, the modern (and more encompassing) term is *parentage*, which I use throughout this chapter. See, e.g., Uniform Parentage Act (2000).

3. See Lawrence M. Friedman, *A History of American Law*, 3rd ed. (New York: Simon and Schuster, 2005), 144. For rulings guaranteeing access to marriage and divorce without regard to wealth, see Boddie v. Connecticut, 401 U.S. 371 (1971) (divorce); Zablocki v. Redhail, 434 U.S. 374 (1978) (marriage).

4. See Loving v. Virginia, 388 U.S. 1 (1967) (invalidating antimiscegenation restriction).

5. See Eisenstadt v. Baird, 405 U.S. 438 (1972) (recognizing an individual constitutional right of access to contraception, regardless of marital status).

6. Nancy F. Cott, *Public Vows: A History of Marriage and the Nation* (Cambridge: Harvard University Press, 2000), 3. Family law centers on marriage, as critics emphasize. See, e.g., Katherine M. Franke, "Longing for *Loving*," *Fordham Law Review* 76 (2008): 2685.

7. For the classic legal formulation of these "separate spheres," see Bradwell v. State, 83 U.S. 130, 141–142 (1872) (Bradley, J., concurring). See also Janet Halley, "What Is

Family Law? A Genealogy, Part I," *Yale Journal of Law and the Humanities* 23 (2011): 1 (criticizing "family law exceptionalism").

8. See, e.g., Gomez v. Perez, 409 U.S. 535 (1973); Clark v. Jeter, 486 U.S. 456 (1988).

9. See, e.g., Uniform Parentage Act (exemplifying model laws); American Law Institute, *Principles of the Law of Family Dissolution: Analysis and Recommendations* (Newark, NJ: Matthew Bender, 2002) (exemplifying law reform recommendations); Griswold v. Connecticut, 381 U.S. 479 (1965) (exemplifying constitutional limits on states' authority to regulate families); Personal Responsibility and Work Opportunity Reconciliation Act of 1996, Pub. L. No. 104–193, 110 Stat. 2105 (1996) (exemplifying federal funding conditioned on state compliance).

10. See, e.g., Stanton v. Stanton, 421 U.S. 7 (1975); Orr v. Orr, 440 U.S. 268 (1979); Kirchberg v. Feenstra, 450 U.S. 455 (1981); Nevada Department of Human Resources v. Hibbs, 538 U.S. 721 (2003). See generally Cary Franklin, "The Anti-stereotyping Principle in Constitutional Sex Discrimination Law," *New York University Law Review* 85 (2010): 83.

11. See Susan Frelich Appleton, "Missing in Action? Searching for Gender Talk in the Same-Sex Marriage Debate," *Stanford Law and Policy Review* 16 (2005): 97, 110–116.

12. Caban v. Mohammed, 441 U.S. 380 (1979).

13. Ibid., 399.

14. Ibid., 394.

15. See Ex parte Devine, 398 So. 2d 686 (Ala. 1981).

16. E.g., ibid.; American Law Institute, *Principles of the Law of Family Dissolution*, sec. 2.12.

17. E.g., Mo. Rev. Stat. sec. 452.375(8) (2011).

18. See, e.g., Marygold S. Melli and Patricia A. Brown, "Exploring a New Family Form—The Shared Time Family," *International Journal of Law, Policy and the Family* 22 (2008): 231. Many joint custody statutes assume one male and one female parent for each child.

19. See, e.g., Michael M. v. Superior Ct., 450 U.S. 464, 469 (1981) (permitting gender classifications that "realistically [reflect] the fact that the sexes are not similarly situated in certain circumstances"); United States v. Virginia ("VMI"), 518 U.S. 515, 533 (1996) (noting "enduring" "physical differences between men and women"); Sylvia A. Law, "Rethinking Sex and the Constitution," *University of Pennsylvania Law Review* 132 (1984): 955, 1004.

20. Cf. *Michael M.*, 471–472 (citing females' capacity to become pregnant as justification for gender-specific statutory rape laws), with ibid., 496 (Brennan, J., dissenting) (finding stereotypes underlying gender-specific statutory rape laws), and ibid., 501 (Stevens, J., dissenting) (finding "traditional attitudes" reflected in gender-specific statutory rape laws).

21. Cf. Nguyen v. I.N.S., 533 U.S. 53 (2001) (upholding different treatment because only mothers must be physically present at birth), with ibid., 86 (O'Connor, J., dissenting) (condemning majority's reliance on "an overbroad sex-based generalization").

22. Mary Anne C. Case, "'The Very Stereotype the Law Condemns': Constitutional Sex Discrimination Law as a Quest for Perfect Proxies," *Cornell Law Review* 85 (2000): 1447, 1449–1450.

23. Ibid.

24. Cf. Planned Parenthood v. Casey, 505 U.S. 833, 895–898 (1992).

25. Carl E. Schneider, "The Channelling Function in Family Law," *Hofstra Law Review* 20 (1992): 495.

26. 29 U.S.C. sec. 2601 et seq. (2006 and Supp. 2011).

27. *Hibbs*, 721.

28. Cleveland Board of Education v. LaFleur, 414 U.S. 632, 639–640 (1974).

29. See, e.g., Goodridge v. Department of Public Health, 798 N.E.2d 941 (Mass. 2003) (invoking liberty and equality to invalidate exclusion of same-sex couples from marriage); Pamela S. Karlan, "Foreword: Loving *Lawrence*," *Michigan Law Review* 102 (2004): 1447.

30. Regarding how unequal treatment can deprive persons of dignity, see *Lawrence*, 558; Roberts v. United States Jaycees, 468 U.S. 609, 624 (1984).

31. Braschi v. Stahl Associates Co., 543 N.E.2d 49, 53 (N.Y. 1989).

32. See generally Nancy D. Polikoff, *Beyond (Straight and Gay) Marriage: Valuing All Families under the Law* (Boston: Beacon Press, 2008).

33. E.g., Weber v. Aetna Casualty and Surety Co., 406 U.S. 164, 175 (1972).

34. See Joseph Goldstein, Anna Freud, and Albert J. Solnit, *Beyond the Best Interests of the Child* (New York: Free Press 1973), 17–20 (developing the concept of "psychological parent").

35. E.g., Elisa B. v. Superior Court, 117 P.3d 660 (Cal. 2005); In re Parentage of L.B., 122 P.3d 161 (Wash. 2005); Marjorie Maguire Shultz, "Reproductive Technology and Intent-Based Parenthood: An Opportunity for Gender Neutrality," *Wisconsin Law Review* 1990 (1990): 297.

36. Lee T. Gettler et al., "Longitudinal Evidence That Fatherhood Decreases Testosterone in Human Males," *Proceedings of the National Academy of Sciences of the United States* 108 (Sept. 2011): 16194.

37. Judith Butler, *Gender Trouble: Feminism and the Subversion of Identity* (New York: Routledge, 1990), 24–25.

38. Susan Frelich Appleton, "Presuming Women: Revisiting the Presumption of Legitimacy in the Same-Sex Couples Era," *Boston University Law Review* 86 (2006): 227.

39. *Hibbs*, 736 (stating that the FMLA is designed to disrupt "stereotypes [creating] a self-fulfilling cycle of [employment] discrimination that forced women to continue to assume the role of primary family caregiver").

40. See Peter Moss, ed., *International Review of Leave Policies and Related Research 2011*, http://www.leavenetwork.org/filcadmin/Leavenetwork/Annual_reviews/ Complete_review_2011.pdf (accessed Jan. 23, 2012), 18.

41. E.g., Martha Albertson Fineman, *The Autonomy Myth: A Theory of Dependency* (New York: New Press, 2004), 182–204.

42. Martha Albertson Fineman, *The Neutered Mother, the Sexual Family and Other Twentieth Century Tragedies* (New York: Routledge, 1995), 235; Barbara Katz Rothman, *Recreating Motherhood* (New Brunswick, NJ: Rutgers University Press, 2000), 155.

43. Laura T. Kessler, "Community Parenting," *Washington University Journal of Law and Policy* 24 (2007): 47.

44. E.g., Appleton, "Presuming Women"; Jennifer S. Hendricks, "Essentially a Mother," *William and Mary Journal of Women and the Law* 13 (2007): 429.

45. Herma Hill Kay, "Equality and Difference: The Case of Pregnancy," *Berkeley Women's Law Journal* 1 (1985): 1.

46. Andrea Doucet, "Can Parenting Be Equal? Rethinking Equality and Gender Differences in Parenting," 266–268 (this volume).

47. *VMI*, 534.

48. Pew Research Center, *The Decline of Marriage and the Rise of New Families*, Nov. 18, 2010, http://pewsocialtrends.org/files/2010/11/pew-social-trends-2010-families.pdf (accessed Jan. 23, 2012), 26–27, 40. See Linda McClain and Daniel Cere, "Introduction," 4 (this volume) (citing relevant data).

49. Despite the Court's equal protection rulings about parents, it has not yet determined the validity of gender-based requirements for marriage. See, e.g., Mary Anne Case, "What Feminists Have to Lose in Same-Sex Marriage Litigation," *UCLA Law Review* 57 (2010): 1199.

50. Nate Silver, "Support for Gay Marriage Outweighs Opposition in Polls," *New York Times*, May 9, 2012, http://fivethirtyeight.blogs.nytimes.com/2012/05/09/support-for-gay-marriage-outweighs-opposition-in-polls/ (accessed June 3, 2012).

51. Daniel Cere, "Epilogue," 363 (this volume).

52. Daniel Cere, "Toward an Integrative Account of Parenthood."

53. Cere, "Epilogue," 363.

54. Elizabeth Marquardt, "Of Human Bonding: Integrating the Needs and Desires of Women, Men, and the Children Their Unions Produce," 325 (this volume).

55. Cere, "Epilogue," 364–365.

56. Marquardt, "Of Human Bonding."

57. See *Orr*, 279 (rejecting as impermissible justification for gender-based alimony rule state's preference for traditional gender roles).

58. Price Waterhouse v. Hopkins, 490 U.S. 228 (1989).

59. Ibid., 235, 251 (plurality opinion).

60. *VMI*, 533. See also, e.g., J.E.B. v. Alabama ex rel. T.B., 511 U.S. 127, 139 n. 11 (1994).

61. *Nguyen*, 76 (O'Connor, J., dissenting).

62. E.g., Louann Brizendine, *The Female Brain* (New York: Morgan Road Books, 2006). But see Rebecca M. Young and Evan Balaban, "Psychoneuroindoctrinology," *Nature* 443 (Oct. 2006): 634, 634 (critique).

63. See Gettler et al., "Longitudinal Evidence."

64. Such "real differences" also reflect social constructions. See, e.g., Alice Domurat Dreger, *Hermaphrodites and the Medical Invention of Sex* (Cambridge: Harvard University Press, 1998).

65. E.g., Hernandez v. Robles, 855 N.E.2d 1, 3–4 (N.Y. 2006).

66. 539 U.S. 558.

67. What happens in "the sacred precincts of marital bedrooms" presumably is no part of the intended role modeling. *Griswold*, 485.

68. The argument resembles those raised against transracial adoption, a practice that federal law supports. See Howard M. Metzenbaum Multiethnic Placement Act, Pub. L. No. 103-382, sec. 553 (a)(1), as amended by Small Business Job Protection Act of 1996, 42 U.S.C. sec. 1996b (2006 and Supp. 2011) (removing "Barriers to Interethnic Adoption"). Experts say that preparation and support can overcome the challenges of

transracial placements. See, e.g., Evan B. Donaldson Adoption Institute, *Finding Families for African-American Children: The Role of Race and Law in Adoption from Foster Care* (New York: Evan B. Donaldson Adoption Institute, 2008), http://www.adoptioninstitute.org/publications/ MEPApaper20080527.pdf (accessed Jan. 24, 2012).

69. E.g., *Caban*.

70. Cere, "Toward an Integrative Account of Parenthood," 21–25.

71. E.g., *Caban*, 380; *Devine*, 686 (invalidating presumption of maternal custody for young children); American Law Institute, *Principles of the Law of Family Dissolution*, sec. 2.12 (making "the sex of a parent or the child" a prohibited factor in custody orders).

72. Marquardt, "Of Human Bonding."

73. E.g., Dorothy E. Roberts, *Shattered Bonds: The Color of Child Welfare* (New York: Basic Books, 2002).

74. See Michael H. v. Gerald D., 491 U.S. 110 (1989) (rejecting a child's claim to continue a relationship with her genetic father over the objection of her mother and her mother's husband, the legal father).

75. Marquardt, "Of Human Bonding," 324 (touting benefits of "the marriage of a child's *own mother and father*"); ibid., 335 (contending that "redefining marriage requires a redefinition of parenthood").

76. E.g., Mary Lyndon Shanley, *Making Babies, Making Families: What Matters Most in an Age of Reproductive Technologies, Surrogacy, Adoption and Same-Sex and Unwed Parents* (Boston: Beacon Press, 2001), 20–24.

77. E.g., Elizabeth Marquardt, "When 3 Really Is a Crowd," *New York Times*, July 16, 2007, A13 (responding to Jacob v. Shultz-Jacob, 923 A.2d 473 (Pa. Super. Ct. 2007)).

78. See, e.g., Personal Responsibility and Work Opportunity Reconciliation Act of 1996, Pub. L. No. 104–193, 110 Stat. 2105 (1996). See 42 U.S.C. sec. 713 (Supp. 2011) (establishing federally funded "Personal Responsibility Education").

79. E.g., David Blankenhorn, *The Future of Marriage* (New York: Encounter Books, 2007), 33 ("human sexiness is fundamentally about creating the couple that will raise the child").

80. Peggy Cooper Davis, "Contested Images of Family Values: The Role of the State," *Harvard Law Review* 107 (1994): 1348.

81. See, e.g., Parham v. J.R., 442 U.S. 584, 618 (1979) (noting that "natural parents [make medical decisions for their children with] a presumed natural affection to guide their action").

82. E.g., Abbie E. Goldberg, *Lesbian and Gay Parents and Their Children: Research on the Family Life Cycle* (Washington, DC: American Psychological Association, 2010); Timothy J. Biblarz and Judith Stacey, "How Does the Gender of Parents Matter?," *Journal of Marriage and Family* 72 (Feb. 2010): 3, 13, 17; Nanette Gartrell and Henry Bos, "US National Longitudinal Lesbian Family Study: Psychological Adjustment of 17-Year-Old Adolescents," *Pediatrics* 126 (July 2010): 28.

83. Fiona Tasker, "Developmental Outcomes for Children Raised by Lesbian and Gay Parents" (this volume).

84. Florida Department of Children and Families v. Adoption of X.X.G., 45 So.3d 79, 87 (Fla. Dist. Ct. App. 2010). See also Perry v. Schwarzenegger, 704 F. Supp. 2d 921, 980, 999 (N.D. Cal. 2010), *affirmed sub nom*. Perry v. Brown, 671 F.3d 1052 (9th Cir. 2012).

85. Palmore v. Sidoti, 466 U.S. 429, 433 (1984).

86. Ibid., 433–434.

87. Tasker, "Developmental Outcomes," 180–184.

88. See, e.g., Robert H. Mnookin, "Child-Custody Adjudication: Judicial Functions in the Face of Indeterminacy," *Law and Contemporary Problems* 39, no. 3 (1975): 226. See also Linda D. Elrod and Milfred D. Dale, "Paradigm Shifts and Pendulum Swings in Child Custody: The Interests of Children in the Balance," *Family Law Quarterly* 42 (2008): 381, 390–392.

89. Marquardt, "Of Human Bonding," 323.

90. E.g., Mnookin, "Child-Custody Adjudication."

91. See, e.g., Meyer v. Nebraska, 262 U.S. 390 (1923); Pierce v. Society of the Sisters of the Holy Names of Jesus and Mary, 268 U.S. 510, 535 (1925).

92. See Appleton, "Presuming Women," 235 and n. 35 (noting that several states invoke best interests to decide whether to apply or rebut the presumption of legitimacy); In re R.M.G., 454 A.2d 776, 795 (D.C. 1982) (Mack, J., concurring) ("In [this transracial] adoption proceeding, we are not concerned with the best interest of children generally; we are concerned, rather, with the best interest of THE child.").

93. See Biblarz and Stacey, "How Does the Gender of Parents Matter?," 13. By "gender performances," I mean to include sexualities. See Clifford J. Rosky, "Like Father, Like Son: Homosexuality, Parenthood, and the Gender of Homophobia," *Yale Journal of Law and Feminism* 20 (2009): 257.

94. See, e.g., *Orr*, 279 (rejecting as an impermissible justification for a gender-based alimony rule the state's preference for traditional gender roles).

95. Biblarz and Stacey, "How Does the Gender of Parents Matter?," 14.

96. For example, in this volume, compare Tasker's acceptance of the findings to date (Tasker, "Developmental Outcomes") with Marquardt's skepticism: "There are serious and important limitations with virtually all the studies so far" (Marquardt, "Of Human Bonding," 326).

97. See, e.g., Ann Fessler, *The Girls Who Went Away: The Hidden History of Women Who Surrendered Children for Adoption in the Decades before Roe v. Wade* (New York: Penguin, 2006).

98. See Goldstein et al., *Beyond the Best Interests of the Child*, 38; Margaret F. Brinig, "Penalty Defaults in Family Law: The Case of Child Custody," *Florida State University Law Review* 33 (2006): 779; Elrod and Dale, "Paradigm Shifts and Pendulum Swings in Child Custody," 397–400.

99. In re Marriage Cases, 183 P.3d 384, 401, 433, 452 (Cal. 2008); *Goodridge*, 964; ibid., 972 (Greaney, J., concurring).

100. See, e.g., *Marriage Cases*, 401. For similar reasoning, see *Perry*, 973; Varnum v. Brien, 763 N.W.2d 862, 873 (Iowa 2009).

101. 1 U.S.C. sec. 7 (2006 and Supp. 2011); 28 U.S.C. sec. 1738A (2006 and Supp. 2011) ("Defense of Marriage Act").

102. Marquardt, "Of Human Bonding," 332.

103. In November 2008, Californians voted in favor of Proposition 8, amending the state constitution to limit marriage to one man and one woman. A federal district court ruled that Proposition 8 violates the federal constitution. Perry v. Schwarzeneg-

ger, 704 F. Supp. 2d 921, 991 (N.D. Cal. 2010). The Ninth Circuit court of appeals affirmed. Perry v. Brown, 671 F.3d 1052, 1064, 1096 (2012). At this writing, the case might still go to the U.S. Supreme Court.

104. Brown v. Board of Education, 347 U.S. 483, 494 (1954).

105. I note the resemblance between my approach to parentage law and Judith Stacey's sociology-based recommendations. Judith Stacey, "Uncoupling Marriage and Parenting," 65–68 (this volume). See Susan Frelich Appleton, "Parents by the Numbers," *Hofstra Law Review* 37 (2008): 11.

106. See, e.g., Polikoff, *Beyond (Straight and Gay) Marriage*.

107. David L. Chambers, "The 'Legalization' of the Family: Toward a Policy of Supportive Neutrality," *University of Michigan Journal of Law Reform* 18 (1985): 805.

108. David B. Cruz, "Disestablishing Sex and Gender," *California Law Review* 90 (2002): 997.

109. David L. Kirp, Mark G. Yudof, and Marlene Strong Franks, *Gender Justice* (Chicago: University of Chicago Press, 1986), 120–123.

110. Martha Albertson Fineman, "The Sexual Family," in *Feminist and Queer Legal Theory: Intimate Encounters, Uncomfortable Conversations*, ed. Martha Albertson Fineman, Jack E. Jackson, and Adam P. Romero (Surrey, UK: Ashgate 2009), 45–63, especially 46, 48; Michael Warner, "Beyond Gay Marriage," in *Left Legalism/Left Critique*, ed. Wendy Brown and Janet Halley (Durham, NC: Duke University Press 2002), 259–289, especially 260.

111. Doucet, "Can Parenting Be Equal?," 266–269.

112. Ibid., 260.

113. Swedish Parliament Report 2008/09: CU19 Gender-Neutral Marriage and Marriage Issues. It would be interesting to learn how gender-specific leave laws apply to same-sex couples.

114. 29 U.S.C. sec. 2612 (Supp. 2011).

115. Doucet, "Can Parenting Be Equal?," 260–261. Further, in the United States, gender equality is a "national constitutional orthodoxy"; Mary Anne Case, "Feminist Fundamentalism on the Frontier between Government and Family Responsibility for Children," *Journal of Law and Family Studies* 11 (2009): 333, 336.

116. E.g., Martin Guggenheim, *What's Wrong with Children's Rights* (Cambridge: Harvard University Press, 2005), 109–132; Anne C. Dailey, "Children's Constitutional Rights," *Minnesota Law Review* 95 (2011): 2099.

117. E.g., James G. Dwyer, *The Relationship Rights of Children* (New York: Cambridge University Press 2006); Barbara Bennett Woodhouse, "'Who Owns the Child?': *Meyer* and *Pierce* and the Child as Property," *William and Mary Law Review* 33 (1992): 995.

118. See, e.g., Emily Buss, "'Parental' Rights," *Virginia Law Review* 88 (2002): 635; Joanna L. Grossman, "Family Boundaries: Third-Party Rights and Obligations with Respect to Children," *Family Law Quarterly* 40 (2006): 1.

119. Joseph Goldstein, Anna Freud, and Albert J. Solnit, *Before the Best Interests of the Child* (New York: Free Press, 1979), 12.

120. Dwyer, *Relationship Rights of Children*, 135; Frances E. Olsen, "The Myth of State Intervention in the Family," *University of Michigan Journal of Law Reform* 18 (1985): 835, 851 n. 46.

Can Parenting Be Equal?

Rethinking Equality and Gender Differences in Parenting

Andrea Doucet

Over the past thirty years, researchers in many countries have pointed to massive, gendered transformations in paid and unpaid work and parenting. Across most Western countries, we have seen more and more breadwinning mothers, stay-at-home fathers, and gay and lesbian parent households. These large demographic and social shifts have engendered equally massive discussions about what a family is, what parenthood is or should be, how to make sense of gender equality and gender differences in parenting, and what institutional, policy, and legal measures might assist those who seek to achieve gender equality in parenting and paid work.

I joined this conversation just over twenty years ago when I was conducting my doctoral research on women and men trying to "share" parenting and housework. That project instigated a two-decade-long research program that has focused on addressing the puzzlingly persistent link between women and primary parenting while also reflecting on what impedes or facilitates active father involvement. My work has constantly scrutinized the fit between gender "equality" and gender differences in parenting. After two decades of ethnographic and theoretical work, I have come to the view that we need a social science approach that focuses less on gender "equality" in parenting and more on making sense of differences, and whether, where, and how those differences matter. That approach informs my contribution to this book.

My chapter is paired with Susan Frelich Appleton's contribution (in chapter 11), which explores "what is parenthood?" as a legal question. I share her location within the diversity model, which recognizes and appreciates the diverse forms that families and parenthood can take. I agree with her support for an approach that "embraces gender equality [and] supports recognition of a diverse range of parent-child relationships, without regard to sex or gender."[1] I approach these questions, however, with a different set of lenses, including sociological, ethnographic, and feminist theoretical work, which, together, combine an aim of gender equality with attention to where, how, and why gender differences can manifest themselves in everyday life.¹

I also take up this book's call to reflect upon some of the "creative tensions" that emerge from attending to both the *integrative model* and the *diversity model* of parenthood. I concur with the book's editors that these models, while posited as "organizing devices," may nevertheless run the risk of ignoring "nuance and plasticity."² In contrast to the integrative model of parenthood, I do not emphasize the "importance of biological connection, the significance of sex difference (in terms of motherhood and fatherhood), and the right of children to their two biological parents."³ At the same time, my chapter recasts some terms from the integrative model, specifically embodiment and the shifting meanings of motherhood and fatherhood to women and men themselves.

This chapter poses two framing questions: (1) Is gender equality possible in parenting?, and (2) How can we take a diversity approach, with its aim of gender equality, and still allow space for gender differences? It also addresses two central questions posed in this part of the volume: (1) Are there gender differences in parenting?, and (2) If so, should difference make a difference?

My response to these questions, and my argument, is threefold. First, in response to the question, Are there gender differences in parenting?, I argue that we need to be clear about what we mean by *parenthood, parenting*, and "differences." I posit parenting as a set of relational, emotional, domestic, community, and "moral" responsibilities. I also argue that gender differences should not be viewed as "real differences";⁴ rather, gender differences, if and when they occur, are socially located, contextual, and time and spatially dependent. As Joan Williams explains, "People have thousands of 'real differences' that lack social consequences. The question is not whether physical, social and psychological differences between women and men exist. It is *why* these particular differences become salient in a particular context and then are used to create and justify women's continuing economic disadvantage," as well as what creates men's disadvantage in care work and parenting.⁵

Second, building from Williams's argument, I attend not only to *why* but also to *how* gender differences become salient in particular contexts. In the flow of everyday family life, for those living it as well as for those observing it, gender differences in parenting alternate between being invisible and insignificant to being magnified and relevant. As feminist sociologist Barrie Thorne argues, from her ethnographic research on children, gender differences can be ignited at a moment's notice and then fade away just as quickly.⁶ I argue that gender differences in mothering and fathering are embodied, relational, and fluid identities and practices; they shift and change over time and within complex webs of social and institutional relationships.

My third argument addresses the question, Should gender differences make a difference? I agree, in general, with Appleton's claim that gender differences "must have limited and time-restricted consequences" and that "attaching any enduring legal effects to a woman's gestational contribution would make biology destiny."⁷ I also agree with her recommendation against any legal rules based on "maternal-infant attachment bonds."⁸ While I agree on the importance of not creating laws based on the assumption of essential, biological differences, I do point to how, *in practice*, many women and men, in heterosexual couples, often attach different meanings to mothering and fathering, especially in the first months of parenting. As a complement to Appleton's chapter, I focus not on the law but on how parents narrate their lived experiences and identities.⁹ While family law may have evolved away from fixed notions of what the sexes do or should do, gender neutrality as a legal matter does not mean that men and women, in actual life, do not experience themselves in gendered ways, particularly with respect to parenting. We need a way of theorizing, and working with, the interplay of gender differences and gender equality in parenting.

In this chapter, I first lay out my methodological and theoretical positioning, which inform my position in this debate; second, I provide a wide definition of parenting as a set of responsibilities for children and put forward a working definition of gender differences; third, I highlight a range of fluid gender differences and similarities in parenting and reflect on how to make sense of such differences; finally, I ask, Should difference make a difference?, with respect to social science work on domestic labor and parental leave policies.

Methodological and Theoretical Positioning

This chapter draws upon two decades of ethnographic research on mothering and fathering in Canada, the United Kingdom, and the United States and a decade-long longitudinal research project on Canadian breadwinning mothers and stay-at-home fathers. My research has also focused on gay father couples, single father families, and divorced and co-parenting families and has emphasized the role of social networks as important dimensions of parenting work. While the majority of individuals in my studies are lower-middle-class and middle-class, of varied white ethnicities, heterosexual, and living with dependent children, my projects also span diversity across class, race, and sexuality. My research has focused centrally on understanding men's fathering narratives. Most of it has occurred with Canadian families.

The Canadian context is important because it provides a different political location from which to approach the central issues of this book. In contrast to Appleton's observations of "culture war" in the United States, where there is a "continuing battle over same-sex marriage," I write from Canada, where the "culture war" is much less visible. Canada has a fairly generous parental leave program that includes maternity leave, gender-neutral parental leave available to heterosexual and same-sex parents, and Scandinavian-style "daddy weeks" (the latter only in the province of Quebec). In 2005, it became the fourth country in the world to legalize same-sex marriage.[10] Comparatively speaking, "Canada is one of the most supportive countries with respect to protections for LGBTQ people . . . and . . . families. . . . In all 13 provinces and territories, LGBTQ people can apply to adopt an unrelated child through the public adoption system."[11]

Theoretical Approaches

In broad terms, my research program is informed by what the late Iris Marion Young called a pragmatic conception of theory, which she describes as "categorizing, explaining, developing accounts and arguments that are tied to specific practical and political problems, where the purpose of the theoretical activity is clearly related to those problems."[12] To understand and explicate the "problem" of gender differences in parenting, I have developed a constantly evolving theoretical position that advocates gender equality while recognizing gender differences.[13] That position initially drew on feminist theories (first developed in the 1990s in France, Italy, and the United States) that call for the constant interplay between gender equality and gender differences; a focus on how context (space, time, and relationships) matters in how equality and differences interact; and analytical shifts from equality to differences, from differences to disadvantages, and to "the difference difference makes."[14]

My theoretical approach also resonates with a contextual approach, which entails close attentiveness to "context and the complexity of women's interests"[15] in concrete situations. This attention to differences, however, does not mean "absolutist categorizations of difference" but rather a recognition that "meanings are always relative to particular constructions in specified contexts."[16] Finally, my recent thinking about theorizing gender equality and differences has been aided by Joan Williams's theory of "reconstructive feminism."[17] This theoretical approach "offer[s] the promise of busting out of the frame of the sameness-difference debate"[18] by "shifting attention away from women's identities onto the gender dynamics within which identities are forged."[19]

In this chapter, my conception of the biological body or embodiment is central. I refer not to any fixed or "essential" notion of the biological in parenting but to a conception of embodiment, which is deeply social and contextual. This conception is informed by feminist understandings of the varied meanings of embodiment in social practices and social contexts,[20] and of the recursive links between biology, culture, discourses, and the social.[21] I also draw on philosopher Merleau-Ponty's well-cited concept of *body subjects* to theorize parenting as embodied subjectivities and sociologist Erving Goffman's insights on public space, social norms, and intersubjective embodied relations to explicate fathers' sporadic difficulties with entering maternal spaces.[22]

I now turn to consider what parenthood is and to attend to the questions of gender differences and where and how they should, or do, make a difference.

What Is Parenthood?

To understand what we mean by gender differences in parenting, we must first clarify what we mean by parenting or parenthood. Parallel to Adrienne Rich's oft-repeated distinction between the experience and the institution of mothering and Selma Sevenhuijsen's distinction between the institutions of motherhood and fatherhood, I maintain that there is a distinction between *parenthood* and *parenting*. Parenthood refers to the broad array of sociocultural, legal, medical, and educational norms, discourses, and ideologies as they relate to and regulate everyday parenting experiences.[23] Parenting, on the other hand, refers to the daily practices and responsibilities of parents. Clearly, these are heuristic, and intrinsically relational, constructs.

My work has developed a conception of primary parenting as a threefold set of responsibilities.[24] These three responsibilities (building from the work of the late feminist philosopher Sara Ruddick) are emotional, community, and "moral."

Emotional responsibility refers to attentiveness and responsiveness, careful "knowledge about the needs of others,"[25] and the steady process of "thinking about" children or "parental consciousness."[26] *Community responsibility* recognizes that parenting is not only domestically based but also community based, interhousehold, and interinstitutional.[27] It connects the domestic realm to the community through social networking, coordinating, balancing, negotiating, and orchestrating those others who are involved in children's lives.[28] Finally, the *"moral" responsibilities* of parenting refer to people's identities as "moral" beings and how they feel they "ought to" and "should" act in society as parents and as workers.[29] This is expressed well by Williams, who notes that "masculine norms create workplace pressures that make men reluctant or unable to contribute significantly to family life" and that women face "hydraulic social pressure to conform to societal expectations surrounding gender."[30]

Gender Differences in Parenting?

I concur with many feminist and family scholars that gender *should not matter* to the ways in which parenthood is undertaken and that men can and do parent in ways that can be viewed as indistinguishable from those enacted by their female partners.[31] Men can and do partake in parenting in "equal" or symmetrical ways, and their contributions as measured by parenting tasks and time have increased gradually with each passing year. However, there have been smaller shifts in the *responsibility* for parenting, especially in heterosexual households.

With regard to *emotional responsibility*, ample studies find that men care and nurture in ways that closely resemble what are considered traditional maternal ways of responding to children.[32] My research confirms those studies.[33] However, my longitudinal research illustrates how men can still rely on women to take the lead in emotional responsibility; additionally, women assume, and feel the social weight of expectation, that they are, and *should* be, the experts in parenting, especially in the first months or years. Put differently, in heterosexual households, emotional responsibility is more often a mother-led than a father-led process; this is mainly due to the many social, relational, institutional, embodied, and ideological forces that coalesce to lead women to "start off" as the primary parent.[34]

There have been some gender shifts in *community responsibilities*, with men being increasingly involved, and accepted, as primary caregivers in schools, health institutions, community organizations, parenting programs, and the sites where adults and children cluster. Nonetheless, my research also demonstrates that mothers, in both joint-custody and stay-at-home-father families, still take on most of the organizing, networking, and orchestrating around children's lives. Part of the problem is that researchers have been using narrow maternal-defined lenses, which overlook the work that fathers are doing. Fathers do take on this responsibility, especially through being involved in coaching, organizing, and participating in children's sports. Nevertheless, this still points to gender differences in the types of community responsibility that women and men undertake.[35]

Perhaps the slowest gender change has been in the *"moral" responsibilities* of parenting, which remain tied to the "shoulds" and "oughts" of what it means to be a good or proper mother and a good or responsible father. One example is the persistence of distinct, gendered, "moral" responsibilities in relation to the still hegemonic ideal of the male breadwinner/female caregiver family. As one American breadwinning mother recently lamented to me in an interview: "Both women and men can be primary breadwinners, and men can be primary caregivers. But there is really no socially acceptable model for mothers who are secondary caregivers." Meanwhile, many stay-at-home fathers have told me that their discomfort about not earning is "a guy thing," thus implicitly highlighting the still-dominant connections between hegemonic masculinity and family provision as their main contribution to parenting.[36] Class also matters. A consistent theme emerging from these interviews is that being a primary caregiver without having achieved success as a breadwinner can be out of sync with what many communities consider as a socially acceptable identity for a male and for a father. Men without jobs or those in low-income jobs can be viewed with particular suspicion within communities; this recurs for both heterosexual and gay fathers.[37]

A second example of the ongoing gendering of parents' "moral" and community responsibilities is how fathers speak about subtle but recurring surveillance when they are in public settings with children. My research has found sporadic, but consistent, articulations of the community surveillance of men who take on care work. While there has been significant change over the past decade, a recurring thread of suspicion remains about the proximity between male bodies and children, especially the children of others. Notable instances of strong community scrutiny can occur around households where single fathers are raising teenage girls (especially when teen sleepovers occur), where men enter female-dominated child-rearing venues or what one father referred to as "estrogen-filled worlds,"[38] where men are babysitting the children of others, and where men in heterosexual households are primary caregivers of infants (and concurrently, where their female partners do not take maternity or parental leave to care for their infants).[39]

Gender differences, thus, do recur in parenting. They are created through interactive relations with persistently gendered social institutions, community norms, and ideologies.[40] These differences are reproduced through deeply rooted gendered habitus,[41] which can still pull women toward care and men toward paid work, especially in infant care,[42] and by hegemonic masculinities,[43] which include a devaluation of activities and identities that have strong connections with traditional femininity. They also recur because of occasional community and social surveillance of close embodied relations between men and children.

Yet change is under way, and the "moral" responsibilities for parenting are especially important in such change. As Kathleen Gerson notes, "Dissolv[ing] the link between gender and moral responsibility" could lead to a "social order in which women and men alike are afforded the opportunity to integrate the essential life tasks of achieving autonomy and caring for others."[44] In fact, we see glimpses of this "social order" in some families that deliberately work to resist gender differences,[45] and in gay and lesbian households where the removal of domestic gender roles and expectations can lead to greater flexibility in approaching parenting and domestic labor.[46]

Should Differences Make a Difference?

There are several ways to approach the question of whether gender differences should make a difference. Is the achievement of gender equality premised on the absence or erasure of gender differences? Are there tensions in giving up differences? Is it possible to adopt a diversity approach while also recognizing gender differences?

I have considered this question in varied contexts over the past two decades.[47] I will address two of these contexts here: theorizing domestic equality and thinking about how best to encourage fathers' take-up of parental leave policies.[48]

Theorizing Parental Equality: Should Differences Matter?

Most social science and feminist studies on gender and parenting and domestic divisions of labor are informed by the view that gender differences are to be avoided, and that gender equality is the gold standard toward which couples should strive. In some earlier, well-known studies on gender divisions of domestic labor, an egalitarian household was defined as one where the man and the woman within it do "share[d] housework equally"[49] or "whose contributions are roughly equal to one another" whether measured by minutes and hours or by division of tasks.[50] Whatever the terms used, the overwhelming consensus by many researchers remains that a fifty-fifty or egalitarian division of domestic labor is the ideal or most successful pattern.[51] As Francine Deutsch put it more than ten years ago, "Equal sharers, of course, were the stars of this study."[52]

An underlying conceptual problem with assessing gender "equality" in household life is that it is tremendously difficult to define and measure domestic life and labor. While equality in employment may be measured and tested by factors like pay, promotions, and the relative status of women and men, equality within the heterosexual couple's home is less straightforward. Does equality in housework mean that women and men perform the *same* household tasks, and/or do they spend an equal amount of *time* performing such tasks? Does it mean doing *everything* even if that means that the woman may learn how to do plumbing and electrical chores for the first time whereas her male partner may have been doing such tasks since he was a boy? Does equality in parenting imply that women and men share all child care tasks from the first day of their first child's life, or, alternatively, do they have periods where one parent does more than the other? Should a father go to toddler groups or playgroup sessions where he might be the only man in the room, and should women spend as much time coaching soccer or baseball as fathers typically do?

Another problem with striving for gender "equality" in parenting is one that I voiced more than fifteen years ago,[53] and which feminist scholars writing critically about "care work" have reiterated: "The employment of equality as a concept and as a goal supposes a standard or a norm which, in practice, tends to be defined as what is characteristic of the most powerful groups in society."[54] The result is that equality *in* household life ends up being that which enables gender equality *outside* household life. Parental equality is viewed in terms of a traditional masculine norm of minimal participation in housework and child care and full participation in continuous employment.

Should gender differences make a difference in how we theorize gender equality in parenting? In my view, they should. By this I mean that we should shift the focus from measuring gender equality in parenting toward making sense of differences. As Thorne notes, such a shift entails seeking to make sense of "how, when, and why does gender make a difference—or not make a difference" and "when gender does make a difference, what sort of difference is it?"⁵⁵ When we take a wide, social relations, and contextual view of differences (within and between gender), the issue is not differences per se but rather why, how, where, and when they recur in parenting; how they affect one's opportunities outside of the domestic sphere; and the interconnections between equality in the workplace and gender "symmetry" in the home. Looking to the importance of challenging masculine norms in the workplace, I concur with Williams's recent point: "If feminists seek to reconstruct gender on the work-family axis, they should focus as much, *or more*, on changing the workplace as on changing the family."⁵⁶

I now illustrate my approach by using the example of parental leave policies.

Parental Leave Policies

From the broad question of whether gender differences in parenting should *matter*, we can ask more specifically whether they should be recognized in parental leave policies. One could argue that policies should be gender-neutral so that fathers in diverse kinds of households can have access to legal entitlement to care for infants. Several commentators who advocate for equal parental leave provision for women and men take this approach. Janet Gornick and Marcia Meyers, for example, have argued for complete parity in American mothers' and fathers' time with infants through six months' *nontransferable* leave each for mothers and fathers.⁵⁷ Another approach integrates gender equality and gender differences, through the provision of gender-neutral leave combined with extra leave directed at fathers. The latter approach has been taken up by several countries in Scandinavia and Europe, and by Canada.⁵⁸

At least four lessons can be gleaned from government policy approaches to parental leave provision that seek to obtain greater gender equality in parenting through explicitly recognizing gender differences. First, where leave is gender-neutral, it is mainly women who take it—and they take most of the leave. Sweden, for example, has the longest established program of parental leave available to women and men, combined with a two-decade-long public promotion of fathers' parental leave entitlement. In spite of significant policy and ideological shifts, Swedish men now still take only about one-fifth (21 percent) of all parental leave days.⁵⁹

Canada is another excellent example. For the past decade, most Canadian men and women have had the option to share up to thirty-five weeks of paid parental leave entitlement (which is an add-on to fifteen weeks of maternity leave). While the number of fathers taking leave initially surged upward (from 3 percent to 10 percent in just one year), men's uptake of parental leave has remained stalled at about 12 percent.[60]

A second lesson concerns the impact of nontransferable father-focused policy on men's uptake of leave. In 1980, only 5 percent of Swedish fathers took parental leave; ten years later, it was just 7 percent. Only when nontransferable and well-paid leave for fathers (also referred to as the "daddy month") was introduced in 1996 did uptake quickly rise to 77 percent. A second "daddy month" was implemented in 2002, and the numbers have risen to above 90 percent.[61] A similar story plays out in neighboring Norway and in one province of Canada. For example, when the Canadian province of Quebec added three to five weeks of nontransferable paternity leave, it quickly translated into 82 percent of Quebecois dads taking an average of seven weeks of leave time.[62]

A third lesson relates to the financial remuneration of parental leave. This has emerged as a strong point in international comparative studies of men's uptake of leave.[63] Indeed, the highest paternal participation rates occur in countries where there are nontransferable leave programs combined with high wage replacement rates; these include mainly the Nordic countries of Sweden (90 percent participation rate), Norway (89 percent), and Iceland (84 percent) and the province of Quebec.[64] Conversely, countries with low replacement wage rates have lower uptake by fathers (e.g., Belgium with under 7 percent; Austria, 2 percent; and France, 1 percent).[65] Given that, on average, men still earn more than women do, well-paid leave is important. This is symbolically important in that it signals a move away from explicit as well as "unspoken masculine norms" in the workplace, especially malestream norms about an ideal male worker, which work against both women and men who desire to spend time caring.[66]

Fourth, it is "striking that fathers' use of leave does respond to policy changes."[67] Yet, as demonstrated earlier, more fathers take leave when policy is informed by recognition of the gender differences that mark women's and men's lives rather than from a position of gender neutrality. Indeed, in addition to the examples given here, there is strong international evidence for the weak impacts on gender equality in countries where only gender-neutral policy is in place. In Australia, for example, where maternity and parental leave are not separate entitlements, Whitehouse, Diamond, and Baird found that "an ongoing barrier to fathers' use of extended leave is that this reduces significantly the amount of leave available to their partners."[68] In my recent research on Canadian fathers, most mothers and fathers within heterosexual households first prioritized the *mother's* leave time and then strategized to maximize *parental* care. Fathers were explicit about "not taking away her leave."[69] Moreover, most fathers did not argue for the greater sharing of gender-neutral leave but rather for extending (in Quebec) or introducing (in the rest of Canada) nontransferable paternity leave.

Should gender differences make a difference in parental leave policy? They do, and I would argue that they should continue to do so. Although many of the heterosexual couples who have participated in my research studies point to how embodiment (in pregnancy, birthing, and breastfeeding) can impart an advantage to women in forming a bond with their infants, fathers who take parental leave also point to the importance of building such a bond with their children. Moreover, my research on fathers and parental leave demonstrates how fathers speak about the importance of getting out of their regular paid work routine to focus on family life, especially in the transition to new, or expanded, parenthood. Some fathers also note that when they take leave, they can see subtle institutional shifts in their workplace cultures around fathers, work, and infant care.[70] Yet, as indicated earlier, gender differences within and across social institutions, including the institution of parenthood, all lead to a situation where it is mainly women who take, and feel entitled to take, parental leave. I concur with researchers who argue this early phase of parenting can entrench women and men into long-standing gender inequalities in their parenting and employment opportunities.[71] My argument here, however, is that researchers who reflect on how to create conditions for long-lasting gender equality in paid and unpaid work may have to consider how to support this early phase of potentially gender-differentiated care work rather than assume that gender differences in infant care can be minimized through gender-neutral policy.[72]

Conclusions

This chapter has centered on two of this volume's questions about gender differences in parenting. I addressed where, when, and why gender differences appear in parenting, especially for heterosexual couples, and reflected on how to make sense of those differences. My overall approach has been more closely aligned with the diversity approach to parenthood, although my chapter also reconfigures some of the terms often used within the integrative model; specifically, I highlight how fluid and contextual approaches to embodiment as well as the recognition of relational and shifting meanings and practices of mothering and fathering might also usefully inform *both* models. As a complement to Susan Appleton's chapter, I focused not on law but on the everyday narratives of women and men. I approached these matters with a multidisciplinary approach combining sociological and feminist theory on gender equality, gender differences, and embodiment.

I made three central arguments. First, I called for a distinction between parenthood and parenting, and for a wide, social, relational, and contextual approach to gender differences. My approach to gender differences in parenting begins with the recognition that the social institution of parenthood remains deeply gendered and this has implications for how parenting practices play out. While much of this chapter's attention was on heterosexual couples, I pointed out how same-sex couples still parent within gendered social institutions of motherhood and fatherhood.

Second, in answering the question, Are there gender differences in parenting?, I argued that attention to gender differences should focus not only on *why* but also on *where* and *how* differences are manifest in social life. I argued that gender differences in parenting are elastic, constantly in motion, embodied, relational, and variable according to time and spatial contexts. Finally, I addressed the question, Should differences make a difference?, by examining studies of gender equality in parenting and parental leave policies.

In sum, arguing for gender neutrality in legal terms does not necessarily translate into an absence or erasure of gender differences in the everyday identities, practices, and responsibilities of parenting. I maintain that we need a way of theorizing, and working with, the interplay of gender differences and gender equality in parenting, in terms of how we theorize domestic life and how we think about family policies.

Notes

1. Susan Frelich Appleton, "Gender and Parentage: Family Law's Equality Project in Our Empirical Age," 237 (this volume).

2. Linda C. McClain and Daniel Cere, "Introduction," 2 (this volume).

3. Ibid., 3.

4. Joan C. Williams, *Reshaping the Work-Family Debate: Why Men and Class Matter* (Cambridge: Harvard University Press, 2010); see also Martha L. Minow, *Making All the*

Difference: Inclusion, Exclusion, and American Law (Ithaca: Cornell University Press, 1990).

5. Williams, *Reshaping the Work-Family Debate*, 128 (emphasis mine).

6. Barrie Thorne, *Gender Play: Girls and Boys in School* (New Brunswick, NJ: Rutgers University Press, 1993).

7. Appleton, "Gender and Parentage," 244.

8. Ibid.

9. A more precise rendering of my position is to point to women's stories or *narrated experiences* rather than *experience* per se. See Andrea Doucet, "'From Her Side of the Gossamer Wall(s)': Reflexivity and Relational Knowing," *Qualitative Sociology* 31 (2008): 73; Andrea Doucet and Natasha S. Mauthner, "What Can Be Known and How? Narrated Subjects and the Listening Guide," *Qualitative Research* 8 (2008): 399–409.

10. In 2005, after an interpretation of the Canadian Charter of Rights and Freedoms by the Ontario Court of Appeal, Canada approved the Civil Marriage Act, which legalized same-sex marriage. Rachel Epstein, ed., *Who's Your Daddy? And Other Writings on Queer Parenting* (Toronto: Sumach Press, 2009).

11. Ibid. In nine of the thirteen Canadian provinces and territories, the nonbiological mother of children conceived through anonymous donor insemination can be named on the birth registration and immediately recognized as a parent. In the other provinces and territories, families have access to second-parent adoption to allow the nonbiological mother (or gay nonbiological father) parental rights. Ibid.

12. Iris Marion Young, "Gender as Seriality: Thinking about Women as a Social Collective," *Signs* 19 (Spring 1994): 713, 717–718.

13. See Andrea Doucet, *Do Men Mother? Fathering, Care and Domestic Responsibility* (Toronto: University of Toronto Press, 2006); Andrea Doucet, "Dad and Baby in the First Year: Gendered Responsibilities and Embodiment," *ANNALS of the American Academy of Political and Social Science* 624 (July 2009): 78; Andrea Doucet, "Gender Equality and Gender Differences: Parenting, Habitus, and Embodiment (The 2008 Porter Lecture)," *Canadian Review of Sociology/Revue Canadienne de Sociologie* 46 (May 2009): 103.

14. For example, Gisela Bock and Susan James, eds., *Beyond Equality and Difference: Citizenship, Feminist Politics and Female Subjectivity* (London: Routledge, 1992); Paola Bono and Sandra Kemp, eds., *Italian Feminist Thought: A Reader* (Oxford: Blackwell, 1991). For an overview, see Andrea Doucet, "Gender Equality and Gender Differences in Household Work and Parenting," *Women's Studies International Forum* 18 (May–June 1995): 271; and Doucet, *Do Men Mother?*; on context and differences, see Thorne, *Gender Play*; Deborah L. Rhode, *Justice and Gender: Sex Discrimination and the Law* (Cambridge: Harvard University Press, 1989), 313. See also Deborah L. Rhode, ed., *Theoretical Perspectives on Sexual Difference* (New Haven, CT: Yale University Press, 1990).

15. Rhode, *Theoretical Perspectives*, 204.

16. Joan Wallach Scott, *Gender and the Politics of History* (New York: Columbia University Press, 1988), 175.

17. Williams, *Reshaping the Work-Family Debate*, 115.

18. Ibid.

19. Ibid., 5.

20. Moira Gatens, *Imaginary Bodies: Ethics, Power and Corporeality* (London: Routledge, 1996); Linda Nicholson, "Interpreting Gender," *Signs* 20 (Autumn 1994): 79; Elizabeth Grosz, *Volatile Bodies: Toward a Corporeal Feminism* (St. Leonards, NSW: Allen and Unwin, 1994); Iris Marion Young, *On Female Body Experience: "Throwing Like a Girl" and Other Essays* (New York: Oxford University Press, 2005); and Williams, *Reshaping the Work-Family Debate*.

21. I am grateful to my colleague Natasha Mauthner for introducing me to "new materialist" understandings of embodiment: e.g., Stacy Alaimo and Susan Hekman, eds., *Material Feminisms* (Bloomington: Indiana University Press, 2008); Susan Hekman, *The Material of Knowledge: Feminist Disclosures* (Bloomington: Indiana University Press, 2010); Samantha Frost, "The Implications of the New Materialisms for Feminist Epistemology," in *Feminist Epistemology and Philosophy of Science: Power in Knowledge*, ed. Heidi E. Grasswick (New York: Springer, 2011), 69–83; Anne Fausto-Sterling, *Sexing the Body: Gender Politics and the Construction of Sexuality* (New York: Basic Books, 2000).

22. Maurice Merleau-Ponty, *The Phenomenology of Perception*, trans. Colin Smith (1962; repr., London: Routledge and Kegan Paul, 1981); Maurice Merleau-Ponty, *Signs*, trans. Richard C. McCleary (Evanston, IL: Northwestern University Press, 1964); Maurice Merleau-Ponty, *The Visible and the Invisible*, ed. Claude Lefort, trans. Alphonso Lingis (Evanston, IL: Northwestern University Press, 1968); Erving Goffman, *Behavior in Public Places: Notes on the Social Organization of Gatherings* (New York: Free Press of Glencoe, 1963); Erving Goffman, *The Presentation of Self in Everyday Life* (London: Allen Lane, 1969); Erving Goffman, *Relations in Public: Microstudies of the Public Order* (Harmondsworth, UK: Penguin, 1972).

23. See Selma Sevenhuijsen, *Citizenship and the Ethics of Care: Feminist Considerations on Justice, Morality and Politics* (London: Routledge, 1998), 26; see also Patrice DiQuinzio, *The Impossibility of Motherhood: Feminism, Individualism, and the Problem of Mothering* (New York: Routledge, 1999). I would also maintain that there are still distinct "institutions" of motherhood and fatherhood.

24. See also Michael E. Lamb, "Introduction: The Emergent American Father," in *The Father's Role: Cross-Cultural Perspectives*, ed. Michael E. Lamb (Hillsdale, NJ: Erlbaum, 1987), 3–25; Rob Palkovitz, "Reconstructing 'Involvement': Expanding Conceptualizations of Men's Caring in Contemporary Families," in *Generative Fathering: Beyond Deficit Perspectives*, ed. Alan J. Hawkins and David C. Dollahite (Thousand Oaks, CA: Sage, 1997), 200–216.

25. Joan C. Tronto, "Care as a Basis for Radical Political Judgments," *Hypatia* 10, no. 2 (1995): 141; Joan C. Tronto, *Moral Boundaries: A Political Argument for an Ethic of Care* (New York: Routledge, 1993).

26. Susan Walzer, *Thinking about the Baby: Gender and Transitions into Parenthood* (Philadelphia: Temple University Press, 1998).

27. Andrea Doucet, "'There's a Huge Difference between Me as a Male Carer and Women': Gender, Domestic Responsibility, and the Community as an Institutional Arena," *Community Work and Family* 3 (Aug. 2000): 163; Andrea Doucet, "'You See the Need Perhaps More Clearly Than I Have': Exploring Gendered Processes of Domestic Responsibility," *Journal of Family Issues* 22 (Apr. 2001): 328.

28. This labor of parents, mainly mothers, and others appears in varied guises in a wide body of feminist research that highlights kin work. Michaela di Leonardo, "The Female World of Cards and Holidays: Women, Families and the Work of Kinship," *Signs* 12 (Spring 1987): 440, 441; Patricia Hill Collins, "Shifting the Center: Race, Class, and Feminist Theorizing about Motherhood," in *American Families: A Multicultural Reader*, ed. Stephanie Coontz, Maya Parson, and Gabrielle Raley (New York: Routledge, 1999), 197–217 (discussing "motherwork"); Sarah Blaffer Hrdy, *Mothers and Others: The Evolutionary Origins of Mutual Understanding* (Cambridge: Belknap Press of Harvard University Press, 2009). For recent work on the role of kin and social networks in carrying out the work of parenting, see Karen V. Hansen, *Not-So-Nuclear Families: Class, Gender, and Networks of Care* (New Brunswick, NJ: Rutgers University Press, 2005); and William Marsiglio, "Men's Relations with Kids: Exploring and Promoting the Mosaic of Youth Work and Fathering," *ANNALS of the American Academy of Political and Social Science* 624 (July 2009): 118.

29. The concept of "moral responsibilities" is rooted in a symbolic interactionist conception of the interactional relational sense. See Kerry J. Daly, *Families and Time: Keeping Pace in a Hurried Culture* (Thousand Oaks, CA: Sage, 1996); Kerry J. Daly, "Time, Gender, and the Negotiation of Family Schedules," *Symbolic Interaction* 25 (2002): 323; Janet Finch and Jennifer Mason, *Negotiating Family Responsibilities* (London: Routledge, 1993); Martha McMahon, *Engendering Motherhood: Identity and Self-Transformation in Women's Lives* (New York: Guilford Press, 1995).

30. Williams, *Reshaping the Work-Family Debate*, 149.

31. See Timothy J. Biblarz and Judith Stacey, "How Does the Gender of Parents Matter?," *Journal of Marriage and Family* 72 (Feb. 2010): 3; Doucet, *Do Men Mother?*; Barbara J. Risman, "Can Men 'Mother'? Life as a Single Father," *Family Relations* 35 (Jan. 1986): 95.

32. See, e.g., Scott Coltrane, *Family Man: Fatherhood, Housework, and Gender Equity* (New York: Oxford University Press, 1996); Nancy E. Dowd, *Redefining Fatherhood* (New York: NYU Press, 2000); William Marsiglio and Kevin Roy, *Nurturing Dads: Fatherhood Initiatives beyond the Wallet* (New York: Russell Sage Foundation, 2012); Donald N. S. Unger, *Men Can: The Changing Image and Reality of Fatherhood in America* (Philadelphia: Temple University Press, 2010).

33. Doucet, *Do Men Mother?*

34. I am grateful to John Hoffman for pointing me to the work of Doherty, Kouneski, and Erikson on this issue and their argument that "fathering can be conceptualized as more contextually sensitive than mothering." William J. Doherty, Edward F. Kouneski, and Martha F. Erickson, "Responsible Fathering: An Overview and Conceptual Framework," *Journal of Marriage and Family* 60 (May 1998): 277, 287; John Hoffman, *Father Factors: What Social Science Tells Us about Fathers and How to Work with Them* (Peterborough, ON: Father Involvement Research Alliance, 2011).

35. Doucet, *Do Men Mother?*

36. Gillian Whitehouse, Chris Diamond, and Marian Baird, "Fathers' Use of Leave in Australia," *Community, Work and Family* 10 (Nov. 2007): 387; Lindsey McKay, Katherine Marshall, and Andrea Doucet, "Fathers and Parental Leave in Canada: Policies, Practices and Potential," in *Engaging Fathers in Social Change: Lessons from*

Canada, ed. Jessica Ball and Kerry Daly (Vancouver: University of British Columbia Press, in press).

37. Doucet, *Do Men Mother?*

38. Ibid.

39. Doucet, "Dad and Baby in the First Year."

40. Bonnie Fox, *When Couples Become Parents: The Creation of Gender in the Transition to Parenthood* (Toronto: University of Toronto Press, 2009); Nancy Folbre, *Who Pays for the Kids? Gender and the Structures of Constraint* (London: Routledge, 1994); Williams, *Reshaping the Work-Family Debate*.

41. Pierre Bourdieu, *Distinction: A Social Critique of the Judgment of Taste* (London: Routledge, 1984); Pierre Bourdieu, *The Logic of Practice* (Cambridge, UK: Polity Press, 1990); Pierre Bourdieu, *Outline of a Theory of Practice* (Cambridge: Cambridge University Press, 1977).

42. Doucet, "Dad and Baby in the First Year"; McKay et al., "Fathers and Parental Leave in Canada."

43. Raewyn W. Connell, *Masculinities* (Berkeley: University of California Press, 1995).

44. Kathleen Gerson, "Moral Dilemmas, Moral Strategies, and the Transformation of Gender: Lessons from Two Generations of Work and Family Change," *Gender and Society* 16 (Feb. 2002): 8, 25–26.

45. See Fiona J. Green, *Practicing Feminist Mothering* (Winnipeg, MB: Arbeiter Ring Press, 2011); Barbara J. Risman and Danette Johnson-Sumerford, "Doing It Fairly: A Study of Postgender Marriages," *Journal of Marriage and Family* 60 (Feb. 1998): 23; Unger, *Men Can*; Doucet, *Do Men Mother?*

46. See Adam L. Benson, Louise B. Silverstein, and Carl F. Auerbach, "From the Margins to the Center: Gay Fathers Reconstruct the Fathering Role," *Journal of GLBT Family Studies* 1, no. 3 (2005): 1; Biblarz and Stacey, "How Does the Gender of Parents Matter?"

47. One context is child custody and equality claims by fathers' rights groups: Andrea Doucet, "Fathers and the Responsibility for Children," *Atlantis: A Women's Studies Journal* 28 (2004): 103; Andrea Doucet and Linda Hawkins, "Feminist Mothers Researching Fathering: Advocates, Contributors, and Dissenters," in Ball and Daly, *Engaging Fathers in Social Change*.

48. On theorizing domestic equality, see Doucet, "Gender Equality and Gender Differences in Household Work"; Doucet, "You See the Need"; Doucet, *Do Men Mother?* On fathers taking parental leave, see Doucet, "Dad and Baby in the First Year"; Lindsey McKay and Andrea Doucet, "'Without Taking Away Her Leave': A Canadian Case Study of Couples' Decisions on Fathers' Use of Paid Leave," *Fathering: A Journal of Theory, Research, and Practice about Men as Fathers* 8 (Fall 2010): 300; Andrea Doucet, Lindsey McKay, and Diane-Gabrielle Tremblay, "Canada and Quebec: Two Policies, One Country," in *The Politics of Parental Leave Policies: Children, Parenting, Gender and the Labour Market*, ed. Sheila Kamerman and Peter Moss (Bristol, UK: Policy Press, 2009), 33–50; McKay et al., "Fathers and Parental Leave in Canada."

49. Arlie R. Hochschild, *The Second Shift* (New York: Avon Books, 1989).

50. Julia Brannen and Peter Moss, *Managing Mothers: Dual Earner Households after Maternity Leave* (London: Unwin Hyman, 1991).

51. Ibid.; Francine M. Deutsch, *Halving It All: How Equally Shared Parenting Works* (Cambridge: Harvard University Press, 1999); Diane Ehrensaft, *Parenting Together: Men and Women Sharing the Care of Their Children* (New York: Free Press, 1987); Hochschild, *The Second Shift*; Gayle Kimball, *50–50 Parenting: Sharing Family Rewards and Responsibilities* (Lexington, MA: Lexington Books, 1988).

52. Deutsch, *Halving It All*, 7; Risman and Johnson-Sumerford, "Doing It Fairly"; Francine M. Deutsch, Amy P. Kokot, and Katherine S. Binder, "College Women's Plans for Different Types of Egalitarian Marriages," *Journal of Marriage and Family* 69 (Nov. 2007): 916.

53. Doucet, "Gender Equality and Gender Differences in Household Work."

54. Elizabeth M. Meehan and Selma Sevenhuijsen, eds., *Equality, Politics and Gender* (London: Sage, 1991), 38; see also Young, *On Female Body Experience*.

55. Thorne, *Gender Play*, 36.

56. Williams, *Reshaping the Work-Family Debate*, 5 (emphasis mine).

57. Janet Gornick and Marcia Meyers, *Families That Work: Policies for Reconciling Parenthood and Employment* (New York: Russell Sage Foundation, 2003); Janet Gornick, Marcia Meyers, and Erik Olin Wright, eds., *Gender Equality: Transforming Family Divisions of Labor* (London: Verso, 2009).

58. Two of the most popular are whole or partial individualized entitlements ("use-it-or-lose-it" quotas) wherein unused leave cannot be transferred to a partner. Another approach is to offer some form of bonus (e.g., additional leave) if fathers take some parental leave. According to the International Parental Leave Network, seven countries offer such a bonus. Sweden is one of the most progressive on this issue, with two "daddy months" available to fathers and the recent introduction of a "gender equality bonus," which provides an economic incentive for families to divide their parental leave more equally. Peter Moss, ed., *International Review of Leave Policies and Related Research 2011* (London: International Network on Leave and Related Research, 2011).

59. The greatest share of paid leave taken by men is, in fact, in Iceland (33 percent). Iceland has a 3/3/3 scheme (i.e., three months each for mother and father and three months of gender-neutral leave). See Guany Bjork Eydal and Ingolfur V. Gíslason, eds., *Equal Rights to Earn and Care: Parental Leave in Iceland* (Reykjavík: Félagsvísindastofnun, 2008). In 2008, for every 100 mothers who took leave, 91 fathers took a period of leave (combined paternity and/or parents' joint rights). Overall, fathers took about a third of all days of leave taken by parents (an average of 103 days leave compared with 178 for mothers). See Thorgerdur Einarsdóttir and Gyda Margret Pétursdóttir, "Iceland," in *International Review of Leave Policies and Related Research 2009*, ed. Peter Moss (London: Department for Business, Innovation and Skills, 2009), 213–221.

60. Doucet et al., "Canada and Quebec."

61. Anders Chronholm, "Sweden: Individualisation or Free Choice in Parental Leave?," in Kamerman and Moss, *Politics of Parental Leave Policies*, 227–241. It is also worth noting that most Swedish men take leave when their children are thirteen to fifteen months of age.

62. McKay and Doucet, "Without Taking Away Her Leave."

63. Kamerman and Moss, *Politics of Parental Leave Policies*; Margaret O'Brien, "Fathers, Parental Leave Policies, and Infant Quality of Life: International Perspectives and Policy Impact," *ANNALS of the American Academy of Political and Social Science* 624 (July 2009): 190.

64. McKay et al., "Fathers and Parental Leave in Canada"; O'Brien, "Fathers, Parental Leave Policies, and Infant Quality of Life."

65. Katherine Marshall, "Fathers' Use of Paid Parental Leave," *Perspectives*, June 2008, http://www.statcan.gc.ca/pub/75-001-x/2008106/pdf/10639-eng.pdf (accessed Jan. 24, 2012).

66. Williams, *Reshaping the Work-Family Debate*, 128.

67. Moss, *International Review of Leave Policies and Related Research 2011*, 38.

68. Whitehouse et al., "Fathers' Use of Leave in Australia."

69. McKay and Doucet, "Without Taking Away Her Leave."

70. See also Barbara Hobson and Susanne Fahlen, "Competing Scenarios for European Fathers: Applying Sen's Capabilities and Agency Framework to Work-Family Balance," *ANNALS of the American Academy of Political and Social Science* 624 (July 2009): 214.

71. E.g., Fox, *When Couples Become Parents*.

72. See Doucet, "Dad and Baby in the First Year"; Ann S. Orloff, "Should Feminists Aim for Gender Symmetry? Why a Dual-Earner/Dual-Caregiver Society Is Not Every Feminist's Utopia," in Gornick et al., *Gender Equality*, 129–160.

Globalization and Parenthood

How Do Family Immigration and Transnational Parenting Shape Parenthood? How Should They Inform Debates over Parenthood?

PART SEVEN

Transnationalism of the Heart

Familyhood across Borders

Carola Suárez-Orozco and Marcelo M. Suárez-Orozco

Global migration is transforming the shape of families as increasingly "familyhood" is experienced and conducted by hundreds of millions of families across national borders. In this chapter, we review the prominence of transnational familyhood and its implications for the meaning of family life in an age of mass migration. We consider what it means to be a parent, a child, or even a "family unit" in transnational circumstances of global migration. Is the biological parent who sends remittances more or less a parent than the grandparent or aunt and uncle who takes care of the child's daily needs across most of his or her childhood? Is the child's attachment to the "functional everyday parent" of a different sort than the attachment to the long-distance parent? Upon reunification how are the legislative, social, and symbolic functions of family life negotiated among members who had lived familyhood at a distance? We consider the reverberations of transnational parenting on children, parents, and extended family dynamics. Finally, we suggest that migration policies should be more attentive to the family—in its enormous diversity and plasticity the world over—as the fundamental unit of migration.

While most think of immigration as driven by labor, demographic, and economic factors, a second look reveals its enduring root in the family. Immigration is, most often, an ethical act *of* and *for* the family.

Shortly after losing her husband to cancer, a Filipina nurse makes the migratory journey to the outskirts of San Diego, working long shifts to support her four young children who have stayed behind in the care of her mother. A Haitian accountant from Port-au-Prince reluctantly leaves his family to find work as a taxi driver in Boston to save for his youngest daughter's costly medical treatment. Countless such sacrifices constitute the ethical logic of family migration all over the world.

Immigration destabilizes and changes the societies in which immigrants settle. Ironically, however, what is most unsettled and changed by the process are the very families that immigration was to safeguard. Many migrations begin tentatively, with a plan of eventually returning home. Most, however, result in protracted family separations that deeply threaten the identity and cohesion of the family, transforming well-established roles, creating new loyalties and bonds, and destabilizing cultural scripts of authority, reciprocity, and responsibility. Even under the best of circumstances, the family is never the same after migration. While one family starts the migration process, an entirely different family completes it. In this chapter, we locate the family at the center of immigration, revealing just how dislocating immigration becomes to its form and coherence.

In the immigrant communities that we studied (Central American, Chinese, Dominican, Haitian, and Mexican), cultural norms tend to hold traditional *integrative* models of "the family." While the family typically places parent-child relationships at the center, it expands to encompass sustained and intimate caretaking provided by extended kin and fictive kin (e.g., *compadres, comadres*). Migrations create extended separations, resulting in biological parents providing financial care and grandparents, or other kin, providing daily care. Extended separations lead to complex attachments to both the symbolic parents (daily caretakers who are typically extended kin) and biological parents who may become abstractions over time. Reunifications lead to complex and poignant adjustments for parties in the caretaking arrangement. These family relationships, while still kin-based, complicate the paradigm of mother/father/children integrative family life.

Global Perspectives on Transnational Separations

Global migrations are transforming the very shape, essence, and definition of family.[1] The experience of transnational migrants can be characterized as a cycle of "separation and reunification of different members of the family unit over time."[2] Generally, long-distance "familyhood" practiced across national borders has been neglected by policy makers, scholars, and nongovernmental organizations working with migrants.[3] The international prevalence of transnational families is finally a matter of growing recognition and interest, however. Indeed, the United Nations Development Programme made the issue of transnational families a priority topic of study in 2009.[4] While it is difficult to establish the extent of immigrant family separations, informed estimates can be made. There were 214 million immigrants and refugees worldwide in 2010. If, on average, each left behind two immediate family members,⁵ then at least 642 million individuals may be involved in transbordered, transnational family formulations.

Typically, migrations take place in a stepwise fashion, with one family member going ahead, followed later by others.⁶ Historically, the male left first, establishing a beachhead in a new land while sending remittances home. Over time, when financially possible, the process of bringing relatives—wife, children, and others—began. But in recent decades, immigration has achieved a nearly perfect gender balance.⁷ The first world's demand for service workers draws women—many of them mothers—from a variety of developing countries to care for "other people's children."⁸ In rapidly aging countries, these immigrant workers are also summoned to care for "other people's aging parents." Large sectors of the "pink-collar" occupations have also attracted immigrant women. When migrating mothers leave their children behind, extended family members, such as grandparents or aunts, often become the primary caretakers with the help of the father (if he remains local and is still part of the family). In many other cases, both parents go ahead, leaving the children in the care of extended family.⁹

As migrant households gain a firmer foot in the country of immigration, new children are born. These complex-blended families incorporate a range of settled migrants, new arrivals, and *citizen children*, as they are born in the new land.¹⁰

In recent years, families with undocumented parents have been involuntarily wrenched apart by workplace as well as in-home raids conducted by immigration authorities. This leaves citizen children behind, sometimes in the care of relatives, sometimes in the care of foster homes, and sometimes forced to relocate to a country they have never known.¹¹

Seemingly in perpetual motion, the immigrant family is destined for separations and, with luck, reunifications. Here, then, is immigration's bittersweet paradox: while it is motivated by the well-being of the family, in reality it wrenches the family apart.

The United Nations Human Development Report of 2009 suggests that family separations are widespread and have lasting repercussions. In a nationally representative survey of documented immigrants within North America, nearly a third of the six- to eighteen-year-olds had been separated from at least one parent for two or more years. Notably, the rates of separation were highest for children of Latin American origin, who account for more than half of all migrants to the United States.¹² Because separation rates are higher among the unauthorized or those who are in the process of regulating their documentation status, this is probably a low estimate.

The Longitudinal Immigrant Student Adaptation Study

In a U.S. bicoastal study we conducted with 400 recently arrived immigrant youth from China, the Dominican Republic, various countries in Central America, Haiti, and Mexico attending public schools, we found that the majority of the immigrant children had been separated from one or both parents for protracted periods—from six months to ten years.[13] Nearly three-quarters of the youth were separated from one or both of their parents during the migration process. We found significant differences between groups in regard to family separations: Chinese families were least likely to be separated over the course of migration (52 percent), while the vast majority of Central American (88 percent) and Haitian children (85 percent) were separated from either one or both of their parents during the course of migration.[14] Approximately 26 percent of children in the study were separated from both parents, for some period of time, a pattern most often occurring in Central American families (54 percent). Separations from mothers only occurred most frequently in Dominican families (40 percent), and separations from fathers only were most frequently found in Mexican families (33 percent).[15]

The length of separation from parents was unexpectedly long, with some children reporting separation from one or both parents for nearly their entire childhood. The length of separation varied widely across regions of origin. Of the youth who were separated only from their mothers, 54 percent of Central American children endured separations lasting four or more years, as did approximately one-third of both the Dominican and the Haitian families. Chinese and Mexican children underwent fewer and shorter separations from their mothers.[16] When separations from the fathers occurred during migration, they were often very lengthy or permanent ones.[17] For those families who were separated, 28 percent had separations from fathers that lasted more than four years. This was the case for 44 percent of the Haitian, 42 percent of the Central American, and 28 percent of the Dominican families.[18]

What are the psychological effects of the separations? When comparing youth who had not undergone family separations with youth who had, we found that those who arrived as a family unit were less likely to report symptoms of depression or anxiety.[19] Those who had undergone the longest separations from their mothers reported the highest levels of these symptoms. Generally, we found that the highest levels of distress were reported by youth who had undergone medium- and long-term separations.

Not surprisingly, we found the lowest rates of psychological distress among youth who had not been separated from their mothers or who had undergone separations of less than two years from their fathers. Youth who had undergone separations of four or more years from their mothers reported the greatest distress. Many of these children had stayed with their fathers rather than with both grandparents or with aunts and uncles. In these cases, we learned that these two-caretaker homes had afforded more stable care as well as better, extended supports.

School Perspectives

The poignancy of separations became clear to us as we listened to teachers, parents, and above all, immigrant youth. Insightful school personnel often spontaneously brought up the issue of family separations and subsequent reunifications as a challenge facing their immigrant students. A veteran high school counselor in California shared with us:

> [In many cases] the family has been separated for many years . . . so when they are reunited sometimes it's a mess in the literal sense of the word. The mother doesn't know the child. . . . Because she knows she's been working, sending money, caring for the child and everything—she's been doing her part. But now it is the child's turn, you know, to show understanding, to show appreciation. . . . Sometimes the mother is in a new relationship. So that kids may be coming to a new family with other siblings and a stepparent.[20]

The director of an international center in a Boston area high school summed up the challenge:

> I feel like I need to give [students] a great deal of personal and emotional support in the transition they are making. . . . You know, the whole issue of family separations. There are a lot of emotional issues, which come into this. . . . We have people here from China, from Brazil, from Haiti, from Central America, and what is interesting is that they are all [talking about] the same issues. "I don't know how to live with my parent."

Family Perspectives: During the Separation Phase

Few topics were more difficult to broach with immigrant families than their time apart. Many of our otherwise talkative informants became monosyllabic when we posed questions about this topic, and many youth admitted that their family simply never discussed their time apart.[21]

The act of separation was often described as one of the hardest things about coming to the United States. Jamisa,[22] a fourteen-year-old Dominican girl, said, "The day I left my mother I felt like my heart was staying behind. Because she was the only person I trusted—she was my life. I felt as if a light had extinguished. I still have not been able to get used to living without her."

In many cases, parents left their children when they were infants and toddlers. Carmen, the mother of thirteen-year-old Central American twins, shared: "It was very hard above all to leave the children when they were so small. I would go into the bathroom of the gas station and milk my breasts that overflowed, crying for my babies. Every time I think of it, it makes me sad."

While the parents told us that they hoped to reunite quickly with their children, the separations turned out to be much more protracted than anticipated. A host of other challenges associated with migration often compounded parents' separation from their children. These included barriers due to language and cultural differences, long working hours typically at low wages, displacement from familiar settings, cultural disorientation, and a limited social support system. Lack of documentation and concerns about security exponentially added to the distress of having the family torn apart.

Rosario, a Salvadoran mother of three, told us:

> I never thought it would be so long. But I had no choice. My husband had been killed and my children had no one else. I had to make the journey to El Norte. I left them with my mother, hoping I could send for them in a few months, but life here is so expensive. I sent money back every month to take care of them and saved every dollar I could and I spent nothing on myself. My life was better in El Salvador. Here I had no friends. I was always lonely. I miss my children desperately and my family. I worked all the time. But a safe crossing was so expensive for three children.

Parents, especially mothers, maintained contact with their children through a series of strategies that included regular remittances, weekly phone calls, the exchange of letters, sending photos and gifts, email and Skype, and occasionally return visits, when finances and documentation status allowed. Over time, these contacts played an ever more important role in nurturing the memory of the absent parent in the child's mind.

The capacity to send remittances to support children and family members is the core motivation behind the majority of the parental absences. Few children, however, seem to have a clear sense of why their parents are away. A fifteen-year-old Guatemalan girl, Amparo, was an exception: "I remember that my grandparents would tell me that my parents had to go to work so they could send money for us to live on."

Children recalled gifts that were sent, sometimes on special occasions, in the form of money so they could buy what they liked, but also in the form of lovingly selected items sent with visitors. Lupita, a twelve-year-old Mexican girl, recounted, "My parents would send dolls, necklaces, clothes, and perfume. Things they thought I would like." For some, the gifts served to salve the absence of the parent. Leandro, a twelve-year-old Mexican boy, explained, "[My grandparents] would say to me, 'Son, do you miss your mother?' I would say, 'Yes,' and then go and play. With the video games she sent I would forget everything."

Staying in touch by sending gifts was a tangible means of maintaining contact. Nevertheless, a few children reported that no amount of material goods could provide what they wanted: a parent's presence and active involvement in their daily life. For example, fourteen-year-old Bao Yu said, "Even though he kept sending me new beautiful clothes—so what? I felt that he is my father, he should *stay* with me, and see how I grow up." While some children had memories of their parents, for others, memories began to fade. For instance, Areceli, a sixteen-year-old Guatemalan girl whose mother left when she was two (and did not see her until eight years later when her asylum papers where finally granted), told us, "I would look at the pictures of my mother, and I would think that I would like to meet her because I could not remember her.... I would say, 'What a pretty mom—I would like to meet her.'" For a number of immigrant youth, the parents in the picture were parents in name only—long-distance benevolent figures ambiguously present but with whom the children had little firsthand experience.

Over time, many families found it difficult to maintain steady long-distance communication—especially those enduring long-term separations. Communication was hardest for parents who had left children behind when they were very young; as the children grew up, the parent became an abstraction. As the mother of a twelve-year-old Salvadoran boy, Manuel, explained: "They lived with my mother in El Salvador. I left when they were babies. I spoke to the eldest once a month by phone. As the little one grew, I spoke to him, too. But since he didn't know me, our communication was quite short. I really had to pull the words out of him."

In listening to parents, it was evident that the absent child remained a daily sustaining presence in their lives. For children, however, the story was different. Especially in cases of long-term absences, for many youth it was a case of out of sight, out of mind. Often, the day-to-day caretakers took on the parenting function along with the psychological role of being the symbolic "mother" and "father."

Family Perspectives: During the Reunification Phase

We might expect that after so many sacrifices, family reunification would be joyful. Indeed, many children, especially those whose separations were short-term or from only one parent, described the moment of reunification with the word *happy*. A thirteen-year-old Guatemalan girl said that on the day she got together with her mother, "[I was] so happy. It was my dream to be with her." Likewise, Yara, a fourteen-year-old Dominican girl, described her family reunification: "We were so happy. We cried, talked a lot, and embraced."

Yet for many children who had endured protracted separations, the reunification was quite complicated. In almost all cases, the children recalled that their parents received them in a highly emotional and tearful, welcoming manner. The child's experience was different—the parent had become a stranger. As Beatriz, a fourteen-year-old Guatemalan new arrival, recalls, "My mother was crying. She hugged me . . . and I felt bad. Like neither my sister nor I *knew* her."

For parents the reunification signified the joyful conclusion of a painful period of sacrifice and struggle to bring the family together. For the children, however, the reunification was the beginning of a new and emotionally laden phase. For them, it meant entering a new life in a new land to be raised by a new set of adults. They reported intense feelings of disorientation. As thirteen-year-old Celeste from Haiti confided, "I didn't know who I was going to live with or how my life was going to be. I knew of my father, but I did not know him." Even under optimal circumstances, migrating to a different country and adopting a new way of life is disorienting. Yet for many youth in our study, the process was complicated by uncertainty about whether they would feel comfortable in their own homes, how they would get along with the people they would be living with, and what their everyday routines would be. These children were experiencing two migrations—one to a new country and another to a new family.

Araceli, a cautious thirteen-year-old from Guatemala whose father left before her birth and whose mother left when she was a year old, not reuniting with her until nine years later, told us:

> I felt very strange, and since I didn't know my mother. I saw a lot of women [at the airport] but didn't know who my mom was. And when she came to hug me, I said to her, "Are you my mom?" I didn't hug her very hard because I didn't know her or anything. I didn't have that much trust or didn't feel that comfortable with her.

Youth display a range of emotions from a short-term sense of disorientation to sadness to anger. For some, the extended absence led to a sustained rejection of the parent they believe abandoned them. In such cases, the damage of the long absence led to rifts that seemed challenging to traverse. Some were unforgiving, and by the time parents reentered their life, it was too late. These youth had grown accustomed to living without the missing parent; they were ready to assert greater independence and were unwilling to submit to the parents' authority after an extended separation. A fourteen-year-old Chinese girl, An, confided that after a nine-year absence, "Suddenly I had another creature in my life called 'father'.... I was too old by then and I could no longer accept him into my life."

Some parents perceived the rupture in trust and patiently worked to rebuild a bridge across the emotional chasm. The mother of a fourteen-year-old Honduran, Felipe, told us: "It was really hard at the beginning because we had been separated for five years.... [H]e barely trusted me, but now, little by little we are building something." But other parents were less patient, hurt, and indeed enraged that their children did not appreciate the sacrifices made on their behalf. A Haitian father, who had worked years to bring over his daughter, said between clenched teeth, "She barely looks at me. All she does is complain that she wants to be back with her aunt, and she just treats me like an ATM."

Parents and adolescents shared with us that reunifications were especially complicated when youth had to adapt to entirely new family members, particularly new stepparents (or partners) or new siblings (or stepsiblings). For example, twelve-year-old Inez from Mexico admitted that she had not wanted to migrate because "I did not know anybody and I was going to live with a man [a new stepfather] I did not like." Many admitted outright jealously. The mother of thirteen-year-old Nicaraguan Enrique disclosed: "We are getting used to each other. We are both beginning a different life together. . . . [T]he kids are jealous of each other and my husband is jealous of them. . . . Jealousy exists between those who were born here and those who were not."

It was not unusual for the youth to envy attention lavished on new siblings (or stepsiblings). As fourteen-year-old Bao Yu articulately stated, "Now whenever I see how my father spends time playing with my younger sister, I always get mad that he never gave me fatherly love. Now I think he is trying to make up to my younger sister." This pattern of envy often led to tension and conflict between family members.

The moment of reunification was thus interlaced with contradictory emotions, as children had to leave the caretakers who became their de facto parents during the absence of the immigrant parent. A sixteen-year-old Guatemalan, Marisol, explained, "I loved living with them [the grandparents] because they were really sweet people. They were wonderful parents. For me they are not like grandparents, they are like my parents because they understand me [and] they love me. . . . I did not want to leave them."

Understandably, many adolescents describe bittersweet feelings upon reunification because of this loss of the caretakers with whom they had daily contact. Marisol told us: "I was sad because I had left my grandparents behind but happy to be together with my mother." Similarly, eleven-year-old Honduran Juan told us: "I was crying because I was leaving my grandfather. I had conflicting feelings. On the one hand I wanted to see my mother, but on the other I did not want to leave my grandfather." Such double separations and losses are major disruptions in these youngsters' lives. In these families, the grandparents also endured two sets of major separations. The elderly had said good-byes to their own children when the family migration began, and then had to bid farewell to their grandchildren whom they had raised as their own children.

Many parents expressed guilt for being away from their children while recognizing that their sacrifice was necessary for the good of the family.

It often dawned on them that their children did not always understand this. The longer the parent and child were apart, the harder it was for the child to make sense of the situation, and the more parental authority and credibility were undermined. Graciela, the insightful mother of a thirteen-year-old Central American girl, reflects that since the reunification,

> our relationship has not been that good. We were apart for eleven years and communicated by letters. Now, we have to deal with that separation. It's been difficult for her and for me. It's different for my son because I've been with him since he was born. If I scold him, he understands where I'm coming from. He does not get angry or hurt when I discipline him, but if I discipline [my daughter] she takes a completely different attitude. I think this is a normal way to feel giving the circumstances.

Disruptions in "Normative" Parenting in Transnational Families

All societies define parenting along shared scripts of safety, security, and emotional care for the children.[23] The idea of "home" connotes familiarity and the sense of being at ease, feeling safe, and being cared for. Providing for the physical security of the child is but the most fundamental of parental responsibilities. The work of protecting children involves a range of domains: providing the basic financial resources needed for feeding and clothing, sending them to school, and meeting their health needs. Parents must also provide the protections afforded to citizens living as members of a larger community.

For immigrants these basic securities may prove elusive. While migrants are renowned for their work ethic and for struggling valiantly to provide for their families, this may not be enough. Poverty among working-class immigrant families remains a protracted problem for newcomers from many countries.[24] Financial security remains a nearly impossible quest for millions of immigrant families.

Millions of immigrant families face a more formidable threat to their basic security—living with unauthorized status. The ethos of safety and security essential to foster healthy family dynamics is unattainable to those families who face a pervasive sense of fear—a culture of fear—driven by the constant threat of being hunted and at risk of apprehension. In the United States, approximately 1.1 million children are unauthorized, and an additional 4 million are citizen children growing up with at least one parent who is an unauthorized immigrant. Amazingly today, the United States—a country with less than 5 percent of the world's population—has approximately 20 percent of the illegal immigrants in the world: 11 million people living in the shadows of society.[25]

Beyond the fundamental physical, social, and economic security parents should provide, there are parental authoritative, socializing, and emotional roles that are essential for optimal child development and well-being.[26] For a variety of reasons, immigrant parents are often robbed of the psychological, social, and cultural resources to engage meaningfully with their children in the new society and fulfill these roles.

Immigrant parenthood is often defined by an ambiguous presence, when parents have gone ahead and left their children behind. Upon reunification the children will experience a new ambiguity. They need to get to know, in new intimate proximity, the rhythms, moods, and expectations of their parents.

Parents, now physically present, may continue to be only ambiguously there.[27] Making ends meet while learning a new language and the ways of a new culture drains parents of their time and energy. Many work multiple jobs for long hours. Others find the stresses of learning a new language while performing on the job overwhelming. Most are mourning the losses of loved ones left behind. Many immigrant parents, with the best of intentions, find themselves unable to provide the physical presence, time, and energy required to meaningfully parent their children. Further, the cumulative stresses and losses of migrations, while tempered by economic gains, leave many parents emotionally exhausted, anxious, depressed, and distracted. They may be physically present but psychologically elsewhere and unavailable to meet their children's emotional day-to-day needs.

Immigration is particularly stressful to parents when they are unable to draw on their usual resources and coping skills, especially when much is at stake for the balance and well-being of the family. Immigration removes parents from many of the supports that are linked to community ties, jobs, and the main institutions of the new society. Stripped of many of their significant supports (extended family members, best friends, and neighbors), immigrant parents may never fully develop the social maps needed to find their way in a foreign land. A lack of a sense of basic competence, control, and belonging leaves many immigrant parents feeling marginalized. A new paradox becomes evident. Even as immigrant parents become more empowered economically by the opportunities in their new homeland, they experience a keen sense of inadequacy in their ability to effectively exercise their parenting authority. At a time when immigrant children and youth need extra guidance in navigating the difficult currents of the new country, many immigrant parents find themselves at a loss in guiding their children.

Further, a loss of parental status is amplified by the multiple social demotions parents experience in the new society. The sources of these demotions are many, and the consequences are profound. Some start with taking a job well beneath their qualifications and skills. The field of immigration is littered with examples of wasted talent: the doctor from China now working as a nurse; the nurse from El Salvador working as a cleaning lady; the engineer from Ghana working as a taxi driver. Even with a better salary, these social demotions are a hard pill to swallow. A Mexican immigrant remembers: "Nothing broke my father except the U.S. He couldn't find his footing here. He could not rise again and he knew it. He tried many jobs—bus boy, cannery worker, bakery truck driver. I often think that he settled on bowling alleys because he was the most erudite man there, even if he was a greaser."[28]

While other immigrants may not suffer a drop in job status, they nonetheless find themselves toiling in the most stigmatized, dangerous, and demeaning work. Narratives of immigrant workers often reveal a deeply felt sense that they, and only they, can and will endure the harshest, most unforgiving working conditions the new land has to offer.[29]

Demoralization, uncertainty, and fear at work are but part of the stress that worms its way into the heart of immigrant family life. Immigration reverses the natural order of parental authority. Typically nonimmigrant parents know the basic rules of socialization and how to guide their children through the moral, social, and cultural etiquette required for membership and belonging.[30] They can wisely impart the basic rules for respectful interaction with others, how to complete school, and how to get a job. In a new society, the rules of engagement change, and immigrant parents are no longer masters (or even sometimes players) of the game. For immigrants, "relinquishing the parental function" is a painful and reluctant process. Some do so out of a sense of helplessness and entrust their children prematurely to responsibility beyond their years. Some youth cherish this role and feel like they are responsible and active contributors to the family.[31] Others, however, feel burdened or are left with a "worm that undermines basic certitude." Eva Hoffman writes that her Polish migrant parents did "not try to exercise much influence over me. 'In Poland, I would have known how to bring you up, I would have known what to do,' says my mother, but here she has lost her sureness, her authority."³²

Parents find themselves turning to their children for help and guidance in the practical, cultural, and linguistic nuances of the new society. Asking children to take on this mature role comes at a cost. A Vietnamese refugee who arrived in the United States as a child recalls:

> The dreadful truth was simply this: we were going through life in reverse, and I was the one who would help my mother through the hard scrutiny of hard suburban life. I would have to forgo the luxury of adolescent experiments and temper tantrums, so that I could scoop my mother out of harm's way and give her sanctuary. Now, when we stepped into the exterior world, I was the one who told my mother what was acceptable and unacceptable behavior . . . and even though I hesitated to take on the responsibility I had no choice.³³

The inability of many immigrant parents to master the language of the new land contributes both to this role reversal and to the undermining of parental authority. The complexity of understanding and making oneself understood will define the lives of new immigrants at work, in dealing with the institutions of the new society (including schools, health care services, and the police and judicial system), and with the very essence of social membership. Language is an overwhelming preoccupation for immigrant parents in the new society because they see it as essential to advancing there. An inevitable period of linguistic inadequacy compounds the difficulty of learning the social rules that smooth interactions in the new society. Some are blessed with the linguistic gifts, previous education, and social contexts that facilitate rapid acquisition of the new language, but many others find themselves linguistically challenged and never fully master its intricacies.

Immigrant children, by contrast, more readily come into more intimate contact with the language and culture of the new society. Schools immerse them in the new values and worldviews and, above all, introduce them to the systematic study of the new language. Teachers are often native-speaking members of the majority culture. Other children who may not be immigrants will become the daily interlocutors with whom immigrant children will develop a new linguistic repartee. The children watch television, see movies, listen to music, and are seeped in the media of their new land's language. Their parents, on the other hand, are more removed from these new cultural realities, particularly if they work long hours, in enclaves with other immigrants who tend to be of the same linguistic, ethnic, and national background. The children's deep immersion in the new culture will facilitate the acquisition of the new language and give them a course to chart in making their way in the new society.

As the children increasingly gain mastery of the new language and culture, many develop feelings ranging from vague to intense embarrassment as they recognize their parents' inability to help them manage what appear like simple tasks. Richard Rodriguez, the son of humble immigrant parents who grew to flourish as an author and National Public Radio commentator, found early success in school. When his teachers would comment, "Your parents must be proud of you . . . shyly I would smile, never betraying my sense of irony: I was not proud of my parents."[34] Instead, like other children of immigrants, he felt embarrassed by his parents' accents, silent ways, and inability to help him understand homework even during the early years of elementary school.

Some immigrant parents rage against their loss of authority; overreaction is not uncommon. Hypervigilance, regimented routines, and policing peer influences, as well as those of the media, become preoccupations in many immigrant households. Parents feel threatened by the encroachment of new cultural values and behaviors in their children. They often respond by tightening the reins. Putting in place disciplinary sanctions from the "old country" will open a new cultural can of worms. While withholding a meal, pulling an ear, or forcing a child to kneel on rice are common practices found in many countries of origin, they may be dissonant with mainstream ideals of proper discipline in the new land. A "good spanking" in the old country can be a reportable offense in another. Children quickly become wise to the spirit and the letter of the law in the new land and threaten their parents with the "911" Sword of Damocles.

If immigrant parents do not learn alternative sanctioning mechanisms, however, they will lose control of their offspring. This may have severe implications for the well-being of the children because it is essential for parents to maintain basic authoritative functions within the family.[35] Parents' authority is not only symbolic but also critical for imposing limits around curfew, values around respectful behavior toward others, expectations for doing homework, and much more. When the voice of parental authority is undermined, and if the children lose respect for their parents, then the very foundation of safety and family coherence is compromised.

Many parents, thus, come to face the paradox of parenting in a promised land. The country that offers them the dream of a better tomorrow and provides them the opportunity to give their children greater economic security becomes a battlefield over the identity of the children and the coherence and cohesion of the family. The profound familial dislocations and the delegitimizing of parental authority can have destabilizing implications for the development of immigrant children, undermining the children's educational and professional pathways in their new society.

Conclusion

If asked, most immigrant parents would likely subscribe to an *idealized* integrative view of the family. The majority come from traditional communities in Latin America, the Caribbean, and Asia, where a household consists of the nuclear family including children and parents—though expansive involvement with extended and fictive kin is not unusual. However, with the process of immigration, the integrative family often becomes little more than a normative ideal. Reunification is often more complicated than anyone anticipates. Under the best of circumstances, immigration represents a huge challenge for the newly reconstituted family.

Our dysfunctional policy architecture compounds these challenges, imposing unnecessary costs on the family. The status quo is in urgent need of repair. First, we must take seriously what we mean when we say that family reunification is at the heart of our immigration policy. We must strive to drain the bureaucratic swamp where millions of families are stuck enduring separations that can stretch more than half a childhood. Our research and other recent work suggest that lengthy family separations extract a serious toll. Indeed, some Organisation for Economic Cooperation and Development member countries are encouraging policies to drastically minimize the length of separation or to simply do away with reunifications if they cannot be conducted in an orderly and timely manner.[36] The costs to families and society have been deemed to be that high.

Beyond the problem of protracted separations, we must once and for all develop a lawful, workable, and humane national plan to put an end to the deforming phenomenon of unauthorized parents raising citizen children.[37] The logic for this is simple and has our national interests in mind. A wealthy advanced democracy simply cannot afford to have millions of citizen children growing up in limbo with unauthorized parents. Why? At the most basic level, illegal immigration undermines the fundamental core functions of the nation-state. Countries come with borders and are in the business of enumerating and accounting for their citizens; 12 million human beings who are unidentifiable represent a tear in the fabric of the nation-state. The reality of unauthorized parents and their citizen children cheapens the value of citizenship for the children, erodes their fundamental protections under the Fourteenth Amendment, and works to create a permanent subcaste of children and youth who are de jure citizens but who de facto operate in the shadows of society.

Finally, our current laissez-faire approach to immigration is anachronistic and out of touch. With the sink-or-swim approach, while some immigrants and their children will thrive, too many are left at risk of drowning. It is time for the premier country of immigration to do its homework and to learn from what other countries have been quietly and successfully putting in place to ease the transition of their new immigrants and families. We need a system of nationally coordinated local supports with beachheads in schools, in community centers, and in places of worship devised to intelligently support immigrant parents and to aid them during a difficult period of transition.

Notes

1. Nancy Foner, "Introduction: Intergenerational Relations in Immigrant Families," in *Across Generations: Immigrant Families in America*, ed. Nancy Foner (New York: NYU Press, 2009), 1–20; Ramaswami Mahalingam, Sundari Balan, and Kristine M. Molina, "Transnational Intersectionality: A Critical Framework for Theorizing Motherhood," in *Handbook of Feminist Family Studies*, ed. Sally A. Lloyd, April L. Few, and Katherine R. Allen (Thousand Oaks, CA: Sage, 2009), 69–80; United Nations Development Programme, *Human Development Report 2009—Overcoming Barriers: Human Mobility and Development* (Basingstoke, UK: Palgrave Macmillan, 2009).

2. Vappu Tyyskä, "Immigrant Families in Sociology," in *Immigrant Families in Contemporary Society*, ed. Jennifer E. Lansford, Kirby Deater-Deckard, and Marc H. Bornstein (New York: Guilford Press, 2007), 83–99, quoted on 91.

3. See Deborah Fahy Bryceson and Ulla Vuorela, "The Transnational Families in the Twenty-First Century," in *The Transnational Family: New European Frontiers and Global Networks*, ed. Deborah Fahy Bryceson and Ulla Vuorela (Oxford: Berg, 2002), 3–30. Economists have made note of the important contributions of remittances in supporting family members and local economies. See, e.g., Leisy Abrego, "Economic Well-Being in Salvadoran Transnational Families: How Gender Affects Remittance Practices," *Journal of Marriage and Family* 71 (Nov. 2009): 1070; Roberto Suro, *Remittance Senders and Receivers: Tracking the Transnational Channels* (Washington, DC: Pew Hispanic Center, 2003), http://pewhispanic.org/files/reports/23.pdf (accessed Dec. 14, 2011). Sociologists in particular have been astutely documenting this phenomenon of late. For interesting analyses, see the work of Joanna Dreby, "Honor and Virtue: Mexican Parenting in the Transnational Context," *Gender and Society* 20 (Feb.

2006): 32; Foner, "Introduction," 1–20; Pierrette Hondagneu-Sotelo and Ernestine Avila, "'I'm Here, But I'm There': The Meanings of Latina Transnational Motherhood," *Gender and Society* 11 (Oct. 1997): 548.

4. United Nations Development Programme, *Human Development Report 2009*.

5. This is likely a conservative estimate. Most migrants tend to originate from settings with large families. Further, estimates of global remittances suggest that in some South/North migration corridors, each migrant in the North who remits funds to the South is supporting an estimated four family members remaining behind. Dilip Ratha and Zhimei Xu, *Migration and Remittances Factbook* (Washington, DC: World Bank, 2008).

6. Hondagneu-Sotelo and Avila, "'I'm Here, But I'm There,'" 548; Pierrette Hondagneu-Sotelo, ed., *Gender and U.S. Immigration: Contemporary Trends* (Berkeley: University of California Press, 2003); Marjorie Faulstich Orellana et al., "Transnational Childhoods: The Participation of Children in Processes of Family Migration," *Social Problems* 48 (Nov. 2001): 572.

7. United Nations Development Programme, *Human Development Report 2009*.

8. Hondagneu-Sotelo and Avila, "'I'm Here, But I'm There,'" 548; Hondagneu-Sotelo, *Gender and U.S. Immigration*; Brian Gratton, "Ecuadorians in the United States and Spain: History, Gender and Niche Formation," *Journal of Ethnic Migration Studies* 33 (2007): 581.

9. Judith K. Bernhard, Patricia Landolt, and Luin Goldring, "Transnational, Multi-local Motherhood: Experiences of Separation and Reunification among Latin American Families in Canada," *CERIS, Policy Matters* 24 (Jan. 2006), http://ceris.metropolis.net/wp-content/uploads/pdf/research_publication/policy_matters/pm24.pdf (accessed Dec. 14, 2011); Foner, "Introduction," 1–20; Scalabrini Migration Center and Overseas Workers Welfare Administration, *Hearts Apart: Migration in the Eyes of Filipino Children* (Manila: Episcopal Commission for the Pastoral Care of Migrants and Itinerant People-CBCP, 2003).

10. In the United States the Fourteenth Amendment grants citizenship automatically at birth to *all born* in the country, irrespective of the citizenship or legal status of parents. Citizenship is not automatically granted at birth in other countries of immigration where children born in the new land typically must wait until they reach legal adulthood before being able to petition for citizenship. Rogers Brubaker, *Citizenship and Nationhood in France and Germany* (Cambridge: Harvard University Press, 1992).

11. Randy Capps et al., *Paying the Price: The Impact of Immigration Raids on America's Children* (Washington, DC: Urban Institute, 2007), http://www.urban.org/UploadedPDF/411566_immigration_raids.pdf (accessed Dec. 14, 2011); Ajay Chaudry et al., *Facing Our Future: Children in the Aftermath of Immigration Enforcement* (Washington, DC: Urban Institute, 2010), http://www.urban.org/uploadedpdf/412020_FacingOurFuture_final.pdf (accessed Dec. 14, 2011).

12. Tim H. Gindling and Sara Poggio, "Family Separation and the Educational Success of Immigrant Children," *Policy Brief No. 7* (Mar. 2009).

13. For details about the sample and the methodology used in the study, see Carola Suárez-Orozco, Marcelo M. Suárez-Orozco, and Irina Todorova, *Learning a New Land:*

Immigrant Students in American Society (Cambridge: Belknap Press of Harvard University Press, 2008).

14. Carola Suárez-Orozco, Hee Jin Bang, and Ha Yeon Kim, "I Felt Like My Heart Was Staying Behind: Psychological Implications of Immigrant Family Separations and Reunifications," *Journal of Adolescent Research* 26 (Mar. 2011): 222.

15. Ibid.

16. Ibid.

17. Ibid.

18. Ibid.

19. Ibid; Carola Suárez-Orozco, Irina Todorova, and Josephine Louie, "'Making Up for Lost Time': The Experience of Separation and Reunification among Immigrant Families," *Family Process* 41 (Dec. 2002): 625.

20. Suárez-Orozco et al., "I Felt Like My Heart Was Staying Behind," 222. Unless otherwise indicated, all quoted statements from participants appear in this same article.

21. For details about the sources of, and coding of, the qualitative data here, see Suárez-Orozco et al., *Learning a New Land*.

22. All names used throughout this chapter are pseudonyms to protect the identity of participants.

23. Robert A. LeVine, "A Cross-Cultural Perspective on Parenting," in *Worlds of Childhood*, ed. Robert H. Wozniak, Mary T. Rourke, and Berit I. Haahr (New York: HarperCollins, 1993).

24. Donald J. Hernandez, Nancy A. Denton, and Suzanne E. Macartney, "Family Circumstances of Children in Immigrant Families: Looking to the Future of America," in Lansford et al., *Immigrant Families in Contemporary Society*; Urban Institute, *Young Children of Immigrants in Two-Parent Families Have Triple the Poverty Rate of Children with U.S.-Born Parents*, Feb. 8, 2005, http://www.urban.org/publications/900779.html (accessed Dec. 15, 2011).

25. Jeffrey S. Passel and D'Vera Cohn, *Portrait of Unauthorized Immigrants in the United States* (Washington, DC: Pew Hispanic Center, 2009), http://www.pewhispanic.org/files/reports/107.pdf (accessed Dec. 15, 2011).

26. Eleanor E. Maccoby, "The Role of Parents in the Socialization of Children: An Historical Overview," *Developmental Psychology* 28 (Nov. 1992): 1006.

27. Pauline Boss, *Ambiguous Loss: Learning to Live with Unresolved Grief* (Cambridge: Harvard University Press, 1999).

28. Luis Alberto Urrea, *Nobody's Son: Notes from an American Life* (Tucson: University of Arizona Press, 1998), 41.

29. Peter Orner and Sandra Hernandez, eds., *En las Sombras de los Estados Unidos: Naraciones de los Immigrantes Indocumentados* (San Francisco: McSweeney's Books, 2009), 30–31.

30. Maccoby, "Role of Parents," 1006.

31. Marjorie Faulstich Orellana, *Translating Childhoods: Immigrant Youth, Language, and Culture* (New Brunswick, NJ: Rutgers University Press, 2009).

32. Eva Hoffman, *Lost in Translation: A Life in a New Language* (New York: Penguin, 1990).

33. Lan Cao, *Monkey Bridge* (New York: Penguin, 1998), 32.

34. Richard Rodriguez, *Hunger of Memory: The Education of Richard Rodriguez: An Autobiography* (New York: Bantam, 1982).

35. Maccoby, "Role of Parents," 1006.

36. Georges Lemaitre, "International Student Assessments, PISA, and the Outcomes of the Children of Immigrants, with Some Implications for Policy" (presentation by representative of the International Migration Division of the OECD, State, School, and Diversity Conference, University of Lisbon, June 7, 2010).

37. Carola Suárez-Orozco et al., "Growing Up in the Shadows: The Developmental Implications of Unauthorized Status," *Harvard Educational Review* 81 (Fall 2011): 438.

Transnational Mothering and Models of Parenthood

Ideological and Intergenerational Challenges in Filipina Migrant Families

Rhacel Salazar Parreñas

An estimated 3,000 workers emigrate from the Philippines every day.[1] As of 2007, there were 8,726,520 Filipinos who live and work outside the Philippines.[2] In the last twenty years, the majority of Filipino migrant workers have been women. From 2000 to 2006, they accounted for more than 70 percent of annually deployed migrant workers.[3] Most of them are employed as care and domestic workers in private households, for instance, constituting 69 percent of those deployed as guest workers from the Philippines in 2006.[4] Indicating the institutionalization of migration from the Philippines, they go not to a few select countries but to an estimated 198 countries around the world, including in Asia, Europe, and the Americas.[5]

Economic globalization and its consequent result of labor migration from developing nations spur tremendous changes in the constitution and maintenance of households in the Philippines. The outburst in labor migration has led to the increasing presence of transnational families, meaning families whose members reside in at least two nation-states. In fact, nongovernmental organizations estimate that more than 9 million children, a figure representing approximately 27 percent of the overall youth population, are growing up in the Philippines with at least one parent working outside the territorial boundaries of the nation. Considering the disproportionate number of women leaving the Philippines every year, we can assume that a sizable number of them are children of migrant mothers.

My chapter examines the rise of transnational mothering in economic globalization. Imposing geographic distance on mothers and children, the practice of transnational mothering ruptures the ideological foundation of a traditional family as it questions not only the idea that biological mothers should raise their children exclusively but also that mothers and children should reside together. This arrangement radically reshapes common ideas of appropriate mothering. First, it expands "definitions of motherhood to encompass breadwinning that may require long-term physical separations."⁶ Second, it involves mothering from a distance, which some would consider the abandonment of one's conventional mothering duties, but others would insist not. Relying on advancements in telecommunication, women compress time and space and use the Internet, telephone, and postal mail to nurture their children from afar and not up close. Regular communication—whether through telephone calls, remittances, letters, voice recordings, emails, SMS messages, or photographs—allows mothers simultaneously to be "here and there."

Without doubt, geographic separation prevents transnational mothers from performing mothering conventionally but instead forces the reconstitution of its practice. Moreover, it requires other adults—and not mothers—to be responsible for the primary caretaking of children. However, this latter phenomenon is neither new nor exclusive to transnational mothers. After all, working women increasingly rely on paid caregivers to free them of housework and child care so they can smoothly enter the workforce. What makes transnational mothers different, however, is not only their geographic distance from their children but also their length of separation from them. In a study on transnational families that I conducted in the Philippines in 2000 and 2001, I found that in ten years, migrant mothers spent a total span of less than six months with their now young adult children.⁷

Addressing the theme of this book, the contrasting *integrative model* and the *diversity model* offer different ways we could view and understand intergenerational relations between migrant mothers and their children in transnational families. The integrative model would insist that the geographic separation of migrant mothers and their children would adversely affect the welfare of children and lead to their delinquency because this perspective prioritizes the biological connection in the family. Perhaps more than this, it emphasizes the importance of a child having both a maternal figure and a paternal figure in their life, with the best scenario being a child raised by a mother and father in an intact marriage. Its vision of gender complementarity often assumes different roles played by mothers and fathers in parenting. Under this perspective, children in transnational migrant families would not fare well because children would not be growing up in close geographic proximity to their married biological parents. Some advocates of this perspective would also frown upon the substitution of the care provided by a biological mother with that given by extended family or hired caregivers. Believing in gender complementarity, they would also question the ability of fathers to perform the duties traditionally assigned to women. Under the perspective of the integrative model, the transnational household arrangement that migration forces on the family threatens to weaken intergenerational relations at the same time that it hurts the well-being of children by jeopardizing marital relations in the family and denying children proximate care from their mothers.

In contrast, the diversity model would not reduce the relationship between mothers and their children to the family form. This means that it would not assume that close geographic proximity is a prerequisite for a healthy family life. Moreover, it does not subscribe to the view that children should grow up with a mother who nurtures emotionally and a father who provides economically. Refusing to reduce good parenting to biological parents, the diversity model recognizes that healthy intergenerational bonds could develop between migrant mothers and their children even from a distance. In acknowledging variations in contemporary family life, the diversity model also recognizes that biological mothers need not be the primary caregiver of children. Other family members, including fathers and female extended kin, could perform mothering as well as, if not better than, biological mothers. A person could provide solid parenting to a child even without a biological connection to the child or if they are not of the proper gender historically associated with family nurturing tasks.

While my chapter engages the concepts of the integrative model and the diversity model, my discussion will not address the question of which is the more accurate model for understanding the well-being of children of migrant mothers in transnational families. Instead, I will address how the maintenance of such families does not occur in a vacuum but is instead shaped by particular ideologies and beliefs of what is supposedly the right kind of family. More specifically, public opinion on transnational families in the Philippines fits the integrative model and rejects the diversity model. I illustrate the negative views of transnational mothering expressed in newspaper accounts and community organization meetings and in the process show how such views fit the integrative model, as they lament the absence of biological mothers from the lives of children and claim that such an absence gives rise to juvenile delinquency. Then I proceed to address not the question of whether the integrative model provides an accurate assessment of the situation of children of transnational mothers but instead the question of the impacts of the views espoused by this model on the welfare of children. I show that this model aggravates the difficulties confronted by children in transnational families because it downplays the care they do receive from substitute mothers (e.g., female extended kin) and encourages feelings of abandonment among children.

As do other family arrangements, transnational families impose a set of challenges on family life. Geographic distance strains marriages and mars intergenerational relations by breeding unfamiliarity, emotional distance, and the pain of family separation. In transnational families, children, for instance, express feelings of loneliness, vulnerability, and insecurity in the absence of their biological mothers.[8] Yet holding onto the values espoused by the integrative model, specifically the timeworn assumption that biological mothers naturally provide the best care for children, does not ease these difficulties. As I show in this chapter, it exacerbates them. Children, for instance, frequently describe their relationship with transnational mothers as one of "abandonment." This is the case for children of both single mothers and married mothers, children who receive optimal care up close from extended kin or older siblings, children who receive regular remittances from their mothers whether cash or in-kind presents, children whose mothers communicate with them by telephone once a week and those that do so once a month, and finally children whose fathers are present in their lives and those who are not. In other words, children equate their mother's reconstitution of mothering and failure to perform traditional forms of mothering, which is the provision of proximate care, with abandonment regardless of the quality of care they receive from substitute mothers up close. We should be mindful that this emotion is ideologically determined and driven by the stronghold of the integrative model in the Philippines, raising the question of whether the acceptance of the diversity model among children would ease their difficulties. I argue that it would, as children would no longer romanticize the proximate care of biological mothers.

My discussion of the emotional difficulties of children in transnational families and the underlying ideological views that shape these difficulties begins with a brief overview of my methodology. Then, I describe efforts of migrant women to mother from a distance and the societal rejection of such efforts. As I explain, Philippine society abides by the integrative model of the family and measures transnational mothering against this model. Proceeding to examine the impacts of holding onto the views of the integrative model on the family, I show that it aggravates the difficulties experienced by children by encouraging them to view their mother's redefinition of mothering as not only an abandonment of traditional duties but also the abandonment of them as children. I end by addressing how following the diversity model not only would facilitate children's recognition of nontraditional forms of care provided by extended kin up close and mothers from afar but also would ease the emotional difficulties imposed on them by the geographic distance in their family.

Methodology

This chapter draws from a larger project on the transnational family life of young adult children in the Philippines. In my larger project, I compare the gender division of labor, intergenerational relations, and the role of extended kin in the lives of the children of migrant mothers and migrant fathers. I do so from the perspective of young adult children whose interpretations of their transnational family life I gathered by collecting one- to three-hour, in depth, open-ended and tape-recorded interviews. I had confined my interviews with "children" to young adults who have spent at least five years of their adolescence in a transnational household and were still in a relationship of economic dependence to a migrant parent. In this way, I interview actual members of transnational families.

For my primary data, I conducted sixty-nine interviews with young adult children of migrant parents between January and July 2000. I interviewed thirty children of migrant mothers, twenty-six children of migrant fathers, and thirteen of two migrant parents. In my discussion, I draw primarily from the interviews with children of migrant mothers. To protect the anonymity of informants, I have used pseudonyms throughout.

By limiting my interviews to adults, I am assured of having gained the perspectives of those who have grown up in a transnational household and have had time to develop well-formulated thoughts and perspectives on the process of adaptation in the transnational family. The interviews with young adult children focus on their family life and relations, emotions, and future goals for family life. The interviews do not seek to generate narrative recollections of childhood experiences. Instead, my queries on transnational family relations focus on relationships that young adults currently maintain with migrant parents and do not look into divisions of labor in the past but the present. Yet, in interviews, children would often refer to their childhood to explain intergenerational relations in the family. During the time of my interviews, all the participants had yet to reunite permanently with their migrant parents.

Because my discussion of transnational intimacy relies mostly on the perspectives of young adult children in the Philippines and leaves out the perspectives of their migrant mothers, my picture of the caring work of transnational mothers relies on the narratives of those at the receiving end of transnational care. Moreover, my perspectives on intimacy are based solely on the feelings and sentiments of the children in the Philippines. How their mothers reciprocate these feelings is unaccounted for in my data. Recognizing these shortcomings, I acknowledge that children of migrant workers may overlook certain caring labors that their migrant parents deem to be important indicators of intimacy, affection, and dependency. Despite this limitation, I consider the interpretation by children of parental caring acts to be a viable glimpse into their understanding of transnational family life and intimacy. The perspectives of children in transnational families and the caring acts of migrant mothers, which they use as the definitive markers of transnational mothering, give us an insight into their gender expectations.

Transnational Mothering: Breadwinning and Nurturing from a Distance

Migrant mothers do not abandon their children. In their absence, they do not even pass down all of their gender responsibilities to other family members left in the Philippines. Instead, they reconstitute mothering by providing acts of care from afar. They struggle to nurture their children from a distance. They do this by (1) remitting funds and (2) keeping abreast of their children's activities with regular communication. In this section, I describe how migrant women mother from a distance.

Remittances play a central role in transnational family maintenance. The money that migrant women remit to the Philippines arguably makes them breadwinners of not only the family but also the nation. Next to electronics manufacturing, labor migration generates the second-largest source of foreign currency in the Philippines.[9] The migration of women ruptures the traditional gender division of labor in the family. Without doubt, the demand for migrant domestic workers in richer countries throughout the world is forcing tremendous social transformations in countries such as the Philippines. While upholding women's traditional role of controlling the purse strings in the family,[10] the maintenance of a shared bank account also allows mothers to redefine mothering to include breadwinning.

Yet mothers do not only remit funds to become breadwinners of the family. They also do so to establish intimacy across borders. According to young adult children, mothers prefer to remit money through the maintenance of a joint bank account that the mother shares with her family in the Philippines and entrusts to one of her children. The management of bank accounts is one way in which migrant mothers stay closely involved with the day-to-day challenges of family life in the Philippines. Through the comanagement of a joint bank account with an entrusted family member in the Philippines, a migrant mother can be immediately accessible to meet the material needs of her family back home. They usually comanage these accounts not with their spouses but instead with an older daughter.

Controlling the purse strings in the family has long been a responsibility held by women in the Philippines, one that is not contested but instead maintained in women's migration as men are not entrusted by migrant women with their remittances. None of the sons who participated in my study comanage bank accounts with their mothers. While many sons receive monthly remittances directly, these funds are often designated for their own personal consumption. The responsibilities of sons do not extend to the well-being of other members of the family. Daughters, by contrast, often have to distribute a mother's remittances to other members of the family. In telephone conversations, mothers would usually ask sons about their school performance, while they would ask their daughters not only about school but also about the well-being of other members of the family, including their father, other siblings, and extended kin.

In addition to micromanaging household finances from a distance, to achieve some semblance of intimacy, migrant mothers make regular communication part of the routine of transnational family life. For instance, the mother of nineteen-year-old Cheryl Gonzaga never fails to call her three children at three o'clock every Sunday afternoon. This routine has been in place since Cheryl's mother migrated fourteen years ago and has yet to be disrupted by the relocation of her mother from one country to the next, beginning with Bahrain, then the United Kingdom, and then most recently Hong Kong.

Migrant mothers achieve intimacy in many ways. Many rely on sending an SMS text to communicate with their children on a daily basis. Some children even told me that they wake up to biblical messages from their migrant mothers every morning; they receive doses of "my daily bread," as they called them. Sending text messages is one system mothers use to make sure that their children are ready for school in the morning. Many are also like the mother of Cheryl Gonzaga and set up a routine of calling at particular times during the week. Other mothers send a box of goods every two months or so. In the boxes would be clothes, goods, and toiletries such as soaps and lotion. Finally, many resort to dropping a letter in the post for their children during set periods of the month. For instance, some children told me that they know when they can anticipate a letter from their mother. These examples suggest that various routines enable transnational families to achieve semblances of intimacy across distances. In turn, they suggest that migrant mothers do not forgo their nurturing responsibilities but maintain them as they also serve as the breadwinner of their families upon migration.

The Dismal View of Transnational Mothers

In the Philippines, the public views children of transnational mothers as victims who have been abandoned by their mothers. The public dismisses women's migration as not just bad for the welfare of children but dangerous to the sanctity of the family. Interestingly, the public does not disdain migrant fathers as it does migrant mothers. The prevailing view in the Philippines is: if one parent must migrate, then it is better that a father and not a mother does so.

How do we explain the vilification of migrant mothers in countries such as the Philippines? Why is there a moralistic compulsion to equate their migration with the abandonment of children? We could speculate that national identity is frequently tied to the idea of women as the reproducers of the nation.[11] Hence, we see the tendency to naturalize mothering as a reaction against the social transformations encouraged by women's labor and migration in countries as diverse as the Philippines. We could also assume that the family in its traditional sense remains a central institution that defines the cultural identity of nations. This latter view would support the integrative model of the family and insist not only on the horizontal foundation of the family being between a husband and wife but also on vertical relations in the family being sustained by a marked gender division of labor that retains the place of women inside the home. Indeed, we see that the ideological views on migrant mothers that are espoused by the media, local community groups, and school officials follow the integrative model of the family.

Illustrating the ideological belief that women's rightful place is in the home, headlines on May 26, 1995, from two of the largest circulating newspapers in the Philippines read, "Overseas Employment a Threat to Filipino Families" and "Ramos Says Pinay OCWs [Overseas Contract Workers] Threaten Filipino Families." In a speech delivered to the Department of Social Welfare the day prior to the release of these newspaper reports, the president of the Philippines, Fidel Ramos, had called for initiatives to keep migrant mothers at home. As President Ramos so stated, "We are not against overseas employment of Filipino women. We are against overseas employment at the cost of family solidarity."[12] By calling for the return migration of mothers, Ramos did not necessarily disregard the increasing economic dependence of the Philippines on the foreign remittances of its mostly female migrant workers. However, he did make clear that it is morally acceptable only for single and childless women to pursue labor migration.

Two parallels with the president's reprimand of migrant mothers are their vilification in public discourse and the media's pathological descriptions of their families.[13] Despite its questionable basis, the media's negative depiction of transnational families, particularly those of migrant mothers, instills in public consciousness the view that migration precipitates a care crisis in transnational families. This crisis supposedly results in the instability of family life and consequently the use of "drugs, gambling, and drinking" among children of migrant workers.[14] Without doubt, sensationalist reports on the well-being of children in transnational families fuel the vilification of migrant mothers, whose migration is equated with the abandonment of children and consequently with children's emotional and psychological difficulties. Yet, in the course of vilifying migrant mothers, news media reports leave fathers free of any responsibility for the care of children. The media presume, as such reports imply, that men are naturally incompetent caregivers of the family.

Public discourse in the media does not disagree with mainstream views in the community. In the course of my fieldwork, I visited eight elementary schools and six high schools in one school district in the central region of the Philippines.[15] Guidance counselors usually welcomed me to the campus and introduced me to teachers. It was during these visits that I evaluated the curriculum for the "values formation" courses required of high school students. The family is frequently addressed in these courses, and I wanted to see the extent to which transnational families are incorporated in lessons and discussions. Not surprisingly, I learned that none of the high schools acknowledged the transnational family in their values formation classes. This had been the case even in schools where the *majority* of students had at least one migrant parent working abroad.

More than just ignoring the situation of transnational families, lessons imparted the message that children in transnational families are prone to delinquency because their arrangement does not abide by the norms advocated by the integrative model of the family. This message is clearly established in the following text, a standard reading assigned to students in the values formation course in a school where 65 percent of students are members of a transnational family. The lesson states:

> If we trace back on [sic] our history, we are proud to say that we are a strong country. Each family goes to mass together, pray [sic] together, ate [sic] together, and happily shares stories before going to bed. The father works for the family. The mother takes care of the children. The parents help the children with their studies. They have enough time to talk to their children on their problems. In return the children showed their love by sharing, helping in the household chores.... They consult their parents before doing anything. Because of this, the children are not influenced by bad friends or peers.[16]

The text more than implies that children in families that do not follow the integrative model of the family would not likely have the strength or know-how to reject negative outside influences. What is significant about this text for the purpose of our discussion is that it sends the message to children in transnational families that they are growing up in the wrong kind of family. The integrative model of the family portrayed in the passage may in turn influence their views on the family. For instance, it may make it difficult for children to imagine their migrant mothers as legitimate breadwinners. Likewise, it may downplay the care provided by their mothers from a distance as well as the care provided by extended kin up close. In general, the normative family depicted in the passage stigmatizes transnational families, which could only hurt the adjustment of children as they face the challenges of growing up in a household physically apart from their mothers.

In addition to schools, I also visited with various community support groups that work with transnational families in the region of my study. I traveled to places far from the city center where I was based, often not in the most comfortable conditions, in order to include in my sample families from both urban and rural areas. I identified community support groups with the assistance of the regional office of the Overseas Workers Welfare Administration (OWWA). In my area of study, there had been fourteen local community organizations registered with OWWA, nine of which remained quite active during the time of my research. My research assistant and I met with members of all nine of these organizations.[17]

Based on our discussions, it was quite clear that migrant community groups had not looked favorably upon the transnational family and its threats to the integrative model of the family, specifically the gender transformations it promotes. This is so despite the fact they were members of such families. Members frowned upon the limited time that migrants spend with their families as well as the transnational family's threat to the family roles of men and women. However, I found that many individuals felt that fathers and not mothers should be the ones who should migrate to economically support the family. A focus-group discussion I conducted with members of migrant families, for instance, left me stunned by the litany of depressing responses that participants gave concerning the effects of women's migration to the family. The participants commented as follows:

1. They are neglected.
2. Abandoned.
3. No one is there to watch over the children.
4. The attitude [*sic*] of children change.
5. They swim in vices.
6. The values you like disappear.
7. They take on vices.
8. Men take on mistresses.
9. Like with the children, when you leave, they are still small, and when you come back, they are much older. But they do not recognize you as their real parents. And what they want, you have to follow. They get used to having a parent abroad and they are used to always having money.
10. That's true. That's true.

Interestingly, these negative sentiments were shared with me by members of the families of migrant fathers, who believe that transnational households with migrant men are more conducive to establishing a healthy family life than are the families of migrant women. In general, opinions of members of community groups reiterated mainstream views of the family. They frequently described the transnational families of migrant mothers as being worse off than those of migrant fathers. Many participants naturalized not only the ineptitude of men to do care work but also their tendency to stray in marriages.

While community representatives conveyed strict gender boundaries of mothering and fathering, they did give greater flexibility to concepts of mothering than to concepts of fathering. For instance, mothers can "mother and father," but fathers can only be breadwinners and cannot take on mothering roles, such as nurturing and caring for children. Often, concepts of fathering are narrowly confined to breadwinning. Moreover, communities do not question but accept the notion that men are incompetent care providers. This conventional view of the family, one that follows the integrative model, resonated in all the interviews and group discussions that I conducted with community representatives.

In this section, I attempted to illustrate the societal rejection of transnational mothering in the Philippines. Society sees this practice as not only a threat to the sanctity of the family but also a danger to the welfare of children. We could assume that the salient support of the integrative model of the family in the Philippines shapes the experiences of transnational family life and likely sends the message to children that they are growing up in the wrong kind of family. Indeed, I found this to be the case as children I met in the Philippines frequently described their relationship with their migrant mothers as one of "abandonment" regardless of the care they receive afar from their mothers and up close from female extended kin. Insisting on the integrative model of the family, I found, intensifies the emotional difficulties of children and does not ease the struggles they face growing up in transnational families.

The Discourse of Abandonment

By questioning the societal lament over transnational mothering, I do not deny the struggles that individuals confront as a result of the forcible separation of the family in migration. Instead, I call attention to the fact that the problems confronted by children are caused not so much by their mother's migration but instead by the resistance against the efforts of migrant mothers to redefine mothering and reconstitute the division of labor in the family. After all, children do receive adequate care in the transnational family. The remittances of migrant mothers, the frequent communication across time and space between mothers and children, and finally the nurturing provided by female extended kin testify to that care.

What I found is that the negative view of migrant mothers, which is premised on the belief that they are the rightful proximate care providers of children, not only absolves fathers of the responsibility to care for their children but also makes it difficult for children to recognize the unorthodox ways that they receive care in light of their mothers' migration. If one were to talk to children of migrant mothers, one would easily assume that they have received no care at all. They often describe their situation as one of "abandonment." One, however, has to read between the lines. A closer look at their situation will show that children are not abandoned and left without adequate care upon the migration of their mothers. Instead, what they often mean by abandonment is not the absence of day-to-day maternal care but the denial of physical intimacy from their biological mothers. Generally, children uphold biological-based views on mothering. In so doing, they believe that it is impossible for mothers to provide care from a distance. Moreover, they assume that the work of extended kin, even those whom they call "mom," cannot adequately substitute for the nurturing acts of a biological mother.

While respondents like Roan Leyritana[18] recognize the care work performed by his aunt, he still assumes that his mother would have provided a greater extent of care. Children often describe the care that their migrant mothers provide from a distance as "not enough." Likewise, they insist that the care extended by other relatives could never match what they assume would just be naturally better care that their mother would have provided if she had not migrated.

Not surprisingly, Roan describes the care that he received from his aunt as "not enough." This is because Roan believes that the care work of his mother would have naturally exceeded the quality of care that his aunt provided him. Although he has yet to experience the same intensive caring acts from his mother as those he has received from his aunt (although his mother did visit him frequently in the Philippines), Roan assumes that the acts of walking him to school, helping him with his homework, cooking him breakfast, and so on would have naturally been better performed by his mother. Roan exclaims: "What is right is for [my mother] to be by my side.... The love that I received from a father and mother was not enough. I received a lot of love from my aunts and my grandmother, but that was it."

Similarly, the affection of fathers is believed not to be interchangeable with that of mothers. The participants I interviewed often assume that the gender division of labor between mothers and fathers is natural. Fathers discipline, and mothers nurture. Fathers provide financial stability, and mothers ensure emotional stability. Not surprisingly, another respondent,

Phoebe Latorre, thinks she would have had a more stable upbringing if her mother had stayed at home. This is regardless of the fact that her mother left behind an alcoholic and jobless husband to work as a domestic worker in Hong Kong, calls frequently enough to know the weekly routine of her children, and has financially supported all of her children through school.

Notably, fathers left behind in the Philippines tend not to take on nurturing responsibilities. Physically present but emotionally absent, fathers forgo the physical caring responsibilities that migrant mothers surely cannot perform due to their geographic separation. Instead, they pass this work on to other women, including daughters, domestic workers, or, more commonly, female extended kin. Fathers are often not stigmatized for rejecting care work. Instead, staunch ideological beliefs in the "cult of domesticity" and society's continued abidance by the integrative model of the family absolve men of responsibility for care.

Due to the ideological stronghold of the integrative model of the family, children likewise often do not recognize the efforts of migrant mothers to redefine mothering, which is to amplify their breadwinning responsibilities and to provide care from a distance. The attitude of Rosette Cabellero, a nineteen-year-old whose single mother works in Qatar, reflects those of most children whom I met in the Philippines. She recognizes the material gains that she has incurred from her mother's migration, but not to the extent that it would free her mother of caregiving responsibilities. For Rosette, mothering cannot be sufficiently satisfied by breadwinning alone. As she poignantly told me, good mothering requires constant nurturing. When I asked her to elaborate, Rosette proceeded to tell me: "What I want is, for example, what I see with other children. I see their mothers get frantic whenever they get hurt. They rush to their child's side, apply ointment on the wound. On my own, I do not get that attention. Then your mother should also brush your hair. You do that on your own without her." Children expect mothers to demonstrate their love via what sociologist Sharon Hays calls "intensive mothering," meaning the work of expending a "tremendous amount of time, energy, and money in raising [one's] children."[19] In the process, children often lose sight of the fact that other individuals, not only their biological mothers, could demonstrate these acts of care. This suggests that the children of migrant mothers are not necessarily denied daily acts of nurturing, but instead they are denied what they think is proper care, which is the proximate care provided by biological mothers. In so doing, they downplay the extent of care they receive from other kin in the Philippines.

The care expectations of children such as Rosette undeniably follow a grid of gender conventions. Children generally expect to be nurtured by their mothers more than their fathers. Yet, in most cases, only the intimacy achieved in the daily routine of family life—one denied transnational families—can provide such reassurances of love. This is reflected in the care expectations of children such as Rosette to be nursed by their mothers. Without doubt, physical intimacy with mothers as a measure of the quality of life in the family places migrant mothers and their children in a no-win situation. Yet, I found that a great number of children define the quality of their family on the basis of how well it fits the integrative model of the family. In this model, fathers provide and mothers nurture in proximity.

Remarkably high care expectations haunt the families of migrant mothers and burden women as they toil in other countries. Mothers may economically provide for their children but not at the expense of their nurturing responsibilities. Children recognize these economic contributions but not to the extent that it would free mothers of their proximate nurturing responsibilities. Weekly phone calls, daily text messages, and letters are considered insufficient means of maternal care. This suggests that, for children, money does not provide for their needs completely. Their disgruntlement over their transnational family arrangement indicates the limits to the satisfaction they achieve with the material gains garnered for the family by their mothers' migration. However, in contrast to the dissatisfaction expressed by the children of migrant mothers is the greater acceptance of the practice of transnational fathering. The twenty-six children of migrant fathers whom I interviewed in the Philippines consistently valorized their fathers as "heroes" who are making sacrifices for the collective good and mobility of the family. Children can accept transnational fathering because this practice agrees with traditional notions of parenting in the Philippines. In other words, it follows the integrative model of the family.

Children of migrant women are not likely to accept a reconstituted form of mothering, one that redefines mothering to be that of a good provider and a distance nurturer. Like children of migrant fathers, they tend to hold on to staunch moral beliefs regarding the family, holding in high regard the conventional nuclear family.

This conventional nuclear family ideology is inculcated in the children of migrant mothers not only by the media and the state, as we saw with the comments by President Fidel Ramos, but also by religious institutions and schools, which, in the state-mandated family values course, does not acknowledge the presence of transnational migrant families. In the community where I did research, churches rarely addressed the plight of transnational migrant families in their weekly services. Consequently, many children of migrant mothers grow up believing they are being raised in the wrong kind of family. Not surprisingly, the children of migrant mothers tend to describe their families as "broken," which is how Philippine public discourse often refers to the "deficiencies" in nonnuclear households. Yet, I wish to point out that families tend to be "broken" not because children have been abandoned in the process of women's migration but because the migration of mothers threatens the organization of gender in society.

Conclusion

In confronting transnational families, the integrative model strongly supports a call for a return to the patriarchal nuclear family. In so doing, it vilifies migrant mothers and sends the message to children that they are not only abandoned but are growing up in the wrong kind of family. As I show, this is the case in the Philippines, where the societal rejection of transnational mothering sets the stage for fathers to reject care work because they believe that this responsibility rightfully remain women's work. Moreover, the vilification of migrant mothers clouds the efforts of mothers to redefine mothering, as it suggests to children the inadequacy of the care they receive from substitute mothers who are not their "real" mothers. Abiding by the views espoused in the diversity model would not necessarily get rid of the emotional difficulties confronted by children in transnational families, but it would ease them. It would pressure fathers to do more care work, in part by finding such paternal care work more socially acceptable, direct children to recognize the care extended by their mothers from a distance and likewise provided by other women from up close, and, finally, ease the feelings of "abandonment" frequently expressed by children of migrant mothers.

We should recognize that the family is not a static institution. As Judith Stacey notes, we are now in the age of the postmodern family in which economic realities can no longer sustain a dominant household structure but instead have ushered in the formation of multiple household forms, including single-parent and dual-wage-earning households.[20] To the diversity of household forms noted by Stacey, I would add transnational migrant households. Indeed, while they are culturally pressured to measure the quality of their transnational family life vis-à-vis the integrative model of the family, children of migrant mothers also seem to accept the reality that diverse family forms are here to stay. When asked to define a family, my interviewees did not respond with a conventional picture of the family. Instead, they stated that a family is composed of individuals whom they love, for whom they care, whom they trust, and with whom they feel comfortable and secure. Hence, they often named a diversity of people when asked to account for their family members. For instance, children did not mention only their parents and siblings; some acknowledged extended kin, distinguishing those who are particularly close to them such as a certain aunt, cousin, or grandmother, while others included their best friends. Needless to say, the flexible account of family members and the expansive definition of the family provided by children could very well include a transnational family.

Children do not necessarily receive optimal care in conventional nuclear households. However, the notion that biological mothers should nurture their children somehow retains its ideological stronghold. Yet, as I have tried to describe in this chapter, holding on to the ideological belief that biological mothers are the most suitable caregivers of children only exacerbates the problems of the children of migrant mothers. Without question, it makes it more difficult for children to adjust to their new family form—the transnational family—spurred on by the process of economic globalization.

Notes

This chapter draws from the author's book *Children of Global Migration: Transnational Families and Gendered Woes* (Stanford, CA: Stanford University Press, 2005).

1. Kanlungan Center Foundation, *Fast Facts on Filipino Labor Migration* (Quezon City: Kanlungan, 2007), 4.

2. Ibid., 1.

3. However, we have seen a marked decline in the number of female migrants since 2006. In 2007, they accounted for only 47 percent of deployed migrant workers. There was an increase in the number of male migrant workers and decline in female migrant workers. Accounting for this decline is the noticeable reduction in the number of migrants going to the Middle East. Ibid., 12.

4. Ibid., 14.

5. Ibid., 12.

6. Pierrette Hondagneu Sotelo and Ernestine Avila, "'I'm Here, But I'm There': The Meanings of Latina Transnational Motherhood," in *Gender and U.S. Immigration: Contemporary Trends*, ed. Pierrette Hondagneu-Sotelo (Berkeley: University of California Press, 2003), 317–340, quoted on 331.

7. Rhacel Salazar Parreñas, *Children of Global Migration: Transnational Families and Gendered Woes* (Stanford, CA: Stanford University Press, 2005), 30–55.

8. Rhacel Salazar Parreñas, "Mothering from a Distance: Emotions, Gender and Intergenerational Relations in Filipino Transnational Families," *Feminist Studies* 27 (Summer 2001): 361.

9. Steven C. McKay, *Satanic Mills or Silicon Islands? The Politics of High-Tech Production in the Philippines* (Ithaca: Cornell University Press, 2006).

10. Belen T. G. Medina, *The Filipino Family: A Text with Selected Readings* (Quezon City: University of the Philippines Press, 1991).

11. Caren Kaplan, Norma Alarcon, and Minoo Moallem, eds., *Between Woman and Nation: Nationalisms, Transnational Feminisms, and the State* (Durham, NC: Duke University Press, 1999).

12. Agence France Presse, "Ramos: Overseas Employment a Threat to Filipino Families," *Philippine Daily Inquirer*, May 26, 1995, 11.

13. Various captions reveal this propensity in the media. While the caption "Overseas Job vs. Family Stability" equates transnational family life with instability, other captions reveal the supposed causes of this instability. See Lorie Toledo, "Overseas Job vs. Family Stability," *People's Journal*, Dec. 15, 1993, 4. For instance, the caption "'Sleeping Beauty' Gets Raped While Her Mom Works as a [Domestic Helper] in Hong Kong" points to the inadequate protection of children in these families. See "'Sleeping Beauty' Gets Raped . . . While Her Mom Works as DH in Hong Kong," *Philippine Tonight*, July 16, 1993. The insufficient guidance of children is established four years later with the caption "Education of OFW's [Overseas Filipino workers] Children Suffers." See Mac Cabreros, "Edukasyon ng mga anak ng OFWs nassaskipisyo" [Education of Children of OFWs Suffers], *Abante*, June 23, 1997, 5. Finally, the absence of emotional security is reported a year later, in the article titled "OFWs' Kids Emotionally Troubled." See Lynette L. Corporal, "OFW's Kids Emotionally Troubled," *Manila Standard*, Aug. 18, 1998, 1.

14. Susan Fernandez, "Pamilya ng OFWs maraming hirap" [Many Hardships in the Families of OFWs], *Abante*, Jan. 27, 1997, 5.

15. To protect the anonymity of my informants, I cannot reveal the city where I conducted fieldwork.

16. Excerpt taken from a handout distributed to high school students for a lesson on family values.

17. With a research assistant, I gathered interviews with officers of each of these organizations and conducted focus-group discussions with members of five organizations. I arranged these discussions weeks ahead of time and with the cooperation of officers arranged to hold discussions with the most active members of each organization. Focus groups ranged from four to fifteen individuals in size. Their discussions were approximately one hour in length and addressed problems and issues family members regularly confront in running a transnational household, for instance, issues concerning the reintegration of the migrant parent and the struggles of raising children single-handedly or from a distance.

18. Roan Leyritana is a seventeen-year-old college student whose never-married mother has worked outside the Philippines for eleven years, first as a domestic worker

for eight years in Kuwait, then as a bookkeeper in the United Kingdom for the last three years. On average, she visits her son every two years and stays in the Philippines for no more than one month.

19. Sharon Hays, *The Cultural Contradictions of Motherhood* (New Haven: Yale University Press, 1996), x.

20. Judith Stacey, *Brave New Families: Stories of Domestic Upheaval in Late Twentieth Century America* (New York: Basic Books, 1990).

Now What?

Given Current Indicators, Can the "Toothpaste Go Back in the Tube"? Should It?

PART EIGHT

Of Human Bonding

Integrating the Needs and Desires of Women, Men, and the Children Their Unions Produce

Elizabeth Marquardt

Social scientists have now had the opportunity to study the positive and negative consequences of widespread family change for more than two decades. In this chapter, I will argue that the weight of the evidence supports the idea that the integration of the mother-child bond, the father-child bond, and the sexual bond between women and men through the institution of marriage is on average good for children, women, and men. I then offer a critical response to June Carbone and Naomi Cahn's "responsible parenthood" proposal (elaborated in the next chapter). I end by examining the list of what I consider to be positive consequences of family change in recent decades and conclude that renewing a strong marriage culture would not compromise those positive changes.

The indicators of family change are familiar. For the average couple, the lifetime probability that their marriage will end now falls between 40 and 50 percent.[1] More than 40 percent of U.S. children are born outside of marriage.[2] Other recent trends point toward a continuing fragmentation of marriage and parenthood. A notable example is the number of children conceived through assisted reproductive technologies using "third-party donors," such as sperm or egg donors or surrogate mothers. These numbers are small overall but appear to be on the rise.[3] These children and young people are only beginning to be studied.

Technologies using third-party donors may now be used by heterosexual married couples, lesbian and gay couples, and single mothers or fathers. It is important to keep in mind that these technologies were pioneered for heterosexual married couples. Dominant trends driving a redefinition of parenthood in recent decades, including divorce, single-parent childbearing, and use of a variety of reproductive technologies, have been led by heterosexuals.

At the same time, the greater visibility of same-sex parenting and the understandable desire of such parents for legal recognition of their families form a unique capstone to these trends driving a redefinition of parenthood. Divorced and remarried heterosexuals pioneered the idea that different kinds of people could be parents or parent figures for children, not just their mom or dad. Social recognition and acceptance of typically heterosexual single mothers first affirmed the idea that children do not necessarily need their fathers. But only same-sex marriage requires a full redefinition of parenthood. With such a change, we can no longer talk about children's needs for their mothers and fathers, but only their need for two "parents." Or maybe one really good parent. Or, if two parents are good, maybe three parents are even better.[4] If we say that children of gays and lesbians do not particularly need their mom and their dad, we cannot very well say that other children *do* need those very same two people.

What's Good about Recent Family Change
Over the last several decades, family trends have evolved in the context of broader social changes in the United States and other parts of the world. Some of the good changes that come to mind, and this list is by no means meant to be exhaustive, include the following:

- Much greater professional, educational, and leadership opportunities for women and girls.
- Greater emotional involvement with children by fathers who live with their children, compared with earlier generations of fathers.
- Greatly reduced tolerance for domestic violence.
- Greater acceptance of racial/ethnic diversity within families through marriage and adoption.
- Growing acceptance of gay and lesbian persons within their families of origin and reduced stigma in society toward gay and lesbian persons.
- More openness about and help for addiction, mental illness, history of sexual abuse, and other traumas that can devastate individuals and families.

What's Harmful about Recent Family Change
Still, harms have resulted from these impulses toward greater openness, equality, and freedom. We now live in a declining marriage culture, one in

which men and women on average are more likely to marry later in life or not at all,[5] more likely to divorce,[6] and more likely to have children outside of marriage,[7] sometimes with multiple partners.

Overall, and after controlling for other variables, the weight of scholarly evidence suggests that having a married mother and father is linked to children's increased physical and mental health, general life happiness, academic and intellectual performance, behavioral success at school, and increased likelihood of graduating from college and successfully entering adulthood.[8] Children whose parents got and stayed married are themselves more likely to build successful family relationships when they reach adulthood.[9] Children growing up with married mothers and fathers are far less likely to live in poverty and suffer its concomitant problems.[10] They are less likely than similarly situated children of unmarried parents to suffer from physical or sexual abuse, to abuse drugs or alcohol, to get involved in criminal or violent behavior, or to engage in early sexual activity and premarital childbearing.[11]

Cohabiting unions tend to be much less stable than married unions. A recent study found that 50 percent of children born to cohabiting couples see their parents split up by the time the child is five years old, while only 15 percent of children born to married couples see their parents split up by this age.[12] Couples who live together on average report relationships of lower quality than do married couples, with those living together reporting more conflict, more violence, and lower levels of satisfaction and commitment.[13] Even biological parents who live together have poorer-quality relationships and are more likely to part than parents who marry.[14] These differences occur in part because people who choose merely to live together seem to be less committed to each other.[15]

The evidence strongly suggests that seeking to integrate the mother-child bond, the father-child bond, and the sexual bond between men and women through this institution called "marriage" is, on average, *good*.

Same-Sex Parenting and Marriage: What We Know, What We Don't Know

While there have been many cultural and policy efforts to address these trends in family change in recent decades,[16] this brief chapter will address in particular the legalization of same-sex marriage. The proposal to legalize same-sex marriage is without question currently the most heated issue among family debates in the United States, and it has, I argue, particularly consequential implications for how we define parenthood.

In the United States, the debate went national when same-sex marriage was mandated by the Massachusetts Supreme Judicial Court in a November 18, 2003, decision.[17] As of mid-2012, at least seven U.S. states or jurisdictions have legalized same-sex marriage, as have some nations around the world.

Those who want legalization of same-sex marriage have good reasons. In addition to lacking some of the legal protections of marriage, they speak of the pain of loving someone you know you can never marry and of relationships sometimes warped because they must take place on the margins of society. Most powerfully, they point out that gay and lesbian couples are already raising children, and those children need legal and social protections.

At the same time, in every other alternative family form we have tried so far, children tell us that lacking a close relationship, or any relationship at all, with their biological father or mother can cause emotional pain. Could the children of gays and lesbians be all that different from the children who have grown up in every other alternative family form we have tried? Might they say, "Yes, absolutely, I love the parents who raised me. But I always wondered about that father or mother out there who could conceive me but didn't seem to want me. Or, I always wondered what in me—my expressions, my gestures, my emotions—came from that parent I barely knew, or never even met." What do we really know about children's experiences when they do not grow up with their mother and father? In many areas we know a great deal. In some, we need to learn more.

In recent decades a powerful consensus among social scientists has emerged about the benefits of marriage for children. Increasing numbers of people realize that marriage has important benefits for children. What many do not realize is that there is something about the marriage of a child's *own mother and father* that brings these benefits. For example, children raised in married stepparent families look more like children of single parents than children of married parents on many important social indicators.[18]

Some who advocate for legalized same-sex marriage claim that it will be good for children because the children will have two married parents. But the stepfamily data suggest that it may not be that simple. We do not know how much the poorer outcomes in stepfamilies are due to the history of dissolution or other unique problems facing stepfamilies, and how much is due to the child being raised in a home with a non–biologically related adult or parent figure. In addition, just as remarriage among heterosexuals does not make a new partner the legal parent of an existing child brought into the union, neither would same-sex marriage make a new partner the legal parent of an existing child brought into the union. Stepparents and same-sex members of a newly married couple must petition for adoption in order to become the legal parent of a child brought into the union, and for adoption to occur, the parental rights of the child's other legal or biological parent must be revoked if they have not been terminated already.

Most stepparents are good people who do their best raising the children in their care, but it is vital for those shaping family policy to be acquainted with the large body of research showing that children raised in the care of non–biologically related adults are at significantly greater risk, in particular, of abuse. Many are not aware of the body of research showing that mothers' boyfriends and stepfathers abuse children much more often on average than fathers do, with children especially at risk when left in the care of their mothers' boyfriends. More than seventy reputable studies document that an astonishing number—anywhere from one-third to one-half—of girls with divorced parents report having been molested or sexually abused as children, most often by their mothers' boyfriends or stepfathers.[19] A separate review of forty-two studies found that "the majority of children who were sexually abused . . . appeared to come from single-parent or reconstituted families."[20] Two leading researchers in the field conclude: "Living with a stepparent has turned out to be the most powerful predictor of severe child abuse risk yet."[21]

The example of adoption, however, is an inspiration. When the state carefully screens prospective adoptive parents and these parents receive social support for their role as parents, and particularly when adopted children can be raised from birth by parents who are committed to one another over the long haul, the outcomes for those children do not look much different than for those raised by their own married parents and are almost certainly better than for those who were unwanted or are being raised in an abusive or neglectful environment. So, again, we see that while biology is not everything—biological parents can fail their children, and adoptive parents are generally highly committed and loving parents—from both the sciences and the voices of children we learn that biology *does* matter.

What relevance does this research have to same-sex marriage and parenting? By definition, the two persons in a same-sex couple cannot both be the biological parents of the child. The family structure most of these families might most closely resemble is that of a stepfamily. Most same-sex couples come together once children are already in the mix and seek to raise those children together. Others use third-party donors to conceive a child, a practice that until recently has not been well studied with regard to outcomes for children, and which will be addressed in this chapter. (Further, some adopt a child as a couple and, in that way, those couples are probably most similar to heterosexual couples who adopt a child. When a couple, whether heterosexual or homosexual, adopts a child together, there is a symmetrical relationship between the parents and the child—neither of them is a biological parent of the child—and both members of the couple have gone through the rigorous legal process of adopting the child.)

Meanwhile, the existing research on same-sex parenting is limited, in part because such parenting is only recently becoming more common and visible, and also because the numbers will always be small in the overall population. In addition, much of the existing research looks at different kinds of questions, such as whether children raised by same-sex couples are more likely to be gay and lesbian themselves, or whether they identify with nontraditional gender roles. On other measures of child well-being, most of the studies find little difference between children of same-sex parents and other children. But there are serious and important limitations with virtually all the studies so far.

One of the most thorough reviews of studies on same-sex parenting was prepared by the late Steven Nock, a sociologist at the University of Virginia. After reviewing several hundred studies, Nock concluded that all of them "contained at least one fatal flaw of design or execution," and "not a single one of those studies was conducted according to general accepted scientific standards of research."[22] Problems and limitations that Nock and other reviewers have noted include the following: there are no nationally representative samples used in studies on same-sex parenting; there are limited outcome measures; the studies often rely on a mother's report of her parenting rather than objective measures of the child's well-being; and there are virtually no long-term studies that follow children of same-sex parents to adulthood.

But the biggest problem by far with these studies is that the vast majority *compare single lesbian mothers to single heterosexual mothers*—in other words, they compare children in one kind of fatherless family with children in another kind of fatherless family.[23] They tell us nothing about how these children compare with those raised by their own mother and father.

More recent work has sought to fill this gap (some of which Fiona Tasker reviews in this volume),[24] but it remains a challenge. The journal *Pediatrics* recently published a paper on the sperm donor–conceived offspring of lesbian mothers, which claimed to find that offspring raised by lesbian mothers are doing better than their peers raised in other family forms.[25] The paper relies on a sample of "154 prospective lesbian mothers" who between 1986 and 1992 "volunteered for a study that was designed to follow planned lesbian families from the index children's conception until they reached adulthood."[26] It is hard to know who volunteers for a study like this, and it could well be higher-functioning couples who do so.

In a review essay, Charlotte Patterson, a developmental psychologist at the University of Virginia and one of the most well-known scholars of lesbian and gay parent families, traces the progression she and her team followed as they constructed first convenience samples and then samples drawn from known populations.[27] She notes the limitations in both methods. She and her team then drew upon the National Longitudinal Study of Adolescent Health (Add Health), a long-running, highly respected study that yields data sets used by scholars all over the country. Both adolescents and their parents are interviewed. Of about 12,000 subjects, a subsample of the parents said they were in a "marriage or marriage-like relationship" with a person of the same gender. Patterson and her colleagues studied their children, a total of forty-four young people, aged twelve to eighteen. Based on the survey responses of that sample, Patterson and her colleagues concluded that "the qualities of family relationships rather than the gender of parents' partners were consistently related to adolescent outcomes." But with only forty-four adolescents, and limited to the kinds of measures that the Add Health study designers used, it is fair to say that the jury is still out on how children of lesbian and gay parents fare.

A New Study of Young Adults Conceived Through Sperm Donation
Meanwhile, with my colleagues Norval Glenn[28] of the University of Texas at Austin and Karen Clark, an author and donor-conceived person, we recently completed a study of young adults conceived through sperm donation, some of whom were conceived by women in couples. The survey research firm Abt SRBI of New York City fielded our survey through a web-based panel that includes more than a million households across the United States. Through this method we assembled a representative sample of 485 adults between the ages of eighteen and forty-five years who

said their mother used a sperm donor to conceive them. We also assembled comparison groups of 562 young adults who were adopted as infants and 563 young adults who were raised by their biological parents.[29]

We learned that, on average, young adults conceived through sperm donation are hurting more, are more confused, and feel more isolated from their families. They fare worse than their peers raised by biological parents on important outcomes such as depression, delinquency, and substance abuse. Nearly two-thirds agree with the statement "My sperm donor is half of who I am." Nearly half are disturbed that money was involved in their conception. More than half say that when they see someone who resembles them, they wonder if they are related. Almost as many say they have feared being attracted to or having sexual relations with someone to whom they are unknowingly related. Approximately two-thirds affirm the right of donor offspring to know the truth about their origins. And about half of donor offspring have concerns about or serious objections to donor conception itself, even when parents tell their children the truth.

Our sample of sperm donor offspring included 262 conceived to heterosexual married parents, 113 conceived to single mothers, and 39 conceived to lesbian couples. There appeared to be similarities and differences among these three subgroups.[30] All three groups of donor offspring appear fairly similar in a number of their attitudes and experiences. For example, they are all about equally likely to agree that they feel confused about who is a member of their family and who is not, that they fear being attracted to or having sexual relations with someone they are unknowingly related to, that they worry their mother might have lied to them about important matters, that they have worried about hurting their mother's or others' feelings if they tried to seek out their sperm donor biological father, and more.[31]

At the same time, there appear to be notable differences among donor offspring born to heterosexual married couples, single mothers, and lesbian couples. Overall, donor-conceived persons born to single mothers seem to be somewhat more curious about their absent biological father, and seem to be hurting somewhat more, than those born to couples, whether those couples were heterosexual or lesbian. Donor offspring born to single mothers are more likely than the other two groups to agree with the statement "I find myself wondering what my sperm donor's family is like." Most (78 percent) born to single mothers agree, compared with two-thirds of those born to lesbian couples or married heterosexual parents. With regard to the statement "My sperm donor is half of who I am,"

71 percent of those born to single mothers agree, compared with 46 percent born to lesbian couples and 65 percent born to married heterosexual parents.

Regarding family transitions, the single mothers by choice appear to have a higher number of transitions, although if the single mother married or moved in with someone, that would count as at least one transition. Still, with about half (49 percent) of the offspring of single mothers by choice in our sample reporting one or more family transitions between their birth and age sixteen, it is clear that family change was not uncommon for them.[32]

Regarding troubling outcomes, even with controls, the offspring of single mothers who used a sperm donor to conceive are almost 2.5 times as likely as those raised by biological parents to report problems with the law before age twenty-five. Similarly, even with controls, the offspring of single mothers who used a sperm donor to conceive are more than 2.5 times as likely as those raised by biological parents to report struggling with substance abuse.[33]

Meanwhile, compared with those born to single mothers or heterosexual couples, those born to lesbian couples seem overall to be somewhat less curious about their absent biological father and somewhat less likely to report that they are hurting. However, substantial minorities of those born to lesbian couples still do report distressing experiences and outcomes, for example, agreeing that the circumstances of their conception bother them, that it makes them sad to see friends with biological fathers and mothers, and that it bothers them that money was exchanged in their conception. Nearly half (46 percent) of the donor offspring born to lesbian couples in our study agree their sperm donor is half of who they are, and more than half (59 percent) say they sometimes wonder if their sperm donor's family would want to know them. Finally, one-third of donor offspring born to lesbian couples in our study agree it is wrong deliberately to conceive a fatherless child.[34]

Regarding family transitions, the donor-conceived children born to lesbian mothers appear only slightly less likely to have had one or more family transitions before age sixteen, compared with the donor-conceived children born to heterosexual married parents.[35] Regarding troubling outcomes, even with controls, the offspring of lesbian couples who used a sperm donor to conceive appear more than twice as likely as those raised by their biological parents to report struggling with substance abuse.[36]

Responding to Carbone and Cahn

In their contribution to this volume, legal scholars June Carbone and Naomi Cahn propose an "alternative model" of "responsible parenthood" that "promotes autonomy not as license but as the acceptance of responsibility."[37] They argue that marriage "follows from the right investments—it does not produce them." As an example, they say that "single parenthood at thirty is a different matter than at seventeen." With regard to persons who use reproductive technologies to achieve pregnancies, they say that, "given the cost and difficulty of assisted reproduction," such persons "tend to be older, more mature, and more financially independent than those who become accidentally pregnant."[38]

At least two responses come to mind. First, it is a simple fact that most childbearing still happens among women in their twenties, and the growth in unwed childbearing is happening among women in that age bracket. Second, it is not clear to me what evidence Carbone and Cahn use to support their argument that people who use reproductive technologies to achieve pregnancies are more mature or independent than others who get pregnant, nor why a single mother at age thirty might be a better single mother than one who is, say, twenty-seven, or twenty-three. I will explain each of my concerns.

First, with respect to twenty-something women, Carbone and Cahn highlight that teen births are a bad idea. America has gotten that message. Until recently, teen pregnancies had been on the decline for well over a decade, and the year 2010 appeared again to show a substantial drop in teen pregnancies. Yet the alternative to teen pregnancies that they suggest seems to depend upon women waiting until they are about thirty to have children. Perhaps that is a wise choice for some, and it is certainly what most of us who are professional or academic women have tended to do. But it is not what the rest of America is doing. The bulk of U.S. births continue to be to women in their twenties, and the growth in unwed pregnancies is happening primarily among women in their twenties, not teenagers.

I think this fact is unlikely to change. Puberty occurs at ever-younger ages. The tide of sexual desire begins to rise in the teenage years—earlier for some than for others, but for most it is a real presence by the late teenage years at the latest. In their late teens or twenties, most young people fall in love with someone of the opposite sex. They feel a deep drive to bond with that person. When you're a woman in your twenties and you're in love, it's neither unusual nor crazy to want to have a baby. This makes sense because, as we know, women's fertility crests in their early twenties, peaking around their midtwenties, and starts to decline a bit after that. By thirty, it can begin a precipitous decline. Thus, women in their twenties are experiencing a kind of perfect storm of fertility, desire, high energy, and, frankly, attractiveness. Compared with this huge tide of heterosexual longing and love that is surging among young people in their twenties, I am not sure if the technocratic interventions of the kind Carbone and Cahn suggest (mainly, widespread contraception with legal abortion as a backup plan, along with a strong social message that young people should aim to be mature and responsible before they have children) are going to make much difference except around the margins. The majority of women probably will not faithfully contracept and abort until they are thirty and have their first child only then. They probably won't do it because they don't *want* to do it. Their bodies and minds and the whole tide of human history are telling them to fall in love and have babies. Some of them who are paying attention have also learned, correctly, how sharply female fertility drops off after age thirty, and how emotionally and physically difficult, and too often ultimately fruitless, the fertility treatment route can be. Carbone and Cahn argue that today's economy no longer supports "early" parenthood, but it does not appear that women in their twenties are checking the stock market before becoming pregnant. Therefore, we could better focus our energy on what we, their elders, would like to say to them about *how* they ought to have and raise the children that so many of them are having and will likely continue to have in their twenties.

Second, it is not clear to me what evidence Carbone and Cahn use to support their argument that people who use reproductive technologies to achieve pregnancies are more mature or independent than others who get pregnant, nor why a single mother at age thirty might be a better single mother than one who is, say, twenty-seven, or twenty-three. They write: "The corollary to delayed childbearing is support for the choices that come with emotional maturity and financial independence. Responsible adults are more likely to act in their children's interests." For this statement they offer a single citation, to a published lecture by sociologist Sara McLanahan.[39] As someone who has observed and studied the field of reproductive technology for the last five years, I think the jury is still out on this question. Anecdotally, I have observed plenty of single mothers and same-sex couples using sperm donors to get pregnant who do not appear to be particularly mature or responsible. If the woman herself is not infertile, the financial bar is not high for getting pregnant this way. The necessary vials of sperm and clinic visits total in the few thousand dollars. Same-sex couples and single women can make unwise, immature choices about using these technologies just as heterosexual persons and couples can make unwise choices about getting pregnant or keeping a pregnancy. There is nothing magical about choosing to get pregnant via a sperm donor rather than through sex with a man that signals "financial and emotional" maturity in a woman, nor are women who get pregnant this way necessarily waiting until their thirties to do so. (In fact, because sperm donor pregnancies are not tracked, we really have no idea who is getting pregnant this way, or how many, or how old they are when they are doing it.)

What should we, the elders, say to these young people having babies in their twenties? How about if we tell them that the best gift they can give their baby is their baby's father and mother, the two people who are most likely to be around and stick around if they are married to one another?

Can Greater Integration Be Achieved? (Can the Toothpaste Go Back in the Tube?)

In conclusion, I believe that greater integration between the needs and desires of men, women, and the children that their unions produce is desirable and achievable. Thus, my answer is yes. The toothpaste *can* go back in the tube, or, at least, it can go in that direction. Currently, about 60 percent of U.S. children are living on any one day with their own, two-married parents. Divorce rates seem to be declining. As of 2006, teen pregnancy had declined dramatically over a decade, and it appeared to drop again in 2010. Marital happiness, after declining for decades, has stabilized and may be improving. And as of 2006, the proportion of black children living in married-couple homes had risen modestly since 1995. Overall, the proportion of all U.S. children living in married-couple homes has stabilized and might be slightly increasing.

While challenges remain—most notably, the U.S. rate of out-of-wedlock childbearing continues to rise sharply—the recent good news shows that there is nothing inevitable about the decline of marriage.

Should Greater Integration Be Sought? (Should We Try to Put the Toothpaste Back in the Tube?)

At the start of this chapter, I listed six *good* developments that, I argue, arise from recent family change. To address the second question, Should greater integration be sought?, it seems wise to revisit that list and consider whether any of these good outcomes of family change might be compromised by seeking to renew a stronger marriage culture, one that resists trends that disintegrate marriage and parenthood.

- Much greater professional, educational, and leadership opportunities for women and girls.

In an earlier era, marriage and especially lack of control over reproduction, coupled with other social attitudes, did conspire to limit women's educational and professional opportunities and opportunities to hold leadership positions in society. Today, however, women who wish to can have much greater control over reproduction, including whether to have children, when, and how many. Meanwhile, social and economic changes have increased pressures on families to have both parents in the workplace. Women now outnumber men on college campuses and increasingly are the majority in at least some areas of formerly male-dominated professions, such as family medicine. Definitely, disparities persist, "glass ceilings" remain, and women on average still do more of the housework. But a woman today who *wants* to have children will be, on average, much better served by being married. By now it is clear that a declining marriage culture has introduced a feminization of poverty and parenting. A woman bearing and raising young children faces unique economic, social, and sometimes physical vulnerabilities that are powerfully offset by being in at least a "good enough" marriage.

- Greater emotional involvement by fathers who live with their children, compared with earlier generations of fathers.

Fathers are much more likely to live with their children if they are married to their child's mother.[40] Thus renewing a marriage culture can only help to increase the proportion of children who are living with loving, emotionally involved fathers.

- Greatly reduced tolerance for domestic violence.

Domestic violence was the secret shame of an earlier era's attitude that marriage is for life. Liberalized divorce laws have grown alongside greater social embrace of the idea that abused spouses should be free to leave their marriages and should have state and social resources available to help them do so. There is still more to be done. It can still be far too difficult for a woman to leave an abusive marriage, and the time when she does leave can be when she faces the most risk. Sadly, too, especially at the national level, those who embrace a renewed marriage culture have too often not engaged with those who advocate against domestic violence (although these conversations and partnerships, I believe, do happen more often at the grassroots level).

In the meantime, some basic assumptions must be challenged. Many people believe that divorce is necessary because it ends violent or dangerous marriages. In fact, research shows that about two-thirds of divorces end low-conflict marriages. Only about one-third of divorces end high-conflict marriages characterized by "abuse or very serious and frequent quarrelling."[41] Further, as noted in this chapter, fathers are far less likely to abuse their children than are stepfathers or boyfriends. Mothers' boyfriends, in particular, on average present a far higher, serious physical risk to children. Women, too, on average are safer in marriages than in informal, living-together relationships.

Divorce is sometimes necessary. But the idea that many marriages ending in divorce are characterized by dangerous levels of conflict is a myth. Similarly, when one considers the data on who is most likely to abuse whom, the idea that deinstitutionalizing marriage will somehow make women and children safer is also a myth.

- Greater acceptance of racial/ethnic diversity within families through marriage and adoption.

There is no reason to think that supporting greater integration—that is, supporting the normative importance of marriage in integrating mother-child, father-child, and male-female sexual bonds—would undo or roll back important gains in acceptance for racial and ethnic diversity within couples and families.

- Growing acceptance of gay and lesbian persons within their families of origin and reduced stigma in society toward gay and lesbian persons.

Advocates for same-sex marriage say one important reason same-sex marriage must be legalized is that it will help reduce social stigma against gay and lesbian persons. Perhaps they are correct that a wider social embrace of same-sex marriage (legally enforced at first, and gradually more broadly accepted in the culture as time goes by) *would* lead to more persons saying there is nothing wrong with being gay.

Because I am concerned about the security and well-being of gay and lesbian persons, and because I realize these persons and couples are and will continue to be raising children, I do support legal and social recognition and protection of their families in areas including jobs, housing, access to health care and other forms of public and private insurance, and the like. I also support adoption rights for gay and lesbian couples, and protections for gay and lesbian persons not to lose custody of their children because of their sexual orientation. But when it comes to marriage, I think we have not yet had a real debate in the United States about how redefining marriage requires a redefinition of parenthood, one that could harm many more children than it might help. Nor have we rigorously studied how children raised by gays and lesbians fare. We need to try to understand what, if any, suffering these children might experience based upon antigay stigma against their parents, and what if any suffering they might experience because their father or mother is absent from their daily lives.

- More openness about and help for addiction, mental illness, history of sexual abuse, and other traumas that can devastate individuals and families.

There is no reason to think that supporting greater integration would, at this point, undo or roll back important gains made in identifying and providing help for persons and families afflicted by addictions, mental illness, history of sexual abuse, or other similar traumas.

Conclusion

Based on the evidence and arguments I have shared in this chapter, I would argue that greater integration between the needs and desires of women, men, and the children their unions produce can and should be achieved.

Notes

1. W. Bradford Wilcox, ed., and Elizabeth Marquardt, assoc. ed., *The State of Our Unions 2011* (National Marriage Project at the University of Virginia and the Center for Marriage and Families at the Institute for American Values, 2011), http://www.stateofourunions.org (accessed Dec. 11, 2011), 67 (Social Indicators section, "Divorce").

2. For percentage of live births to unmarried women, by year, in the United States, see ibid., 92 (Figure 13).

3. The U.S. Centers for Disease Control and Prevention counts the number of pregnancies achieved through egg donation and embryo transfer, but neither it nor any other U.S. agency tracks the number of pregnancies achieved annually through sperm donation. Experts estimate that perhaps 30,000 to 60,000 children are conceived via sperm donation annually in the United States. It appears that pregnancies achieved via sperm donation may be increasing among single women and lesbian couples. Due to improved treatments for male infertility, pregnancies achieved via sperm donation may be decreasing among heterosexual couples. However, the latter still make up the majority of patients presenting at fertility treatments.

4. See Elizabeth Marquardt, "When 3 Is Really a Crowd," *New York Times*, July 16, 2007, A13. See also Elizabeth Marquardt, *One Parent or Five: A Global Look at Today's New Intentional Families* (New York: Institute for American Values, 2011).

5. W. Bradford Wilcox, ed., *The State of Our Unions: Marriage in America 2009* (Charlottesville, VA: National Marriage Project at the University of Virginia and the Institute for American Values, 2009), 66.

6. Ibid. 75.

7. Ibid. 99.

8. In this section, I draw on the social science literature summarized in W. Bradford Wilcox et al., eds., *Why Marriage Matters, Third Edition: Thirty Conclusions from the Social Sciences* (New York: Institute for American Values [Broadway Publications], 2011); Steven Stack and J. Ross Eshleman, "Marital Status and Happiness: A 17–Nation Study," *Journal of Marriage and Family* 60 (May 1998): 527; Deborah A. Dawson, "Family Structure and Children's Health and Well-Being: Data from the 1988 National Health Interview Survey on Child Health," *Journal of Marriage and Family* 53 (Aug. 1991): 573; David Popenoe, *Life without Father: Compelling New Evidence That Fatherhood and Marriage Are Indispensable for the Good of Children and Society* (New York: Martin Kessler Books, 1996*)*; Glenn T. Stanton, *Why Marriage Matters: Reasons to Believe in Marriage in Postmodern Society* (Colorado Springs, CO: Pinon Press, 1997); Ronald P. Rohner and Robert A. Veneziano, "The Importance of Father Love: History and Contemporary Evidence," *Review of General Psychology* 5 (Dec. 2001): 382; Sara S. McLanahan and Gary Sandefur, *Growing Up with a Single Parent: What Hurts, What Helps* (Cambridge: Harvard University Press, 1994) (cited in Wilcox et al., *Why Marriage Matters*, 10, 17).

9. Judith S. Wallerstein, Julia M. Lewis, and Sandra Blakeslee, *The Unexpected Legacy of Divorce: A 25 Year Landmark Study* (New York: Hyperion Books, 2000) (cited in Wilcox et al., *Why Marriage Matters*, 33).

10. McLanahan and Sandefur, *Growing Up with a Single Parent (cited in Wilcox et al., Why Marriage Matters*, 10*)*.

11. Popenoe, *Life without Father*; Stanton, *Why Marriage Matters*; Frank W. Putnam, "Ten-Year Research Update Review: Child Sexual Abuse," *Journal of the American Academy of Child and Adolescent Psychiatry* 42 (Mar. 2003): 269; Michael N. Stiffman et al., "Household Composition and Risk of Fatal Child Maltreatment," *Pediatrics* 109 (Apr. 2002): 615.

12. Wendy D. Manning, Pamela J. Smock, and Debarun Majumdar, "The Relative Stability of Cohabiting and Marital Unions for Children," *Population Research and Policy Review* 23 (Apr. 2004): 135; Pamela J. Smock and Wendy D. Manning, "Living Together Unmarried in the United States: Demographic Perspectives and Implications for Family Policy," *Law and Policy* 26 (2004): 87 (cited in Wilcox et al., *Why Marriage Matters*, 14, 17).

13. Scott M. Stanley, Sarah W. Whitton, and Howard J. Markman, "Maybe I Do: Interpersonal Commitment Levels and Premarital or Nonmarital Cohabitation," *Journal of Family Issues* 25 (May 2004): 496; Susan L. Brown and Alan Booth, "Cohabitation versus Marriage: A Comparison of Relationship Quality," *Journal of Marriage and Family* 58 (Aug. 1996): 668; Renata Forste and Koray Tanfer, "Sexual Exclusivity among Dating, Cohabiting, and Married Women," *Journal of Marriage and Family* 58 (Feb. 1996): 33; Steven L. Nock, "A Comparison of Marriages and Cohabiting Relationships," *Journal of Family Issues* 16 (Jan. 1995): 53; Larry L. Bumpass, James A. Sweet, and Andrew Cherlin, "The Role of Cohabitation in Declining Rates of Marriage," *Journal of Marriage and Family* 53 (Nov. 1991): 913; Jan E. Stets and Murray A. Straus, "The Marriage License as Hitting License: A Comparison of Assaults in Dating, Cohabiting, and Married Couples," *Journal of Family Violence* 4 (June 1989): 161 (cited in Wilcox et al., *Why Marriage Matters*, 18).

14. Manning et al., "Relative Stability of Cohabiting and Marital Unions"; Thomas G. O'Connor et al., "Frequency and Predictors of Relationship Dissolution in a Community Sample in England," *Journal of Family Psychology* 13 (Sept. 1999): 436; Brown and Booth, "Cohabitation versus Marriage" (cited in Wilcox et al., *Why Marriage Matters*, 18).

15. Stanley et al., "Maybe I Do" (cited in Wilcox et al., *Why Marriage Matters*, 18).

16. For example, the focus of the first decade of my own work was on the experience of children of divorce, and much of our work at the Center for Marriage and Families at the Institute for American Values addresses problems and possible solutions related to heterosexual marriage, divorce, relationships, and childbearing. See the publications page at FamilyScholars.org, and Elizabeth Marquardt, *Between Two Worlds: The Inner Lives of Children of Divorce* (New York: Crown, 2005).

17. Goodridge v. Department of Public Health, 798 N.E.2d 941 (Mass. 2003).

18. Girls in stepfamilies are slightly more likely to have a teenage pregnancy than girls in single-parent families, and much more likely to have a teenage pregnancy than girls in intact, married families. Children who grow up in stepfamilies are also more likely to marry as teenagers, compared with children who grow up in single-parent or intact, married families. See W. Bradford Wilcox et al., *Why Marriage Matters: Thirty Conclusions from the Social Sciences, Third Edition Endnotes*, http://www.americanvalues.org/pdfs/why-marriage-matters3-notes.pdf, 3 n. 36 (citing McLanahan and Sandefur, *Growing Up with a Single Parent*, 70) and n. 56 (citing Nicholas H. Wolfinger, *Understanding the Divorce Cycle: The Children of Divorce in Their Own Marriages* [Cambridge: Cambridge University Press, 2005]). In regard to educational achievement, children whose parents remarry do not fare better, on average, than do children who live with single mothers. See Wilcox et al., *Why Marriage Matters Endnotes*, 11 n. 127 (citing William H. Jeynes, "Effects of Remarriage Following Divorce on the Academic

Achievement of Children," *Journal of Youth and Adolescence* 28 [June 1999]: 385). One recent study finds that boys raised in single-parent homes are about twice as likely, and boys raised in stepfamilies are more than two and a half times as likely, to have committed a crime that leads to incarceration by the time they reach their early thirties. See Wilcox et al., *Why Marriage Matters Endnotes*, 17 n. 204 (citing Cynthia C. Harper and Sara S. McLanahan, "Father Absence and Youth Incarceration," *Journal of Research on Adolescence* 14 [Sept. 2004]: 369). Teens in both one-parent and remarried homes display more deviant behavior and commit more delinquent acts than do teens whose parents have stayed married. See Wilcox et al., *Why Marriage Matters Endnotes*, 17 n. 205 (citing Chris Coughlin and Samuel Vuchinich, "Family Experience in Preadolescence and the Development of Male Delinquency," *Journal of Marriage and Family* 58 [May 1996]: 491). Children living with single mothers, mothers' boyfriends, or stepfathers are more likely to become victims of child abuse. See Wilcox et al., *Why Marriage Matters Endnotes*, 20 n. 236 (citing Martin Daly and Margo I. Wilson, "Evolutionary Psychology and Marital Conflict: The Relevance of Stepchildren," in *Sex, Power, Conflict: Evolutionary and Feminist Perspectives*, ed. David M. Buss and Neil M. Malamuth [Oxford: Oxford University Press, 1996], 9–28); 20 n. 237 (citing Martin Daly and Margo I. Wilson, *Homicide* [New York: Aldine de Gruyter, 1998]; Martin Daly and Margo I. Wilson, "Some Differential Attributes of Lethal Assaults on Small Children by Stepfathers versus Genetic Fathers," *Ethology and Sociobiology* 15 [July 1994]: 207); and 20 n. 238 (citing Martin Daly and Margo I. Wilson, "Child Abuse and Other Risks of Not Living with Both Parents," *Ethology and Sociobiology* 6 (1985): 197).

19. See Robin Fretwell Wilson, "Children at Risk: The Sexual Exploitation of Female Children after Divorce," *Cornell Law Review* 86 (2000): 251, 256.

20. Joseph H. Beitchman et al., "A Review of the Short-Term Effects of Child Sexual Abuse," *Child Abuse and Neglect* 15 (1991): 537, 550.

21. Daly and Wilson, "Evolutionary Psychology and Marital Conflict," 22.

22. Affidavit of Steven Lowell Nock, Halpern v. Attorney General of Canada, 60 O.R. 3d 321 (2002).

23. See Maggie Gallagher and Joshua K. Baker, "Do Mothers and Fathers Matter? The Social Science Evidence on Marriage and Child Well-Being," *iMAPP Policy Brief* (Washington, DC: Institute for Marriage and Public Policy, 2004), http://www.marriagedebate.com/pdf/Do%20Mothers%20and%20Fathers%20Matter.pdf (accessed Dec. 18, 2011).

24. Fiona Tasker, "Developmental Outcomes for Children Raised by Lesbian and Gay Parents" (this volume).

25. Nanette Gartrell and Henny Bos, "US National Longitudinal Lesbian Family Study: Psychological Adjustment of 17-Year-Old Adolescents," *Pediatrics* 126 (July 2010): 28.

26. Ibid.

27. Charlotte J. Patterson, "Children of Lesbian and Gay Parents," *Current Directions in Psychological Science* 15 (Oct. 2006): 241.

28. With much sadness I wish to inform readers that Professor Glenn passed away on February 15, 2011.

29. The study, with full marginal frequencies available in the publication, was first reported in Elizabeth Marquardt, Norval D. Glenn, and Karen Clark, *My Daddy's Name Is Donor: A New Study of Young Adults Conceived through Sperm Donation* (New York: Institute for American Values, 2010). The 135-page report is available as a PDF online at FamilyScholars.org as well as in hard copy. The study has since been reported in Elizabeth Marquardt and Leah Ward Sears, "Fathers Matter: Anonymous Sperm Donation and the Age-Old Problem of Father Absence," *John Marshall Law Journal* 4 (2011): 113; and Elizabeth Marquardt, "The Child as Gift or Commodity," in *Whither the Child? The Causes and Consequences of Low Fertility*, ed. Eric Kaufmann and W. Bradford Wilcox (Boulder, CO: Paradigm Press, forthcoming).

30. Regarding sample sizes, due to the size of the sample of offspring of lesbian couples, most reported findings related to that particular group can only suggest differences or similarities, although where significant differences emerge they are noted in our report. The size of the single mother by choice and heterosexual married couple subsamples were, however, large enough to make meaningful comparisons.

31. Marquardt et al., *My Daddy's Name Is Donor*, 109–110.

32. Ibid., 116, Figure 3b.

33. Ibid., 115, Figure 2.

34. Ibid., 109–110.

35. Ibid., 116, Figure 3b.

36. Ibid., 115, Figure 2.

37. June Carbone and Naomi Cahn, "The Other Side of the Demographic Revolution: Social Policy and Responsible Parenthood," 344 (this volume).

38. Ibid., 340–341, 352, 355.

39. Ibid., 351 (citing Sara S. McLanahan, "Diverging Destinies: How Children Are Faring after the Second Demographic Transition," *Demography* 41 [Nov. 2004]: 607).

40. Wilcox et al., *Why Marriage Matters*.

41. Paul R. Amato and Alan Booth, *A Generation at Risk: Growing Up in an Era of Family Upheaval* (Cambridge: Harvard University Press, 1997), 220.

The Other Side of the Demographic Revolution

Social Policy and Responsible Parenthood

June Carbone and Naomi Cahn

At the core of the family values debate is a central irony. In the more liberal (and "blue") regions of the United States where public institutions make little effort to preach traditional sexual values, the traditional two-parent marital family is alive and well. Teen birthrates have dropped dramatically, divorce rates have fallen, and children enjoy greater material and emotional resources than they did in earlier eras.

In contrast, the "redder" parts of the country that most loudly proclaim the importance of family values and insist on the need to reinforce the commitment to marriage are experiencing a profound sense of moral crisis. These families continue to have much higher teen birthrates, continually rising divorce rates, and worsening circumstances for the next generation.

We believe that the contrast between the two systems is not accidental. Underlying the different approaches to family structure are wholesale changes in the economy and the relationship between work and family. The new information economy rewards education and investment in the market potential of both men and women. Realizing the benefits of that investment, however, delays readiness for family life into the middle to late twenties, if not later. At the same time, the era of globalized competition has largely eliminated the male premium that made a husband's earning capacity indispensable to family life and the relatively high-paying jobs for the unskilled that sustained young couples of a different era. The secret to the stable families in more successful communities? Embrace change. This new "blue" model, which we dub the *responsible parenthood model*, depends on a set of critical principles: Emphasize education for both men and women. Postpone childbearing until the adults have reached a measure of financial independence and emotional maturity. Adopt more flexible attitudes toward gender: with a decline in job stability, fathers and mothers need to be able to trade off family responsibilities and employment. Respect the life and reproductive choices of the mature and the independent; single parenthood at thirty is a different matter than at seventeen. The more troublesome consequences of the new system become ones of management: later childbearing inevitably means lower overall fertility (for better or ill) and longer high-fertility periods when pregnancy is unwelcome. And failure requires redoubling the effort: the solution to an improvident birth is not a shaky marriage but greater investment in the mother's workforce potential, the child's education, and avoidance of the second birth in close proximity to the first.

This new model has been most thoroughly embraced by the college-educated middle class, and it has increasingly become the foundation for assistance to struggling families in the more liberal and Democratic regions of the country. The more Republican and traditionalist heartland, however, has emphasized promoting marriage. These efforts treat marriage as a matter of will and have focused most systematically on fighting abortion and containing sexuality without addressing the underlying economic and gender issues driving marriage and divorce rates. Yet, the shotgun marriage, which provided the stopgap for youthful indiscretions of old, does not work in the new economy: men are unlikely to earn enough to support a family and, indeed, have been harder hit by the recession,[1] and women have greater ability to walk out in the face of infidelity, insensitivity, or violence—factors that increase with financial stress. Almost all of the proposals associated with the *integrative model* will fail to bolster the traditional family if the net result is to increase the number of children born to parents who are not prepared to care for them. Those who would place greater emphasis on marriage fail to ask the hard questions of whether their proposed exhortation can actually produce more stable relationships in a more unequal economy that writes off a high proportion of men as effectively unmarriageable because of high rates of chronic unemployment, imprisonment, violence, mental illness, and substance abuse.

We suggest, therefore, that while societal changes have sparked profound disagreement between those who would continue to privilege two-parent biological, marital families (the integrative model) and those of us who seek responsible parenthood irrespective of family form (the responsible parenthood model), our disagreement is less about the ideal and more about the means for achieving healthy families. Even in an era of family change, almost 60 percent of today's children live with their married biological parents, and another 10 percent live in two-parent families with their adoptive parents, remarried parents, or nonmarital cohabiting parents.[2] The question of why more people do not create two-parent married families—and why American marriages and cohabitations are more likely to dissolve than those abroad—involves the issue of what happens when ideals meet reality. Most adults would choose a stable, committed, two-parent arrangement over the alternatives if they could succeed in making it work; in this chapter we focus on the alternatives for a world in which marriage either must be carefully chosen or is likely to fail.

This chapter, first, explains why emphasis on marriage as an end in itself is misguided. Second, it argues for a focus on better child outcomes; we live in a society that cannot make marriage universal without bringing back the subordination of women. Finally, we consider the policies that best support responsible parenthood, focusing on efforts that discourage early birth, provide support for families in the workplace, foster independence for single mothers, and encourage caretaking through custody rules at family dissolution that recognize function rather than biology.

Fundamentally, however, the changing landscape for American families starts with the economy. What once made marriage close to universal was socialization into a system that provided jobs that paid a family wage, did so only for men, and simultaneously restricted women's economic and reproductive autonomy. Today, the college-educated middle class has successfully combined women's independence with family stability while the changing economy is effectively destroying the pathways of upward mobility for the working class. Debates about parenthood and family forms too often examine the family in isolation. Until the study of the family is reintegrated into a larger discussion of social and economic forces, true understanding of the changing nature of family structure is impossible.

The Landscape for Responsible Parenthood

This book's examination of parenthood proposes, as an orienting framework, a disagreement between two ideals: one based on promotion of marriage as the most effective locus for child rearing (the *integrative model*) and the second embracing a variety of family forms as equally valid ways to conduct family life (the *diversity model*). In this chapter, we argue that the real conflict is less the ideal than the means of getting there. Most adults, all other things being equal, can and do choose a committed, two-parent household as the preferred way to manage child rearing and, indeed, the majority of couples still undertake child rearing within such unions.

Instead, the true differences concern which unions deserve support and what fallback actions to accept. The model of marriage that arose in northwestern Europe combined two notions: the restriction of childbearing to marriage and the restriction of marriage to financially independent adults. In the era following World War II, a prosperous economy made it possible for most adults to be financially independent with a single male breadwinner. In that era, the shotgun marriage reached highs last seen in 1800 (with 30 percent of brides giving birth within 8.5 months of the nuptials), the average age of marriage fell to twenty for women and twenty-two for men, the youngest ages in a century, fertility rates rose dramatically, and class differences in income and family structure fell.[3]

Since then, the high-paying manufacturing jobs for unskilled men that made these marriages viable have disappeared. At the same time, women's educational achievement has outpaced men's, and women's economic opportunities have dramatically expanded. Successful middle-class families today overwhelmingly depend on two incomes and a re-creation of family roles. More traditional working-class families may have difficulty securing a single stable income and face greater difficulties in renegotiating appropriate roles. Given greater women's independence and changing economic realities, a large part of the change in family structure proceeds from the clash between men's and women's expectations about family life.

Why We Can't Get There from Here

The integrative model rests on the notion that lifelong marriage between two heterosexuals constitutes the optimum place for child rearing. One branch of this ideal—championed by the Christian right, traditionalists in many faiths, and the consensus model of the last century—celebrates the unity of sex, marriage, and procreation. This branch has historically united the stigmatization of nonmarital sexuality (according a scarlet letter for nonmarital births and denying "illegitimate" children access to support, condemning adultery, and denouncing homosexuality and encouraging gays and lesbians to enter heterosexual unions if they wish to produce) with celebration of marriage as the institution designed for reproduction. A second branch, to which many integrationists subscribe, would leave sexuality as a matter of private choice but still see a traditional heterosexual marriage as the only appropriate setting for childbearing. The tension between these two branches is not so much the ideal—both agree that lifelong, heterosexual unions are the best places for child rearing—but how to get there. Adherents to the first branch respond that marriage can achieve universality as the locus for child rearing only if sexual access is limited to marriage and remains the reward for forgoing carnal temptation.[4]

We suspect that critics are right that stigmatization of nonmarital sexuality and celebration of heterosexual marriage as the ideal locus for child rearing are inextricably linked for two reasons. The first is political. While both religious and secular justifications exist for the emphasis on marriage, the religious justifications all emphasize marriage as the dividing line between acceptable and sinful sex, and religious groups are an indispensable part of the coalition promoting marriage as an essential institution.[5] Accordingly, they tend to dominate the political debate and to insist on measures that also restrict access to abortion and contraception. The second reason is instrumental: adherents argue that religious understandings promote marital stability, that sex needs to be the reward that lures men into marriage and keeps them there, and/or that the unacceptability of child rearing outside of marriage depends on the unacceptability of the sexual activity that stigmatizes the pregnancy. Without these measures, it is hard to channel childbearing into marital unions.

Adherence to these arguments has consequences. The areas of the country most committed to traditional marital and moral ideals have the highest teen birthrates, and the lowest average ages of marriage, and it is these youthful beginnings to family that we believe pose the real obstacle to healthier family life. Our alternative model, of blue families and responsible parenthood, promotes autonomy not as license but as the acceptance of responsibility. We accordingly turn to an examination of what works—and what doesn't—in promoting family stability.

The Demographics of Family Instability
AGE, CLASS, DIVORCE, AND RESPONSIBLE PARENTHOOD

Underlying the statistics on greater family instability is a more complex story of class and regional division. We agree with Elizabeth Marquardt (in this volume) that the story of family dissolution is one of emerging class divisions, and the results increase class divisions and societal inequality.[6] As Princeton University sociologist Sara McLanahan explains, for those who have embraced the new pathways to middle-class success, life is rosy. Their secret: an increase in the average age of women with children under the age of five from twenty-six to thirty-two, and with that increase in the age of reproduction, a greater tendency for the successful to marry the similarly successful.[7]

Accompanying these improvements in family stability is more time and money spent on children. McLanahan argues that the single biggest difference in the family formation patterns of the well-off is delay in childbearing, with the age of mothers of young children in the top group rising by five years, compared with two years for the middle group, and hardly at all for the bottom quartile.[8]

What does the age of family formation have to do with family life? The interactions are almost certainly multidirectional. First, the age of childbearing itself reflects education. Women who complete graduate school are likely to begin childbearing later than high school dropouts.[9] Second, later age of marriage correlates with lower divorce risk. Teen marriages have always been risky, and almost all studies find that the increase in maturity from the teen years to the early twenties promotes more stable relationships.[10] Earlier studies, however, found that the effect waned after the early twenties.[11] In 2009, Paul Amato showed a dramatic change. Looking at measures of divorce proneness rather than divorce rates, Amato's research indicated that in 1980, marital stability increased with an increase in the age of marriage from the teens into the twenties, but the advantages of age leveled off after the early twenties.[12] In 2000, however, every increase in the age of marriage produced a decline in divorce proneness through the late thirties.[13] The increase in the age of marriage, which in the 1990s rose substantially for college graduates but not for anyone else, appears to play a much more important role in marital stability today.

Economist Stéphane Mechoulan's research provides some insight into reasons for the change. He compared marriage and divorce rates in different states and found that divorce rates were the same across different legal regimes, whether or not the regimes permitted consideration of fault.[14] He suggested, however, that states that made divorce easier also tended to produce later ages of marriage, and that age was a protective factor in marital stability. Using regression analyses to tease out the effects of different factors, Mechoulan found that age of marriage had a small but statistically significant effect on the likelihood of divorce. The much bigger effect was the impact of selection effects. Today, college graduates have become more likely to marry other college graduates, and later age of marriage also provides greater certainty—it is easier to determine who is going to be successful at twenty-nine than at twenty-one.[15] The economist summarized these as "search costs": with greater marital fragility, engaging in a more extensive search for the right mate appears to pay off, but it lengthens the time spent searching.[16]

Amato and colleagues explained why it pays off. In a thorough study of family relationships, they found that several things had changed by 2009 that were likely to affect the class-based nature of marital stability. First, the effect of financial stress had increased. Their data from 1980 found that those experiencing financial distress were more divorce-prone than those who did not experience financial distress. No surprise there. By 2000, however, those experiencing financial distress reported twice the divorce risk of those who were financially stressed in 1980. At the same time, those who were not financially stressed had become even less divorce-prone. Moreover, by 1980, almost all of those marrying in their twenties reported financial distress, increasing the disadvantages of early marriage in comparison with other eras.[17]

Second, Amato and colleagues discovered that one of the factors that exacerbated the relationship between financial distress and divorce was women's employment.[18] For higher-income families, there were two patterns that produced stable relationships. The first involved a traditional, breadwinning husband and a wife who worked outside the home part-time or not at all. The second involved dual-earner couples, both committed to their jobs. These couples spent relatively little time together but reported little conflict.[19] In contrast, among the least happy couples were those where the wife preferred to work outside the home part-time or not at all but needed to work full-time because the family needed the income.[20] The study also found the following:

> Dual-earner arrangements are linked with positive marital quality among middle-class couples and with negative marital quality among working-class couples. Although the additional income provided by working-class wives helps ... their families, these financial benefits come with a steep price in the form of greater marital tension, low job satisfaction, and a desire ... to decrease their hours of employment or return to ... homemaking.[21]

Amato and colleagues observed that these differences explain one of the great mysteries in studies of marital quality. Between 1980 and 2000, the average levels of marital happiness seemed to stay about the same despite the smaller number of people who married. In fact, Amato explains that the averages are misleading. During that period, the number of both stable *and* unstable marriages increased while the middle diminished. Two-career couples reported spending less time together, with less conflict, fewer problems, and greater stability. At the same time, the number of unhappy couples also increased.[22] At least part of the reason was the mismatch in gender expectations and roles. Both those who wanted traditional marriages and those who wanted dual-employment marriages were doing well if their relationships lived up to their expectations.[23] Less-educated women, however, were more likely both to prefer a traditional division of family responsibilities and to be married to men who did not earn a family wage.[24]

These findings suggest that this mismatch is at least part of the explanation of the divergent rates of marital happiness that emerged in the nineties. During the period between 1980 and 2007, college graduates were the only men whose earnings increased in real dollar terms.[25] Families farther down the socioeconomic ladder lost ground. Men's wages stagnated at best, employment instability increased, adding to family stress, and women's earnings changed from a boon to the foundation of many families' well-being.[26] The result may affect not only the economic well-being of their families but also the terms on which men and women understand their relationships.[27]

AGE, FAMILY INSTABILITY, AND MARRIAGE PROMOTION

The erosion of blue-collar men's income and the increasing divorce rates may further affect the likelihood of marriage. Among the least educated Americans between the ages of twenty-five and forty-four, more than half (53 percent) believe that "'marriage has not worked out for most people [they] know,'" compared with 17 percent of those who are highly educated.[28] Statistics on nonmarital births, which have increased markedly for everyone but white college graduates, bear out the impressions. For the country as a whole, the figures now reach 40 percent, but they vary. A startling 96 percent of the births to African Americans without a high school degree are nonmarital, in comparison with 2 percent of the births to white college graduates; the latter figure has barely changed over the last thirty years.[29]

Perhaps the most common explanation for the increase in nonmarital births to poor women involves the idea that Sara McLanahan and Christine Percheski refer to as a "marriage bar," defined as "the standard of living a couple is expected to obtain before they marry."[30] The idea is that the marriage bar is not an absolute standard—the minimum necessary to maintain a household—but a relative standard that ties marriage to the ability to maintain "a certain standard of living, which includes a house, a car, and stable employment."[31]

This analysis, however, though it has empirical support tying the level of marriage to greater income equality among males, is not convincing in itself as an explanation of why lower-income women are willing to have children. Amy Wax, by contrast, ties the decline of marriage to standards of behavior rather than standards of income.[32] With their greater economic independence, women have become less willing to put up with abusive, unfaithful, and unreliable men. Sociologists, however, turn the question around, asking whether growing unemployment does not in turn affect standards of behavior.[33] The breadwinner role continues to define male success, and the loss of both status and income that comes with lesser employment may cause many men "to be deemed as failures by society, themselves, and their partners."[34] Indeed, *Newsweek* reports that the American Time Use Survey shows that "laid-off men tend to do less—not more—housework, eating up their extra hours snacking, sleeping and channel surfing (which might be why the Cartoon Network, whose audience has grown by 10 percent during the downturn, is now running more ads for refrigerator repair school)."[35] According to the same study, unemployed women spend twice as much time taking care of children and doing chores as do men. Unemployed men rank right behind alcoholics and drug addicts as the group most likely to assault their female partners.[36] Moreover, as a larger percentage of the potential marriage pool become unmarriageable because of chronic unemployment, substance abuse, or incarceration, the remaining men acquire greater ability to play the field. Many studies find that whether considering the African American middle class,[37] the urban poor,[38] or cross-cultural comparisons, the greater the ratio of marriageable women to marriageable men, the lower the overall marriage rates in the region.[39]

Today's economy effectively serves to write off a high percentage of men as unmarriageable due to chronic unemployment, high rates of imprisonment, and increasing rates of mental illness and substance abuse in poor communities—rates that disproportionately affect men rather than women and the poor and working class rather than college graduates.[40] At the same time, working-class men have consistently lost ground both to the college-educated middle class and to the women in their communities. Working-class family patterns increasingly resemble those of the poor, with marriage rates declining with the loss of good jobs for the men. The result affects both divorce and nonmarital birthrates. To prescribe marriage as the solution—even if in fact children would be better off if their parents stayed together—begs the question of how to encourage marriage in an era of economic decline and increasing class differences.

What Policies?

Given the changes we have described, there are only two effective ways to increase stable two-parent unions: improve male economic prospects or increase women's subordination to men. If we were philosopher-kings, we would propose redirecting the emphasis on family to an emphasis on jobs, and we predict that marriage rates would rise. Sadly, however, we view that outcome as politically improbable. That leaves two alternatives. The first is purportedly pro-marriage policies that in fact promote women's subordination by punishing their sexuality.[41] This has been the subtext of efforts to outlaw abortion, restrict access to contraception, and extend parental rights on the basis of biology alone. The second is greater investment in the well-being of prospective mothers and fathers, in accordance with a responsible parenthood model.

The new system of responsible parenthood (the "blue family" approach) focuses on the parent-child tie rather than adult unions. It seeks to secure reproductive and workplace autonomy and reward the acceptance of responsibility. Rather than ask what is the ideal family, as though there were only one acceptable model, it asks what policies most effectively empower prospective parents to make responsible choices. It accordingly requires four types of policies: first, deter *early* parenthood; second, support *later* parenthood; third, promote commitment between adults who assume parenting responsibilities; and, fourth, keep parental development on track in the event of a nonmarital birth or the dissolution of adult relationships.

Prevent Early Parenthood

The United States leads the developed world in the number of unplanned pregnancies. For all races, unplanned pregnancies correlate inversely with education and income, and the disparities have grown worse in recent decades. In addition, race is an independent risk factor, even after controlling for education and income, with African American women having the highest rates of unplanned pregnancies.[42] As contraceptive methods have improved in safety and efficacy, access to a doctor has become more important in securing the most effective methods. The most conscientious—and those most likely to avoid unwanted births—begin contraceptive use before they become sexually active, use multiple methods, and back up contraceptive failure with the morning-after pill or abortion. The failure to promote comprehensive birth control use as a rite of passage into adulthood exacerbates class-based inequalities in family structure.

The international development literature indicates that the most effective contraceptive is support for women's autonomy (including freedom from sexual coercion) and belief in a promising future. While such investment involves a broad range of measures, a critical priority is discouraging early childbirth.[43] In the United States, this requires a commitment to comprehensive sex education, contraceptive promotion and access, and greater willingness to acknowledge the trade-off between abortion and support for single parenthood.

ABSTINENCE VERSUS ABSTINENCE PLUS EDUCATION

Education for autonomy and delayed family formation requires preparation for making the choices that allow self-determination. Principal among them is the ability to manage sexuality through what may be a long transitional period to adulthood. In an era in which the average age of marriage has increased, abstinence until marriage is unrealistic as a majority strategy.

Abstinence programs, when mandated as the exclusive form of sex education in public schools, abdicate their responsibility to prepare teens realistically for adulthood.[44] Abstinence-only education has proved ineffective in delaying the beginning of sexual activity,[45] and it exacerbates class-based disadvantages as the teens from the best-educated families have broader sources of information than other teens. We accordingly recommend that states mandate abstinence-plus (comprehensive) sex education that stresses both abstinence and contraception.[46]

SYSTEMATIC PROVISION OF CONTRACEPTION

Both the European and the American experience in the 1990s demonstrate that comprehensive access to contraception reduces births, and that poorer and minority women show disproportionate increases in unplanned pregnancies when contraception becomes harder to obtain. Moreover, public opinion polls show that the economic downtown has produced both less ability to afford additional children and a shift away from the most effective contraceptives because of their costs.[47]

The U.S. Supreme Court has guaranteed access to contraception to married women, unmarried women, and teens.[48] Yet, states routinely attempt to restrict access by requiring parental notification or consent or defunding popular programs such as Planned Parenthood.[49]

The recommendations here are straightforward: systematize contraceptive use by promoting accurate information, allow minors access without parental notification or consent, encourage low-cost or free access for all women, and make emergency contraception available without restriction.

AVAILABILITY OF ABORTION

One of the factors that has facilitated greater acceptance of nonmarital childbearing is the declining availability and acceptability of abortion. The college-educated middle class has held the line on single parenthood in part because of the willingness to terminate improvident pregnancies.[50] While abortion rates have fallen for college graduates, they have done so overwhelmingly because of improvements in contraceptive usage; abortions remain higher as a percentage of unplanned pregnancies than for any other group. Other groups have much higher abortion rates, but increasingly the women electing to abort are older, and they are doing so to prevent the birth of additional children. State restrictions have made abortion systematically less available to those who need it most, including teens,[51] the poor, those in isolated rural areas,[52] and those who because of poverty or lack of sophistication have difficulty acting quickly to end their pregnancies.[53] These differential patterns of access to contraception and abortion aggravate regional, age-based, and other inequalities.

Support Later Childbearing

The corollary to delayed childbearing is support for the choices that come with emotional maturity and financial independence. Responsible adults are more likely to act in their children's interests.[54] More women, however, are likely to have difficulty conceiving, due to fertility declining with age, and may choose to raise the resulting children in a wider variety of circumstances and with a wider variety of partners.

WORK/FAMILY SUPPORT?

Despite all the benefits that come from delayed childbearing, biology and economics are on a collision course. The irony may be that women's ability to provide for their children peaks in the early thirties after overall fertility, defined in terms of the ability to bear a child, has already begun to decline. A second irony is that those women most in need of the income that comes from employment—poor and single mothers—have the greatest difficulty reconciling the needs of their children with the demands of the workplace.

Work/family balance is accordingly critical to the newer, responsible parenthood model. Family support policies, such as family leave, state-supported preschools and longer school years, and flextime, can help balance the needs of society and families. Indeed, in Europe, those countries that have better family leave policies are more likely to have higher fertility rates.[55] Because women who defer childbearing are reacting to the difficulty of combining employment and motherhood under existing work/family policies, this may even alleviate some of the pressure to offer better coverage of assisted reproductive technology.

Several states—California, Minnesota, and Washington (all blue)—have enacted paid family leave legislation.[56] Other states should enact paid family leave and make it available to both men and women.

FERTILITY SUPPORT

Today, family formation is diverging along class lines.[57] The college-educated middle class postpones childbearing until they form the right partnerships and secure the right financial support, but they risk being unable to reproduce at all if they wait too long. The working class is becoming more likely to give up on the search for the right mate and proceed with childbearing without waiting for marriage.[58] For those who wait, support for reproduction is appropriate.[59]

Given the cost and difficulty of assisted reproduction, those who use it tend to be older, more mature, and more financially independent than those who become accidentally pregnant.[60] Moreover, just as limits on the reproductive rights of the excessively fertile are deeply offensive to our society morally and constitutionally, so too would be limits on access to assisted reproduction. The other half of discouraging premature (and unplanned) reproduction is providing greater assistance to those experiencing difficulties with reproduction. It is, of course, possible that some of those who will seek access to assisted reproduction will be less than ideal parents, just as many of those who become accidentally pregnant are less than ideal parents. We argue, instead, that creating an ethic that discourages early childbirth requires greater support for reproduction as fertility may be waning—and we confidently predict that the support for the resulting children will be greater than in a system that encourages birth of the children at younger ages.[61]

We would like to see greater equity in access to fertility services in the context of comprehensive health care reform that also provides more treatment for the diseases that contribute to infertility. We also support the development of guidelines for safe practices, testing, counseling, and considerations related to age or physical condition in accordance with the type of approach used for other medical treatments.

Support Commitment

Adult commitment has traditionally taken the form of marriage between a man and a woman. Women's economic dependence together with the societal stigma against divorce and nonmarital childbearing have been important components of marital stability in years past. The same coercion does not exist once women obtain the ability to leave abusive, alcoholic, or simply immature or inattentive mates. Reengineering commitment requires reconsidering what keeps couples together.

In the clash between traditionalists, who continue to insist on marriage because it is right, and modernists, who long for increased stability without reviving male domination, same-sex marriage has become a flash point for the differences between the two systems. For traditionalists, same-sex marriage is often associated with license. In the integrative system, heterosexual marriage, with its identification with reproduction and monogamy, is the necessary precondition for childbearing. Same-sex marriage, in contrast, suggests the ability to have sexuality on "sinful" terms and still enjoy the benefits of family life. Moreover, such marriages enable a family form in which a child—by design—will not have *both* a biological mother and a biological father; for advocates of the new model, on the other hand, same-sex marriage epitomizes responsible parenthood and is part of a needed reconsideration of the relationship between marriage and child rearing.

For all couples, strategies to promote equal respect between partners, greater realism about parenting, more secure financial foundations for family life, and greater recognition of the importance of preparation and maturity will do more to ensure two-parent child rearing than any emphasis on institutional form alone. In the process, stigmatization of single-parent families or nonmarital sexuality is likely to be counterproductive, because of both the immediate impact on the affected children and the association of such strategies with improvident early unions. We recommend support for educational efforts that focus on the factors that promote relationship stability.

Fallback Options and Continued Adult Development

We believe that the integrative model has historically rested on the need to channel improvident reproduction into institutions designed to provide for the resulting children. Early marriage is likely to be no longer sufficient to do so. Instead, whether or not young mothers marry and stay married, their children's well-being depends on their parents' continued education, workforce participation, and contributions to the children's upbringing.

EDUCATION FOR WELFARE PARENTS, INVESTMENT IN CHILDREN

Studies show that poor teens often welcome an initial pregnancy; it is a second birth in close proximity to the first that has the most negative consequences on the life chances of mother and child. The reactions to a teen's initial pregnancy should accordingly focus on both parties and the child: the mother needs support to continue her education and prevent further pregnancies; the father needs counseling and education to be able to contribute to the new family; and the child needs health care and childhood education programs.[62] Thus, for the mother, this must include access to birth control, efforts to keep her in school and provide labor force training, and the availability of affordable and high-quality child care. Ensuring that employment is feasible for single mothers also involves the recognition that employers of poor women cannot realistically subsidize family leave or health benefits *on their own*.[63] Similar funding could also extend to health benefits to ensure that former welfare recipients have adequate access without employers assuming the full responsibility.

TWO-PARENT INVOLVEMENT IN A RELATIONSHIP THAT DOES NOT LAST

Pregnancy at young ages is more likely to produce single parenthood whether through nonmarital births or divorce. Nonetheless, insisting on contributions by both parents, even if unlikely to be sufficient, is important in reaffirming the principle of responsibility for children. Accordingly, identification of the biological father and child support enforcement efforts make sense. So does encouraging fathers as well as mothers to contribute to child care. Indeed, studies indicate that fathers are substantially increasing the amount of time they spend with children.[64]

Conversely, the instability of early relationships (and the high correlation of domestic violence with income and class) makes recognition of functional parenthood that much more critical. McLanahan's research on fragile families, for example, indicates that where single mothers fail to marry the fathers of their children and later marry someone else, the man they marry provides greater material and/or emotional support than the biological father.[65] States as diverse as California,[66] Louisiana,[67] and Washington[68] recognize the adults who have played parental roles in the child's life over those who claim legal recognition on the basis of biology alone. Children benefit from this greater flexibility in recognizing husbands, stepparents, and other adults who have made a commitment to the child. The American Law Institute's *Principles of Family Dissolution* provides appropriate guidelines distinguishing parental figures who have merited recognition from more transitory figures.[69]

Conclusion: Investment and Norm Creation and Acceptance

In today's world, investment in young adults is critical, and mature adults make good decisions. Freedom is not license, however, because it involves the internalization of norms of responsibility. And internal norms as opposed to external constraints come from valuing each individual. The "blue" model of responsible parenthood and the implications for children are better suited to the needs of a postindustrial economy. The toothpaste cannot—and should not—be put back in the tube. Ironically, it is the responsible parenthood/college-educated middle-class morality that realizes the values of the integrative approach because this group's marriages are more stable and their children are more likely to be raised in a two-parent household. By focusing on the well-being of mothers, good things follow for children. Marriage, however, follows from the right investments—it does not produce them.[70]

Notes

We thank Linda McClain and Elizabeth Marquardt for asking us to participate in the conversation that led to this volume.

1. Heather Boushey, "Women Breadwinners, Men Unemployed," *Center for American Progress*, July 20, 2009, http://www.americanprogress.org/issues/2009/07/breadwin_women.html (accessed Dec. 5, 2009); see also, e.g., Elizabeth Warren and Amelia Warren Tyagi, *The Two-Income Trap: Why Middle-Class Mothers and Fathers Are Going Broke* (New York: Basic Books, 2003).

2. See Rose M. Kreider, "Living Arrangements of Children: 2004," *Current Population Reports* P70-114, Feb. 2008, http://www.census.gov/prod/2008pubs/ p70-114.pdf (accessed Dec. 5, 2009), 4.

3. Linda R. Hirshman and Jane E. Larson, *Hard Bargains: The Politics of Sex* (New York: Oxford University Press, 1998), 92 (the number of brides who gave birth within eight and a half months of the nuptials rose to 30 percent in 1960); Andrew J. Cherlin, "American Marriage in the Early Twenty-First Century," *Future of Children* 15 (Fall 2005): 33, 35 (on the fall in the age of marriage); Stephanie Coontz, *The Way We Never Were: American Families and the Nostalgia Trap* (New York: Basic Books, 1992), 25–26 (on the fifties more generally).

4. For critiques of this ideology, see Judith E. Koons, "Motherhood, Marriage, and Morality: The Pro-marriage Moral Discourse of American Welfare Policy," *Wisconsin Women's Law Journal* 19 (2004): 1, 22–25; see also Angela Onwuachi-Willig, "The Return of the Ring: Welfare Reform's Marriage Cure as the Revival of Post-bellum Control," *California Law Review* 93 (2005): 1647, 1663; Kristin Luker, *When Sex Goes to School: Warring Views on Sex—and Sex Education—since the Sixties* (New York: Norton, 2006).

5. Gary J. Simson and Erika A. Sussman, "Keeping the Sex in Sex Education: The First Amendment's Religion Clauses and the Sex Education Debate," *Southern California Review of Law and Women's Studies* 9 (2000): 265, 286–288; John Tuskey, "The Elephant in the Room—Contraception and the Renaissance of Traditional Marriage," *Regent University Law Review* 18 (2005–2006): 315, 318–322.

6. Elizabeth Marquardt, "Of Human Bonding: Integrating the Needs and Desires of Women, Men, and the Children Their Unions Produce" (this volume).

7. Sara McLanahan, "Diverging Destinies: How Children Are Faring under the Second Demographic Transition," *Demography* 41 (Nov. 2004): 607.

8. Ibid., 608–609.

9. Ibid.

10. June Carbone, "Age Matters: Class, Family Formation, and Inequality," *Santa Clara Law Review* 48 (2008): 901, 930–931 n. 138.

11. Ibid.

12. Paul R. Amato et al., *Alone Together: How Marriage in America Is Changing* (Cambridge: Harvard University Press, 2007), 79.

13. Ibid.

14. Stéphane Mechoulan, "Divorce Laws and the Structure of the American Family," *Journal of Legal Studies* 35 (2006): 143, 152.

15. Many studies show that the highly educated have become more likely to marry each other. For a summary, see Leslie McCall and Christine Percheski, "Income Inequality: New Trends and Research Directions," *Annual Review of Sociology* 36 (June 2010): 329, 336. Economists argue further that the greater the economic inequality among males, the bigger the potential payoff for search efforts, and thus the greater the incentives for later marriage. In empirical tests of this hypothesis, Loughran found that increases in male wage inequality over time in geographically, educationally, and racially defined marriage markets can account for between 7 and 18 percent of the decline in marriage between 1970 and 1990 for white women, but for considerably less of the decline for black women. David S. Loughran, "The Effect of Male Wage Inequality on Female Age at First Marriage," *Review of Economics and Statistics* 84 (May 2002): 237. Gould and Paserman estimate that differences in male wage inequality

can account for approximately 25 percent of the decline in marriage over the past few decades. Their findings hold across a variety of educational groups and suggest that both men and women delay marriage in response to greater male inequality, but not greater female inequality. Eric D. Gould and M. Daniele Paserman, "Waiting for Mr. Right: Rising Inequality and Declining Marriage Rates," *Journal of Urban Economics* 53 (Mar. 2003): 257.

16. Mechoulan, "Divorce Laws," 167.

17. Amato et al., *Alone Together*, 132.

18. Ibid., 138 (distinguishing between college graduate women in the professional and managerial ranks and less educated women).

19. Ibid. (concluding that the workforce participation of these women, which contributes to economic security, has generally beneficial consequences for marriages).

20. Ibid. (concluding that the labor force participation of working-class wives, without college degrees, adds to marital stress).

21. Ibid., 139.

22. Ibid., 68.

23. Ibid., 137.

24. Ibid., 138. Compounding these changes are changes in employment stability. Men's employment stability, measured by changes in jobs, has steadily declined for most of the period since World War II while women's has increased through much of that period, and the implications of layoffs tend to be different for men and women. See Henry S. Farber, "Is the Company Man an Anachronism? Trends in Long-Term Employment in the United States, 1973 to 2006," in *The Price of Independence: The Economics of Early Adulthood*, ed. Sheldon Danziger and Cecilia Elena Rouse (New York: Russell Sage Foundation, 2007), 56–83.

25. Richard Fry and D'Vera Cohn, *Women, Men and the New Economics of Marriage*, Jan. 19, 2010, http://pewsocialtrends.org/files/2010/11/new-economics-of-marriage.pdf (accessed Sept. 1, 2011), 1, 8. According to the Pew study, women college grads saw their incomes increase by 30 percent between 1970 and 2009. Ibid. All men, in contrast, have shown steady declines in income since 1980, except for college graduates. Ibid.

26. That is, they became more dependent on women's income to maintain the same standard of living. Ibid., 16.

27. Sara McLanahan and Christine Percheski, "Family Structure and the Reproduction of Inequalities," *Annual Review of Sociology* 34 (2008): 257.

28. Institute for American Values and the National Marriage Project, *When Marriage Disappears: The New Middle America*, Dec. 2010, http://www.virginia.edu/marriageproject/pdfs/Union_11_12_10.pdf (accessed Sept. 1, 2011), 41.

29. Ibid., 56.

30. McLanahan and Percheski, "Family Structure," 261.

31. Ibid.

32. Amy L. Wax, "Engines of Inequality: Class, Race, and Family Structure," *Family Law Quarterly* 41 (2007): 567, 590.

33. See, e.g., McLanahan and Percheski, "Family Structure," 261.

34. Ibid.

35. Tony Dokoupil, "Men Will Be Men: When Guys Lose Jobs, the TV, Den and Gym Win. Women? Sex? Not so Much," *Newsweek*, Mar. 2, 2009, 50.

36. Ibid.

37. Ralph Richard Banks, *Is Marriage for White People? How the African American Marriage Decline Affects Everyone* (New York: Dutton, 2011); see also Gould and Paserman, "Waiting for Mr. Right," 257, on gender ratios.

38. See, e.g., William Julius Wilson, *When Work Disappears: The World of the New Urban Poor* (New York: Knopf, 1996).

39. Gould and Paserman, however, find that the level of male inequality in a city affects the marriage rates of all men, such that the same man, even if at the top or bottom of the income scale, becomes more likely to marry in a city with less male inequality. They attribute the effect to women's choices rather than men's. Gould and Paserman, "Waiting for Mr. Right," 279.

40. See, e.g., Richard G. Wilkinson and Kate Pickett, *The Spirit Level: Why Greater Equality Makes Societies Stronger* (New York: Bloomsbury Press, 2010), 69 (tying mental illness to inequality and showing U.S. rates at the top of the developed world); 71 (tying illegal drug use to inequality, though less strongly than mental illness); 135 (tying homicides to inequality); 148 (tying imprisonment to inequality and showing U.S. rates above those of the rest of the developed world).

41. Carol Sanger, "Regulating Teenage Abortion in the United States: Politics and Policy," *International Journal of Law, Policy and the Family* 18 (2004): 305.

42. Lawrence B. Finer and Mia R. Zolna, "Unintended Pregnancy in the United States: Incidence and Disparities, 2006," *Contraception* 84, no. 5 (2011): 478, Figure 1, also published online at http://www.guttmacher.org/pubs/journals/j.contraception.2011.07.13 (accessed June 9, 2012).

43. See Cynthia Dailard and Chinué Turner Richardson, "Teenagers' Access to Confidential Reproductive Health Services," *Guttmacher Report on Public Policy*, Nov. 2005, http://www.guttmacher.org/pubs/tgr/08/4/gr080406.pdf (accessed Dec. 7, 2009): 6.

44. See generally Guttmacher Institute, "Sex and HIV Education," *State Policies in Brief* (as of Dec. 1, 2011), http://www.guttmacher.org/statecenter/spibs/spib_SE.pdf (accessed Dec. 17, 2011) (report describes sex education policies in the states).

45. Rob Stein, "Panel Says Evidence Is Insufficient to Know Effectiveness of Abstinence Programs," *Washington Post*, Nov. 7, 2009, http://www.washingtonpost.com/wp-dyn/content/article/2009/11/06/AR2009110601208.html (accessed Dec. 8, 2009).

46. The Obama administration has changed the basis for federal funding to an evidence-based approach. See Sexuality Information and Education Council of the United States, *Appropriations for Coming Year Prioritize Sexual Health and Education*, Dec. 9, 2009, http://siecus.org/index/ (accessed Oct. 1, 2011); Consolidated Appropriations Act, 2010, Pub. L. No. 111–117, 123 Stat. 3034, 3253 (2009).

47. Guttmacher Institute, *A Real-Time Look at the Impact of the Recession on Women's Family Planning and Pregnancy Decisions* (New York: Guttmacher Institute, 2009), http://www.guttmacher.org/pubs/RecessionFP.pdf (accessed Dec. 10, 2009), 3, 5–7.

48. See, e.g., Griswold v. Connecticut, 381 U.S. 479 (1965); Eisenstadt v. Baird, 405 U.S. 438, 452–453 (1972).

49. Dailard and Richardson, "Teenagers' Access," 6; Guttmacher Institute, "Minors' Access to Contraceptive Services," *State Policies in Brief* (as of Dec. 1, 2011), http://www.guttmacher.org/statecenter/spibs/spib_MACS.pdf (accessed Dec. 12, 2011); Guttmacher Institute, "Emergency Contraception," *State Policies in Brief* (as of Dec. 1, 2011), http://www.guttmacher.org/statecenter/spibs/spib_EC.pdf (accessed Dec. 12, 2011).

50. Banks, *Is Marriage for White People?*

51. Planned Parenthood, *Parental Consent and Notification Laws*, Aug. 3, 2009, http://www.plannedparenthood.org/health-topics/abortion/parental-consent-notification-laws-25268.htm (accessed Dec. 10, 2009). The states are California, Connecticut, Hawaii, Montana, Nevada, New Hampshire, New Jersey, New Mexico, New York, Oregon, Vermont, and Washington.

52. See, generally, Lisa R. Pruitt, "The Geography of the Class Culture Wars," *Seattle University Law Review* 34 (2011): 767.

53. Lawrence B. Finer et al., "Timing of Steps and Reasons for Delays in Obtaining Abortions in the United States," *Contraception* 74 (2006), http://www.guttmacher.org/pubs/2006/10/17/Contraception74-4-334_Finer.pdf (accessed December 10, 2009): 334, 340–342, 344.

54. McLanahan, "Diverging Destinies," 609.

55. Russell Shorto, "No Babies?," *New York Times Magazine*, June 29, 2008, http://www.nytimes.com/2008/06/29/magazine/29Birth-t.html?pagewanted=all (accessed Oct. 17, 2011).

56. See, e.g., National Partnership for Women and Families, *Expecting Better: A State-by-State Analysis of Laws That Help New Parents* (2nd ed., 2012), 12, 44, http://www.nationalpartnership.org/site/DocServer/Expecting_Better_Report.pdf?docID=10301 (accessed May 23, 2012); see generally, National Conference of State Legislatures, *State Family and Medical Leave Laws That Differ from the Federal FMLA*, Sept. 2008, http://www.ncsl.org/Portals/1/documents/ employ/fam-medleave.pdf (accessed Dec. 8, 2009).

57. See, e.g., June Carbone and Naomi Cahn, *Family Classes* (New York: Oxford University Press, forthcoming).

58. See ibid.

59. Implementing our proposals, including those about work-family conflict, would likely have the effect of moving the age of first birth down a bit; we are not advocating that women wait until the age of thirty to have children, contrary to the claim of Elizabeth Marquardt. See Marquardt, "Of Human Bonding" 330–332.

60. See Lawrence B. Finer and Mia R. Zolna. "Unintended Pregnancy in the United States: Incidence and Disparities, 2006," *Contraception* 84 (Nov. 2011): 478.

61. See June Carbone and Naomi Cahn, "Embryo Fundamentalism," *William and Mary Bill of Rights Journal* 18 (2010): 1015, 1033–1037 (noting religious differences toward the acceptability of in vitro fertilization and lack of agreement on an overall approach).

62. On the efficacy of Head Start, see, e.g., U.S. Department of Health and Human Services, *Strengthening Head Start: What the Evidence Shows*, June 2003, http://aspe.hhs.gov/hsp/StrengthenHeadStart03/report.pdf (accessed Oct. 17, 2011).

63. Ann O'Leary, "How Family Leave Laws Left Out Low-Income Workers," *Berkeley Journal of Employment and Labor Law* 28 (2007): 1, 59–62.

64. See, e.g., Ruth Davis Konigsberg, "Chore Wars," *Time*, Aug. 8, 2011, http://www.time.com/time/magazine/article/0,9171,2084582-1,00.html (accessed Dec. 17, 2011); Suzanne M. Bianchi, *Family Change and Time Allocation in American Families* (Washington, DC: Alfred P. Sloan Foundation, 2010), http://workplace flexibility.org/images/uploads/program_papers/bianchi_-_family_change_and_time_ allocation_in_american_families.pdf (accessed Dec. 17, 2011).

65. Marcia J. Carlson, Sara S. McLanahan, and Jeanne Brooks-Gunn, "Coparenting and Nonresident Fathers' Involvement with Young Children after a Nonmarital Birth," *Demography* 45 (May 2008): 461, 479.

66. In re Nicholas H., 28 Cal. 4th 56 (2002).

67. Smith v. Cole, 553 So. 2d 847 (La. 1989).

68. In re Parentage of L.B., 122 P.3d 161 (Wash. 2005).

69. American Law Institute, *Principles of the Law of Family Dissolution: Analysis and Recommendations* (St. Paul, MN: American Law Institute, 2002).

70. See generally Linda C. McClain, *The Place of Families: Fostering Capacity, Equality, and Responsibility* (Cambridge: Harvard University Press, 2006).

Epilogue

Daniel Cere and Linda C. McClain

In this epilogue, each of us will offer some reflections on this book's investigation of critical questions about parenthood.

Daniel Cere—
This book began as an attempt to contribute to the public conversation about parenthood by teasing out basic tensions in academic discourses and identifying unresolved questions that could orient further analysis and research. As it developed, participants expressed concerns that framing the conversation as a debate between two broad approaches could result in a narrow stereotyping of the intellectual complexity of the arguments at play in interdisciplinary work on parenthood. To that end, I conclude by addressing some misleading critiques of both the diversity perspective and the integrative perspective.

Stereotypical Critiques of Diversity Accounts
Proponents of diversity advance a corrosive form of relativism. Some proponents of diversity happily endorse a thoroughgoing cultural relativism. However, many gravitate toward "normative pluralist" accounts of parenthood. Such accounts do not deny the existence of integral human goods in the domain of parenting and child development but argue that a diverse flora of parental forms can foster a variety of basic goods critical to child well-being and flourishing. Martha Nussbaum clearly takes a diversity approach to the family, yet her theory would require that all forms of parenthood contribute to promoting certain basic goods or "central human capabilities," including life, bodily integrity, cognitive and psychological development, freedom, autonomy, and self-respect.[1] Normative pluralists would express moral outrage at forms of parenting that involve neglect or abuse. Pluralist accounts are sensitive to the growing body of research highlighting the critical importance of strong, stable attachments and high parental investment for healthy child development. They stress the importance of responsible adulthood, including the capacity to handle the

daily social and financial challenges of raising children in difficult times and the critical value of dyadic or collaborative forms of adult bonds in parenting.

Diversity accounts represent the imposition of a form of comprehensive liberalism, namely, a state-driven project to reengineer parenthood by penetrating liberal values deep into the soft-shelled texture of family life. Some pluralist accounts have a pronounced normative edge. Pluralists raise serious moral concerns about the array of traditional forms of parenthood that foster patterns of gender inequalities. They frequently argue for a channelling of public discourse on parenthood along lines that reflect a commitment to core values such as freedom, equality, capacity, autonomy, and respect for diversity. However, pluralist accounts are not wedded to strong versions of comprehensive liberalism. Softer versions argue the liberal state needs to exercise caution in this important domain of interpersonal life. Decisions relating to family matters and child rearing involve "the most intimate and personal choices a person may make in a lifetime, choices central to personal dignity and autonomy."[2] Accordingly, the state must tread gently, seeking to persuade and educate rather than to force or coerce. Finally, some accounts celebrate the rich diversity of family forms and resist political imposition of any liberal vision of parenthood. Strong multicultural accounts resist the promotion of Western liberal models of the family, arguing that this undermines rather than enriches meaningful diversity.[3] In short, there are tensions within the diversity approach over the role of the state.

Proponents of diversity are committed to sustained critique of the traditional heterosexual form of parenthood. Some diversity proponents may hope for a revolutionary deconstruction of the forces of heterosexism and heteronormativity, but most acknowledge the legitimate place of the traditional heterosexual parental bond in the ever-expanding map of family diversity. However, they dismiss the contention that parenting hinges critically on kin connections between children and their opposite-sex parents and maintain that good parenting practices can blossom in a variety of familial contexts. Some may provide social frames connecting children to opposite-sex pair-bonded parents; others may not.

Diversity accounts promote the ongoing social disintegration and fragmentation of the various components of parenthood. Normative pluralist accounts aim at promoting social cohesion through including the diverse array of parental forms and fostering a shared ethos of responsibility, commitment, and caregiving. They argue that attempts to impose a more restrictive institutional framework on parenthood may contribute to social divisiveness because important sectors of the community may find themselves marginalized and excluded. Cohesion is built around common values and best parenting practices, not selective privileging or penalizing of specific family forms.

Diversity accounts betray an individualizing anti-institutional bias. This critique is misleading. Pluralist accounts do not repudiate the need for institutional contexts for diversity but resist imposing one monolithic institutional model. They focus on the common norms and best practices that should inform good parenting in diverse social contexts. From another angle, such accounts do not discount the significance of institutionality but emphasize the need to recognize the "political" nature of these institutional forms.

Stereotypical Critiques of Integrative Accounts

Arguments for integrative approaches mask convictions that are ultimately based on religious conviction, not public reason. Certainly, some academic advocates of integration appeal to reasoned religious or theological arguments in advancing their case, just as some advocates for diversity do.[4] Such appeals do offer a limited and problematic basis to build a reasoned public argument. However, more substantive interdisciplinary lines of argument may be found in academic fields like evolutionary psychology, sociology, or biological anthropology, disciplines that adopt a stance of methodological skepticism toward religious or theological arguments. This line of critique also assumes a strong correlation between religious adherence and commitment to integrative conceptions of the family and parenthood. Research indicates that the situation is more complex. A survey of various Christian denominations indicated strong support for integrative conceptions of the family in conservative evangelical churches. However, more than 83 percent of Roman Catholic pastors and 88 percent of mainline Protestant clergy supported family diversity perspectives.[5]

Integrative conceptions put forward a biological model of parenthood. Integrative accounts argue for the integration of the diverse aspects of parenthood: biological, intentional, gestational, paternal, maternal, social, sexual, and psychological. Freestanding "biological" conceptions of parenthood pose as many dilemmas for an integrative conception of parenthood as do freestanding psychological, social, or intentional conceptions. Integrative accounts resist the fragmentation of parenthood into its diverse components.

The integrative approach lends support to soft or strong forms of patriarchy by insisting on substantive distinctions between the sexes, sex complementarity, and distinct maternal and paternal roles. Commitments to gender equality are critical concerns, but they do not define either diversity or integrative approaches to parenthood. On the diversity side, proponents of strong versions of multiculturalism have come under fire from feminist pluralists for their dedication to the protection of all forms of cultural diversity, including traditional patriarchal forms of culture.[6] Some versions of the integrative approach gravitate toward a soft patriarchy, but other accounts stress equality. Important trajectories of liberalism embrace both integrative conceptions of the family while affirming gender equality.[7] Moreover, the Universal Declaration of Human Rights implicitly embraces this perspective when it weds a robust affirmation of gender equality to an equally robust affirmation of the "natural" family as the fundamental social basis of human society.[8] In this view, commitment to gender equality is not only compatible with but also critical to modern conceptions of integrative parenthood.

Integrative accounts advance a narrow and restricted view that is little more than nostalgia for the "love/marriage/baby carriage" nuclear family package of the 1950s. Critical integrative approaches acknowledge the rich cultural diversity of family forms and that a plurality of kinship systems can meaningfully integrate sexual mating, exogamous pair-bonding, procreation, bilateral kin relations, and committed parental investment in stable and enduring forms of family. In principle, diverse monogamous, polygynous, polyandrous, nuclear, and extended kinship systems fit the integrative profile to the extent that they address these core elements. However, some proposed models of the family might be viewed as too restrictive and one-dimensional insofar as they foster social forms that fail to include the complex tapestry of social relationships characteristic of most human kinship systems. The integrative approach would argue against reducing parenthood to simpler and more disparate fragments that delete core dimensions in the complex of kin-connected parenting.

Could more innovative approaches to parenthood address this integrative concern about an inclusive nexus of core bonds? Advocacy for more complex integrative parenting is surfacing in some sectors of the gay and lesbian community. Such proposals suggest that the genetic links between parents and children, and the intergenerational bonds they create, are worth taking seriously. These families would involve at least three parental participants: the two married same-sex parents and the surrogate mother or the sperm-donor father. Such arrangements do not constitute a form of polygamy, since the *conjugal* bond remains monogamous, but they do constitute a complex integrative form of the family. In short, modern forms of kin complexity that integrate, rather than fragment, parental bonds merit serious consideration.

Integrative accounts propose the use of coercive legal sanctions to exclude or penalize alternative family forms. Debates over integrative and diversity conceptions of parenthood should be cautious about sliding too quickly into debates about the particular legal or political mechanisms aimed at advancing either account. Pluralist accounts often assume that integrative accounts are bent on advancing their vision by creating coercive legal frameworks that would stigmatize or even criminalize alternative family forms. Proponents of integrative conceptions of the family worry that diversity advocates will use the state's coercive power to enforce or "channel" their particular vision of familial relationships and censure alternative forms of discourse by throwing them under the legal cloud of discriminatory speech. Addressing these troubling and conflicting concerns about freedom and tolerance in the domain of family life is a central challenge for law and public policy in liberal democracies. There is considerable diversity within both lines of discourse concerning possible policy implications of theoretical accounts of parenthood. For example, some integrative scholars argue for the critical importance of cultural norming and legal channelling. In this view, law is constitutive of human kinship systems.[9] However, it is also feasible for integrative proponents to argue that the modern state and the coercive power of law are inappropriate mechanisms to advance integrative forms of family life. Historically, integrative kinship systems found ways of encoding norms and practices long before the advent of the modern state and its uniform systems of law. In this view, integrative family forms may do best when left to evolve in the free market of social evolution. Curtailing state intervention may provide the most creative environment for the innate integrative dynamisms of evolving human kinship systems to flourish.

Partisan positions on family structure offer little in terms of meaningful scholarly contribution to public debates on parenthood. Sustaining a creative debate spanning the tensions of diverse intellectual and interdisciplinary perspectives requires a certain amount of self-critical intellectual honesty along with open engagement and argument. It is our hope that these qualities mark this collection.

Linda C. McClain

Reading through the rich and varied contributions to this book's investigation of critical questions about parenthood suggests several themes warranting further exploration. Some illuminate points of agreement between the integrative and diversity models; others highlight disagreement. The interplay of the various disciplinary perspectives also reveals challenging methodological and normative questions that require attention in considerations of shaping the law of parenthood and family policy.

The Fact and Value of Family Diversity—and the Role of Law

Proponents of the integrative and diversity approaches to parenthood readily concur on the *fact* of family diversity in the contemporary United States (and more globally), but *how* family law should manage family diversity is an important issue on which integrative and diversity proponents differ. Should the law accept and even facilitate newer pathways to parenthood, or should it try to "put on the brakes"? This in turn implicates the intractable question of the relationship between law and culture, or law and social practice. Should law reflect social practice or seek to construct it?

Undoubtedly, family law and policy shape family life by setting parameters such as who may enter marriage, how parental rights and responsibilities are assigned, and the like. Parenting by lesbian and gay couples becomes more feasible in a legal regime that facilitates and protects their adult-adult relationships along with their parent-child relationships than in a legal regime that deems homosexuality immoral and gay men and lesbians unfit to be parents. But social practice also pushes family law and policy to respond to the growing diversity of family life—for the growing visibility of diverse families seems to call for legal support and recognition of such families as a matter of basic fairness and equality. What people believe about the proper role of law in the face of family diversify depends, in turn, on why they believe a particular model of parenthood is preferable. This implicates two further issues: the relevance of natural science and social science in telling us "what to do," and the role of public values and constitutional commitments (such as to equality) in shaping family law and policy.

The Relevance of Natural Science and Social Science

Many contributions to this volume appeal to findings from the natural or social sciences to argue in support of either an integrative or a diversity approach. For example, proponents of the integrative model routinely appeal to a supposed consensus among social scientists that a heterosexual marital, low-conflict, two-parent family is, on average, best for children. However, "on average" does not reveal significant differences based, for example, on race. Moreover, studies of developmental outcomes for children reared by gay and lesbian parents strongly suggest that parenting quality is more determinative of child well-being than family type. Expert opinion and testimony on child outcomes has played a pivotal role in litigation over access by same-sex couples to marriage, with courts stressing the basic sameness of heterosexual and homosexual parents and the irrelevance of gender to parenting. Legislatures, as well, stress this sameness and a state interest in protecting and supporting all families. And the literature on attachment suggests that the quality of attachment does not depend critically on a biological relationship between parent and child. From a transnational perspective, the experience of family migration entails both periods of separation between children and their parents, and children forming deep attachments to various kin who function as parents. So, too, a biological relationship alone (even in a marital family) does not vouchsafe good parenting, secure attachment, or other positive child outcomes. I believe that one conclusion this volume supports is that public policy should attend to what we do know about good parenting—and conditions that facilitate it—and about the constraints many families face, be they economic obstacles to stable family life, the absence of generous parental leave policies, legal obstacles to family recognition, or the challenges experienced by transnational families.

This does not mean that further scientific investigation of parenting and attachment would not inform discussion of family law and policy. There is work to be done, for instance, on the relationship between attachment and fatherhood. The integrative model often relies upon a narrative about human nature and sexuality, drawing on evolutionary theory, which envisions the social construction of fatherhood, through marriage, as society's solution to the vexing problem of getting men to invest in the children they produce. This leads to truncated views of the "goods" of marriage, such as reducing it to a mechanism for handling accidental pregnancy and as having nothing to do with adult-adult commitments or with parent-child relationships not anchored in genetics or biology. However, it is important to realize that there are other narratives that one could construct about the human family and the problems societies need to solve. Indeed, Cere himself notes this in discussing Sarah Blaffer Hrdy's work on the evolution of cooperative breeding and the critical role of "alloparenting."[10] There is more than one story of origins that one could glean from the evolutionary record in seeking to argue about how the past should shape present family law and policy.

Some contributors to this volume counsel that social science cannot tell us what to do, that our basic differences over models of parenting may rest more on our underlying normative convictions and values, and that appeals to empirical claims about child well-being must be considered within the framework of broader societal and legal commitments and value judgments. Otherwise, family law—as well as the families whose lives it touches—is at the mercy of the vicissitudes or pendulum swings of the changing consensus of what social science "tells" us about parenthood and what is best for children. A significant issue this volume foregrounds is the need to reflect on how empirical research and data should inform family law and policy and what kind of normative framework should guide this consideration.

The Role of Public Values

At its heart, the debate over parenthood turns on underlying debates about "family values," as well as broader public values and constitutional commitments. In expounding the integrative model, Cere mentions the issue of pluralism, suggesting that both models of parenthood embrace pluralism to a degree. I believe that a diversity model allows more room for reasonable moral pluralism, as it supports and recognizes a variety of family forms, not only the "conjugal" model at the core of the integrative approach. Curiously, even though some proponents of the integrative model view polygamy as within its umbrella, in principle, because it integrates heterosexual intimate bonds with parenting bonds, they are troubled by extending marriage to an intimate bond formed by a same-sex couple who are parenting a child because it departs from the one-man/one-woman understanding of marriage.[11] (This willingness to fit polygamy into the integrative model creates a notable tension with the claim that it is legalizing same-sex marriage that would offer no limiting principle against the slippery slope to polygamy, group marriage, and the like.) By contrast, at least some adherents of a diversity model (and here I include myself) are troubled by polygamy—at least as currently practiced in fundamentalist religious communities—because of the extreme sex hierarchy and the risks of harm to women and children.[12]

The critical question, then, is, What ends should family law promote? Sex equality, for example, is a basic value in contemporary family law and constitutional law, and it is appropriate to employ family law's channelling function to promote that value. This does not mean that sex equality is the only relevant value in shaping the contemporary law of parenthood and, more broadly, family policy, or that such policy would not benefit from empirical research (of the sort Doucet offers) on gender differences in parenting. The role of family in shaping identity and bestowing a sense of belonging and membership touches on other important values of freedom of association and personal autonomy. So, too, religious liberty is a relevant concern. It is not accidental that when states expand their marriage laws to allow same-sex couples to marry, they couch such laws in the dual terms of promoting marriage equality and protecting religious freedom.

Recognizing that issues of parenthood and family definition implicate an array of public values and goods, as well as the rights and needs of adults and children, helps us to appreciate their complexity. Working through such public values and goods may also facilitate evolution in our understanding of how to do justice to these values and goods and point to possible common ground. One instructive example is David Blankenhorn's recent account of why he now supports same-sex marriage even though he continues to endorse the good of an integrative view of marriage and parenthood. That good, he concludes, should be viewed not in isolation from, but in relationship to other goods, such as the equal dignity and worth of same-sex relationships, fairness to same-sex couples and their children, rejecting animus as a reason for opposing same-sex marriage, and comity.[13] Blankenhorn thus resolves an evident conflict of goods — or among public values — in a different way than he did previously, when he opposed same-sex marriage.

Another instructive example is Naomi Cahn's thoughtful exploration of how family law might be adapted to regulate ART in light of the needs, interests, and rights of donor-conceived persons. A supporter of family diversity and (in this volume) of a model stressing "responsible parenthood" rather than family form as such, Cahn seeks to respect parental rights and donor privacy while also taking seriously the expressed needs and arguable rights of donor-conceived persons to learn about who they are and even to find and form family relationships with half-siblings or their genetic parents.[14] In this Epilogue, Cere ponders whether there could be more "innovative approaches" to parenthood, where ART is used, so that more than two persons might be part of an "inclusive nexus of core bonds." For both Cahn and Cere, concern over children's needs and rights is pressing and may point to a place where integrative and diversity approaches to parenthood might meet. Innovations in the law of parenthood will continue to be subject to debate. As this volume goes to press, the California legislature is considering a bill that would allow a court to recognize that a child has more than two legal parents; its sponsor defends it as "putting the welfare of the child above all else" while its opponents warn that it will open the door to a child having "a dozen parents" and to messy child custody and support battles.[15]

We should not deny that there are genuine clashes of rights at issue in questions about parenthood and family rights and responsibilities. Nonetheless, a point of common ground between both models is a paramount concern for child well-being. As I have worked on this book, I have been struck by the genuine concern contributors have about fostering child well-being and family welfare. Yet, I have also been struck by contributors' different convictions about how best to secure those ends. Is there a way forward? My hunch is that it will start with careful reflection on issues like those I note here: assessing the fact of diversity and how to evaluate it; considering the relevance of the natural and social sciences for family law and policy; and looking to important public values and the normative commitments of family law and constitutional law to help frame the conversation.

Notes

1. See Martha C. Nussbaum, *Women and Human Development: The Capabilities Approach* (Cambridge: Cambridge University Press, 2000), 241–297 (discussing the family). See also Linda C. McClain, *The Place of Families: Fostering Capacity, Equality, and Responsibility* (Cambridge: Harvard University Press, 2006).

2. Planned Parenthood v. Casey, 505 U.S. 833 (1992).

3. Feminist multiculturalist conceptions of gender, diversity, and equality are debated in Susan Moller Okin (with respondents), Joshua Cohen, Matthew Howard, and Martha C. Nussbaum, eds., *Is Multiculturalism Bad for Women?* (Princeton: Princeton University Press, 1999).

4. For an overview of contemporary theologies of the family, see Adrian Thatcher, *Theology and Families* (Oxford: Blackwell, 2007).

5. Andrew J. Cherlin, *The Marriage-Go-Round: The State of Marriage and the Family in America Today* (New York: Knopf, 2009), 109.

6. For critical discussion of the issues, see Ayelet Shachar, *Multicultural Jurisdictions: Cultural Differences and Women's Rights* (Cambridge: Cambridge University Press, 2001).

7. Locke rejected Filmer's patriarchal view of the family and the state but viewed the family as a natural social form that should be protected *by* the state and protected *from* state interference. John Locke, *Two Treatises of Government*, ed. Peter Laslett (Cambridge: Cambridge University Press, 1988).

8. On the drafting of the UDHR clause on the family, see Daniel Cere, "Human Rights and the Family," *Academic Questions* 22 (Winter 2008/2009): 63.

9. See Leslie White, *The Evolution of Culture* (New York: McGraw-Hill, 1959), 94, on the importance of institutionalization in human kinship bonds.

10. See Cere, "Toward an Integrative Account of Parenthood, 23–24 (this volume) (discussing Sarah Blaffer Hrdy, *Mothers and Others: The Evolutionary Origin of Mutual Understanding* [Cambridge: Belknap Press of Harvard University Press, 2009]).

11. See, e.g., Daniel Cere's observations about polygamy in this epilogue. Although David Blankenhorn is critical of polygyny because it promotes "social inequality" and is "inconsistent with full human flourishing for women," he argues that, "conceptually, a polygynous marriage conforms to the principal [*sic*] that each marriage unites one woman with one man"—his suggested, universal definition of marriage. David Blankenhorn, *The Future of Marriage* (New York: Encounter Books, 2007), 254–255; see also Perry v. Schwarzenegger, 704 F. Supp. 2d 921, 948 (N.D. Cal. 2010), *affirmed sub nom* Perry v. Brown, 671 F. 3d 1052 (9th Cir. 2012) (noting that "David Blankenhorn explained that despite the widespread practice of polygamy across many cultures, the rule of two is rarely violated because even within a polygamous marriage, 'each marriage is separate'"). Blankenhorn has subsequently announced that he supports same-sex marriage, as I discuss in Chapter 2 of this volume. See David Blankenhorn, "How My View on Gay Marriage Changed," *New York Times*, http://www.nytimes.com/2012/06/23/opinion/how-my-view-on-gay-marriage-changed.html?_r=2&hp&pagewanted=print (accessed June 23, 2012).

12. On these harms, after a lengthy trial and on a comprehensive record, the Supreme Court of British Columbia concluded that Parliament's "reasoned apprehension of harm" to women, children, society, and the institution of marriage justified Canada's criminal ban on polygamy and survived a challenge under the Canadian Charter of Rights and Freedoms. Reference re: Section 293 of the Criminal Code of Canada, 2011 BCSC 1588.

13. Blankenhorn, "How My View on Gay Marriage Changed."

14. Naomi Cahn, *The New Kinship: Constructing Donor-Conceived Families* (NYU Press, 2012).

15. Ian Lovett, "Measure Opens Door to 3 Parents, or More," *New York Times*, July 14, 2012, A9.

About the Contributors

SUSAN FRELICH APPLETON is the Lemma Barkeloo and Phoebe Couzins Professor of Law at Washington University School of Law. She has published numerous law review articles on family law and coauthored two casebooks: *Adoption and Assisted Reproduction: Families under Construction* and *Modern Family Law: Cases and Materials*. She is a member of the Council of the American Law Institute.

MARGARET F. BRINIG is the Fritz Duda Family Professor of Law at Notre Dame Law School. She has published the coauthored casebook *An Invitation to Family Law*; numerous articles and book chapters; two edited collections; and two books: *From Contract to Covenant: Beyond the Law and Economics of the Family* and *Family, Law, and Community: Supporting the Covenant*.

DON BROWNING was Alexander Campbell Professor of Religious Ethics and the Social Sciences, Emeritus, Divinity School, University of Chicago. His numerous publications on the relevance of the social sciences to religious ethics, and of both to family life and family law, include the coauthored *From Culture Wars to Common Ground: Religion and the American Family Debate* and *Equality and the Family*.

NAOMI CAHN is the John Theodore Fey Research Professor of Law at George Washington University Law School. Her publications include *Test Tube Families: Why the Fertility Market Needs Legal Regulation* and *The New Kinship: Constructing Donor-Conceived Families* and the coauthored (with June Carbone) *Red Families v. Blue Families* and *Family Classes* (forthcoming). She is a board member of the Donor Sibling Registry.

JUNE CARBONE is the Edward A. Smith/Missouri Chair of Law, the Constitution and Society at the University of Missouri at Kansas City. She is the author of *From Partners to Parents: The Second Revolution in Family Law*, and coauthor of the *Family Law* casebook and (with Naomi Cahn) *Red Families v. Blue Families* and *Family Classes* (forthcoming).

DANIEL CERE is associate professor of religion, law, ethics, and public policy in the Faculty of Religious Studies at McGill University. He founded a Canadian think tank, the Institute for the Study of Marriage, Law and Culture. He coedited *Divorcing Marriage* and authored the research monographs *The Future of Family Law* and *The Experts' Story of Courtship*.

ANDREA DOUCET is professor of sociology and gender studies at Brock University and holds the Canada Research Chair in Gender, Work, and Care. She is the author of *Do Men Mother?* and editor of the international journal *Fathering*. A central focus of her work is enduring gender differences in responsibility for care work, domestic life, and community work.

TERENCE E. HÉBERT is associate professor in the Department of Pharmacology and Therapeutics at McGill University. He has published more than eighty articles with a focus on molecular pharmacology and has received a Chercheur National Award from the Fonds de la Recherche en Santé du Québec and the John J. Day Award from the Heart and Stroke Foundation of Canada.

ELIZABETH MARQUARDT is vice president for family studies and director of the Center for Marriage and Families at the Institute for American Values. She is editor of the FamilyScholars.org blog. The author of *Between Two Worlds: The Inner Lives of Children of Divorce*, she was coinvestigator of the study *My Daddy's Name Is Donor* (on adult offspring of sperm donors) and a study on college dating.

LINDA C. McCLAIN is professor of law and Paul M. Siskind Research Scholar at Boston University School of Law. Her books on family law, gender and law, and jurisprudence include *The Place of Families: Fostering Capacity, Equality, and Responsibility*; *Ordered Liberty: Rights, Responsibilities, and Virtues* (with James Fleming); and *Gender Equality: Dimensions of Women's Equal Citizenship* (coedited with Joanna Grossman).

DAVID D. MEYER is Dean and Mitchell Franklin Professor of Law at Tulane University Law School. He lectures and writes on the intersection of family law and constitutional law and is coauthor of the casebook *Contemporary Family Law*. He has served as the U.S. national reporter on family law for the last three congresses of the International Academy of Comparative Law.

ELLEN MOSS is full professor of developmental psychology at the University of Quebec at Montreal. Her current research investigates the effects of attachment relationships on cognitive, social, and emotional development. She is director of the Centre for Study of Attachment and the Family. She has published numerous articles and presented papers at international and local conferences.

RHACEL SALAZAR PARREÑAS is professor of sociology at the University of Southern California. She has published extensively on issues of the family, gender and globalization, and migration. She is the author of three books, including *The Force of Domesticity: Filipina Migrants and Globalization*, and coeditor of three anthologies, including, most recently, *Intimate Labors: Cultures, Technologies and the Politics of Care*.

HYUN SONG is a graduate student in epidemiology at McGill University. She holds a bachelor of arts and science from McGill. Her research interests include health policy, public health ethics, and children's rights. Her current research explores the association between health insurance and access to care for children from low-income families.

JUDITH STACEY is professor of sociology and professor of social and cultural analysis at New York University. She has written extensively on changes in family, sexuality, and society, including, most recently, *Unhitched: Love, Marriage, and Family Values from West Hollywood to Western China*. She has served as an expert witness in same-sex marriage, lesbian adoption, and gay family rights cases.

HOWARD STEELE is professor and director of graduate studies in psychology at the New School for Social Research. He is senior and founding editor of *Attachment and Human Development*. He coedited the book *Clinical Applications of the Adult Attachment Interview* and has authored more than seventy journal articles and book chapters.

MIRIAM STEELE is professor and director of clinical training at the New School for Social Research. Her work bridges the world of psychoanalytic thinking and clinical practice with contemporary research in child development. She is currently researching the efficacy of an innovative attachment-based intervention with high-risk families and the intergenerational transmission of body and attachment representations.

CAROLA SUÁREZ-OROZCO is professor of psychological studies of education at the Graduate School of Education and Information Studies, University of California Los Angeles. She was formerly a professor of applied psychology at New York University's Steinhardt School of Culture,

Education, and Human Development and codirector of Immigration Studies at NYU. She has coauthored numerous books addressing immigrant families and youth, most recently *Learning a New Land: Immigrant Students in American Society*.

MARCELO M. SUÁREZ-OROZCO is the dean of the Graduate School of Education and Information Studies at the University of California Los Angeles. He was formerly the Courtney Sale Ross University Professor of Globalization and Education at New York University and codirector of Immigration Studies at NYU. He founded the Harvard Immigration Project. His extensive publications include the coauthored book *Learning a New Land: Immigrant Students in American Society* and the coedited *Educating the Whole Child for the Whole World*.

FIONA TASKER is senior lecturer, Department of Psychological Science, Birkbeck University of London. Coauthor (with Susan Golombok) of *Growing Up in a Lesbian Family: Effects on Child Development* and coeditor (with Jerry J. Bigner) of *Gay and Lesbian Parenting: New Directions*, she also edits the *Journal of GLBT Family Studies* and is on the editorial board of *Psychology and Sexuality*.

PETER WOOD is president of the National Association of Scholars. He is the author of *A Bee in the Mouth: Anger in America Today* and *Diversity: The Invention of a Concept*. He previously served as a college provost and a professor of anthropology. His writings on American culture and higher education have appeared in numerous academic journals.

Index

Abortion:
   constitutional right to, 44
   family values conflicts and, 41
   as response to rape, 97
   restricting access to, 341, 344
   role in supporting "responsible parenting," 331, 349–351
Adoption:
   attachment in adoptive families, 216, 217–218
   child outcomes and, 51, 150, 152, 183–184, 325–326
   as contributing to family diversity, 124, 132
   by co-parents (non-birth or social parents), 176
   by de facto parents, 132
   "equitable adoption," 126
   as establishing legal parent-child relationship, 130
   ethnographic record of reliance upon, 98–99
   human rights challenge to France's anonymous adoption law, 138–139
   integrative model of parenthood and, 2, 4, 46–47, 80n1, 167, 242, 325
   by lesbians and gay men, 9, 124, 51, 173, 176–177, 183–184, 260, 335
   open adoption, 55, 244, 247
   second-parent adoption, 3, 46, 176, 270 n11
   sexual orientation and, 177
   stranger adoption, 176
   timing of adoption and developmental milestones, 196, 201
   transracial adoption, 150, 177, 247, 253–254n68
   versus voluntary acknowledgment of paternity, 127
Adult Attachment Interview. *See* Attachment research methods
Adultery, 77, 343

Age:
   at childbearing, 344–353, 359n59
   family instability and, 347–348
   at marriage, 344–345
AIDS, 73, 78
Ainsworth, Mary, 20, 25, 202, 216–217, 219
Alloparents, 23–24, 34–35, 89–90
   See also Grandmothering
Amato, Paul, 148, 345–346
American Law Institute's *Principles of the Law of Family Dissolution*, 106, 114–117, 126, 355
Animus, opposition to same-sex marriage and, 45, 53
Appleton, Susan Frelich, 11–12, 47, 49, 51, 257, 259, 260, 269
Aquinas, Thomas, 106, 110–114, 117–118
Aristotle, 105–107, 109–112, 118–119
Assisted Reproductive Technology (ART):
   access by unmarried women, 98, 176
   arguments for policies supporting access to, 351–353
   attachment by children born through, 216
   as contributing to family diversity, 51, 124
   criticisms of, from perspective of integrative model of parenthood, 3, 45–46, 107
   donor gametes, 173–174, 175, 176, 369
   donor insemination, 173, 181, 244
   egg donation, 175
   embryo donation, 175
   increasing use of, 321
   intentional parenthood and, 51
   planned lesbian and gay parenting and, 9, 51, 173, 174–176, 184
   regulation of, 174–176
   sperm donation, 327–328
   use of known versus unknown sperm donors, 175
   views of donor-conceived young adults, 327–329

Attachment:
adequate parenthood, 193
in adopted children, 217
adverse parenting (AP), 224–225
ambivalent-dependent attachment, 203
attachment-based intervention models, 201
attachment needs as basis for children's rights, 32–34
"attachment parenting," 227–228
avoidant attachment, 203, 204, 219
biological bases of, 193–201, 207
caregiver sensitivity and, 202
in children born by ART, 218
child welfare policy and, 201, 205–206
disorganized attachment, 204, 205, 206, 220–221, 227, 228
in foster children, 217
functions of, 193, 201–206
insecure attachment, 203–204
insecure-avoidant, 220, 227
insecure-resistant, 220, 227, 228
institutionalized orphans and, 20, 193, 216–217
interventions to enhance maternal-infant attachment, 228–229
maternal-infant patterns of, 20–25, 194–198, 226, 229
maternal sensitivity and, 225–226, 228
optimal parenting (OP), 224–225
parental-infant, 218, 219
parental sensitivity and, 206
paternal-infant, 198
patterns of, 202, 218–219
and post-traumatic stress disorder, 221
psychological dimensions of, 207
reflective functioning, 215
role reversal, 206
secure attachment, 205–206, 216, 217, 220, 221
"self-righting" tendency, 206
therapeutic interventions and, 205–206
transnational parenting and children's, 279–280
Attachment bonds, 20–22, 25, 34, 35, 205, 207
Attachment parenting movement, 227
Attachment research methods:
Adult Attachment Interview, 216–220, 221–229
the Strange Situation, 217, 219, 220–224, 229
adverse childhood experience studies, 224, 226–228
import for public policy, 215, 226
reflective functioning, 222–226
as supporting diversity model, 216
Attachment theory:
Bowlby's influence on, 193–194, 202, 214, 216–217, 229
evolution and, 19–20, 206
import for law and public policy, 215, 229
parent's internal working model of attachment, 219–220
patterns of attachment in, 202–205, 218–226
resonance with integrative approach to parenthood, 19–20, 32, 245
shift away from kinship theory and studies, 20, 25–26
supports diversity model of parenting, 216, 229
Augustine, 117

Bailey, J. Michael, 180
Bailey, Martha, 78
Baird, Marian, 268
Bakersmans-Kranenburg, Marian J., 221
Barrett, Helen, 180
Becker, Gary, 118
Beebe, Beatrice, 227
Best interests of the child:
as a fact-sensitive standard, 246
integrative tradition and approach to, 105–114
as a paramount value, 249
parents' constitutional rights and, 131, 133,
as rationale for functional approach to parenthood, 51
role in human rights law, 107–114,
role in law of family dissolution, 115–117, 133, 173
Biblarz, Timothy, J., 183
Bigamy, laws against, 77, 78
Bigner, Jerry J., 180
Biology:
biological bases of attachment, 194–201, 205–206

biological kin selection in social systems, 90
See also Attachment; Definitions of parenthood; Diversity model of parenthood; Integrative model of parenthood
Blankenhorn, David, 15n5, 45, 66, 68, 82n25, 369, 371n11
Boas, Franz, 86
Bonobos, 23, 29
Bowlby, John:
  criticisms of Bowlby's focus on mothers, 23–25
  emphasis on evolutionary biology and kin connection in, 22–23, 25, 193, 229
  on how early childhood experiences shape adults' parenting, 226–229
  on newborns' "hardwired" responses, 217
  research on attachment by, 10, 20–23, 113, 193, 202, 214–215, 216–218
  on role of social parenting influences on children, 214–215, 216–218, 226, 227, 228, 229
Bowman, Cynthia Grant, 54
Brinig, Margaret, 9, 106, 117–119
British Longitudinal Study of Lesbian Mother Families, 179
Brown v. Board of Education, 248
Browning, Don, 7–8, 124–125
Burnstein, Eugene, 25, 27
Butler, Judith, 240

Caban v. Mohammed, 238–239, 244
Cahn, Naomi, 13–14, 321, 330–331, 369, 370
Canada:
  research on Canadian parents, 172–173, 259–266
  parental leave policies in, 249, 260, 266–268
  polygamy in, 78–79, 84n52, 371n12
  rights of gay and lesbian parents in, 249, 260
  same-sex marriage in, 249, 260
Carbone, June, 13–14, 41–42, 106, 116–117, 321, 330–331
Caregiving, legal support for, 55 *See also* Care work; Child care
Care work:
  gender equality and, 264–266
  gender-neutral versus father-focused parental leave policies and, 264–269
  legal efforts to combat gender stereotypes about, 239–240
  performed by extended kin in transnational families, 310–312, 314
  relevance of differences between women and men to, 257–264
Carsten, Janet, 26
Case, Mary Anne, 239
Case of E.B. v. France, 137
Cash, Scottye, 184
Cere, Daniel, 2, 6, 10, 14, 41–43, 214, 242, 244, 245, 249, 367–368, 369–370
Chambers, David, 249
Channelling function of family law, 42–43, 46, 55, 57, 125, 239, 242, 247, 344, 362, 365, 369
Chapais, Bernard, 28–31, 34
Charter of Fundamental Rights of the European Union, 129, 133, 135–138
Cherlin, Andrew, 156, 171
Child abuse, prevention of, 214
Child care:
  by alloparents, 23–24, 34–35, 89–90
  care expectations of immigrant children, 310–314
  and cultivating empathy, 35, 228
  by extended family in transnational families, 280–289, 310–312, 314
  father's engagement in, 332, 354
  maternal care for children, 23–24, 96, 100, 197–199, 226, 311, 313
  paternal care for children, 96, 100, 314
  See also Caregiving; Care work
Child custody:
  antidiscrimination goals and, 246
  attachment theory and, 214,
  by extended kin in transnational families, 300
  gender not legitimate factor in, 238–239
  joint custody, 159–160, 247, 263
  lesbian and gay parenting and custody disputes, 173–174
  the nexus test, 174
  parental relocation cases, 158–159
  and parental sexual orientation, 174
  shared parenting, 159–160
  "tender-years" doctrine, 238

Child development. *See* Attachment; Child outcomes
Childhood:
  abuse during childhood as linked to epigenetic changes, 199
  attachment bonds and disorders as affecting, 20–21, 203–204, 207, 221
  impact of childhood attachment experience on parenting, 219–220, 223–225, 226, long period of dependency in, 116–117
  parental influence during, 164
  reflective functioning as nascent capacity in, 215
  rights associated with, 6, 32–34
  separation from parents during childhood in transnational families, 279, 282–283, 294
  as stage of vulnerability, 32–34
  as subject of human rights protection, 24
Child outcomes:
  adoptive parents and, 51, 150, 152, 183–184, 325–326
  African American children and, 147–154, 164–165
  as argument for marital, mother-father family, 322–323
  cohabitation and, 119, 148–157, 164, 323
  divorce and, 148–149, 158–163
  family forms and, 147–160, 171
  foster care and, 150–154, 185–186n13
  heterosexual two parent families and, 41, 53, 182
  impact of legal regime on, 247–248
  interracial marriage and, 150
  lesbian and gay parents and, 41, 53, 171, 173, 177–185, 247–248
  lesbian mother families and, 182–183
  parenting quality as most relevant to, 171, 327
  single heterosexual mothers and, 179, 182
  stepparent families and, 38n61, 154–157, 324–326
  unequal family resources and, 56–57
Child protection, 214
Children. *See* Childhood; Child outcomes; Children's rights
Children's Act of 1989 (England and Wales), 173, 184

Children's rights:
  capacity-based rights, 134
  choice-protecting rights, 134
  conflicts with adults' rights, 33
  constitutional protection of parent-child relationship, 130–135
  definitions of parenthood and, 124–139
  as human rights, 33–34, 105–111, 124–125, 128–130
  interest protecting rights, 134
  as multiple and conflicting, 133–136
  needs-based rights, 134
  to their biological parents, 46, 126
  vulnerability of children and, 32–34
  See also Convention on the Rights of the Child; Rights, of children
Child support, 51, 127, 160
Child well-being:
  as argument against same-sex marriage, 44
  as argument for same-sex marriage, 44
  as supporting adoption, 46
Civil marriage, 3, 5, 41–42, 44, 52–53, 71 *See also* Marriage; Same-sex Marriage
Civil registration, 54
Civil unions, 45, 52–54, 124, 127, 183, 248
Clark, Karen, 327
Class:
  differences in family stability and, 344–348
  marriage gap based on, 56–67, 365n15
Cohabitation:
  among the Mosou or Na, 70, 92,
  child outcomes and, 119, 148–157, 164, 323
  growing rates of, 171, 174, 323
  lack of community support for, 164
  proposals for legal recognition of, 55, 115–116
  stability of, 119, 341–342
Commission on Parenthood's Future, 46, 124
Conjugal model of marriage. *See* Marriage
Consanguinity, 109
Constitutional law (U.S.):
  barring racial discrimination in custody rulings, 246
  birthright citizenship under Fourteenth Amendment, 295, 296n10
  doctrines about gender-based classifications, 239–245

Equal Protection Clause and same-sex marriage, 53
the parent-child relationship in, 130–137, 237–240
on "real differences" between men and women, 239–240, 242–245
rejection of gender-based roles and stereotypes in, 238–245
See also Children's rights; Fundamental rights of parents; Rights
Constitution of the Republic of South Africa, 71
Contraception:
constitutional right to use, 44
and preventing early parenthood, 331, 349–351
restrictions on access to, 344–350
Convention on the Rights of the Child:
Article 7 (right to know and be cared for by one's parents), 128, 134, 136, 142n48, 139
Article 27(2), 128
family rights and, 112, 116, 119, 134
relevance to definition of parenthood, 7–8, 33–34
role of integrative, natural law tradition in, 105–109, 116, 117, 124–125
as taking due account of traditions and cultural values, 137
U.S. refusal to ratify, 133
Coontz, Stephanie, 23, 66
Cordy, Robert J. (Justice), 47
Council on Family Law, 43
Critical race feminism, 78
"Culture wars," 65, 127, 129, 247, 249, 260
Customary marriages, 71

Dawkins, Richard, 27
De facto parenthood. *See* Definitions of parenthood
Defense of Marriage Act (U.S. federal), 5, 41, 43–45, 47, 52–53, 248
Defense of marriage acts (state), 44
Definitions of parenthood:
as contentious issue in family law, 41
de facto parents, 126, 240
functional approach to, 240
in loco parentis and, 126, 140
intentional parenthood, 51

legal recognition of multiple parents, 55–56, 126
lesbian and gay parents affected by, 172–173
parents by estoppel, 240
presumption of legitimacy, 244, 247
psychological parents, 127, 240
relevance of attachment theory to, 206–207
rights of children and, 124–139
role of empirical evidence in, 245–248, 366–358
same-sex marriage and, 323–327
Deutsch, Francine, 265
De Waal, Frans, 23
Diamond, Chris, 268
Disestablishment:
of marriage, 55
of sex and gender, 249
Diversity:
fact of diversity of family life, 3, 47–54, 87–90
radical diversity (in kinship studies), 87, 95
value of diversity of family life, 3, 48–54, 65–68
See also Family diversity
Diversity model of parenthood:
anthropological studies and, 87–88
child outcomes and, 9, 171, 177–184, 245–248, 366–367
constitutional law as supporting, 237–240
a continuum approach and, 6–7, 42, 57
contrasted with integrative model, 2–5, 43–54, 237–250, 342–344
defined, 3–4, 47–48
diversity within the diversity model, 54–56
as easing challenges faced by transnational families, 13, 314–315
on fact and value of diversity, 47–54, 366
family inequality and, 56–57
family law's embrace of, 50–54, 114–117, 240
functional approach to defining family and parenthood and, 51
gender differences and, 11–12, 257–259, 264–269
gender equality and, 11–12, 237–242, 258–269

Diversity model of parenthood (*Continued*):
  gender equality and difference in parenting, 257–269
  as lens on transnational families, 13–14, 300–303
  modernity and, 106–107, 114
  as organizing device in debates over parenthood, 2, 41–43
  public opinion and, 4–5, 49–50
  relationship to "pluralist" approach to parenthood, 65–66, 248–249
  relevance of natural and social science to, 366–368
  "responsible parenthood" model as form of, 14, 342–343
  rights of adults and, 8, 114–116, 124–139
  rights of children and, 8, 114–116, 124–139
  in social practice, 47–50
  supported by attachment theory and research, 216, 229
Divorce:
  blended families following, 48, 55, 70
  class and rates of, 56
  and conflict over family values, 66
  decline of "marriage culture" and rise of, 322–323, 332–333
  "the divorce revolution," 75
  domestic violence and, 333–334
  effects upon children, 148–151, 154–158, 323, 325
  impact on family structure, 126, 171, 194, 321–322,
  lesbian and gay parenting after, 173–174, 179–181, 184
  parental responsibilities post-divorce, 116, 119, 259, 353–354
  rates of, 14, 332, 340–341
  and reasons for marital instability, 345–348
  relocation by custodial parent after, 158–160
  single-parent families following, 48, 126
Domestic partnership laws, 52–54, 115, 117, 127, 248
Domestic violence, 322, 333–334
Doucet, Andrea, 11–12, 241, 249
Dowd, Nancy, 55
Downing, Jordan B., 177
Dozier, Mary, 217
Dwyer, James, 131, 134, 136

Economy:
  economic policies to support responsible parenthood, 344, 349, 351
  impact on family structure and marriage, 340–348
Edwards, John, 77
Eichner, Maxine, 55
Eisler, Riane, 86
Embodiment, 12, 258, 261, 268–269
Embryo and egg donation, 175. See Assisted Reproductive Technology (ART).
Employment:
  impact of men's job instability on family life, 340–341, 342–347
  policies supporting work/family balance, 351–352
  women's contribution to family income, 333, 343, 345–347
Epigenetics, 21, 193, 198, 199, 200, 201:
Equal citizenship, 45
Equality:
  family law's embrace of gender equality, 49, 237–245, 248, 249, 250
  formal equality and, 241
  gender differences in parenting and, 257–269
Erich, Stephen, 183
Erikson, Erik, 107
Ertman, Martha, 106, 116
Ethnographic research:
  anthropological study of human groups, 86–90 96–97, 99, 100
  on Canadian fathers and mothers, 259–266
  ethnographic diversity, 87–88
Ethology, 216
European Convention on Human Rights, 8, 129–130, 135, 137–139, 173, 174
European Court of Human Rights, 129–130, 136–139, 173, 174, 184
Evolutionary biology, 131, 193
Evolutionary psychology, 6, 22, 110, 118
Evolutionary theory:
  biological bases of attachment and, 194, 201, 226
  as relevant to integrative model of parenthood, 19, 34, 367
  on significance of kinship, 19, 25, 27–28, 32, 34
Exogamous breeding patterns, 29

Family diversity:
  ambivalence about, 4–5, 42, 49–50
  diversity model of parenthood approach to, 3–4, 47–57
  fact of, 3, 47–52, 57, 79, 87–90, 171
  family law's evolving embrace of, 4–5, 50–54, 124
  in family structure, 171
  growing acceptance of, 4–5, 42, 47–50
  moral neutrality in family law about, 114–116
  transnational migrant households as form of, 314
  value of, 47–52, 57, 65–68
  See also Diversity model of parenthood
Family Fairness Act (Oregon), 52
Family formation:
  adoption as path to legal parenthood, 9, 176–177
  early versus later parenthood, 330–332, 344–355
  human rights documents concerning, 105–116, 119–120
  law and policy concerning diverse pathways to, 13–14, 321–326, 332–335
  pathways to parenthood by lesbian and gay parents, 9, 171–177
  "responsible parenthood" as supporting later parenthood, 349–355
  use of assisted reproductive technology in, 3, 46, 51, 174–176, 321, 327–330, 352
Family forms:
  African American children and, 148–164
  blended families, 48, 50, 281
  diversity of, 47–48, 207
  households with gay or lesbian parents, 171–184
  multigenerational families, 50
  nuclear, 48, 65, 76, 96, 126, 294, 313–314, 364
  public opinion about, 4–5, 47–50
  quality of parenting as more relevant to child well-being than, 171, 178, 218
  "responsible parenthood" model and, 341–342
  single mothers, 49
  single parent, 48–49, 353
  stay-at-home father families, 263
  transnational family as among contemporary, 50, 314–315
Family law:
  embrace of pluralism, 246
  equality project in, 49, 237–245, 248–250
  functional approach of, 240
  growing embrace of diversity model of parenthood, 50–54
  irrelevance of gender to parental rights and responsibilities, 47
  law of family dissolution, 106, 114–115, 119
  protective function of, 51, 53
  role of gender-based roles and stereotypes, 238
  role of "real differences" between men and women in, 239–240, 242–245
Family life:
  factors leading to stability and instability, 340–355
  immigration and, 279–295
Family and Medical Leave Act (U.S.), 239, 241, 243, 249
Family migration:
  as a cycle of separation and reunification, 280–289
  impact on family life and parenting, 279–295
Family privacy, 134, 137, 139
Family values:
  among the Mosuo people, 68–70, 73–77
  blue and red states contrasted, 14, 340, 344
  conflict over abortion and, 41
  contrasting views of family structure and, 65–69
  family diversity and, 51–52
  same-sex marriage and, 41, 51–53
Fatherhood:
  embodiment and men's experience of, 258, 260–266
  fraternal polyandry and, 96
  as institution, 261, 269
  lack of acknowledged fathers among the Mosuo (or Na), 68–70, 74–76, 91–95
  legal presumption of paternity, 127
  marriage as necessary to secure paternal investment, 46–47, 367
  multiple fatherhood, 55–56
  paternal recognition in human kinship systems, 30–31

Fatherhood (*Continued*):
  planned gay fatherhood, 174–184
  social fatherhood by mother's brother among the Mosou (or Na), 69, 93
  as societal construction, 30, 367
  voluntary acknowledgment as establishing legal, 127
Father-infant bonding, in animals and humans, 198
Fatherlessness, 68–70, 75, 97–98
Fathers:
  Canadian, 268
  class differences and stay-at-home fathers, 263
  constitutional rights of unwed biological fathers, 130–131, 238
  gay fathers, 172–184, 263
  heterosexual fathers, 181
  masculine norms in workplace and, 262, 266–267
  migrant, 303, 306, 309, 313
  practices of taking parental leave, 266–269
  as primary caregivers, 262
  roles played in immigrant family, 311–312
  single fathers, 7, 259, 263
Feminist theory:
  on gender differences and gender equality in parenting, 257–264, 269
  liberal feminist approach to family, 48–49
  perspectives on polygamy, 71
  reconstructive feminism, 261
Filiation:
  bilateral filiation, 30
  "complementary filiation," 93
  in hunter-gatherer groups, 88–89
  impact on assisted reproductive technology on, 107
Fineman, Martha Albertson:
  on caretaker-dependent relationship and family law, 54–55
  critique of gender neutrality in family law, 241
  critique of the "sexual family," 70, 75, 116
  on mother-child dyad, 117
  on single motherhood as "deviant," 49
Fortes, Meyer, 30, 88, 93
Foster care, 11, 25, 55, 150, 177, 193, 216, 217
Foster children, 1, 79, 152, 205, 217. *See also* Child outcomes
Fostering children, 98–99
Foster parenting, 201
Fragile families, 167, 355
Fraiberg, Selma, 224
Frazer, James George, 85–86
French National Assembly's *Parliamentary Report on the Family and the Rights of Children*, 137
Freud, Sigmund, 216
Functional parenthood, recognition of, 46, 354–355. *See also* Parenthood
Fundamental rights of parents, 130–132, 136. *See also* Rights

Gallagher, Maggie, 45
Garrison, Marsha, 115–116
Gates, Gary J., 172
Gender complementarity:
  diversity model of parenthood not dependent upon, 4
  in integrative model of marriage and parenthood, 47, 49, 300
  public opinion about, 49
Gender differences:
  contextual approach to, 260, 266
  integrative model's emphasis on two differently-sexed parents, 47
  parental leave policies and, 266–269
  in parenting, 11–12, 79, 257–269, 369
Gender equality:
  constitutional protection for (in South Africa), 71
  difficulty of measuring in parenting, 265
  and gender differences in parenting, 257–269
  impact of polygamy on, 78–79
  in law of parentage (U.S.), 237–242
  integrative model of parenthood and, 242–245, 364
  and parenting, 11–12, 19
  sameness-difference debate, 261
Gender neutrality:
  in constitutional equality jurisprudence, 49, 241
  in contemporary family law, 49, 241, 243
  gender differences and, 269
  gender equality as requiring, 11, 243
  parental leave policies and, 11–12, 249, 266–269

parenting and, 259
Gender roles:
  changing family structure and, 343
  children's attitudes towards, 182, 326
  expectations concerning roles in marriage, 49, 242, 248, 346–347
  family law's revolution away from fixed, 4, 49
  flexibility concerning roles in home and workplace, 14
  flexibility in same-sex households concerning, 264
  ideal of male breadwinner/female caregiver family, 263
  marital quality and, 345–346
Gender stereotypes, 11, 237, 240, 247, 250, 348
Gene expression, 21, 197–200, 215
Genetics, 32, 88, 193, 198, 237, 244, 248, 367
Gerson, Kathleen, 264
Giddens, Anthony, 74–75
Giuliani, Rudy, 77
Glenn, Norval, 327
Goffman, Erving, 261
Goldberg, Abbie E., 177
Golombok, Susan, 178–179, 182
Goodridge v. Department of Public Health, 15n10, 47–48, 324
Gornick, Janet, 266
Gough, Kathleen, 90
Grandmothering:
  the grandmothering hypothesis about role in evolution, 24, 33, 89–90
  grandmothers as providing "allomaternal" care, 24, 33
  See also Grandparents
Grandparents:
  as caregivers in transnational families, 290–291
  grandparent-headed families in U.S., 76
  parenting by, 50, 76
Graves, Robert, 86
Green, Richard, 179
Green, Tom, 78
Greenfeld, Dorothy A., 175
Griswold v. Connecticut, 44
Group marriage hypothesis, 85–86

Hale, Brenda (Baroness), 128
Hamilton, William D., 27
Hays, Sharon, 312
Hazan, Cindy, 21
Hébert, Terence, 10, 214
Hernandez v. Robles, 47
Hesse, Erik, 220, 223
Hinde, Robert, 217
Holy, Ladislav, 26
Homophobia, 173–174
Household division of labor:
  difficulty of measuring equality in, 264
  in immigrant families, 310
  more equitable in lesbian couple than heterosexual couple families, 181–182
  mothers as breadwinners, 263–264
  need for flexibility in, 340
  public opinion concerning, 49
Hrdy, Sarah, 23–24, 35, 89, 367
Hua, Cai, 90
Human rights:
  intellectual history of, 8, 105–114, 119
  as protecting motherhood and childhood and, 24
  relevance to conceptions of parenthood, 7–8, 124–139
  vulnerability of children as central to, 32–33
Hunter, Rielle, 77
Hunter-gatherers, 88–90

Imanishi, Kinji, 28
Immigrant children:
  care expectations of, 310–314
  as citizen children, 294–295
  discourse of abandonment, 310–314
  effects of separation from parents, 282–286
  experiences by and views on transnational mothers, 302–314
  experiences in schools, 282–283, 292–293
  from Central America, 282–291
  from China, 282–291
  from the Dominican Republic, 282–291
  from Haiti, 282–291
  from Mexico, 282–291
Immigrant families:
  child discipline in, 293
  economic and cultural challenges faced by, 289–294
  idealized integrative view of the family held by parents in, 294

Immigrant families (*Continued*):
    language barriers faced by parents in, 292–293
    loss of parental status and authority in, 290–294
    unauthorized immigrant parents in, 289–290
Immigration:
    as destabilizing and dislocating families, 279–280
    family as fundamental unit of, 279
    from the Philippines, 299–315
    laws, 78, 239
    migrating mothers, 280–289
    public policy on, 279, 294–295
    transnational parenting and, 279–295
Incest avoidance, 28–29, 31, 95
Indian joint family, 96
Inequality, and class-based marriage gap, 56–57
"In loco parentis." *See* Definitions of parenthood
In re G, 127
Institute for American Values, 45–46
Integrative model of parenthood:
    as aggravating challenges faced by transnational families, 300–315
    anthropological study of kinship and, 85–100
    biological sex differences and, 42
    as channeling reproduction and parenting into marriage, 3, 43, 46–47, 242, 354
    children's rights and, 32–35, 124, 128, 132
    critiques of, 65–80, 237–250, 340–348
    critiques of assisted reproductive technology, 46, 321–322, 323–329
    critiques of "responsible parenthood" model, 330–332
    as cultural norm in immigrant communities, 280
    defined, 2–3, 43–44
    gender complementary as feature of, 42, 47, 49, 300
    as including polygamous kinship systems, 364, 368
    kinship bonds as vital feature of, 2–3, 25–32, 245
    lack of congruence with contemporary constitutional and family law, 44–45, 50–54, 114–120, 237–245
    marriage and child outcomes, 147–167, 245–248, 323, 367
    on marriage as uniting biological, legal and social parenthood, 2, 45
    opposition to same-sex marriage, 3, 5, 42–44, 323–326
    as organizing device in parenthood debate, 2, 41, 258
    public opinion and, 4, 6, 422, 48–49
    as singular and universalist, 65, 77, 94
    support for same-sex marriage, 45, 369
Intentional parenthood. *See* Definitions of parenthood
International Covenant on Civil and Political Rights, 108
International Covenant on Economic, Social, and Cultural Rights, 24, 108

Jacobsen, R. Brooke, 180
Jacobvitz, Deborah, 204
Jones, Doug, 28

Kant, Immanuel, 107
Kegan, Robert, 107
Kessler, Laura, 55, 241
Kin altruism, 8, 26–27, 109, 116
Kindle, Peter, 183
Kindregan, Charles P. Jr., 175
Kin recognition, 27–28, 30, 31
Kinship bonds, 25–26, 31, 34, 99, 205, 245
Kinship care, 152, 167
Kinship studies:
    anthropological research, 87–99
    cultural relativism in, 28
    features of human kinship, 28–32
    relevance of primatology to, 28–29
    relevance to parenthood debates, 3, 6, 25–35
    social constructionist approach to, 25–28
    structuralism in, 28
Kinship systems:
    among the Mosou, 74
    fundamental features of human, 28–32
    import for integrative model of parenthood, 6, 31–32, 34–35, 364–365
    incest taboo as basis for, 28
    matrilineal, 87
    role of attachment in, 194, 201

role of fictive kinship, 23
Kurtz, Stanley, 96

Lawrence v. Texas, 132, 137, 174, 244
Lesbian parents. *See* Parenthood; Parenting
Letsas, George, 138
Leung, Patrick, 183
Lévi-Strauss, Claude, 28–29
Lobola (bridewealth), 71
Lombard, Peter, 114
Lorenz, Konrad, 217
Loving v. Virginia, 132
Luintel, Youba Raj, 96
Lurquin, Paul, 32
Lyons-Ruth, Karlen, 204

MacCallum, Fiona, 182
Magassa, Moussa, 78
Main, Mary, 204, 220, 223
Male problematic, 113
Malik, Charles, 106, 108–111
Malinowski, Bronislaw, 86
Mandela, Nelson, 79
Manhattan Declaration, 43–44
Margin of appreciation, 138–139
Maritain, Jacques, 106
Marquardt, Elizabeth, 13, 46, 242, 244, 245, 246, 248, 249, 344
Marriage:
  accidental pregnancy as rationale for traditional marriage, 47
  as attaching fathers to mother-child dyad, 113–114, 120
  channelling function of, 46–47
  child outcomes and, 147–157
  child well-being and, 148
  class-based decline in, 56–57
  as close relationship model of, 43
  cohabiting partnerships equated to in ALI *Principles*, 115–116, 117
  commitment as purpose of, 48
  conjugal model of, 43–45, 53
  as contract, 118
  as covenant, 114–115, 117–118
  deinstitutionalization of, 116, 171
  de-legalization of, 117
  economic obstacles to, 347–348, 356–357n15
  as firm or franchise, 118

  group marriage, 85, 98
  as integrating biological, social, and legal dimensions of parenthood, 43–45
  interracial, 150
  marital presumption (of paternity), 127
  marriage promotion, 347–348
  optimal child-reading as purpose of, 44–45
  remarriage, 55, 70, 156–158, 171, 324
  renewing a marriage culture, 333
  responsible procreation as purpose of, 41, 43–37
  romantic love-based, 76
  as sacrament, 114, 122n27
  sexual complementarity in, 44
  as social institution, 43–45
  traditional marriage, 237
Marriage equality laws, 52. *See also* Same-sex marriage
Maternity leave. *See* Parental leave policies
Matrifocal societies, 97
Matrilineal families, 68–70, 76
Matrilineal societies, 68–70, 76, 87, 90–95
McBrien, Maureen, 175
McClain, Linda, 3, 6, 14
McGlynn, Clare, 135
McKinley, Robert, 26
McLanahan, Sara, 56, 331, 344–345, 347, 355
Mechoulan, Stephane, 345
Merleau-Ponty, Maurice, 261
Metz, Tamara, 55
Meyer, David, 7–8, 42, 51, 105
Meyers, Marcia, 266
Modernity, 70, 74, 106
Monogamy, 66, 194, 353
Moral theology, 106, 110–144
Morgan, Lewis Henry, 85–86, 88
Moss, Ellen, 10, 204, 214
Mosuo:
  family values among, 69
  matrilineal households, 69
  matrilineal kinship, 69–70, 75
  matrilineal parenting, 76
  as separating parenthood from marriage, 7, 68–70, 73–76, 94
  plural parenthood and, 75–77
  tisese, 69–70, 74–77
  See also Na

Mother-infant bonding:
  disorganized attachment and, 205
  impact of maternal deprivation, 196–198, 205
  in humans, 195–198
  in mammals, 194–195
  See also Attachment
Motherhood:
  assisted reproductive technology as legitimating later, 33
  embodiment and meaning of, 258
  fatherhood contrasted as social construction, 30
  lesbian mothers, 171–183, 218, 326–327, 329
  protected in human rights document, 24
  public concern over single motherhood, 49–50, 66
  redefinition by transnational mothers, 299–300
  relevance of Bowlby to expanded definitions of, 202
  as social institution, 261, 269
Moynihan, Daniel Patrick, 66
Mularoni, Antonella (Judge), 129
Multiethnic Placement Act, 149
Multiple parenthood, 55–56
Murphy Brown, 98

Na:
  approach to fatherhood, 92–93
  disdain for marriage, 92–95
  incest avoidance, 95
  matrilineality among, 90, 91–95
  role of *ewu*, 95
  See also Mosuo
Naru, 69
Natural family, 106, 125, 138, 364
Natural law, 8, 105, 109–114, 119–120, 124, 131
Natural parents, 108–109, 111, 127
Natural rights, 105, 109, 111–114, 119, 120
Nayars, 7, 90–91, 95, 97
Netherlands, 173, 181
Neurogenesis, 196, 197
Nevada Department of Human Resources v. Hibbs, 239, 243
Nock, Steven, 119, 326
Nontraditional families, 9, 11, 136, **171**, 218
Nuclear family, 48, 65, **76**, 96, 126, 294, 313–314, 364

Nussbaum, Martha, 32–33, 361
Obama, Barack (President), 53, 79
Odièvre v. France, 138–139
Oneida Community, 98
Opie, Kit, 89
Oxytocin, 194, 195

Pair-bonding:
  as central feature of kinship, 26, 29, 31–32
  child rearing as reason for emergence of, 66
  integrative model of parenthood and, 3, 6, 25, 364
  relevance to rights of children, 34–35
  relevance to secure human attachment, 21
  role of hormones in, 194–195
  studies of physiology in animal, 194–195
Palin, Bristol, 76
Palmore v. Sidoti, 246
Parentage:
  depiction of parentage as contentious issue in family law, 41
  diversity approach to defining, 42, 47–57
  laws concerning, 237–242, 245–250
  presumption of legitimacy, 247
  relevance of gender to law of, 237, 243, 245
  See also Definitions of parenthood
Parental investment:
  contribution to healthy child development, 361–362
  diverse family forms and, 364
  as form of kin altruism, 27
  marriage as rectifying gender asymmetry in, 46–47
  parental rights as encouraging, 131
  paternal kin recognition and, 30
  relevance to political commitments, 32
  in stepchildren, 38 n61
Parental leave policies:
  in Australia, 267–268
  in Canada, 249, 266–268
  the "daddy week" and "daddy month," 260, 267, 274n58
  equal parental leave, 266
  in Europe, 249, 266–268
  gender differences in parenting and, 259, 266–269
  gender neutral, 11–12, 249, 260, 266
  gender specific, 11–12, 249

masculine norms and, 266–267
nontransferable leave, 266–268
paternity leave as "affirmative action," 241
as supporting "responsible parenthood," 351–352, 367
in the United States, 249, 362
Parental responsibility:
attachment security from adult assuming, 10, 216
best interests of the child as guide concerning, 173
as community, emotional, and moral responsibilities, 261–264
legal enforcement of, 117
to meet children's basic attachment needs, 22
parental responsibility orders and same-sex parents, 184
voluntary assumption at birth by men, 127
Parental warmth, 9, 147, 151, 155. *See also* Attachment
Parent-child bonds, 3, 4, 6, 25, 43, 57, 99, 193. *See also* Attachment; Father-infant bonding; Mother-infant bonding
Parenthood:
Bowlby's work on, 214, 226–229
child well-being and forms of, 247
continuum of approaches to, 42, 57
definitions of, 1, 2–4, 41, 124–139, 172, 240, 244, 247, 323–327
doctrine of psychological parenthood, 46
epigenetic changes and, 200–201
gender differences and, 257–269
gender equality and, 237–245, 257–266
gender stereotypes and legal rules concerning, 238–24-
as institution, 261, 268–269
legal recognition of functional parenthood, 46, 240, 354–358
rights of, 130–132, 136
as social institution, 43, 261
See also Definitions of parenthood; Diversity model of parenthood; Integrative model of parenthood
Parenting:
"attachment parenting," 227–228
child developmental outcomes and gay or lesbian parenting, 177–185

as community responsibility, 261–264, 272n28
as emotional responsibility, 261–264
as experience, 261
by gay fathers, 172–184
gender equality and differences in, 257–269
gender roles and role modeling in, 242–245
genetic influences on, 214
by lesbian mothers, 172–184, 326–327
as moral responsibility, 261–264
multiple parents, 55–56, 242
parenting experiences in transnational families, 279–295
quality of parenting and child developmental outcomes, 178, 181, 218, 229
"real differences" and, 258
same sex couples and, 181–182, 269, 326
social influences on, 214
stepparents and, 324–326
transnational mothers as redefining, 299–315
Parenting plans, 115. *See also* Child custody
Parreñas, Rhacel Salazar, 12
Paternal kin recognition. *See* Kin recognition
Paternity, 30, 69, 77, 85, 91–92, 127
Paternity laws, 50
Paternity leave. *See* Parental leave policies
Patterson, Charlotte, 327
Perry v. Brown, 58n15, 61n65, 255–256n103
Perry v. Schwarzenegger, 58n15, 61n65, 255–256n103, 371n11
Pew Research Center, 4, 49, 242
Philippines:
immigration of female Filipino migrant workers, 299–315
migrant mothers' reconstitution of mothering, 304–306
public opinion about transnational mothering, 13, 301–315
Plato, *The Republic*, 16, 19, 106, 109
Pluralism:
family law's embrace of, 239–240, 246
pluralist approaches to family structure, 7, 65–68, 94, 361–362
reasonable pluralism as value in diversity model, 48–49, 368
as a value in crafting a law of parentage, 11, 248–249

Plural marriage, 71–72, 77–78, 96–97. *See also* Polygamy; Polygyny
Plural parenthood, 70–73, 76–77. *See also* Mosou; Polygyny
Polikoff, Nancy, 184
Political liberalism, 32, 48–49
Polo, Marco, 92–93
Polyandry, 96
Polygamy:
　Black Muslim women and, 78
　child's need for care within polygynous households, 96–97
　among Fundamentalist Latter-Day Saints, 78–79, 81n16
　Islamic forms of polygamy, 78, 82n22
　multiple pair-bonds in, 29
　polygynous marriage in South Africa, 7, 70–73,
　suppression and persistence in United States, 77–79
　as within integrative model of parenthood, 73, 365, 368, 371n11
Polygyny, 66, 68, 70–73, 77–78. *See also* Polygamy
Pope Leo XIII, 110–111
Posner, Richard (Judge), 118
Poverty, 49, 147, 150, 158, 289, 323, 333, 351
Power, Camilla, 89
Precautionary principle, 34, 207
Pregnancy:
　delaying childbearing, 330–332, 349–353
　teen, 56–57, 332, 340–341, 349–351, 354
　unplanned, 76, 349–351
Price Waterhouse v. Hopkins, 243
Primatology, 22, 27–29
Primitive matriarchy, 85–86
Primitive patriarchy, 85
Principle of proportionality, 136–138
Private ordering (in family law), 112, 114, 116
Procreation, 41, 43–47
Proposition 8 (California), 5, 15–16n11, 58n15, 61, 255–256n103

Ramos, Fidel (President), 306–307, 313
Rawls, John, 48
Recognition of Customary Marriages Act, 71
Religion:
　delinquency and, 164
　parental religiosity and child outcomes, 154, 164
　peers' religiosity, 164
　support by religious institutions for families, 157
Remittances, 97, 279, 281, 285, 295n3, 300, 302, 304–305, 307, 310
Reproductive rights, 8, 33, 352
Rerum Novarum, 110
Resilience, 206, 225
Responsible parenthood:
　autonomy as aim of, 344
　as "blue" state model, 340–341
　contrast with integrative model, 340–341
　criticism of, 330–332
　definition of model of, 340–341
　public policies for supporting, 349–355
Rich, Adrienne, 261
Rights:
　of adults, 46, 127–133
　of children, 32–35, 105, 127–139
　conflicts among, 125, 128, 133–135
　of the family, 108–112, 119, 138
　of parents, 108, 124–139
　of parenthood, 124, 131
　See also Children's Rights
Rivers, W. H. R., 86
Rodriguez, Richard, 293
Rodseth, Lara, 30
Roman Catholic Church social teachings, 109–114, 118
Roman law, 105–106, 112, 119
Rothman, Barbara Katz, 241
Ruddick, Sara, 261
Rutter, Michael, 22
Ryan, Scott D., 183–184

Sahlins, Marshall, 27–28
Salgueiro Da Silva Mouta v. Portugal, 174
Same-sex marriage:
　child outcomes asserted as reason for opposing, 248, 324–327
　child outcomes asserted as reason for supporting, 41, 44, 67, 324
　as "culture wars" and family values issue, 41, 75, 237, 242, 260
　definitions of parenthood and, 322–325
　marital presumption applicable to, 127
　nations allowing, 249, 324

opposed by proponents of integrative parenthood model, 3, 13, 44–46, 242–243, 369
public values and, 369
rejection in "red" state family model, 353
relevance of social science to debates over, 67, 183, 245–248
second-class citizenship and denial of, 248
state and federal laws (U.S.) prohibiting, 44–47, 174
state laws allowing, 52–54
support for in "responsible parenthood" model, 353
Sauck, Christine C., 177
Schneider, David, 25–26, 28, 87
Schuengel, Carlo, 221
Schwenzer, Ingeborg, 139
Sears, William, 227
Seli, Emre, 175
Sevenhuijsen, Selma, 261
Sex education, 349–350
Sexual division of labor, 89
Sexual equality, 71
Sexuality, stigmatization of nonmarital, 341, 343–344
Sexual orientation:
  access to assisted reproductive technology and, 175
  children's development and, 171
  parental sexual orientation and child outcomes, 183–184, 218
Shepher, Joseph, 19
Slade, Arietta, 226
Social capital, 107, 156
Social cooperation, 35
Social justice, 71
Social reproduction, 49
Solomon, Judith, 204
Song, Hyun, 10, 214
South Africa, 7, 68, 71–73, 77–79
Sperm donation. *See* Assisted reproductive technology
Stacey, Judith, 7, 54, 91, 94, 183, 314
Steele, Howard, 10
Steele, Miriam, 10
Stepparents. *See* Child outcomes; Parenting
Stone, Linda, 32
Suárez-Orozco, Marelo, 12

Subsidiarity, 109, 110–111
Surrogacy, 66, 173, 175–176, 202. *See also* Assisted reproductive technology
Sweden, 249, 266, 267

Tasker, Fiona, 9, 67, 148, 180, 245–246, 327
Thorne, Barrie, 259, 266
Tierney, Brian, 111–112
Tiger, Lionel, 19
Traditional marriage. *See* Defense of Marriage Act (federal); Marriage
Transnational families:
  caretaking by kin in, 286–288
  challenges faced in, 286–289, 302
  challenges of parenting in, 289–295
  forms of nurturing in transnational parenting, 285–286
  as growing family form, 48, 279
  negative views of in Philippines, 306–310
  as neglected by policy makers, 280
  patterns of migration, 280
  perspectives on family separation and reunification, 284–294
  role of remittances in maintaining, 279, 281, 285, 304–306
Transnational mothering:
  as challenge to idea of traditional family, 299–300
  children's expectations of "intensive mothering," 312
  gender role ideology about, 306–310
  mothering and nurturing from a distance, 304–310
  as reconstituting practice of mothering, 300–307
  role of remittances, 304–305, 307, 310
Transnational parents, 283–294
Trobriand Islanders, 30, 66
Troxel v. Granville, 50, 133, 137
Trust, 156
Turner, Bryan, 32–33
Tylor, Edward, 85–86

Uniform Parentage Act, 175, 250n2
United Kingdom, 173, 178, 180, 182, 184, 220, 259, 305
Universal Declaration of Human Rights:
  Article 16 (1), 128, 129
  Article 16 (3), 108, 128

Universal Declaration of Human Rights (*Continued*):
   family as "natural and fundamental group unit," 108–109, 128–129, 364
   limitations on rights in, 136–137
   natural law and natural rights foundations of, 105–112, 116, 117, 119, 125

Van Ijzendoorn, Marinus H., 221
Vasopressin, 194–195, 198
Vulnerability, 32–34, 112, 131, 302

Wainright, Jennifer L., et al, 178
Whitehouse, Gillian, 268
Williams, Joan, 258, 261, 262, 266
Wing, Adrien, 78
Wood, Peter, 7, 68
Woodhouse, Barbara Bennett, 134–135, 137
Wyers, Norman L., 180
Yearning for Zion, 70, 81n16
Young, Iris Marion, 260

Zeifman, Debra, 21
Zulu, 71–**72**
Zuma, Jacob, 71, 77